W9-BVY-332

LIBERATING THE BIBLE

SALZMANN LIBRARY
St. Francis Seminary
3257 South Lake Drive
St. Francis, Wis. 53235

BS
511.3
.M325
2008

LIBERATING THE BIBLE

A Guide for the Curious and Perplexed

Linda M. MacCammon

WITHDRAWN

SALZMANN LIBRARY
St. Francis Seminary
3257 South Lake Drive
St. Francis, Wis. 53235

ORBIS BOOKS
Maryknoll, New York 10545

Founded in 1970, Orbis Books endeavors to publish works that enlighten the mind, nourish the spirit, and challenge the conscience. The publishing arm of the Maryknoll Fathers and Brothers, Orbis seeks to explore the global dimensions of the Christian faith and mission, to invite dialogue with diverse cultures and religious traditions, and to serve the cause of reconciliation and peace. The books published reflect the views of their authors and do not represent the official position of the Maryknoll Society. To learn more about Maryknoll and Orbis Books, please visit our website at www.maryknoll.org.

Copyright © 2008 by Linda M. MacCammon.

Published by Orbis Books, Maryknoll, New York 10545-0308.
Manufactured in the United States of America.

All rights reserved. No part of this publication may be reproduced or transmitted in any form or by any means, electronic or mechanical, including photocopying, recording or any information storage or retrieval system, without prior permission in writing from the publisher.

Queries regarding rights and permissions should be addressed to: Orbis Books, P.O. Box 308, Maryknoll, New York 10545-0308.

Library of Congress Cataloging-in-Publication Data

MacCammon, Linda M.
  Liberating the Bible : a guide for the curious and perplexed / Linda
M. MacCammon.
      p. cm.
  ISBN 978-1-57075-775-4
  1. Bible—Criticism, interpretation, etc. I. Title.
  BS511.3.M325 2008
  220.6—dc22
                              2007036459

For Roger Haight, SJ
and
for my brother, Arthur

CONTENTS

PREFACE

Liberating the Bible grew out of my experiences as a religious studies professor and Christian ethicist. Prior to entering the teaching profession, I was unaware that the Bible needed liberating. My graduate years at Yale Divinity School and Boston College had instilled in me a deep love, appreciation, and respect for the Bible that I was anxious to share with others. Once removed from the "ivory tower," however, I quickly discovered serious obstacles in teaching the Bible that prevented many of my students and adult learners from engaging scripture in an authentic way. My rude awakening began in the classroom.

For several years now, I've taught undergraduate courses in religion and the Bible at private liberal arts colleges. As part of the core curriculum, all students are required to take courses in religious studies. As might be expected, many arrive in my classroom with less than enthusiastic attitudes. They don't understand why they have to study religion or the Bible, especially since these things seem to have little to do with their chosen disciplines. After all, what possible significance can the Bible have for pre-med students or accounting majors?

Their general apathy and sometimes downright hostility are understandable given their sketchy knowledge of the subject matter. Many students are not practicing Christians (or Jews or Muslims for that matter) and many others have no religious affiliation whatsoever. Consequently, they feel lost and intimidated by the Bible's lofty status as the "Word of God." Its culture, history, language, and mode of communication are completely alien to them. Christian students generally feel less intimidated, but their knowledge is also limited because few have studied the Bible with the established tools of modern biblical criticism. While many look upon college-level Bible study as an opportunity to expand their knowledge and understanding, others (a small and often vocal minority) believe they know all there is to know about the Bible and are confident in their reading of it, particularly on questions of morality and salvation. The general consensus among this latter group is that if you're a Christian you'll be saved, if not, well . . .

As their teacher, my challenge is to mediate these different perspectives and attitudes so that students can explore the Bible together with open minds and with a spirit of discovery, yet many students resist the process for a variety of reasons. Christian students—particularly fundamentalist and very conservative Christians—are often afraid to question or engage the biblical texts in a critical way because they think it will be a betrayal of their belief system. They cling to their traditional presuppositions and beliefs out of fear for their souls. It troubles some of them to learn, for example, that the disciples did not actually write the gospels; rather, they were the product of a long history of oral transmission, which culminated in the written texts. For these students, the historical process of textual formation somehow threatens the Bible's veracity. It takes some time and study for them to realize that literary artistry does not compromise revelatory truth.

Non-Christian students are just as resistant to new ways of thinking. With few exceptions, they struggle to reflect critically about the meaning of their lives and about spirituality generally. Many have confided to me that the life of the soul is rarely discussed in junior-high or high-school classrooms. It is simply uncharted territory for them. They have no idea what they believe about life, death, evil, suffering, or other ultimate realities. If they have any spiritual sense at all, they're often hard pressed to articulate it in a clear and meaningful way, especially in front of their peers. Most of them are confused and a little bewildered by the whole process. In working with these students, I've become convinced that our educational and religious institutions teach students what to think—whether the content is scientific data, historical facts, or religious dogma—but they don't teach them how to think. I encountered a slightly different but equally distressing set of problems in working with adult learners in the community.

As a Christian theologian and ethicist, I'm often asked to speak to local church and civic groups on a range of topics, from the teachings of Islam and the morality of stem-cell research to church-state relations and the meaning of biblical texts. In discussing these topics, Christians and non-Christians alike have voiced deep concerns about the breakdown of the traditional family, rapid changes in technology, a creeping ethical relativism, a fragile environment, and a materialistic and increasingly pluralistic culture. Moreover, the tragic events of September 11th and the global "War on Terrorism" have shaken their beliefs and have generated a fear of other peoples, other cultures, and other faiths. Opposition to the war in Iraq has only added to their sense of anxiety and confusion. Many Christians turn to their faith and the Bible to help them cope with these new and frightening realities. Unfortunately, the way in which many faith communities study the Bible is precisely where the system of religious education begins to break down.

In the churches, the Bible is read during worship services, marriages, funerals, baptisms, and other events, but while the texts are regularly read, the majority of churchgoers do not carefully study them. The reasons are simple. Like college students, they also feel intimidated by the Bible. Many rely on the interpretive expertise of the clergy while others turn to the writings of Christian ethicists for guidance, yet not all clergy or ethicists are trained in biblical criticism. They tend to read the Bible through the interpretive lens of their theological traditions, which often results in narrow or dogmatic readings that blunt scripture's revelatory content and critical edge. While some churchgoers participate in Bible study groups, they are only as good as the commitment of their members and the training and organizational skills of the group leaders. Despite the array of scholarly books and academic journals on biblical interpretation, the use of these advanced and often esoteric sources by the laity is impractical—at least initially—because such sources often confuse and discourage more than they enlighten.

The obstacles are even greater for those who have left the church for one reason or another or who have no religious affiliation whatsoever. Many of these folks have pulled me aside after presentations to tell me that they're very interested in the Bible, but like college students and churchgoers they, too, feel intimidated by it. Their interest is undercut further by the lack of opportunity to read and study the Bible outside of a church setting. Many colleges, both private and state, don't offer any courses in religious studies much less the Bible, and if they do, the cost is often prohibitive. And so the "Bible-curious," as I like to call them, are left to their own devices or, worse, to the apocalyptic programming and sales pitches of TV evangelists or the pulp fiction that fills the "religion" sections in most bookstores. Granted, my experiences in the classroom and the community are anecdotal, but I believe they are representative of the extremes that many religious educators encounter today. On the one hand, college students have the opportunity to study the Bible with some degree of exegetical depth, but they are either apathetic or resistant to the process. On the other hand, adult learners are eager to study the Bible but are often denied the exegetical expertise or educational opportunity to move beyond simplistic or overly dogmatic readings. Given these extremes, sustained and critical engagement with the Bible is inconsistent at best and non-existent at worst, making the Bible a badly hobbled resource for spiritual and moral guidance. This book attempts to liberate the Bible—and the Bible-curious—from these obstacles so that the divine-human encounter can truly begin.

ACKNOWLEDGMENTS

I want to acknowledge my debt to all those who have offered their help and support during the research and writing of this manuscript. A generous grant from the Wabash Center enabled me to travel from the wilds of Montana and spend the summer in the libraries of Boston. I am especially grateful to Jim Skypeck and Jim Taber for their friendship and gracious hospitality during the early stages of research, and to John Hart, who has been a dear friend, colleague, and mentor through it all. I also want to thank Daniel Harrington, SJ, and Warren Carter who read early drafts of the manuscript and offered cogent and constructive advice. I am also deeply grateful to my friends and colleagues at Carroll College and St. John Fisher College, and to John Wall, Lenore Field, Katherine Greiner, Steve and Jackie Brehe, Del Bouafi, and Ashley Oliverio. Their friendship and unwavering support over the years made my writer's solitude bearable. Finally, I want to thank Susan Perry and Catherine Costello at Orbis Books, whose patience and unerring editorial judgment helped me improve the manuscript and survive this crazy process.

INTRODUCTION
Why Does the Bible Need Liberating?

Why does the Bible need liberating? The answer to this provocative question becomes readily apparent when we consider the way many Christians use (or misuse) the biblical texts. Putting aside for the moment its status as a divinely inspired text, the Bible is an excellent resource for spiritual and moral reflection because it welcomes and encourages critical engagement. The biblical world offers a vision of reality that actively challenges our presuppositions and prejudices, sparks our imagination, and introduces values, standards, and alternative modes of living that readers can consider and adopt. In short, the Bible teaches us *how to think*.

Ironically, the way many Christians perceive and use the Bible would seem to suggest otherwise. With few exceptions, Christians do not regard the Bible as a dynamic, thought-provoking text that challenges their beliefs, values, and assumptions. On the contrary, most view the Bible as an unchanging, divinely sanctioned rulebook that requires unquestioned acceptance and obedience. The most vocal proponents of this view are fundamentalist and very conservative Christians, whose numbers are growing within Protestant and Catholic denominations. When considering such complex issues as homosexuality, the status of women, abortion, stem-cell research, and the validity of other religions, for example, such individuals will often quote chapter and verse with little consideration of the cultural, historical, and literary contexts that determined biblical prohibitions and sanctions. In their view, the laws, values, and ethical teachings of the Bible should be interpreted as written and obeyed without question. Simply put, the Bible says what it means and means what it says and that's that!

While such righteous certainty may be comforting, these simplistic and overly literal interpretations not only ignore the complexities of the biblical texts but they also fly in the face of biblical reality, for the Bible's pages are filled with flawed human beings who wrestle with uncertainty and doubt—and with their God—as they struggle to act morally and find truth, value, and meaning in their lives. Doubt, struggle, and critical questioning are central to the Bible's revelatory message, yet many Christian clergy, theologians, and religious educators have failed to recognize and incorporate these strategies adequately into their theologies and ethical teachings. The result is a tragic loss of biblical wisdom and a crippling inability on the part of many Christians to think critically about how their

1

faith informs their ethics, as well as their relationship to other religions. Christianity's checkered history and, more recently, the extreme beliefs and politics of the Christian Right in America offer compelling evidence of this universal failure.

A particularly destructive and timely example is the Bible-based tradition of Christian supersessionism, an influential teaching that emerged during the second century CE. Supersessionism holds that with the coming of the promised Messiah, the Christian Church assumes the place of Israel in fulfilling God's plan, hence the traditional division of the canonical scriptures into the "Old" and "New" Testaments, as well as the assumption that conversion to Christianity is necessary for salvation. While supersessionist thinking has been roundly criticized and largely discredited over the centuries, many Christians continue to embrace it in one form or another, generating divisive and exclusionary beliefs and doctrines that condemn Jews and other non-Christians to the hellfires of damnation—unless they convert, of course. Such Bible-based intolerance is not only destroying the fabric of our country, but it is sabotaging the Bible's central intention.

The thesis of this book is that the Bible does not promote a rule-oriented ethic of obedience or an exclusionary, supersessionist theology; rather, the Bible has existential significance for all human beings because it challenges them to perceive and think about God and the faith-ethics relation differently. God's intention—both inside and outside the biblical world—is not to produce unreflective rule-followers who parrot the dictates of a divine command morality, but to transform human beings into spiritual and moral discerners who think critically about their faith and who have the ability to construct moralities that are relevant to their own time and place. Throughout the biblical narrative God and his many agents employ this pedagogical strategy, forming a crucial part of the Bible's revelatory message.

Liberating the Bible thus has three distinct but interrelated purposes. It aims first to make the Bible less intimidating and more accessible to all the Bible-curious, regardless of their spirituality or religious affiliation; second, to liberate the Bible from Christian interpretive traditions that limit and distort its revelatory message; and, third, to liberate the Bible from its reputation and use as a divinely sanctioned rulebook. To achieve these aims, the book begins by exploring the nature and function of the Bible as a revelatory text and then presents a series of biblical readings that offer a new approach for developing Christian ethics and that establish the Bible's relevance and universal significance for all people of faith and good will.

My interpretive approach to the Bible is an integrated, eclectic one that has been greatly influenced by the work of the French philosopher Paul Ricoeur, whose writings are cited frequently in this book. Ricoeur's groundbreaking work on language and the nature of biblical revelation establishes the importance of understanding how religious language functions as a revelatory medium before one attempts to interpret biblical texts. Adopting the biblical framework that Ricoeur calls the *economy of the gift*, my readings explore the multi-layered dimensions and intertextual dynamics of the biblical texts, using the accepted tools of biblical criticism. Although my training is in Christian theological ethics, I try to avoid "smuggling in" or imposing theological viewpoints on the biblical texts as much as possible—I'll leave it to my readers to judge how well I have succeeded.

There has been much scholarly debate in recent years about which title to use to designate the first collection in the Christian Bible. The term "Old Testament" has fallen out of favor with many Christian scholars because of the theological "baggage" mentioned above. Many use alternative titles, such as the Hebrew Bible, the Jewish scriptures, the Tanakh, the First Testament, and the Jewish Bible, but for simplicity's sake and to avoid unnecessary confusion for general readers, I use the traditional designation of "Old Testament" for the Jewish scriptures and "New Testament" for the Christian scriptures. In citing biblical verses, I use the New Revised Standard Version (NRSV). Longer passages are presented in block quote form for easy reading and reference. While I'm not a scholar of ancient languages by any means, I frequently offer translations and explanations of important words and phrases to clarify meaning in the texts. For ease of discussion, I use gender-specific pronouns for God, but only when necessary, and with the full understanding that God is not a gender-specific deity. My readings also rely heavily on scholarly sources that students and adult learners have found interesting and accessible. My hope is that many of the Bible-curious will seek out these sources to further their own Bible study.

Undoubtedly, my approach to the Bible and to biblical interpretation will draw criticism from clergy, Christian theologians, and ethicists. Many will argue that the Bible is the book of the church and should not be used for guidance outside of an ecclesiastical setting. Jewish rabbis and scholars may also object to my approach as yet another attempt to subsume Judaism under Christianity. Nevertheless, I'm willing to go out on the proverbial limb because I believe the signs of the times warrant bold initiatives, especially from religious educators. Today, we live in a pluralistic age in which competing values, lifestyles, economic systems, political ideologies, and religious and philosophical perspectives vie for our attention and our allegiance. It is also an age of increasing division, hatred, and violence among the nations and religions of the world. Faced with these grim realities, many people are actively searching for spiritual meaning and moral guidance, but they're confused and fearful about the process. I can think of no better place to begin than with the Bible, but we must be willing to liberate it from the restrictions, limitations, and distortions that we and our predecessors have purposely or inadvertently placed upon it.

In offering this work, my intention is neither to weaken the religious identities of Christians or Jews or to minimize the importance of religious tradition; rather, it is to extend an invitation to all those who are curious about the Bible and who wish to explore its pages in an open, inclusive, and non-threatening way. "Pick up and read!" were the words of a child that prompted Saint Augustine's religious conversion. Those of us who are Christians are obliged to continue extending this invitation, but we must also be wise enough and trusting enough to let the Bible do its own work and not stifle or narrow its unique voice and redemptive vision.

Reflection

1. Before proceeding to chapter one, write a brief paragraph on what you think the Bible is and how you have studied it in the past.

1

WHAT IS THE BIBLE ANYWAY?

The Bible is a dangerous book. It is without question one of the most misinterpreted, misunderstood, and misapplied books on the planet. Over the centuries, it has been used as a rationale for economic and social exploitation, the oppression of women and minorities, slavery, war, and genocide. It has fostered anti-Semitism, misogyny, racial animus, homophobia, a variety of extremist movements within Christianity, and every sort of crackpot cult imaginable. Yet the Bible has also been the driving force behind numerous social and political reform movements, as well as the inspiration for some of the greatest art, music, architecture, and literature ever produced. It has influenced our culture's legal codes, philosophy, and ethics, and it continues to be a spiritual and moral guide for millions of people. With such a checkered history, it seems clear that many people are confused about what the Bible is and how it should be used. Thus, before we embark on our journey through the biblical world, it's important and necessary to clarify what the Bible is (and is not), the nature of biblical revelation and biblical truth, and how we should approach the task of interpreting biblical texts.

Some Basic Facts about the Bible

The most obvious thing we know about the Bible is that it is a priceless cultural artifact. The Bible (a term taken from the Greek *ta biblia*, meaning "little scrolls") is an ancient collection of texts composed principally in Hebrew and Greek with a smattering of Aramaic (a Hebrew dialect). Within its pages readers discover a variety of writings composed over many centuries by many different people in a variety of cultural contexts. The rich diversity of the biblical texts provides us with a unique window into the cultural institutions, values, lifestyles, and practices of the peoples of the ancient Near East. The Bible's Old and New Testaments bear witness, for example, to the social and political evolution of the people of Israel, as well as the beginnings of the early Christian movement after the death of Jesus.

The Bible is also universally recognized as a classic collection of stories that offer profound insights into the human condition. The books abound with great tales of action, romance, political intrigue, war, and apocalyptic destruction. While the God of Israel is the Bible's principal player (at least in the Old Testament), the men and women who populate the biblical world are equally fascinating. They are cowardly and compassionate, barbaric and brilliant, tragic and triumphant. Yet they are not caricatures by any means. These are complex and full-blooded human beings who struggle with God and each other and in the process reveal fundamental truths about the human condition. In engaging their stories, we come to understand better who we are and why we do some of the crazy things we do.

Arguably the most significant (and potentially dangerous) thing we know about the Bible is its status as a divinely inspired text. For Christians, the Bible's authority is grounded in the fundamental belief that God's intentions for humanity are purposely and explicitly revealed there and that they should be honored and obeyed. We are all familiar with the Ten Commandments (or Decalogue), which list prohibitions against murder, theft, adultery, and so on, and there are literally hundreds of other prescriptions found throughout the biblical corpus—613 *mitzvot*, or commandments, to be exact. The Christian Church uses these and other biblical teachings to influence and shape the lives of the faithful, giving them a sense of identity, purpose, and certainty. They can be confident that the way of life presented there is authentic and true because it is revealed (and thus ordained) by God. The problem with this traditional view of the Bible's authority is that it often leads to the mistaken assumption that biblical teachings can be extracted and applied directly to contemporary situations. While a majority of Christian theologians and ethicists reject this approach as uncritical and illegitimate, many practicing Christians continue to use the Bible as a divinely sanctioned rulebook for contemporary morality, citing the biblical texts on questions of divorce, homosexuality, stem-cell research, the status of women in society and religious institutions, the validity of other religions, and other complex issues. Yet the will of God rarely comes to us with the clarity and force of the Decalogue; hence the danger, for the Bible is a notoriously ambiguous text that can be easily misconstrued.

The Ambiguity of the Bible

One of the main sources of ambiguity is the mixed nature of the biblical materials. In addition to narratives, the Bible offers an array of literary genres, including poetry, legal codes, letters, songs, proverbs, parables, and apocalyptic visions. Each genre has its own unique form and content, with the consequence that the messages generated are often contradictory. For example, the misfortunes of Job, a righteous and prosperous patriarch, radically challenge the central message of Proverbs, which teaches that if you "play by God's rules" you will be blessed. Job and his friends are understandably perplexed because Job's unjust suffering throws a sizeable monkey wrench into this religious worldview. The kind of tension found within these wisdom writings runs throughout the Bible, confusing many readers, and prompting some to practice "selective reading," which excludes awkward or troublesome texts from consideration. Adding to the confusion is the biblical practice of mixing historical events with theological reflection.

Contrary to popular opinion, the Bible is not a history book. When we read histories of the Roman Empire, the American Civil War, or the Irish Rebellion, for example, we expect historians to present the material in an objective manner and to get the facts straight. The Bible cannot meet these standards because it is a theological work that is not objective or historically accurate and doesn't pretend to be. On the contrary, the Bible is unapologetically biased. The authors of the book of Exodus, for instance, use their considerable literary and rhetorical skills to persuade their audience that *Yahweh*, Israel's patron deity, is more powerful than any earthly ruler and is responsible for the Hebrews' miraculous escape from Egyptian bondage. Similarly, the writers of the gospels use the basic facts of the life of Jesus and oral traditions about him to construct a religious biography that promotes their understanding of the significance of his life and mission. For these biblical writers, the *facts* of the events are not as important as their *meaning*.

This is not to suggest that the Bible is pure fiction, by any means. Trace memories of historical events are embedded in the biblical accounts. Most historians acknowledge, for example, that the exodus from Egypt, the Babylonian exile, and the crucifixion of Jesus did occur.[1] Yet few would suggest that the biblical writers depicted these events objectively and in historically accurate terms. The Bible, therefore, is not historical in the modern sense of the term. It is more accurately understood as a theological reflection on the divine-human relation in various historical and cultural contexts. The Bible does not present an objective statement of facts and does not strive for historical accuracy; rather, it strives to articulate the experience of God as lived by the people of Israel and the early Christian communities.

The mixed nature of the biblical materials raises the central issue of biblical revelation. Once again, the Bible has a knack for generating extremes. On the one hand, agnostics and atheists often argue that biblical revelation is nothing more than subjective speculation and that the biblical writers were simply deluding themselves—God doesn't reveal himself in history, only in their fertile imaginations. On the other hand, many faithful readers of the Bible insist that God does communicate to human beings and that the miraculous events of the exodus and the miracles of Jesus occurred exactly as depicted in the Bible. In these cases, biblical revelation is reduced to either subjective fantasy or magic, neither of which is an accurate or acceptable position. In truth, biblical revelation is a much more complex phenomenon that involves intricate connections between faith, human knowing, religious experience, language, and the biblical canon.

The Intricacies of Biblical Revelation

A key component of biblical revelation is faith, which is a fascinating dimension of human subjectivity. Most people understand faith as a pious disposition of religious people, but religious faith is only one example of a complex and universal dimension of human existence. All human beings display faith in one form or another. But what *is* faith, exactly? The always quotable H. L. Mencken once described faith as "an illogical belief in the occurrence of the improbable." Many people would agree with that assessment, but a more positive and useful description of faith is a fundamental attitude of openness to reality. All of us are thrust into a dynamic and ever-changing environment that requires some degree of faith if we are to function in it. For instance, we all have faith that the sun will rise tomorrow and we plan our lives accordingly, but faith involves more than the confidence needed to get out of bed in the morning.

Roger Haight has explored the nature of faith and sheds some welcome light on the subject. He describes faith in more substantive terms as a human response to reality that signals "an acceptance of and loyalty to something that commands the whole of human personality in a central and centering way. Faith as such is an existential reality; it consists in the dynamic commitment of the entire person in action."[2] Marriage is a good example of the kind of faith Haight is talking about.

When two people marry, they mutually commit themselves and their individual freedoms to the reality of marriage. They enter into the union with the expectation (i.e., with the faith) that the marriage will endure. From the moment they take their vows, they become part of this new reality and perceive the world and each other differently. As a married couple they must adjust their behaviors as individuals in light of the new reality of marriage. In other words, they must "act married." No more singles bars and all-night parties for them! They must live, work, and plan together as a couple, make joint decisions about finances and family, fulfill each other's emotional and physical needs, and accept each other's weaknesses with patience and compassion. Their willingness to work with and accommodate each other indicates their commitment to the marriage, which is the object of their faith. The strength of their commitment will ultimately determine whether the marriage endures or becomes another unfortunate divorce statistic. Similar kinds of commitments are found in friendships, business partnerships, and creative collaborations. The length of the commitment may vary, but the essential structure of the faith response is the same. Thus, faith, at its very core signifies a *relational* mode of being in the world. Faith simply cannot exist without having a relationship of some kind with the object of faith.

Central to any kind of faith relation is knowledge. We have faith in something because we know things about it that warrant our trust. Knowledge of the object of faith is acquired through our engagement with the material world and with the people around us. We know the sun will rise tomorrow because it always has in the past, so we take a leap of faith and scamper (or trudge) out of bed in the morning. Many of us are willing to enter into committed relationships with others because experience has shown us that they are reliable and trustworthy and deserving of our loyalty. We thus enter into relationships in "good faith." Religious faith is very different in this regard. While the commitment is the same, the basis for the commitment is not. We can't acquire knowledge of God in the traditional sense because God is not of this world, but that doesn't mean that religious faith is pure fantasy or devoid of cognitive content. Knowledge of God's reality comes to us in a unique way through the experience of revelation.

The Experience of Revelation

In its simplest terms, revelation is God's self-disclosure and self-communication to human beings in history. God initiates the encounter and the effect on human beings is powerful indeed. In a classic statement on the subject, Rudolf Otto describes the *mysterium tremendum* that is the human encounter with the Wholly Other:

> The feeling of it may at times come sweeping like a gentle tide, pervading the mind with a tranquil mood of deepest worship. It may pass over into a more set and lasting attitude of the soul, continuing, as it were, thrillingly vibrant and resonant, until at last it dies away and the soul resumes its "profane," non-religious mood of everyday experience. It may burst in sudden eruption up from the depths of the soul with spasms and convulsions, or lead to the strangest excitements, to intoxicated frenzy, to transport, and to ecstasy. It has its wild and demonic forms and can sink to an almost grisly horror and shuddering. It has its crude, barbaric antecedents and early manifestations, and again it may be developed into something beautiful and pure and glorious. It may become the hushed, trembling, and speechless humility of the creature in the presence of—whom or what? In the presence of that which is a *mystery* inexpressible and above all creatures.[3]

As Otto's description suggests, the experience of revelation takes many forms. God is revealed through nature, historical persons, and events. Revelation also finds expression in religious worship and in the symbolic language of oracles, songs, prayers, and written texts. What is important to understand here is that revelation doesn't simply drop from the sky as a fully formed message. Human beings experience the divine and then try to make sense of it, articulating the meaning of the experience through language, art, music, dance, and other creative forms. The encounter is a dynamic and thoroughly historical one that involves reflection, articulation, dialogue, refining reflection, and so on until there is insight or "revelation."

This process is found in all the major world religions. For Jews, God is disclosed in the long and turbulent history of their survival as a people. Christians believe that God is definitively revealed in the life, death, and resurrection of Jesus of Nazareth. For Taoists, divine revelation is equated with the all-encompassing reality of the Tao, whereas Muslims encounter the eternal word of Allah in the Qur'an. But how are human beings able to detect God's self-communication? Is there a special kind of divine radar or something? Well, the answer is yes and no. The ability of human beings to detect the divine requires a different kind of knowing that involves the human imagination and our lived experience. Roger Haight describes how the faith response to revelation interacts with the imagination.

> Let us assume that imagination consists in the human mind forming and projecting images of reality, culled from experience of this world, in a creative way to illuminate further data of experience. Not to be equated with fancy or fantasy in any pejorative sense, imagination functions constructively to creatively react to the data of experience by interpretation of it. One cannot know the transcendent object of faith, but one necessarily forms images of it. There is no "pure" faith experience, for all experience is at the same time interpreting or interpreted experience. One cannot have faith in God without imagining or constructing images of God.... Through imagination all human knowledge about this world enters into the process of forming concepts of transcendence within consciousness, of construing, imagining, and interpreting what the object of faith is.[4]

In other words, when we encounter the divine, our imagination constructs images of this encounter with the materials at hand, making God conceptually present to us. In each case, revelation is never direct but is mediated through material objects and modes of expression that are historically and culturally conditioned. This is significant, because it means that the message of revelation is always influenced to some extent by the medium of communication. A useful analogy is found in the encounter with a work of art.

When we gaze upon Vincent van Gogh's "The Potato Eaters," for instance, the painting becomes the medium through which van Gogh communicates his vision of the world, but we also gain insight into van Gogh as a creative artist and as a human being. In interpreting his work, we quickly recognize the artistic talent and passionate nature that drove him to break free from the representational art of his day, but closer inspection also reveals his love and respect for common working people, as well as his own sense of sadness and despair. These insights are not revealed directly, but come to us indirectly through the medium of brush, paint, and canvas. In detecting the artist through these materials, our imagination conjures images of van Gogh laboring in his studio, or walking alone through the French countryside, or conversing with the local villagers who would eventually become "The Potato Eaters." When we leave the art gallery, we feel that we know something about van Gogh, but our knowledge is far from complete. There are aspects to his personality that are not visible through his work but are revealed through other media, such as letters. Reading van Gogh's many letters to his brother, Theo, would reveal more about the man, but our knowledge of him would still remain incomplete. Divine revelation works in a similar fashion. In encountering the divine, the world is God's brush, paint, and canvas, you might say, and our imagination constructs the images that make God conceptually present to us. The knowledge that we acquire about God is genuine, but it is always indirect, varied, and partial.

Acquiring knowledge of God in such a manner is unique, yet there is one more amazing aspect to this process. In detecting the divine in material objects, we perceive and understand the objects themselves differently. As Haight explains,

> faith's interpretation of its object bends back to interpret the world. Although the object of faith transcends the world, still, being in relation to this transcendent object floods light on one's understanding of the world. Faith has implications not only for how one lives in the world, but also for a qualitative appreciation of the whole realm of finite reality that can be strictly speaking known. For example, from one point of view faith in God as personal does not change the content of one's understandings of the workings of nature. But from another point of view the interpenetration of this faith with knowing can yield an entirely new context for appraising the same understanding. It is construed differently because of this new expanded horizon and content of consciousness.[5]

In essence, the eyes of faith transform our perception of the material world. It takes on a new appearance and a new significance. Suddenly, a patch of earth, a waterfall, a building, an event can acquire new meaning. For the thousands of men and women who contributed to the traditions of the Bible, their encounters with the divine helped them perceive, interpret, and understand the meaning of their liberation from Egyptian bondage, the horrors of the Babylonian exile, and the life and death of Jesus of Nazareth. Put another way, their encounters with the divine helped them make sense of the non-sense. Yet it's important to understand that while the sacred is revealed through the material world, it can't be equated with it—the sacred and the profane are two distinct realms that are held in tension, thus ensuring the integrity of each. Unfortunately, readers of the Bible often collapse this distinction, leading to serious misinterpretations. To understand how this happens, we must consider how language operates as a material medium and as a vehicle for revelation.

Language as a Material Medium and Vehicle for Revelation

One of our unique traits as human beings is our ability to develop and use language. English, Russian, Sanskrit, Swahili, and French are a few examples, and there are literally hundreds of regional dialects. From these languages, we construct verbal and written speech to communicate with each other. As the noted philosopher Paul Ricoeur so aptly phrased it, all human discourse has the intention or purpose of "saying something to someone about something."[6] This common experience of language is what allows us to read an ancient text like the Bible and still have some sense of what the various authors intended to say. Yet our understanding of any text is greatly hampered if we don't understand the form of discourse the author is using. Discourse is not uniform; it varies according to the subject matter. For instance, a scientist who wants to describe fluctuations in humidity, soil temperature, and plant growth in a field experiment will use a form of discourse very different from that of a poet who wishes to express his impressions of a rain-washed meadow. While both authors may communicate in English and observe the same object (the meadow), their subject matter is very different. The scientist wants to communicate facts about the meadow; the poet wants to communicate its meaning. Thus they use different styles, words, phrases, and sentence structures to communicate with their respective audiences. Similarly, the biblical writers use their own form of discourse to express their experiences of God to their audiences.

The kind of discourse used by the biblical writers is similar to the poet's in that they both use symbolic forms to communicate meaning. We are all familiar with symbols. The American flag, a Christmas wreath, a totem pole, and a swastika are all symbols; yet we rarely give any thought to how they function or what they represent. Sandra M. Schneiders offers a helpful description.

> It must be realized that symbol is not merely a sign, that is, an indicator of something that is other than itself, like an exit sign pointing to a door or a label identifying an object. Nor is a symbol a stand-in, a substitute, for an absent reality like a promissory note representing a future payment. A symbol is, rather, the mode of presence of something that cannot be encountered in any other way. The body, as a person's way of being present, is a prime instance of a symbol. It focuses our attention on several important notes of the symbol, the most obvious of which is perceptibility. Whether a symbol appeals directly to the senses or is an idea or image in the mind, it is essentially a perceptible reality that mediates what is otherwise imperceptible.[7]

In a religious context, symbols are the linguistic medium through which God reveals God's self to us. God becomes present—becomes perceptible—through the symbol.

The imperceptibility of God means that all discourse about God is necessarily symbolic. Statements about God are not statements of *fact* (what is perceptible in the material world); they are statements of *meaning* (what we experience and feel when we encounter God). In the Bible, knowledge of God is a symbolic knowledge that is revealed through engaging the symbolic language of the texts. To understand how this process works, we must once again consider the faith response, only this time in relation to the Bible.

THE SWISS ARMY KNIFE THEORY OF LANGUAGE

A Swiss Army Knife is a pocket knife that contains within its handle a number of special-purpose tools, such as a screwdriver, a nail file, a bottle opener, a wire stripper, a corkscrew, scissors, and so on. Each tool is specially designed to perform a specific task. For example, the corkscrew is designed to uncork wine bottles. Although we could cut away the cork with the knife blade, it wasn't designed for that. The corkscrew is the proper and most efficient tool for that particular job.

Language is like a Swiss Army Knife. As a form of communication, language offers a variety of literary forms (poem, prose, farce, sermon, essay) and categories of discourse (scientific, historical, poetic, instructional, satirical, and so on). Each form uses an appropriate category of discourse to communicate its message. For example, satire is a literary form that uses comedic wit, irony, or sarcasm to expose and ridicule social hypocrisy and other human failings. While it may make interesting reading, we would never consider using satirical discourse for developing an instruction manual; it's not designed for that purpose. Similarly, the biblical writers used religious literary forms (poem, prose, parable, apocalyptic) and categories of discourse (such as poetic, parabolic, prophetic) to communicate truths about God, the divine-human relation, the human condition, and the ultimate destiny of God's creation. To read the Bible as literal history or as pure fantasy is to misconstrue the authors' form of communication.

The Bible and Symbolic Knowing

Most of us read the Bible, and any religious text for that matter, because it purports to say something to us about God, human existence, and our ultimate destiny as human beings. We bring questions about these subjects to the texts and read them with the expectation that we'll find some meaningful answers. Our willingness to engage the Bible indicates that we are open to—we have faith in—the subject matter presented in the text. Without some degree of openness to ultimate realities, religious discourse cannot speak to us; it becomes mute. If we enter into the symbolic world in "good faith," however, we encounter a host of religious symbols (e.g., the creation accounts, the story of the exodus, the parables of Jesus, the cross and resurrection) that demand our participation and interpretation.

Our openness to and relationship with the biblical world allows the symbolic forms to draw us into their realm, energizing and activating our minds and our imaginations in the quest for meaning. The parables of Jesus, for example, describe the kingdom of heaven in images of a mustard seed (Mt 13:31-32), baker's yeast (Mt 13:33), and a farmer's field (Mt 13:24-30). The kingdom of heaven *is like* these things, and our imagination works on the symbols, generating a variety images and memories of mustard trees, baking bread, and pesky weeds, all of which reveal something about the kingdom. Yet there is always a surplus of meaning that escapes each symbol, revealing their individual inadequacy in expressing the divine. Thus, while we know symbolically that the kingdom of heaven *is like* a mustard seed, it is *more than* a mustard seed. It is also like baker's yeast and a farmer's field, and many other symbolic images that swirl within the biblical world. In each case, the "is" of the symbol is always shadowed by the "is not" that reveals its incompleteness.

In interpreting religious symbolism, we are thus confronted with many potential meanings, none of which are wholly adequate or definitive. Unfortunately, many readers of the Bible are unaware of the dynamics of religious discourse, and this often leads to literal readings of religious symbols. The miracle stories are the most obvious example. Interpreting biblical miracles as literal statements of fact ignores the manner in which knowledge of God is revealed to us. As was noted above, God's self-communication does not destroy the laws of nature; it transforms our perception of nature. Roger Haight explains this distinction in relation to Jesus of Nazareth.

> Something becomes a hierophany, a revealer of the sacred, or a receptacle of the holy, and at the same time it continues to participate in its proper worldly environment.... Any attempt to break this tension, to resolve it in favor of either the sacrality or divinity of the symbol on the one hand, or the worldliness or humanity of the symbol on the other, will destroy it as a religious symbol. The theologian encounters God in Jesus; for the historian, Jesus is a human being. The mediating truth of these opposites lies in the symbolic interpretation of Jesus as the Christ.[8]

The dynamic interplay of the "is" and "is not" is clearly at work here. The exodus, the feeding of the five thousand, the life, death, and resurrection of Jesus—all of these events were experienced indirectly and expressed symbolically. They are grounded in history, yet they transcend the historical in their function as symbolic vehicles or receptacles of the divine. God was experienced in all of these events, but not in the literal, magical way that most people understand. Thus, properly understood, biblical revelation is neither fantasy nor magic. It is grounded in human experiences of the divine that are genuine and that do not defy the laws of nature. There is, however, one more dimension of biblical revelation that must be explored if we are to understand how the Bible communicates to us, and it involves the dynamic relationship among the many books that constitute the biblical canon.

Biblical Revelation and the Canon

Within a religious context, *canon* refers to a list of books that the religious community considers authentic and authoritative for their lives. There are several canons of the Bible, including the Jewish canon, the Protestant canon, and the Roman Catholic/Orthodox canon. Each canon arranges the biblical texts in a certain order and includes only those texts that the religious traditions consider authentic and authoritative.[9] There are notable differences among the lists. The Jewish canon, for example, does not include the New Testament. For Jews, the Bible is the *Tanakh,* which consists of *Torah* (Law),[10] *Nevi'im* (Prophets), and *Kethuvim* (Writings). The Catholic/Orthodox canon includes the texts of the Jewish canon and the New Testament, as well as apocryphal/deuterocanonical books (e.g., Tobit, Ecclesiasticus, Judith, 1 and 2 Maccabees) not included in the Jewish and Protestant canons. The reasons for these variations are complex and interesting, but are not pertinent to our study. What is important to understand, however, is how the canon influences biblical revelation.

As an authoritative list of sacred texts, the canon marks out the parameters of biblical revelation. In the Christian canons, biblical revelation begins with the book of Genesis and ends with the book of Revelation. These canonical boundaries influence biblical revelation by establishing a kind of "symbolic playground" in which the various texts interact. Paul Ricoeur, who has written extensively on this issue, explains that once the texts are apprehended as a canonical whole, "these texts of different origins and intentions work on one another, displacing their respective intentions and points, and they mutually borrow their dynamism from one another. So read, the Bible becomes a great living intertext, which is the place, the space for a labor of the text on itself."[11] Grasping the intertextuality of the Bible is important because it means that the tensions and textual contradictions that trouble so many readers are in fact part of the Bible's revelatory strategy.

To use yet another analogy, we could liken the global dimension of biblical revelation to an orchestra performing a symphonic work. Each of the instruments has a distinctive sound and makes a unique contribution to the music as a whole. The composer uses these differences to create certain effects and to communicate the message of the music. One moment we might hear the delicate sounds of flutes, cellos, and violins, blending their voices to create a melodious interlude; the next moment our senses are assaulted by the clash of trombones, clarinets, kettledrums, and piccolos as the orchestra races toward a thunderous crescendo. The interplay between harmony and discord are vital to the composer's musical message. But what if the brass section suddenly stopped playing during a performance? We would undoubtedly lose an important dimension of the work. Imagine Tchaikovsky's *1812 Overture* or Stravinsky's *Firebird Suite* without trombones and French horns! The Bible is very much like a symphonic work in this regard. The canon is the musical score and the individual texts are the instruments that work together—in harmony and conflict—to tell us a story. Our study will focus on the story communicated in the Old and New Testaments of the Christian canon.

The Story of the Christian Canon

As noted above, the Christian canon begins with Genesis and ends with Revelation. They are the *alpha* and the *omega*, the beginning and the end of the biblical story. Within the biblical world resides an active and providential Creator God, who governs the universe and who takes an active interest in all the inhabitants of his creation. Among the human population there are a host of leading characters (e.g., Adam and Eve, Abraham and Sarah, David, Jesus, and Paul), with hundreds of lesser characters lending their voices to the narrative.

Like all great stories, the biblical narrative is energized by a central conflict that has important existential and ethical dimensions. The plot revolves around the ongoing struggle between God's authority as the creator and sustainer of the universe, and the freedom of his human creatures. While the Genesis creation accounts depict the human condition as one of essential goodness, the willful disobedience of Adam and Eve introduces the reality of sin, which requires God's redemptive activity (and human cooperation) to overcome. The central question that pushes the narrative along is: Will human beings be redeemed from their fallen state? The question hovers in the background as the narrative unfolds. With the first sin of Adam and Eve comes a long and tragic procession of human beings who perform all kinds of despicable deeds: Cain kills his brother Abel; Jacob tricks his brother out of his rightful inheritance; the people of Israel repeatedly commit idolatry; King David has one of his most loyal soldiers murdered so he can claim the man's wife; Judas Iscariot betrays his friend and teacher to the Jewish authorities. The possibilities for human redemption look pretty bleak, but the biblical God is not just the Creator God, he is also the God of hope.

Throughout the narrative, God offers human beings a variety of gifts to help them overcome their sinful tendencies. Paul Ricoeur calls this method of divine governance the *economy of the gift*.[12] In a religious context, "economy" denotes God's governance, maintenance, and ultimate transformation of creation in accordance with the divine plan. A gift economy is a governance structure of pure grace in which human beings receive God's unconditional love and care without a *quid pro quo* or equal exchange between God and human beings. In the Bible, God's unstinting generosity begins with the gift of creation and continues with the gifts of the covenant, the Law, the prophets, the gospel, and many others. All of the gifts are intended to help human beings learn how to be in right relation with God, with each other, and with the created order. For Christians,

God's quintessential gift is the sending of the Savior, Jesus Christ, who defeats death and returns at the *eschaton* (Gr. "the last thing") to destroy evil, judge the living and the dead, and usher in a new age of righteousness and justice.

The central truth claim of the biblical narrative is a hopeful one, proclaiming that redemption will indeed be accomplished. The evil and sin that dominate the world will not defeat God's good intentions for creation, which are established in the Genesis creation accounts and renewed in the final pages of Revelation:

> Then I saw a new heaven and a new earth; for the first heaven and the first earth had passed away, and the sea was no more. And I saw the holy city, the new Jerusalem, coming down out of heaven from God, prepared as a bride adorned for her husband. And I heard a loud voice from the throne saying, "See, the home of God is among mortals. He will dwell with them; they will be his peoples, and God himself will be with them; he will wipe every tear from their eyes. Death will be no more; mourning and crying and pain will be no more, for the first things have passed away." (Rev 21:1-4)[13]

This is the overarching narrative (complete with "happy ending") that arises within the Christian canon. While the overall structure takes a narrative form, the canon does not prevent the voices of the individual genres from being heard. On the contrary, the canonical structure depends upon textual diversity—as well as textual harmony and conflict—to tell the whole story. After all, redemption is but one of the many truths proclaimed in the Bible's "musical score." There are others, which we will explore in the chapters that follow. Before leaving the topic of biblical revelation, however, it is vital that we have an understanding of the nature of these biblical truths.

The Nature of Biblical Truth

Often people think that the "truth" of the Bible rests on whether the stories can be historically or scientifically verified, but such a standard is inappropriate for the Bible because of its symbolic nature. It would be like judging whether our poet's impressions of a rain-washed meadow are consistent with the scientist's data or whether the colors van Gogh uses to portray "The Potato Eaters" are true to their historical counterparts. So how do we assess the validity of the Bible? The answer lies in understanding the kinds of truth claims symbolic texts make.

As was mentioned above, we all use language with the understanding that its primary intention is to relate human existence to the world, that is, to say something to someone about something. While the literary genres of the Bible are quite diverse, they all speak about the lives of fallible human beings who grapple with common experiences of suffering, death, fear, doubt, peace, and joy, and who recognize a transcendent source of value and goodness in their encounter with the Wholly Other. The significance or truth value of biblical revelation is based on how well their experiences speak to and illuminate our own struggle as human beings. Clarence Walhout explains the reasoning behind this comparative process:

> Our interest in the people, places, and plots of stories is related to our insatiable curiosity about how people act in situations of conflict. That interest is natural, of course, because that is so much of what life is about: how to deal with problems and stressful situations that come our way. Our uncertainties and fears drive us to seek answers beyond ourselves and our immediate circumstances..., [thus] we look to fictional stories as well as to actual life and history to give us examples that will confirm or guide or explain or point out new directions for our actions. We read for many reasons, but underlying them all is that in fictional narratives we are encountering patterns of action that help us understand or come to grips with conflicts and issues that we face in real life.[14]

Although Walhout is speaking of fictional texts, his description pertains to the Bible as well. We continue to turn to the Bible as a spiritual and moral guide because the voices of the various characters "ring true" with our own experience, and the attitudes and behaviors of the characters (both good and bad) provide us with possible alternatives for our own lives. The Christian canonical narrative offers a helpful example.

The central message of the narrative is the promise of future redemption, which is based on the experience of biblical characters with their God. They have faith in their God and hope in future redemption because they have lived and fought and prayed with their God. They have come *to know* this God through their many encounters and are in a position to trust the promise. In engaging the biblical texts, we naturally compare and assess their experience of God with our own. Their God is our God; their experience is analogous with and illuminates our own experience. Thus we, too, can believe in God's promise, because even though redemption is a future possibility, the experience of God we share with the biblical characters makes the promise worthy of belief. The biblical claim that human redemption will be accomplished is thus judged to be a truthful one.

Biblical truth is not always so comforting or pleasant, however. The Bible has a nasty habit of throwing a mirror up to the human condition and showing us some very ugly truths about ourselves. Our souls are also laid bare in the stories of Adam and Eve, Cain and Abel, Jacob, and David, showing us that we are just as selfish, cruel, and unjust as they were. Similarly, the teachings of Jesus often force us to see ourselves from a new and often unflattering perspective. Such is the nature of biblical truth. Whether the claims are about God, good and evil, or the human condition, biblical truths are not statements of empirical fact that can be verified through scientific or historical data; rather, they are insights into human existence that we understand as true because we *recognize* their truth in our own experience.

The existential nature of biblical truth has important implications for understanding the nature of biblical authority. As was mentioned at the beginning of this chapter, Christians have traditionally recognized the Bible as authoritative because of its divine origin. The laws, values, and norms found in the Bible are regarded as normative in the strong sense, that is, they are intended to structure and guide the spiritual and moral lives of the faithful. Yet the dynamic nature of biblical truth suggests that the Bible's authority is derived principally not from its normative function but from its illuminative function, from its ability to offer alternative visions of reality that have ultimate significance for human beings. When taken as a whole, these symbolic images establish the necessary foundation for other truth claims that have yet to be experienced by human beings, such as the final judgment and the resurrection. The existential truths proclaimed in the biblical texts thus pave the way for a life of faith and hope.

The existential nature of biblical truth also has important implications for the potential audience of the Bible. Can people from other faiths or people who have no particular spiritual sense engage the Bible in any meaningful way? The nature of biblical truth would seem to suggest that they can and should, because at its very core, the Bible reveals what it means to be fully human, despite the evil and suffering that afflict all human beings. While the Christian canons make very specific truth claims about the life and work of Jesus as prophet and Messiah, these claims cannot be assessed until readers encounter them in the biblical world and compare them with their own experience. Whether the readers are Christians, Jews, Buddhists, or Taoists is not as crucial as whether they trust in the ability of the biblical texts to disclose fundamental truths about the meaning of human existence. Thus, the Bible, the Tao Te Ching, the Qur'an, the Bhagavad Gita and other sacred texts are books that all people should read, reflect upon, and potentially appropriate for their spiritual and moral lives.

To summarize thus far, this chapter has attempted to liberate the Bible from the many misconceptions and misunderstandings people have about its revelatory content, its method of communication, its source of authority, and its truth claims. Of course, understanding the inner workings of the Bible raises the critical issue of interpretation. How do we approach such a complex and multi-dimensional text? The initial answer is simple: with the proper attitude! Given its controversial history, we must recognize and acknowledge that the Bible is indeed a dangerous book, and, as such, it confronts all readers with a challenge and an obligation. We'll conclude the chapter with a brief discussion of these dimensions of biblical interpretation and how we will approach the Bible in the chapters that follow.

The Challenge of Biblical Interpretation

The challenge the Bible presents to all readers—regardless of interest, experience, or faith (or lack thereof)—is to interpret the texts thoroughly, which means not only understanding the nature of biblical revelation, but also employing some of the established tools of biblical criticism. In making this statement, we're not suggesting that all readers become fluent in the Bible's original languages of Greek, Hebrew, and Aramaic. On the contrary, many biblical interpreters depend on translations of the Bible, as well as on biblical commentaries, Bible dictionaries, and other resources for biblical interpretation. Armed with these tools, readers are ready to perform the first task of biblical interpretation, which is *exegesis*. Exegesis is a Greek word that means "to lead out." It is an appropriate term, because the aim of biblical exegesis is to lead out or explain what the text meant for its original audience. Michael J. Gorman describes the nature of the work:

> To engage in exegesis is to ask historical questions of the text, such as "What situation seems to have been the occasion for the writing of this text?" Exegesis also means asking literary questions of the text, such as "What kind of literature is this text, and what are its literary aims?" Furthermore, exegesis means asking questions about the religious, or theological, dimensions of the text, such as "What great theological question or issue does this text engage, and what claims on its readers does it make?" Exegesis means not being afraid of difficult questions such as "Why does this text seem to contradict that one?" Finally, exegesis means not fearing discovery of something new or puzzlement over something apparently insoluble. Sometimes doing exegesis means learning to ask the right questions, even if the questions are not immediately resolved. In fact, exegesis may lead to greater ambiguity in our understanding of the text itself, of its meaning for us, or both.[15]

As Gorman's summary suggests, the exegetical task can be a daunting one, but thorough exegesis is a critical first step in the interpretive process because understanding what a text meant for its original audience acts as a standard and check against *eisegesis* (from the Greek *eis* meaning "into"). Eisegesis occurs when an exegete (the one who is doing the "leading") reads meaning into a text rather than allowing the text to reveal its own meaning, which is embedded in the historical, literary, and religious dimensions of the text. Eisegesis is one of the primary reasons why the Bible is misapplied; eisegesis should be avoided as much as possible.

With an adequate grounding in the meaning of the text for its original audience, the exegete then proceeds to the task of *hermeneutics*. The term is derived from the mythical character Hermes, the messenger of the Greek gods. Once again, the designation fits, for hermeneutics attempts to carry the meaning of the biblical text into a contemporary setting. The practice combines exegetical investigation with critical reflection and imaginative construal to effect a "conversation" between the world generated by the biblical texts and the world of the reader. Although the text and the reader bring very different perspectives and questions to the encounter, the goal is to orchestrate a "fusion of horizons" between the two worlds, a fusion that generates meaning. For instance, a reader's conversation with the story of Cain and Abel would inquire into the historical, literary, and religious elements that produced the texts (the exegetical task), as well as introduce questions about sin, jealousy, pride, punishment, and mercy as they are experienced in Cain and Abel's world and in the world of the reader (the hermeneutical task). When the dialogue is completed, the reader then assesses the significance and relevance of the text's meaning for his or her life.

If the conversation with the text is performed properly, it is always lively and thought-provoking, but never "objective." That is to say, all interpreters bring presuppositions to the text that invariably influence the result. Theologians and clergy, for example, often read the Bible through the lens of their theological traditions, feminists read it from a liberationist perspective, archaeologists from a historical viewpoint, and so on. Moreover, factors such as gender, race, age, education, political persuasion, and life experience all influence the conversation. Part of the challenge in reading the Bible is to be clear and forthcoming about what these presuppositions and factors are and how they will influence the interpretive process.

Two critical points must also be kept in mind. First, the symbolic nature of religious discourse and the diversity of interpretive perspectives mean that no person or religious tradition can lay claim to a definitive or "correct" reading of the Bible. That is not to suggest that all readings are created equal. On the contrary, judgments about legitimacy and adequacy must be made to guard against eisegesis and other abuses. Nevertheless, the exegete must be willing to acknowledge that the Bible has a revelatory integrity and autonomy that transcends all historical locations and individual perspectives. We encounter the biblical texts just as Moses encountered Yahweh in the burning bush—they are revealed at the very moment of encounter.

The second point is related to the first and has to do with interpreting the religious experience of others. Many of the contributors to the Bible were the recipients of original revelation, which they expressed through symbolic language. Thousands of years later, we, as interpreters, are reading and interpreting these symbolic forms. Although we are several steps removed from the original experience of revelation (as were many of the biblical writers), the process that accompanies symbolic knowledge still holds. In engaging the biblical texts, we are encountering God through the symbols, which are the material marks or traces that make God present to us. Although the original authors selected the symbols, our imagination plays with them, generating images from a twenty-first-century world, images that the authors may or may not have considered or even intended. This means that with each new reader comes the possibility of new insight within the symbolic playground of the canon. Such is the dynamic nature of biblical revelation. It is always indirect, varied, partial, and *ongoing*. The challenge for all exegetes is to assess the validity of the new insight in light of the old and strike the proper balance between tradition and innovation.

The Obligation of Biblical Interpretation

The obligation that the Bible presents to all its readers is to apply the texts responsibly. Given the Bible's complexity, this is easier said than done. The difficulties in using the Bible as a moral source are numerous and complex. The most obvious difficulty is cultural. As an ancient text, the Bible is a product of its own time, customs, values, and religious perspectives that are quite different from our own. We have argued in this chapter that a responsible exegete cannot extract biblical morality from the Bible's literary and theological contexts and apply it directly to contemporary situations without considerable risk of misapplication. Complicating the task is the diversity of the ethical materials. The Bible's many legal codes, prophetic oracles, wisdom writings, and teachings are unique and often require different approaches to interpretation and use. The parables of Jesus, for example, cannot be interpreted and applied in the same manner as the commandments, and even they have their own theological and literary contexts that must be considered. Still another problem is the sheer number of ethical materials. Selections have to be made and reasons given as to why certain texts are chosen and others excluded. The danger, of course, is "selective reading" for the sake of theological or ethical consistency.

The Bible is also limited by the kinds of questions it can address. Scripture is simply not equipped to consider some contemporary issues, such as the morality of stem-cell research or same-sex unions—at least not directly. So, what are responsible exegetes to do? The answer lies in how we perform the hermeneutical task, because the results of the interpretive process largely determine the method we use to apply the texts.

Often when the Bible is used for moral guidance, readers bring an ethical issue to the text (such as war, divorce, sexuality), and then try to find relevant passages to determine what the Bible has to say on the matter. If pertinent passages are found, they are read and assessed and judged in conjunction with other acknowledged sources for moral reflection, such as reason, religious tradition, and human experience. The problem with this selective approach is that it does not adequately consider the symbolic and global nature of biblical revelation. Ethical content is still being extracted from its original context, with all the dangers and complications that such a move entails. In considering what the moral teachings of the Bible might mean for contemporary audiences, this study will employ a different approach.

Interpreting Scripture from a Global, Theocentric Perspective

In engaging the biblical texts, we shall shift our gaze away from specific moral issues and discrete texts and adopt a more global, theocentric (God-centered) perspective. Paul Ricoeur provides the guiding principle for our analysis in his descriptions of the intertexuality of the Bible and its economy of the gift. As was noted above, he understands the biblical canon as a "great living intertext" that provides a space for "a labor of the text on itself." Our journey through the biblical world will focus on the intertextual dynamics of the Christian canon with the purpose of discovering God's intentions in the texts as a whole. In reviewing the canonical narrative, we know that God's ultimate intention for humanity is redemption, but there are other, more practical goals. God also enters into relationship with human beings to teach them how to live fully human lives with God, with each other, and in community. This divine strategy is revealed in the Bible's economy of the gift, which will be the subject for the chapters that follow.

The book will analyze major portions of the Bible's canonical narrative, including Genesis, Exodus, Isaiah, the Gospel of Matthew, Paul's letter to the Galatians, and key passages in Romans. As the narrative unfolds, the God of Israel offers Adam and Eve, Noah, Abraham, Moses, the Hebrew slaves, and the people of Israel a variety of gifts to help them overcome their sinful tendencies and achieve some degree of righteousness before God. In reading the texts, we will consider the meaning of the gifts for the Bible's original audience and for contemporary readers. We will reflect on the historical, theological, literary, ethical, and canonical dimensions as we wend our way through their stories. While our textual analyses consider the content ("the what") of biblical morality, our main focus will be on God's approach to developing biblical morality ("the how"). The central question guiding the reading is thus a methodological one: How does God develop and use these gifts to help human beings fulfill the divine intentions, grow and mature in their faith, and construct their own moralities within the biblical world? The basic strategy is to highlight the pedagogical dimensions of God's redemptive activity and then assess their value as a model and method for constructing contemporary Christian ethics.

Chapters 2 through 5 explore the divine gifts of creation, covenant, the Mosaic Law, and the prophets as presented in Genesis, Exodus, and Isaiah. The readings in the Old Testament focus on God's relationship with Adam and Eve, Cain and Abel, Noah and his progeny, Abraham, Moses, and the people of Israel. They reveal that Yahweh is a mysterious but accessible deity who creates and continually hones a progressive program for human development that coincides with the divine plan for salvation. This structural frame combines universal values and norms with concrete practical strategies to address the needs (and failings) of the biblical characters within their particular literary contexts. Although the framework is foundational, it's hardly static. Yahweh frequently revises the structure, offering, as the need arises, new gifts to guide and shape his creatures as they move toward spiritual and moral maturity. In each case, God presents them (either directly or through his agents) with an ethical ideal and then provides a practical program (a biblical morality) to help them realize it.

Moving to the New Testament, we find God's pedagogical strategies and plan for salvation jeopardized (at least momentarily) by the conflict between Jews and Jewish Christians over the identity of Jesus of Nazareth. This bitter and often violent family feud is reflected in the anti-Judaism of the New Testament and other Christian writings—a shameful legacy that continues to divide the human family today. To understand how the conflict influenced the formation and content of early Christian writings, chapter 6 explores the development of Palestinian Judaism, the emergence of the Jesus movement, and the breakdown in Jewish-Christian relations in the first centuries. Analysis of the conflict shows that the impasse between Jews and Christians is the result of their theological and interpretive biases, which blind both groups to the possibility that God's salvific initiative in Jesus might take multiple forms; that is to say, at one moment in time God calls the prophet, Jesus, to show his chosen people the path to true righteousness under the Law, and then, at another moment in time, God raises his dead prophet, transforming him into a concrete symbol of universal salvation—an initiative first introduced in Isaiah and extended in the prophetic mission and sacrificial death of Jesus.

Chapters 7 and 8 make this case, exploring the dual roles of Jesus as Jewish prophet and Christian Messiah as presented in the Gospel of Matthew and Paul's letters to the Galatians and Romans. Reading these texts from a global, theocentric perspective reveals how God's gift of the prophet-Messiah mediates their differences. In this configuration, the dual roles of Jesus are held in creative tension, extending their salvific power to both groups, offering Jews and Christians the possibility of salvation through faith in God, a faith that Abraham first introduced and modeled and that Jesus perfectly realized, a faith that makes both the Mosaic Law and the Christ-event effective vehicles of salvation, a faith that grounds and unites both traditions without privileging one over the other. The final chapter considers the implications of our study for the interpretation and use of the Bible for Christian ethics and for furthering interfaith dialogue.

Our journey of discovery will begin—as all things do—with Genesis and the divine gift of creation.

Questions for Reflection and Discussion

1. Return to the brief paragraph you wrote after reading the Introduction. Now reconsider your answers. How has this chapter affirmed, challenged, or altered your understanding of the Bible and how it functions as a revelatory text? How do you understand the challenge and responsibility of biblical interpretation?

2. Roger Haight states that "One cannot have faith in God without imagining or constructing images of God." What does he mean? What images of God have you constructed over the years? How have your images changed? What do these changes (or what does the lack of changes) suggest about your relationship with God?

Recommended Reading

Alter, Robert, and Frank Kermode, eds. *The Literary Guide to the Bible.* Cambridge: Harvard University Press, 1987. A valuable collection of essays from literary and biblical specialists that explores different literary approaches to reading the Bible.

Gorman, Michael J. *Elements of Biblical Exegesis: A Basic Guide for Students and Ministers.* Peabody: Hendrickson Publishers, 2001. A user-friendly introduction to the art and science of biblical interpretation.

Livingston, James C., ed. *Anatomy of the Sacred: An Introduction to Religion.* 5th ed. Upper Saddle River, NJ: Pearson Prentice Hall, 2005. A comprehensive, accessible, and well written introduction to the study of religion in a variety of cultural contexts.

McKim, Donald K. *Westminster Dictionary of Theological Terms.* Louisville: Westminster John Knox Press, 1996. A handy dictionary for biblical and theological study.

Schneiders, Sandra M. *The Revelatory Text: Interpreting the New Testament as Sacred Scripture.* New York: HarperCollins Publishers, 1991. A highly regarded analysis of the process of biblical interpretation, the nature of religious language and scripture, and use of the Bible as a book of the church.

2

THE ECONOMY OF THE GIFT
Establishing the Ethical Context

Genesis is the first book of the Pentateuch, which also includes Exodus, Leviticus, Numbers, and Deuteronomy. The Pentateuch, which means "five scrolls," is the first major block of material in the Christian canon. It presents a theological narrative that begins with the creation and ends with the death of Moses, Israel's prophet, liberator, and lawgiver. One of the more startling facts that students of the Bible learn about the book of Genesis is that despite its position in the canon it was not the first book written. The biblical writers constructed Genesis as a preface to the book of Exodus. Its purpose was to establish God's creative activity, introduce the major characters of the biblical narrative, and explain how the people of Israel, who originally lived in the region of Canaan, came to reside in Egypt prior to the exodus.

The patchwork nature of the Bible raises important questions about the origins of the Pentateuch that are vital to understanding the revelatory content of the books, both for their original audiences and for contemporary readers. Thus, before exploring the economy of the gift established in Genesis, we shall first briefly consider the historical background and literary sources of the Pentateuch, how the books were formed, and why the biblical editors (or redactors) arranged the materials in the order that we find today.

The Origins of the Pentateuch

As an ancient text, the Bible could be likened to an archaeological dig; its pages contain many layers, or strata, that must be carefully unearthed from their original ground and studied for insight into the people who produced those pages. In the case of the Pentateuch, the earliest layers can be traced to the ancient ancestors of Israel, a mixed peoples of Northwest-Semitic (possibly Amorite) stock who migrated to Canaan from the region of Mesopotamia (the land between the Tigris and Euphrates Rivers) during the first half of the second millennium BCE.[1] Many of these Bronze Age ancestors were pastoral nomads, moving their herds of sheep and cattle along seasonal grazing routes and interacting with local village settlements. Some tribal groups camped for extended periods around the settlements, conducting trade and even farming small plots of land. Archaeological evidence suggests that relations between the pastoral nomads and the villagers were cordial, each providing necessary goods and services to the other. Groups that didn't mesh well with established commercial arrangements continued their migration, settling in northern Egypt as refugees, asylum seekers, or guest workers. Some of these migrant workers would eventually become state slaves to the pharaohs, thus setting the stage for the events of the exodus. It was during this time of nomadic wandering, early village settlement, and sporadic migration that the first traditions about God's revelation to Israel's ancestors emerged.

It's often difficult for contemporary readers of the Bible to understand the worldview of the ancients, particularly in their attitude toward the divine. Religion in the ancient Near East was dominated by geographical location, politics, and polytheism. The sacred universe was populated by a multitude of gods who acted as local patrons and protectors for fortified settlements, city-states, and regional empires. In the dangerous and uncertain world of the ancients, sacrifices of small animals and foodstuffs were offered to the gods in the hopes of a stable food supply, good weather, fertility, success in war, and other common concerns. To ensure divine favor, it was not unusual for nomads and settlers entering into a new region to adopt the local gods and to worship them alongside their own. Such cultural borrowing would often result in the blending of religious traditions and deities. This is most likely what happened when a small group of former Hebrew slaves entered Canaan from Egypt around 1250 BCE.

At the time of the exodus, the land of Canaan was a prosperous region of Palestine that carried on extensive trade with Egypt, Lebanon, and Syria. Lawrence Boadt describes the religious system of the Canaanites, which was polytheistic and centered on the cycles of rainfall and fertility.

> Typically their religion pictured the gods as little more than the *personified power* of the storm, the drought, the growing crops, sexual fertility and the like. Around these gods and goddesses myths and rituals were developed which tried to reflect an orderly and proper way to bring such natural forces into proper balance during the year, so that rain and dryness alternated without an excess of one or the other. ...Many rituals dealt with sacrifices or duties toward dead parents and ancestors, but among the chief concerns was fertility, both of the soil and of the animal and human populations. Failure in crops or flocks could mean starvation, while human birth rates had to remain high to offset the terrible infancy and childhood mortality rate.[2]

Principal Canaanite deities included El, the father of the gods, creator of the world and ruler of the divine assembly; Baal, the god of storm, who controlled the cycles of rainfall and fertility; Asherah, the wife of El and ruler of the sea, and Astarte, the goddess of fertility.

In entering Canaan, the Hebrew slaves introduced new religious ideas that were closely associated with their leader, Moses, and that centered on

Yahweh, a tribal God from the land of Midian.[3] A distinctive feature of the new religion was its emphasis on Yahweh as the warrior god of liberation. This god was very attractive to the native inhabitants, many of whom were under the thumb of the local rulers of Canaanite city-states. Another distinctive feature was the covenant relation. For the Hebrew slaves, the covenant represented an unbreakable bond with a personal, providential God who demanded worship, fidelity, and obedience to the divine will. In return, Yahweh promised the people divine aid and protection from disease, famine, foreign enemies, and other common calamities.

While many Canaanites found Yahwism appealing, conversion to the new religion was hardly uniform or total. The convergence and eventual blending of the two traditions produced an interesting religious hybrid. Recent archeological digs have discovered prayers inscribed on pieces of clay that addressed Yahweh and his wife Asherah. Apparently, Yahweh and Asherah were an item! In one fragment, Yahweh is shown wearing a bull mask (a common Canaanite symbol) and Asherah is wearing a cow mask.[4] Similarly, the book of Exodus presents Yahweh in powerful storm-god imagery that strongly resembles that used for Baal, who would become a major competitor of Yahweh in Canaan and in the biblical record. Despite pressure from priests and prophets to abolish the practice, the blending of Yahwist and Canaanite traditions persisted for centuries, prompting the biblical writers—many of whom were priests and prophets—to wage an all-out war on Baal and his followers (1 Kings 18:1-46), with Yahweh as the unquestioned victor.

In the centuries that followed the slaves' entry into Canaan, stories about Yahweh and other local gods, as well as tribal songs, myths, sagas, and folklore circulated around the region in oral form, evolving (as all good stories do) with the telling. During this period, traditions about Moses and the exodus, as well as tales of the tribal judges and the patriarchs, took shape. As more Canaanites converted to Yahwism, loyalty to individual tribes was replaced with allegiance to Yahweh, thus forging new alliances that would ultimately result in the birth of Israel as a nation. As Lawrence Stager notes,

> Israel developed its self-consciousness or ethnic identity in large measure
> . . . through its religious foundation—a breakthrough that led a subset
> of Canaanite culture coming from a variety of places, backgrounds,
> prior affiliations, and livelihoods, to join a super-tribe united under
> the authority of and devotion to a supreme deity, revealed to Moses
> as Yahweh. From a small group that formed around the founder
> Moses in Midian, other groups were added. Among the first to join
> was the Transjordanian tribe of Reuben, firstborn of the "sons of
> Jacob/Israel." Later, this once powerful tribe was threatened with extinction (Deut 33.6). But by then many others had joined the Mosaic
> movement. . . .[5]

What this evidence suggests is that in its earliest form Israelite religion was not monotheistic but henotheistic; in other words, while Yahwism acknowledged the existence of other gods, it demanded allegiance to Yahweh alone. Many years would pass before monotheism dominated Israel's religious consciousness.

Although exact dates are elusive, most scholars believe that it was during the eleventh and tenth centuries BCE that the super-tribe of Canaan evolved into a united monarchy under the leadership of Saul, David, and Solomon. The city of Jerusalem became the political and religious center of the kingdom, serving as the official home of the royal house of David and the site for Yahweh's Temple. During the reigns of David and Solomon, writers were commissioned to collect, write down, and edit the various oral traditions, forming a narrative about Israel's origins that reflected and promoted the kingdom's political and religious worldview. From the tenth century onward, priestly and prophetic schools generated additional narrative materials, reflecting the changing fortunes and theological development of the people of Israel.

Modern biblical scholars have used a variety of analytical methods in an effort to determine who these various writers were. Although the issue of authorship continues to be debated, most biblical scholars hold to the Documentary Hypothesis that posits four different literary sources for the Pentateuch: the Yahwist (J), the Elohist (E), the Deuteronomist (D), and the Priestly writer (P).[6] German scholars developed the names for the sources based on characteristics of the writings themselves. The Yahwist and Elohist are derived from the name each writer used for the God of Israel. The Yahwist source used the deity's personal name *YHWH* (Eng. "LORD God"). Vowels were eventually added to the name (Yahweh) for ease of pronunciation. The abbreviation "J" instead of "Y" is a bit of a misnomer, resulting from the mistranslation of YHWH to "Jehovah." The Elohist source used the more generic term *Elohim*, which is the plural form of the Hebrew word *El* (Eng. "God") and was used to denote either non-Israelite "gods" or the singular God of Israel. The Deuteronomist and the Priestly writer are names derived from the religious schools that produced the writings.

The final form of the Pentateuch did not appear until the fifth century BCE, after Israel had survived the brutal occupations of Assyria and Babylonia and many years of political and social upheaval. The history is worth recounting, if only briefly, because it explains why the biblical editors arranged the Pentateuchal materials in their present order.

The Evolution of the Pentateuch and Its Original Audience

Between the tenth and sixth centuries BCE, the united monarchy of Israel experienced severe reversals of fortune. In 922 BCE, internal squabbles between Solomon's successor (his inept son, Rehoboam) and the northern tribes split the empire into the Northern Kingdom of Israel and the Southern Kingdom of Judah (1 Kings 12). To distinguish themselves from their southern kinsmen, the newly liberated Israelites established their own capital city of Samaria and developed traditions that reflected their own religious outlook. Reworking the materials of the Yahwist, the Elohist (the E source) constructed a theological narrative for the Northern Kingdom that was highly critical of the monarchy (which was headquartered in the southern capital of Jerusalem) and that stressed the centrality of the covenant for proper worship and righteous governance.

Israel's existence as a sovereign state was short-lived, however. In the latter part of the eighth century BCE, the Assyrian empire began a systematic campaign of conquest in the region, eventually crushing the Northern Kingdom in 722–721 BCE. In a policy designed to minimize rebellion and maximize control, the Assyrians deported the bulk of the Israelite population to other parts of their empire while moving foreign peoples into Israel. This ancient form of "ethnic cleansing" was highly effective—a homeless, disoriented people were ill-equipped to launch any kind of resistance movement. Some of the survivors who escaped deportation fled to the Southern Kingdom of Judah, taking their Elohist traditions with them. Facing the Assyrian juggernaut, Judah had little choice but to become a vassal state, complying with Assyrian demands for taxes and tribute. The uneasy alliance ended in the late seventh century BCE, when the Babylonians and Medes challenged Assyrian dominance in the region. Weakened by years of war, political intrigue, and assassinations, the Assyrians were vulnerable to attack. In quick succession the combined armies of Babylonia and Media sacked the Assyrian religious capital of Ashur (614 BCE) and the imperial capital of Nineva (612 BCE), effectively destroying the empire. Any dreams of Judean independence were quickly dashed, however, by the Babylonians and the Egyptians, who vied for domination in the region. After several see-saw battles, Babylonia finally gained the upper hand in 605 BCE.

The religious leadership of Judah was hardly passive during this tumultuous period. Priests, prophets, and other leaders organized a religious reform movement that stressed a return to the covenant requirements. In their view, the destruction of the Northern Kingdom by the Assyrians had been God's punishment for the people's failure to uphold the Mosaic Law. Judah's survival thus depended upon the willingness of the people and the Judean kings to repent and return to the covenant requirements. Under royal sponsorship, the reformers collected and copied the bulk of the legal materials found in the book of Deuteronomy (the D source). These materials stressed obedience to the Mosaic Law, the centrality of the Jerusalem Temple for proper worship, and fidelity to Yahweh alone.

While some reforms were enacted by the Judean kings (most notably, Hezekiah and Josiah), the results were mixed, especially in the political arena. The controversial priest and prophet Jeremiah, whose teachings were deeply rooted in Deuteronomy, believed that the Babylonians were instruments of Yahweh's righteous punishment (Jer 7:1–9:26). In his view, intercession on Judah's behalf was futile. God was determined to punish

Judah for past iniquities, and so Jeremiah advised cooperation with the Babylonians. Not surprisingly, Judah's nationalistic kings rejected Jeremiah's advice outright, initiating repeated rebellions against their Babylonian overlords. Weary of Judah's recalcitrance, the Babylonian King Nebuchadnezzar began a systematic campaign of deportation and destruction. Beginning in 598 BCE, the elite of the Judean population were exiled in successive waves to Babylon, where they settled in border towns north of the capital city. Others fled to Egypt, dragging Jeremiah with them (Jer 42–44). The few who remained in Judah eked out a meager existence in the countryside. The end came in 587 BCE, when the Babylonians sacked Jerusalem, destroyed the Jewish Temple and sent the last Judean king in chains to Babylon. This national catastrophe was the setting for the truly inspiring story of cultural survival by a people who had lost their king, their Temple, and their homeland.

The Babylonian Exile and Its Aftermath

For more than forty years the Judeans lived in exile. While their actual number is unknown, it is likely that there were tens of thousands of exiles. By all accounts, the Babylonians were merciless in war, yet they were benevolent captors by ancient standards, allowing the exiles to have homes and businesses, to govern themselves, and to worship Yahweh without hindrance. The Babylonian strategy was one of cultural assimilation, and there is evidence that it was working. Mordechai Cogan notes that Babylonian influence is clearly witnessed in the exiles' use of language.

> Aramaic, the lingua franca of the Near East, replaced Hebrew in daily discourse and commerce; and though Hebrew seems to have remained the preferred literary vehicle, parts of Ezra-Nehemiah and the late biblical book of Daniel are written in Aramaic. Babylonian month-names, in their Aramaic renditions, replaced the common Hebrew ones ... and in just one generation, Babylonian personal names, some including the names of Babylonian deities, were adopted by the exiles; even among the family of the Davidides, one finds names like Zerubbabel ("seed of Babylon") and Shenazzar (the god Sin protects").[7]

For the Jewish leadership, these trends were a harbinger of a greater and more direct threat. In a world where gods were worshiped for their effectiveness, the Babylonian gods were an understandable temptation to the exiles. The destruction of Judah by the Babylonians attested to the power of their gods and presented a formidable challenge to Yahwism. Fearing a loss of religious and ethnic identity, Judah's religious leaders gathered their traditions, which at this time included the combined materials of J and E (what biblical scholars refer to as the JE epic) and the core legal materials of Deuteronomy (the D Source). They also collected hymns, poems, liturgical and cultic requirements, genealogies, temple lists, and legislation not found in these earlier works. A member (or members) of the Priestly School (the P source) edited these materials, forming a continuous narrative from Genesis to Deuteronomy that preserved Israel's beliefs and cultic practices, and that reminded the exiles of their unique identity as the chosen people of Yahweh, a warrior God who would surely not abandon them in their time of trial.

The people's loyalty to Yahweh was soon rewarded. In 539 BCE the Persian king, Cyrus, conquered Babylon, ending the exile and permitting the Jews to repatriate to Jerusalem and rebuild the Jerusalem Temple. It was during the Persian period that the editorial work on the Pentateuch was completed. Many scholars believe that the priest Ezra's reading aloud of the "book of the law of Moses" (Neh 8:1) to the assembly in Jerusalem marks the official unveiling of the Pentateuch. The extent of Babylonian influence is witnessed in Ezra's reliance on Levites (assistants to the priests) to translate the book orally from the Hebrew into Aramaic so that the people could understand its meaning (Neh 8:7-8). Thus, in its final form, the Pentateuch was addressed to Israel's exilic and postexilic communities. The writer-redactors crafted the writings to speak to a people who had lost everything but their religious and cultural identity and their hope in the future. It is with this historical background that we begin our analysis of the book of Genesis, focusing first on the structure and the editorial intent of the biblical writers.

The Book of Genesis

As was noted at the beginning of this chapter, the biblical writers constructed Genesis (which means "origins") as a preface to the book of Exodus. A major literary genre in Genesis is myth. For ancient peoples, myths were more than fantastic and entertaining stories about the origins of things. Their essential function was to explain the way the world worked; much like science does for us today. As Lawrence Boadt explains,

> [m]yth allows us to speak of events of primal importance at the very beginning of time because it does not depend on knowing the scientific facts, but upon understanding the inner meaning of what happened and what purpose stands behind the event. It especially concerns itself with divine beings and their relation to the human world. It is not history in the strict sense, but it surely is not anti-historical either. It is at least profoundly historical in *outlook*, for all ancient peoples knew the gods acted according to their relation with humanity. Past events and experience formed the *grounds* for future *expectations* of divine acts.[8]

The biblical writers understood this, structuring the Genesis myths into two major blocks of material: a primeval history (chapters 1–11), which details the origins of humanity, and an ancestral history (chapters 12–50), which recounts the origins of Israel through the stories of the patriarchs, Abraham, Isaac, and Jacob.

In reading these stories, it is important to understand that initially many of the oral traditions had no religious significance whatsoever. Religious meanings were grafted onto them when they made the transition into the written narrative. In the primeval history, for example, the biblical writers collected mythical folk tales about the creation of the world and the introduction of evil, the struggles between cattlemen and farmers (Cain and Abel), the origins of different peoples and languages (the Tower of Babel), and other mythical lore. They placed these materials within an overarching narrative structure that promoted the power and exploits of Yahweh, often adding their own writings to fill in narrative gaps, to reinforce the cultic rituals and traditions of Yahwism, and to present their own theological point of view. Thus, what first appears to be a seamless tale about Israel's origins and the people's ongoing relationship with their God is actually the product of a long editorial process that involved many anonymous storytellers whose diverse contributions span many centuries. The significance of this process cannot be overstated, because it indicates that the biblical writers were well aware of and very comfortable with the dynamic and evolving nature of biblical revelation. A classic example of intertextual influence is found at the beginning of the primeval history where we encounter two creation accounts.

The consensus among scholars is that the first account (Gen 1:1–2:3) was written by the Priestly writer (P). The second (Gen 2:4-25) was composed by the Yahwist (J), whose writings provide the bulk of the material found in Genesis, as well as its basic plotline and theological outlook. But why are there *two* creation accounts? Certainly the Yahwist account of creation is a vivid, entertaining, and insightful story, so why did the Priestly writer find it necessary to add another one? The answer lies in the cultural threat posed by the Babylonians during the exile and how the Priestly writer's theology responded to that threat.

As was noted above, the Yahwist source was developed during the monarchy, when Israel had reached the height of its prestige and power in the region. The Yahwist creation account reflects this status, presenting a powerful "hands-on" deity who provides many gifts and blessings to Israel's primeval ancestors. The historical situation confronting the Priestly writer is quite different. He is working during the Babylonian exile, when the people are badly demoralized and understandably tempted by the power of the Babylonian gods. Thus, while the Yahwist's theological message is valid (i.e., Yahweh is a powerful Creator God who greatly favors the people of Israel), it requires a little tweaking to address the Babylonian threat and to provide a more adequate conception of God—at least from the Priestly point of view. The Priestly writer (who, like the Elohist, refers to God as *Elohim*) thus offers a supplemental creation narrative that asserts the superiority of Israel's God and directly challenges the cosmogony found in the Babylonian creation myth, the *Enuma Elish*.[9] A brief synopsis of the myth will show its influence on the Priestly writer's theological vision.

The Enuma Elish *and the Priestly Creation Account*

The *Enuma Elish* is much older than the Genesis creation accounts, dating to at least 1700 BCE. In this creation myth, the world is born from the freshwater god Apsu and saltwater goddess Tiamat. From their union other gods are born, but the divine children are incredibly noisy, preventing Apsu from getting any sleep. In a fit of anger, Apsu decides to murder the unruly wretches, but before he can carry out his plan, the children discover his plot and murder him instead. Tiamat is naturally furious and declares war against them. Terrified of their murderous parent, the divine children choose a young warrior god, Marduk, to lead them against Tiamat and her few loyal offspring. In return for killing Tiamat, Marduk demands that he be made king of the gods. A bloody battle ensues, with Marduk killing Tiamat and dismembering her body, but his ghoulish behavior is not without purpose.

> The Lord rested, and inspected her corpse. He divided the monstrous shape and created marvels [from it]. He sliced her in half like a fish for drying: Half of her he put up to roof the sky.... He fashioned stands for the great gods. As for the stars, he set up constellations corresponding to them. He designated the year and marked out its divisions, apportioned three stars each to the twelve months. When he had made plans of the days of the year, [h]e fashioned the stand of Neberu to mark out their courses, so that none of them would go wrong or stray. He fixed the stand of Ellil and Ea with it, opened up gates in both ribs, made strong bolts to left and right. With her liver he located the heights; [h]e made the crescent moon appear, entrusted night [to it]. And designated it the jewel of night to mark out the days.[10]

Thus, Marduk fashions the structures and courses of the heavens from Tiamat's body. Afterward, in a moment of whimsy, he decides to form a human being out of the blood of Qingu, a god who incited Tiamat to attack her children. These lowly creatures are created for one purpose only: to be slaves to the gods so that they may enjoy lives of leisure.[11]

The *Enuma Elish* is a creation myth that reflects the worldview and mentality of the predatory empire of Babylonia. To the Babylonians, the world was truly a battleground, and their gods reflected this perspective, showing no mercy for either divine parents or children, and placing little value on human life. In contrast, the Priestly creation account (Gen 1:1–2:3) depicts a single, all-powerful God, who peacefully brings order out of chaos through the power of the spoken word.

> In the beginning when God created the heavens and the earth, the earth was a formless void and darkness covered the face of the deep, while a

wind from God swept over the face of the waters. Then God said, "Let there be light"; and there was light. And God saw that the light was good; and God separated the light from the darkness. God called the light Day, and the darkness he called Night. And there was evening and there was morning, the first day. (Gen 1:1-5)

This orderly process continues, culminating in the creation of human beings. But in contrast to the Babylonian epic, human beings are not made of the blood of gods, nor are they to be slaves to the gods. Instead, human beings are created in the divine image and are given a special mission.

So God created humankind in his image, in the image of God he created them; male and female he created them. God blessed them, and God said to them, "Be fruitful and multiply, and fill the earth and subdue it; and have dominion over the fish of the sea and over the birds of the air and over every living thing that moves upon the earth." God said, "See, I have given you every plant yielding seed that is upon the face of all the earth, and every tree with seed in its fruit; you shall have them for food. And to every beast of the earth and to every bird of the air, and to everything that creeps on the earth, everything that has the breath of life, I have given every green plant for food." And it was so. God saw everything that he had made, and indeed, it was very good. And there was evening and there was morning, the sixth day. (Gen 1:27-28)

Greatly pleased with his creation, God rests from his labors. Here the Priestly writer deftly weaves traditional sabbath observance into the narrative, establishing it as part of God's creative activity from the very beginning: "So God blessed the seventh day and hallowed it, because on it God rested from all the work that he had done in creation" (Gen 2:3). The Priestly writer effectively employs this strategy throughout the Pentateuch, integrating central tenets of Israel's faith, as well as its ancestral lineage and traditional ritual practice, into the narratives.

As a supplement to the Yahwist myth, the Priestly version serves several important functions. It counteracts the temptation that the Babylonian gods might have for the exiles (the God of Israel is clearly a superior God), while preserving Israel's religious heritage. It also provides the exiles with an important message of hope. The many blessings bestowed upon the primeval parents are a sign that God has not abandoned them in spite of their present situation. The Priestly version also affirms the dynamic and evolving nature of biblical revelation, for the Priestly writer does not hesitate to expand upon the theology of the Yahwist (and J's conception of God) to address his own situation. In this sense, the Priestly writer was relying on intertextual dynamics to flesh out his understanding of Israel's God.

The Yahwist/Priestly (J/P) accounts are just one example of the skillful editorial work of the biblical writers. There are many others, each reflecting the values, beliefs, and practices of the people of Israel and the development of their God. As we continue exploring the literary world of the primeval history, we shall focus on God's character, his developing relationship with human beings, and the ethical foundations that constitute the global economy of the gift.

The Primeval History of Genesis

One of the most striking features of the primeval history is the often contrasting portraits of God. While some readers may find the differences disconcerting, they reflect the complexity and ultimate mystery of a God that cannot be categorized or wholly defined. The deity who emerges from these different renderings is a powerful Creator God who transcends creation and yet is radically present within it.

As the Priestly creation account makes clear, Elohim is a rather distant, disembodied God who initiates the creative process from some mysterious location beyond the "formless void and darkness" that covers the earth. For this deity, the act of creation is effortless and wholly gratuitous. God speaks and the primordial chaos is immediately transformed into the orderly divisions of day and night, evening and morning, earth and sky (Gen 1:1-19). From the very beginning, God places a value upon creation, declaring each new phase and element of the process to be good and ultimately "very good" (Gen 1:31). The process culminates in the creation of male and female beings, who are born in the divine image and who are blessed by God.

In its most fundamental sense, to bless is to confer favor upon someone or something. In blessing human beings, God is acknowledging his intention to be in relationship with them and to assist them in all their endeavors. Thus, while Elohim is a distant deity, the blessing signifies a long-term, "good faith" commitment on his part. But the divine generosity doesn't stop there. Immediately after the blessing, Elohim commands human beings to "Be fruitful and multiply, and fill the earth and subdue it; and have dominion over the fish of the sea and over the birds of the air and over every living thing that moves upon the earth" (Gen 1:28). Clearly, God intends to sustain creation and human beings are an integral part of the providential plan. Such responsibility requires that they share in the divine attributes, albeit to a limited degree. Thus the man and woman are created as free, rational, creative, loving, powerful, relational beings who are instructed to care for creation. These additional blessings are gifts from a proud deity who is pleased with his handiwork and who trusts his creatures to such an extent that he is willing to relinquish care of creation to them. As creatures made in the divine image, human beings are thus born with an innate dignity and purpose.

While the Yahwist account shares this fundamental theology, the Yahwist's God is an immanent deity depicted in anthropomorphic terms (i.e., as having human characteristics). In this version, Yahweh is a "hands-on" deity who labors to bring creation into being.

[T]hen the LORD God formed man from the dust of the ground, and breathed into his nostrils the breath of life; and the man became a living being.

And the LORD God planted a garden in Eden, in the east; and there he put the man whom he had formed. Out of the ground the LORD God made to grow every tree that is pleasant to the sight and good for food, the tree of life also in the midst of the garden, and the tree of the knowledge of good and evil. (Gen 2:7-9)

Yes, Yahweh is both a talented sculptor and avid gardener! The intimacy of the divine-human relation is evident. This is a deity who is so close to the creature that he literally breathes life into him. Another obvious difference from the Priestly version is the order of creation. Here the man is created first and without a partner, but this is hardly a demotion in creaturely rank or a sign of divine indifference. On the contrary, Yahweh seems to be centering his creative activity on the essential needs of the man, making to grow "every tree that is pleasant to the sight and good for food." The man is also given the task of caring for creation, but with one crucial difference:

The LORD God took the man and put him in the garden of Eden to till it and keep it. And the LORD God commanded the man, "You may freely eat of every tree of the garden; but of the tree of the knowledge of good and evil you shall not eat, for in the day that you eat of it you shall die." (Gen 2:17)

This verse is the first instance of divine command, an ethic that imposes strict limitations on human freedom. Given God's unstinting generosity thus far, why would he want to keep the man ignorant of good and evil? Perhaps Yahweh is attempting to spare the man the pain that must accompany such wisdom. Whatever his reasons, God quickly changes the subject (perhaps as a diversion), observing that "It is not good that the man should be alone; I will make him a helper as his partner" (Gen 2:18). Clearly, the fundamental goodness of creation is marred by this glaring omission. How is this possible? What follows is a rather comic scene in which the deity churns out one creature after another, feverishly trying to create the perfect mate for the man, acting much like an overly indulgent parent with a finicky child. As Yahweh presents each creature to the man, he is given the power to name it, but after cataloguing all the animals a fitting companion has not been found. Casting a deep sleep upon the man, God extracts a rib to form a woman. With great relief (a feeling no doubt shared by God), the man joyfully exclaims, "This at last is bone of my bones and flesh of my flesh; this one shall be called Woman, for out of Man this one was taken" (Gen 2:23).

The appearance of the woman thus marks the culmination of the creative process. The Yahwist concludes the myth with a statement that establishes the nature of the relationship between the sexes: "Therefore a man leaves his father and mother and clings to his wife, and they become one flesh. And the man and his wife were both naked, and were not ashamed" (Gen 2:24-25). Biblical commentators commonly note that the nakedness of Adam and Eve symbolizes a pre-civilized state, but it may also indicate the degree of intimacy between them. In the joy of sexual union, the man and woman are naked both physically and psychologically. In this sense, nakedness means that they are truly open to each other, with nothing to hide.

The Bible's Economy of the Gift

While the Genesis creation accounts provide fascinating reading, they also make certain claims about the nature of existence. Whether the claims are explicit or implied, they reflect values and beliefs that are shared by the biblical writers and that are foundational to the Bible's salvation narrative. In the biblical world, the existence of God is assumed—there is no debate on this issue. In a world where God exists, creation is an unmerited gift and everything that flows from it is inherently good. It is brought into being by a powerful, providential God who desires to be in relationship with human beings and his creation for the foreseeable future; yet, this God is a complicated, unpredictable deity, with many faces and many moods. One moment he is frightening, remote, and otherworldly; the next he is hovering over his creation, anxious to please. The multifaceted and utterly mysterious nature of God is a constant throughout the biblical canon.

As creatures made in the divine image, human beings have an innate goodness and dignity, as well as powers and abilities that make the divine-human relationship possible. Yet they are not created simply to entertain or serve God. Human beings are meant to live together as equal partners, creating and nurturing families and acting as stewards for creation, thus fulfilling God's providential plan. This means that justice, respect, mutuality, and solidarity are core values within the biblical world. The only external limitation placed on human beings at this point is the command not to eat from the tree of the knowledge of good and evil. Unquestioned obedience to a higher power is thus also expected.

Together, the blessings, beliefs, values, and obligations presented in the creation myths constitute a divine governance structure—an economy of the gift—that is used as a guide and standard for judgment throughout the biblical canon. Ideally, human beings are to conform themselves to this governance structure, and thus live fully human lives in communion with God, with each other, and with the created order. Although these ethical building blocks seem simple and straightforward enough, Yahweh's efforts to instill them in human beings are met with active resistance. As a result, flexibility becomes a crucial part of God's pedagogical strategy and is subtly foreshadowed in the divine command itself. The threat of death attached to the command seems to indicate a fear on the part of the deity, and perhaps even a bit of naiveté. As with all inexperienced parents, Yahweh is hoping that the threat of harsh punishment will be frightening enough to curb the freedom of his creatures. Alas, the Yahwist stories of Adam and Eve and Cain and

Abel will confirm God's fear, shatter his naive hope, and force him to change his tactics.

The Fall and Its Aftermath

The story of humanity's fall from grace (Gen 3) occurs immediately after the story of creation, which is hardly coincidental. The Yahwist wants to show how the movement toward civilization invariably results in conflicts and divisions that destroy the primordial harmony God established in the beginning. In this sense, the fall reflects the Yahwist's conviction that evil will always be present in the world, even in the midst of God's blessings and mercy. Yet God has a plan for redeeming creation, a plan that cannot be stopped despite the evil that human beings commit. Given the historical situation of the Yahwist, it's not surprising that he would pen such an optimistic theology. From where he was sitting, God had indeed blessed the people of Israel and their monarchy. Yet the Yahwist is more than a gifted theologian of the royal house of David. From a contemporary perspective, he is also an astute observer of the human condition, offering an insightful study in human psychology that reveals fundamental truths about the nature of temptation and the destructive effects of evil on relationships, whether human or divine.

As the tempter, the serpent is described as "more crafty than any other wild animal that the LORD God had made" (Gen 3:1). Here the serpent's craftiness (Heb. *arum*) plays against the naked innocence (Heb. *arumim*) of the man and the woman established in the previous verse. The encounter between the serpent and the woman occurs while she is alone—all the better to confuse and entice her. Probing for any weakness, the serpent asks her, "Did God say, 'You shall not eat from any tree in the garden'?" (Gen 3:1). The question seems innocent enough, but its phrasing is subtly designed to discover what the woman knows while at the same time drawing her attention to what is forbidden. She parrots back the divine prohibition, but with an interesting addition: "We may eat of the fruit of the trees in the garden; but God said, 'You shall not eat of the fruit of the tree that is in the middle of the garden, nor shall you touch it, or you shall die'" (Gen 3:2). God's command did not ban touching the fruit, so why does the woman mention it? Some commentators suggest that since the command was initially spoken to the man, the addition may be the result of mistakes the man made in relaying the information to the woman, or it could be the result of the woman's contemplation of the forbidden fruit. Perhaps she wondered what it would be like to touch it, and inadvertently added her own thoughts to the prohibition. Whatever the case, the serpent exploits this opening perfectly, assuring her that "You will not die; for God knows that when you eat of it your eyes will be opened, and you will be like God, knowing good and evil" (Gen 3:4). With these words, the serpent cleverly places in the woman's mind a seed of doubt about God's intentions. It quickly takes root, partly because in instituting the command Yahweh never explains his motives; the man and woman are simply expected to obey it. To make matters worse, the serpent's explanation (albeit a presumptuous and erroneous one) makes the woman aware that she is missing something, thus igniting a terrible desire within her. Is it possible that God's command is designed to prevent her and her mate from attaining the full powers of divinity? Confronted with such a possibility, the woman gazes upon the object of desire, constructs the necessary rationale in her own mind for her rebellious act, and then carries it out swiftly and decisively.

> So when the woman saw that the tree was good for food, and that it was a delight to the eyes, and that the tree was to be desired to make one wise, she took of its fruit and ate; and she also gave some to her husband who was with her, and he ate. Then the eyes of both were opened, and they knew that they were naked; and they sewed fig leaves together and made loincloths for themselves. (Gen 3:6-7)

The man is depicted as a passive but very willing player in the crime. There is no attempt on his part to talk the woman out of it or to stop her from eating the fruit and he doesn't refuse it when it is offered to him. While the wisdom they desired is given to them, it comes at a terrible price. For the Yahwist, their loss of innocence (represented by the loincloths) symbolizes the move toward civilization, as well as a loss of intimacy between the man and woman, for now they truly have something to hide, not only from each other, but from God as well. Immediately afterward, the pair hears the "sound of the LORD God walking in the garden at the time of the evening breeze" (Gen 3:8). Like all guilty children, they hide themselves, hoping to avoid Yahweh and the inevitable consequences of their actions.

It's always fun to speculate about the kind of "sound" Yahweh is making. Perhaps he is whistling or singing as he walks about the garden, pleased with his handiwork and proud of his accomplishments. His mood quickly changes, however, when he realizes that the man and woman are hiding.

> But the LORD God called to the man, and said to him, "Where are you?" He said, "I heard the sound of you in the garden, and I was afraid, because I was naked; and I hid myself." He said, "Who told you that you were naked? Have you eaten from the tree of which I commanded you not to eat?" The man said, "The woman whom you gave to be with me, she gave me fruit from the tree and I ate." Then the LORD God said to the woman, "What is this that you have done?" The woman said, "The serpent tricked me, and I ate." (Gen 3:9-13)

Yahweh's questions to the man are meant to draw him out and find out why he is hiding. Readers know that the man's fear is not of other creatures or of something new or strange growing in the garden. There is the obvious fear of punishment, but the man is also afraid because his guilt makes him feel exposed and vulnerable, hence the desire to hide. God picks up on this immediately, for he understands that the man's awareness that he is naked—that he has something to hide—can mean only one thing: he has disobeyed the divine command. God's follow-up questions are designed to elicit a confession from the man and woman so that they can accept responsibility for their actions, but they choose to deny any responsibility. The man blames Yahweh and the woman, the woman blames the snake, and the snake has no comment. So much for harmonious relations in the garden!

The verses that follow present a number of "curses" (Gen 3:14-19). These ancient *etiologies* (which are explanations of the origins of place names and traditional practices) explain why human beings have an ingrained fear of snakes, why there is pain in childbirth, why men dominate and oppress women, why survival requires ceaseless labor, and why human beings are mortal. Placed within the context of the fall, these etiological explanations become the consequences of the trio's actions, but it's important to note that they are not imposed by Yahweh. "Because you have done this," is a causal statement. In presenting the punishments, God is simply affirming the timeless yet terrible truth that "actions have consequences." The oppression, pain, and death human beings suffer were never part of the divine plan. Punishment is the unavoidable result of their rebellion against it. In this sense, the serpent was not deceptive, for the man and woman did not die from eating the fruit. It was their disobedience to Yahweh's command that ultimately sealed their fate. Yet, despite their rebellion, God is merciful. Before sending the man and woman out of the garden, he made "garments of skins for the man and for his wife, and clothed them" (Gen 3:21). This very maternal gesture is reminiscent of a wise and loving mother who bandages her children's scraped knees and then sends them back outside. While they will undoubtedly get hurt again, she knows that's the only way they'll learn. In this sense, Yahweh, too, is learning that he can't protect his children indefinitely. They must experience the reality of evil and learn its painful lessons themselves.

The Lessons of the Garden

On one level, the myth of the fall symbolically depicts the development of human beings from a state of primordial innocence to civilization, but it also throws a mirror up to human behavior, and the image is not terribly flattering. Like Eve, most of us suffer from a basic insecurity. We are unhappy with the limitations of our creaturely state and desire something to fill the void or to compensate for what we feel we lack. We reason that if we were just a little smarter, or prettier, or thinner, or wealthier, or more powerful then we'd feel complete and happy. It's this sense of inadequacy that sparks our desire and that tempts us to abuse our freedom and do whatever it takes to get what we want. When we're caught with our "hands in the cookie jar," our reactions mirror those of Adam and Eve perfectly. We, too, feel shame and want to hide. We quickly point an accusing finger at everybody and everything else to deflect attention away from the real culprit. This all too human tendency to deny responsibility reveals a fundamental paradox in the human condition, for as human beings we claim that we are free, and yet when we yield to temptation and abuse our freedom, we claim that we are not free, that we are under the spell or power of someone or something else that forces us to behave badly. "The devil made me do it!" is the sheepish excuse that we've all used at one time or another, but we can't have it both ways. We are either free or enslaved—there is no middle ground. If we believe we are free (and most of us do), then we have an obligation to use our freedom responsibly and accept the consequences when we don't. Clearly this is Yahweh's hope when he sends Adam and Eve out into the world. Unfortunately, they fail to learn from their mistake, leading to the tragic tale of Cain and Abel.

The First Homicide

Originally, the mythical story of Cain and Abel (Gen 4:1-16) explained the ancient and ongoing tension between farmers and herdsmen. Within the Yahwist's narrative structure, however, the story is transformed into a murderous tale of sibling rivalry that reveals how evil spreads and intensifies over time. It also marks a significant shift in Yahweh's pedagogical approach, for keeping evil in check will require a more flexible deity who is willing to explain more and command less. The story begins on a positive note.

> Now the man knew his wife Eve, and she conceived and bore Cain, saying, "I have produced a man with the help of the LORD." Next she bore his brother Abel. Now Abel was a keeper of sheep, and Cain a tiller of the ground. In the course of time Cain brought to the LORD an offering of the fruit of the ground, and Abel for his part brought of the firstlings of his flock, their fat portions. And the LORD had regard for Abel and his offering, but for Cain and his offering he had no regard. So Cain was very angry, and his countenance fell. (Gen 4:1-5)

It appears that Adam and Eve are taking God's command to "be fruitful and multiply" to heart. In bearing Cain, Eve readily acknowledges her dependence upon Yahweh for her fertility, a sign of reverence and humility that is quickly rewarded with a second child. The central conflict arises when Yahweh reacts negatively to Cain and his offering. No explicit reason is given, yet the text offers some clues. The first appears in the contrast between the brothers' offerings. There is nothing to distinguish Cain's offering, it is simply "an offering from the fruit of the ground." In contrast, Abel brings the very best from his flock, "their fat portions." Perhaps this disparity had been happening for some time and God finally decided to confront Cain. But why is God displeased? No doubt the quality of the offering has something to do with it. Perhaps Cain was momentarily tired of competing with Abel (sibling rivalry is a common theme in the biblical narrative), or he may have slipped into a minimalist work ethic, doing only what was necessary to gain God's favor. Whatever the reason, Cain's lackluster offering is a symptom of a more deep-seated problem, which reveals itself in Cain's reaction. For Cain is not merely disappointed in God's judgment, he is *angry* and he has no qualms about showing it. Yahweh understands the implication of Cain's anger. He has dealt with it before. Cain desires what Abel has and Cain's anger is a sign and a warning that anything can happen.

God immediately intervenes with some pointed questions: "Why are you angry, and why has your countenance fallen?"(Gen 4:6). As with Adam and Eve, Yahweh's questions are designed to help Cain examine his feelings and his actions. If Cain thinks about why he is jealous of his brother, then he might understand that the problem lies in his own motives. Why is he working in the fields and why is he making the offering? Are his efforts for the sake of the work itself and for his love of God, or are they motivated by a desire to best his brother and win praise from God with a minimum of effort? Yahweh already knows the answers to these questions—they are apparent in the quality of Cain's offering and in his reaction to Abel's success. But instead of simply commanding Cain to quell his anger, God poses another question: "If you do well, will you not be accepted? And if you do not do well, sin is lurking at the door; its desire is for you, but you must master it" (4:7). Linking the question with a warning and an instruction is designed to teach Cain fundamental truths about desire, temptation, punishment, and moral growth. Yahweh is assuring Cain that if he is doing well, that is, if he's working out of pure motives (as Abel apparently was), then Cain and his offering will be accepted regardless of how it compares to his brother's, but if he is working only for self-serving ends and doesn't get what he feels he deserves, then jealousy and anger will tempt him to take matters into his own hands—just as his parents did in the garden. While the temptation to sin will always be "lurking at the door," Cain can master it if he understands that God's regard for Cain and the acceptance of his offering are determined by the quality of his motives. Cain's response to such wise and loving instruction is swift and disappointing.

> Cain said to his brother Abel, "Let us go out to the field." And when they were in the field, Cain rose up against his brother, Abel, and killed him. Then the LORD said to Cain, "Where is your brother Abel?" He said, "I do not know; am I my brother's keeper?" And the LORD said, "What have you done? Listen; your brother's blood is crying out to me from the ground. And now you are cursed from the ground, which has opened its mouth to receive your brother's blood from your hand. When you till the ground it will no longer yield to you its strength; you will be a fugitive and a wanderer on the earth." Cain said to the LORD, "My punishment is greater than I can bear! Today you have driven me away from the soil, and I shall be hidden from your face; I shall be a fugitive and a wanderer on the earth, and anyone who meets me may kill me." Then the LORD said to him, "Not so! Whoever kills Cain will suffer a sevenfold vengeance." And the LORD put a mark on Cain, so that no one who came upon him would kill him. (Gen 4:8-15)

Enticing his brother into a position of vulnerability (much like the serpent did with Eve), Cain kills Abel. Further echoes of the fall resound in Yahweh's interrogation of Cain and in his cynical denial of any responsibility. In refusing to be "his brother's keeper," Cain rejects the role of steward that was established by God when human beings were created. The resulting curse (which further alienates human beings from the goods of the earth) and the mercy that God shows Cain reinforce key themes; yet, the story also reveals important characteristics of evil that were not present in the previous story. Here we see evil spreading from one generation to the next, and as the contagion spreads, its effects become even more destructive. Adam and Eve's disobedience in the garden is the seed that spawns Cain's murderous act in the field.

As the primeval narrative progresses, the situation continues to deteriorate. In Genesis 4, the Priestly writer adds genealogies to the Yahwist's narrative, not only to remind the people of their religious lineage, but to emphasize the downward spiral of humanity. From Adam to Methuselah to Noah, the "begetting" continues unabated, yet the primeval ancestors (with the notable exception of Enoch) continue to ignore God's instruction. The effects of evil are reflected in the diminishing life spans of the ancestors. Stubborn in their desire to be like God, some of them mate with beings of the heavenly court to produce the *Nephilim* (Heb. "fallen ones"), ancient warriors who are larger and stronger than ordinary human beings. God is further alarmed to see that "the wickedness of humankind was great in the earth, and that every inclination of the thoughts of their hearts was only evil continually" (Gen 6:6). No longer can he look upon creation and declare it to be "very good." Grief-stricken and angry, God impulsively decides to destroy his creation, much like Tiamat and Apsu, but with far greater success.

Destruction and Recreation

The story of Noah and the flood (which has striking parallels with the Babylonian epic of *Gilgamesh* and the *Atrahasis* myth) depicts God's destruction and recreation of the world and his second attempt at the human experiment.[12] The narrative consists of two interwoven accounts from the Yahwist and Priestly writers. As the final editor, the Priestly writer preserves the Yahwist's dark assessment of human nature, but tempers it with material that emphasizes God's mercy and blessings amid the destruction. Together, the two versions introduce important changes into the divine-human relationship, beginning with the figure of Noah. Unlike the majority of his ancestors, Noah is described as "a righteous man, blameless in his generation" (Gen 6:9). Despite his unrestrained love of the grape (Gen 9:20-27), Noah is presented as a model of righteous conduct, obeying God's numerous commands without question. He builds the ark (to Yahweh's exacting standards), gathers pairs of animals from every species, and then waits for the next command. He doesn't have to wait long.

Then the LORD said to Noah, "Go into the ark, you and all your household, for I have seen that you alone are righteous before me in this generation. Take with you seven pairs of all clean animals, the male and its mate; and a pair of the animals that are not clean, the male and its mate; and seven pairs of the birds of the air also, male and female, to keep their kind alive on the face of all the earth. For in seven days I will send rain on the earth for forty days and forty nights; and every living thing that I have made I will blot out from the face of the ground." And Noah did all that the LORD had commanded him. (Gen 7:1-5)

For forty days and nights, primordial chaos is unleashed, flooding the earth and blotting out every living thing. The ordeal must have been terrifying for humans and animals alike, but Noah's faith in God does not waiver. When the deluge finally subsides and God commands Noah and his family to leave the ark, he immediately shows his respect and gratitude for the divine mercy by erecting an altar and making sacrificial offerings from "every clean animal and every clean bird" (Gen 8:20). Noah's pattern of behavior establishes a righteous model of faith, obedience, and worship that will be repeated with and later challenged by Abraham.

The interweaving of the Yahwist and the Priestly material also introduces another layer of complexity to the divine portrait. The Yahwist's depiction of a grieving, volatile deity is tempered by the rather detached God of the Priestly account. In the Priestly version, God informs Noah that "I have determined to make an end of all flesh, for the earth is filled with violence because of them; now I am going to destroy them along with the earth" (Gen 6:14). There is no anguished soul-searching here, just an honest, straightforward assessment. In the face of mounting violence, God's justice demands that creation simply be "un-created." Yet God is not ready to abandon the experiment entirely. After the deluge, both the Yahwist and the Priestly writer include God's promise not to destroy creation through a flood again, but the Priestly writer adds the central concept of covenant, a formal, binding agreement that marks the beginning of a new relationship between God, Noah, and the entire created order.

God said, "This is the sign of the covenant that I make between me and you and every living creature that is with you, for all future generations; I have set my bow in the clouds, and it shall be a sign of the covenant between me and the earth. When I bring clouds over the earth and the bow is seen in the clouds, I will remember my covenant that is between me and you and every living creature of all flesh; and the waters shall never again become a flood to destroy all flesh. When the bow is in the clouds, I will see it and remember the everlasting covenant between God and every living creature of all flesh that is on the earth." God said to Noah, "This is the sign of the covenant that I have established between me and all flesh that is on the earth." (Gen 9:12-17)

Clearly, God realizes that the divine punishment was a bit excessive. In instituting the covenant, he promises to preserve and care for creation, regardless of the evil that human beings commit. God's willingness to enter into a binding agreement with his creation is unusual, to say the least, but it is representative of the evolution of this deity. Biblical scholars have commented on the divine transformation.

> This God: expresses sorrow and regret; judges, but doesn't want to; goes beyond justice and decides to save some, including animals; commits to the future of a less than perfect world; is open to change in view of experience with the world and doing things in new ways; promises never to do this again. What God does here "recharacterizes" the divine relation to the world. God ameliorates the workings of divine judgment and promises an orderly cosmos for the continuation of life. God will never do this again! God is the one who has changed between the beginning and end of the flood, not human beings.[13]

SIN AS A RELIGIOUS REALITY

Sin has no meaning outside of a religious context, but in the Bible it is the fundamental source of conflict and suffering. In the biblical stories, sin is not merely breaking God's law; it is a rebellious, selfish act that purposely erodes the divine-human relation. Sin has several destructive characteristics and effects that the biblical characters reveal and that we all experience as human beings:

- Sin alienates and divides us from others. There is a loss of connection to and respect for other life (both human and non-human) and for creation.

- Sin is an abuse of power. It results in the manipulation, exploitation, and oppression of other life.

- Sin is repetitious and contagious. We often commit the same sin over and over again and indoctrinate others (either purposely or inadvertently) into the selfish mindset that prompts sin.

- The mindset of sin becomes embedded in society's beliefs, activities, and institutions, leading to large-scale abuses, such as discrimination in all its forms, environmental destruction, and genocide.

How do you think the mindset of sin becomes embedded in society? What is the process? How do we know that it is present? What should we do as individuals and as a society to counteract this tendency?

Yahweh is hardly the omnipotent, omniscient deity of later Christian theology. This God is a sadder and wiser deity who has learned through bitter experience that human beings are a handful (anthropomorphically speaking, of course) and that they require a great deal of attention, guidance, and periodic punishment. The final story in the primeval history reinforces this harsh reality and sets the stage for yet another change in the divine strategy.

The Tower of Babel

Immediately after the establishment of the covenant, Noah's sons follow the divine command to "be fruitful and multiply, and fill the earth" (Gen 9:1). Their numerous offspring are recorded in the Table of Nations (Gen 10:1-32), a composite of Yahwist and Priestly genealogical materials that list the various ethnic groups in the ancient Near East. As an early attempt at ethnography, the narrative suggests that the diversity among the groups is the result of kinship relations and the natural migratory movements of the ancestors as they establish settlements in the region. The Priestly writer, as the final redactor of these materials, wants to show that the divine blessings have indeed been renewed after the flood and that the people are prospering (and multiplying!). The Tower of Babel story (Gen 11:1-9) immediately follows the listings and offers a less optimistic and more theological explanation for the region's ethnic diversity.

As a product of the Yahwist, the story is an etiological myth that parallels the events of Genesis 3, suggesting that the different ethnic, linguistic, and territorial groups in the region are the result of the sin of pride and humanity's stubborn refusal to accept creaturely limits. In reinforcing his theological vision, the Yahwist also takes some good-natured swipes at Babylonian culture, mocking their penchant for building ziggurats (terraced pyramids) as lasting monuments to their greatness. As with most stories in the primeval history, the Tower of Babel story begins on a promising note.

> Now the whole earth had one language and the same words. And as they migrated from the east, they came upon a plain in the land of Shinar and settled there. And they said to one another, "Come, let us make bricks, and burn them thoroughly." And they had brick for stone, and bitumen for mortar. Then they said, "Come, let us build ourselves a city, and a tower with its top in the heavens, and let us make a name for ourselves; otherwise we shall be scattered abroad upon the face of the whole earth." (Gen 11:1-4)

The unity that was established in the garden and lost in the fall is now realized—at least linguistically—at Shinar. Yet all is not well in this Babylonian Eden. The first ominous sign is the noticeable absence of Yahweh. For some unknown reason, the covenant relation established with Noah and his sons has eroded to the point that the residents of Shinar do not need or want divine aid. In fact, their decision to stay together and build a city with a great tower contradicts the divine command to disperse and "fill the earth." The residents' statements indicate that the dark side of humanity has once again gained the upper hand, leading them to defy the divine plan, corrupt the ideal of a unified humanity, and conjure up frightening possibilities that are voiced by Yahweh when he pays the settlers an unexpected visit.

> The LORD came down to see the city and the tower, which mortals had built. And the LORD said, "Look, they are one people, and they have all one language; and this is only the beginning of what they will do; nothing that they propose to do will now be impossible for them. Come, let us go down, and confuse their language there, so that they will not understand one another's speech." So the LORD scattered them abroad from there over the face of all the earth, and they left off building the city. Therefore it was called Babel, because there the LORD confused the language of all the earth; and from there the LORD scattered them abroad over the face of all the earth. (Gen 11:5-9)

The distance Yahweh must travel to view the site cleverly underscores the settlers' inflated sense of pride in their own accomplishments and symbolizes the severe alienation that now exists between God and human beings. The reference to the divine "us" in the passage undoubtedly reflects to the polytheistic roots of this ancient myth. The text gives the impression that the entire heavenly court is alarmed at the turn of events and supports God's intervention. As in the case of Adam and Eve, the residents of Shinar refuse to accept their creaturely limits. Their efforts to "make a name" for themselves by constructing monuments of brick and mortar reflect their desire for the omnipotence and immortality of God. Interestingly, when Yahweh discovers their intent, he does not interrogate the people so that they may see the error of the ways. Perhaps his previous conversations with human beings have shown the futility of reasoning with those who lust after power and acclaim. Whatever his thoughts on the matter, Yahweh realizes that such hubris cannot go unchallenged or unchecked. Since talking does no good, and destruction is no longer an option, he resorts to the trick of confusing their language—at best a stop-gap measure that buys a little time. Abandoning the tower project, the residents of Shinar disperse over the face of the earth, conforming to the divine plan and completing the transition from innocence to civilization.

The final verses of the story display the Yahwist's talent for puns. The Hebrew, *balal*, which means "to mix or confuse," is presented as the etiological source for the name "Babel" (in some textual translations it is "Babylon"). This is a clear slap at the Babylonians, who understood the name to be derived from the Akkadian, *Babel*, which meant "the gate of the god."[14] In the editorial hands of the Yahwist, however, the great city is so named because God "babbled" or confused the language of its residents. And so it goes.

Conclusion

The writer-redactors of Genesis combined their own writings with collected pieces of tradition to give expression to their understanding of the world and their experience of God. The revelation embedded in the stories of Genesis is the combined product of the materials at hand, the creative imagination of the writer-redactors, and the people's history. By the time the Pentateuch was compiled in the fifth century BCE, the God of Israel had delivered the people from Egyptian bondage, given them the Torah (the Mosaic Law), established an eternal covenant with the house of David, and remained loyal to the people, despite their repeated idolatry and subsequent exile and return. As a preface to the book of Exodus, the primeval history provided theological and ethical contexts that were foundational for interpreting the pivotal events in Israel's history. Equally important, the myths offered an alternative to the often violent polytheism that characterized the Egyptian, Canaanite, Assyrian, and Babylonian cultures. As Lawrence Boadt explains,

> [t]he authors of Genesis consciously intended to refute and contradict [the pagan religious worldview] by reworking the traditional stories to remove any idea that there is more than one God, that the world is subject to chaos, that God is callous or uncaring. . . . By telling the story of Genesis 1–11 as they did, stressing Yahweh's freedom and power versus human refusal of responsibility, the Israelites demythologized the myths—they destroyed the heart of pagan belief and reinterpreted the real meaning of the world in light of the one God who had revealed himself as Savior and Ruler to Moses.[15]

While we cannot grasp the full significance of these stories for their original audience—we can never fully enter their world—we can understand the basic revelatory intent of the primeval history, which is to assert the existence and superiority of Israel's God, explain the nature of creation and the divine-human relationship, introduce certain norms and core values, and establish the basic plotline for the remainder of the Pentateuch.

From a contemporary perspective, the stories continue to resonate with readers because they reveal fundamental truths about human existence. We see ourselves in these stories and recognize their universal validity. We, too, strive for the ideals of the garden, feel the enslavement of desire and the shame of sin, and dare to hope for future redemption. As participants in the quest for ultimate meaning, we, too, understand that human beings are brought into existence to live in peaceful union with God, with each other, and with the created order. The primeval myths reveal that God's economy of the gift is directed toward these ends. God's love and care are witnessed in the diverse gifts he bestows upon creation, in his repeated attempts to enlighten human beings through interrogation and dialogue, and even in the rash decision to destroy what he has created and begin again. All of these actions reflect the ongoing efforts of a volatile yet loving deity who realizes that his designated stewards are ill-suited for programmed rule-following—at least in any consistent way. As the primeval history comes to a close, it is clear that a more radical change in pedagogical strategy is in order, one that Yahweh is more than willing to consider for the sake of saving his creation. The new and improved model is introduced in the next chapter with Abraham, Israel's greatest patriarch.

Questions for Reflection and Discussion

1. The two creation accounts in Genesis were written many years apart and present two very different portraits of God. Discuss their similarities and differences. When viewed together, what personality emerges from these accounts? What does the time lapse between the two accounts suggest about how we experience, understand, and express the divine? Are you comfortable with the notion of an evolving, changing God?

2. The story of Adam and Eve depicts the destructive effects of sin and reveals the paradox that evil presents to human freedom. As human beings, we claim we are free, but as soon as we give in to temptation and abuse our freedom, we claim that we are not free, that something or someone else *made us* act badly. The belief that we are free and yet enslaved is the paradox of evil. What is your position on this paradox? Do you think we are both free and enslaved? How might human beings overcome this paradox?

3. Collectively, what portrait of humanity emerges from the primeval history? In other words, what kind of creatures are human beings? What are their good points and bad points? What desires do they have? How do they go about satisfying them? How does God respond to their efforts? What do these stories reveal about the nature of the divine-human relation? What do these insights tell us about the nature of biblical truth?

An Exercise in Self-Knowledge

Recall the last time you were really angry. Write down how you felt. Why were you angry? What did you want? Who or what was standing in your way? What did you do about it? Did you abuse your freedom? How? What was the result? How is your experience similar to or different from the experiences of Adam, Eve, and Cain?

Recommended Reading

Boadt, Lawrence. *Reading the Old Testament*. New York/Mahwah, NJ: Paulist Press, 1984. One of the most readable and entertaining introductions to the Old Testament in print.

Coogan, Michael D., ed. *The New Oxford Annotated Bible with the Apocryphal/Deuterocanonical Books*, 3rd ed. New Revised Standard Version. Oxford: Oxford University Press, 2001. One of the best translations for Bible study, with annotations, maps, essays, and other educational materials.

Dalley, Stephanie, ed. *Myths from Mesopotamia: Creation, the Flood, Gilgamesh, and Others*. Oxford: Oxford University Press, 1989. A translation of ancient Mesopotamian myths that influenced the early biblical writers.

Harris, Stephen L., and Robert L. Platzner. *The Old Testament: An Introduction to the Hebrew Bible*. Boston: McGraw-Hill, 2003. A comprehensive textbook for students and adult learners, offering interesting and informative treatments of Israel's history and the books of the Bible, Apocrypha, and Pseudepigrapha.

Ricoeur, Paul. *The Symbolism of Evil*. Boston: Beacon Press, 1967. A landmark study of the myths and symbols of evil in the ancient world that offers an illuminating analysis of the Adamic myth.

3

THE GIFT OF THE COVENANT

God and Abraham's Rocky Road to Righteousness

The ancestral history presented in Genesis 12–50 is a collection of mythical stories that recount the lives of Israel's patriarchs, Abraham, Isaac, and Jacob. Compiled and edited during the exilic and postexilic periods, the primary purpose of the history is to present the origins of Israel's ancestors and to explain how they came to reside in Egypt before the exodus. The shifting fortunes of the patriarchs and their relationship with Yahweh are vividly portrayed in the history, but their literary adventures should never be mistaken for historical fact. As Wayne T. Pitard explains,

> There are many reasons to be skeptical of these narratives as historically accurate accounts of the lives of Israel's progenitors. Indications within the narratives suggest that they had a substantial prehistory as oral literature. Modern studies of oral transmission demonstrate that stories preserved in this manner do not primarily serve a historical or antiquarian purpose; rather, they are meant to present cultural values that must be passed on to younger generations. In modern parlance, their function is sociological rather than historical. Usually, historical facts quickly become garbled in an oral tradition, which adapts such information to make whatever point the story is intended to convey. Events and characters are often manufactured for the narrative purposes, and variant versions of a single story develop alongside one another.[1]

In the ancestral history, a classic example of this phenomenon is the story of a patriarch who claims that his wife is his sister. This story occurs twice with Abraham (Gen 12:10-20; 20) and once with Isaac (Gen 26:6-11). The consensus among biblical scholars is that the repetitions are the result of multiple versions of a single story that evolved in the telling and that eventually made their way into the writings of the Yahwist (J), the Elohist (E), the Priestly writer (P).

The evolving, piecemeal nature of myth-making would seem to undercut the value of the Genesis myths for contemporary readers, but that is hardly the case. While the patriarchal stories are limited as a historical record, they still provide us with an intriguing glimpse into the cultural values, beliefs, and practices that influenced and shaped the worldview of ancient Israel. From an intertextual perspective, the carefully crafted stories also show dramatic changes in God's relationship with human beings, changes that indicate an evolving pedagogical strategy within the biblical canon. Taking a more literary approach to biblical interpretation (while including pertinent historical and cultural data), this chapter will explore God's relationship with Abraham, who is presented as the first and greatest of Israel's patriarchs.

In the Judeo-Christian tradition, Abraham is revered as the "father of faith"; in the Islamic tradition, he is often called *khalil Allah*, the friend of God. For centuries Jews, Christians, and Muslims have viewed the life of Abraham as a model for righteous living that should be embraced and emulated by all believers. But what kind of model does Abraham actually present? What characteristics does he display that make him an example of righteousness? Most believers would immediately answer that Abraham is righteous because he has faith in God. But what does that mean exactly? Why does Abraham have faith in God, and what is the content of that faith? The answer to these questions lies in the unique and often turbulent relationship between Yahweh and Abraham. In establishing a series of covenants with Abraham, God essentially abandons the rule-centered ethic of obedience introduced in Genesis, opting instead for a more flexible, developmental model that encourages critical thinking, debate, and even religious doubt. Exploring the dynamics of their relationship will illuminate the nature of faith and show how Yahweh's new model influences and shapes Abraham's religious consciousness, ultimately helping him grow and mature as a faithful, God-fearing human being.

The Beginning of Patriarchal History

The patriarchal history begins with a rather long genealogy (Gen 11:10-32) that traces Israel's ancestors back to Shem, the eldest of Noah's sons. This Priestly addition to the Yahwist narrative is intended to remind the Judean exiles of their ancestral heritage. Robert Alter notes that

> [t]his genealogy, which constitutes the bridge from the Flood to the beginning of the Patriarchal Tales, uses formulas identical with those of the antediluvian genealogy in chapter 5, omitting the summarizing indication of life span and the report of death of each begetter. Longevity now is cut in half, and then halved again in the latter part of the list, as we approach Abram. From this point, men will have merely the extraordinary life spans of modern Caucasian mountain dwellers and not legendary life spans. The narrative in this way is preparing to enter recognizable human time and family life. There is one hidden number-game here, as the Israeli Bible scholar Moshe Weinfeld has observed: the number of years from the birth of Shem's son to Abram's migration to Canaan is exactly a solar 365.[2]

The transition to human time is not the only reason for the decreasing life spans, however. They also symbolize the continued estrangement between God and humanity reflected in the Tower of Babel story (Gen 11:1-9). By the time Abraham arrives on the scene, several generations have passed, and yet the people's relationship with Yahweh has hardly improved. Evidence of this appears when we first encounter Abraham (who is initially called Abram) and learn a startling bit of news about his wife, Sarai: "Now Sarai was barren; she had no child" (Gen 11:30). Barrenness was generally interpreted in the ancient world as a sign of divine disfavor, but, ironically, Sarai's condition becomes a critical factor in Abraham's transformation from a mere tribal patriarch to the father of faith. The saga begins with Yahweh's first words to Abram in Genesis 12.

> Now the LORD said to Abram, "Go from your country and your kindred and your father's house to the land that I will show you. I will make of you a great nation, and I will bless you, and make your name great, so that you will be a blessing. I will bless those who bless you, and the one who curses you I will curse; and in you all the families of the earth shall be blessed." (Gen 12:1-3)

As the verses suggest, Yahweh has decided to try again, to redeem creation through a hand-picked successor to Adam. As with the primeval history, God initiates contact and issues a direct command to his creature, yet the order Abram receives is very different from Adam's. Instead of a negative prohibition ("You shall not . . ."), Yahweh's command is a positive instruction. He tells Abram to leave his homeland and go to the land of Canaan, but God doesn't stop there. He sweetens the offer with some very generous incentives. In return for Abram's obedience, Yahweh promises to give the patriarch an heir, enough land to accommodate a "great nation," unstinting care, and protection from his enemies. God even suggests that Abram will become so great that "all the families of the earth" will benefit from his obedient example. Abram's response to Yahweh's gracious offer is instantaneous and revealing.

> So Abram went, as the LORD had told him; and Lot went with him. Abram was seventy-five years old when he departed from Haran. Abram took his wife Sarai and his brother's son Lot, and all the possessions that he had gathered, and the persons whom they had acquired in Haran; and they set forth to go to the land of Canaan. When they had come to the land of Canaan, Abram passed through the land to the place at Shechem, to the oak of Moreh. At that time the Canaanites were in the land. Then the LORD appeared to Abram, and said, "To your offspring I will give this land." So he built there an altar to the LORD, who had appeared to him. From there he moved on to the hill country on the east of Bethel, and pitched his Tent, with Bethel on the west and Ai on the east; and there he built an altar to the LORD and in-

voked the name of the LORD. And Abram journeyed on by stages toward the Negeb. (Gen 12:4-9)

As the verses indicate, leaving Haran is no easy undertaking. As the head of a large household, Abram has many possessions and persons under his care, yet he never asks Yahweh for some time to talk to his wife or to get his affairs in order; he simply obeys. Given his wealth and position in society, why would Abram suddenly pick up, lock, stock, and barrel, and move to a foreign land? While Abram doesn't offer the reader an explanation for his behavior, it seems plausible that his response to Yahweh's command is based on his faith in the power of this God. Clearly, Yahweh has made quite an impression on Abram, so much so that he believes this deity will somehow make good on his promises. Abram thus departs from Haran in "good faith" without a second thought or backward glance.

At this point in the story, Abram is seventy-five years old, a number that denotes wisdom and maturity rather than strict chronological age. As Abram leads his household to Canaan, Yahweh reassures him that the promise of land will be fulfilled, despite the presence of Canaanites (i.e., the local inhabitants) of the land. Abram responds by building altars and invoking God's name, thus making a public affirmation of his loyalty to Yahweh. In performing these acts of worship along the travel route, Abram is acknowledging his continued faith in Yahweh, as well as his dependence upon God for his household's present survival and future prosperity.

The Bible's Call-Response Pattern

The initial encounters between Yahweh and Abram reaffirm a call-response pattern that was initiated with Noah and that is repeated throughout the biblical canon. From Genesis to Revelation, God calls many persons (e.g., the patriarchs, the prophets, the disciples) and each response reveals something about the character of the individual. Like that of Noah, Abram's response to God's offer reveals three fundamental characteristics of a righteous life: faith, obedience, and worship. Like that of Noah, Abram's behavior is immediate and unquestioning. He does not rebel against the divine command, nor does Yahweh have to explain or teach Abram how to respond. He does everything quite naturally. Clearly, Yahweh has chosen well, for Abram appears to be a perfect model of righteousness—at least at this point. Abram's sojourn in Egypt, however, tests the divine-human relationship and reveals another, quite unexpected characteristic of the righteous life.

Now there was a famine in the land. So Abram went down to Egypt to reside there as an alien, for the famine was severe in the land. When he was about to enter Egypt, he said to his wife Sarai, "I know well that you are a woman beautiful in appearance; and when the Egyptians see you, they will say, 'This is his wife'; then they will kill me, but they will let you live. Say you are my sister, so that it may go well with me because of you, and that my life may be spared on your account." When Abram entered Egypt the Egyptians saw that the woman was very beautiful. When the officials of Pharaoh saw her, they praised her to Pharaoh. And the woman was taken to Pharaoh's house. And for her sake he dealt well with Abram; and he had sheep, oxen, male donkeys, male and female slaves, female donkeys, and camels. (Gen 12:10-16)

The first occurrence of the wife-sister stories is prompted by famine, which necessitates Abram's move to unfamiliar territory. Perhaps his fear of the unknown prompts his scheme to trick Pharaoh, but whatever the reason, one thing is certain. His deception is the act of a man who has doubts, who is wavering in his belief that Yahweh will protect him against his enemies. Rather than depend on Yahweh (as he did in his earlier travels), Abram takes matters into his own hands. Interestingly, Abram's fears regarding the Egyptians are not without merit. Pharaoh takes Sarai into his house and attempts to buy Abram's approval with numerous gifts. Although Abram seems to have "dodged the bullet" himself, his self-serving meddling has disastrous implications, for Pharaoh's intention to have carnal knowledge of the future mother of the promised heir jeopardizes the divine plan. The child of the promise is to come from no other woman but Sarai. Yahweh quickly intervenes to foil Pharaoh's plans.

But the LORD afflicted Pharaoh and his house with great plagues because of Sarai, Abram's wife. So Pharaoh called Abram, and said, "What is this you have done to me? Why did you not tell me that she was your wife? Why did you say, 'She is my sister,' so that I took her for my wife? Now then, here is your wife, take her, and be gone." And Pharaoh gave his men orders concerning him; and they set him on the way, with his wife and all that he had. (Gen 12:17-20)

Although God does not address Abram directly, his actions speak volumes. By afflicting Pharaoh and his household with severe plagues (later echoed in the exodus story), God is upholding the promise to protect Abram and his household from his enemies. Yahweh is thus showing Abram that he can be trusted. Equally telling is Yahweh's restraint. He does not punish Abram for his lack of faith or for placing the promise in jeopardy; instead, Abram is allowed to leave Egypt, taking with him Pharaoh's generous bribes.

Given Yahweh's demanding track record with human beings thus far, why would he appear to reward such behavior? Some clues emerge as the patriarchal history unfolds, for in working with Abram, Yahweh's pedagogical approach shifts from that of the strict disciplinarian of the primeval history to one of being a patient and tolerant mentor to Abram. In taking on this new role, Yahweh gives Abram the freedom to make mistakes, to doubt his faith in Yahweh's power and providence, so that he can learn what it truly means to be righteous. The new approach is immediately put to the test in Genesis 15, when Yahweh establishes the first explicit covenant with Abram.

> After these things the word of the LORD came to Abram in a vision, "Do not be afraid, Abram, I am your shield; your reward shall be very great." But Abram said, "O Lord GOD, what will you give me, for I continue childless, and the heir of my house is Eliezer of Damascus?" And Abram said, "You have given me no offspring, and so a slave born in my house is to be my heir." (Gen 15:1-3)

"After these things" refers to a series of adventures in which Abram (in true swashbuckling fashion) rescues his nephew, Lot, from foreign kings and receives a blessing from the mysterious king-priest, Melchizedek of Salem (later Jerusalem). Abram's triumphs are a clear indication of divine favor, yet Yahweh's continued reassurance is met with a sharp rebuke from Abram. Blessings and protection are all well and good, but where is the child of the promise? Abram is worried that his considerable wealth and family name will become the property of Eliezer, a trusted steward and possible adopted son. As much as he cares for Eliezer, Abram wants a son from his own loins, and he wants him now! Once again, Abram is showing signs of doubt in Yahweh's promises. In the face of such uncertainty and presumption (has he forgotten who he's talking to?) God responds in a way that combines patience with pedagogy.

> But the word of the LORD came to him, "This man shall not be your heir; no one but your very own issue shall be your heir." He brought him outside and said, "Look toward heaven and count the stars, if you are able to count them." Then he said to him, "So shall your descendants be." And he believed the LORD; and the LORD reckoned it to him as righteousness. (Gen 15:4-6)

Rather than punish Abram for his audacity, Yahweh offers comfort as he takes him outside to look at the stars. Abram's faith in God is immediately renewed, but why this sudden about-face? What did Abram see in the stars that prompted his radical switch from doubt to faith? The answer lies in Abram's changed sense of perspective and proportion. As with many human beings, Abram's vision is narrow, extending only to what he sees and wants at the moment. Yahweh promised him a son, but the child is nowhere in sight. Abram's patience is at an end and who can blame him? He's not a young man any more and the years are quickly slipping away. But Abram's obsession with fathering a child has blinded him to the "big picture" of the promise. In leading him outside to look at the stars, Yahweh draws Abram out of his narrow perspective, shifting his gaze from the immediate moment to a vast new horizon that transcends his own time and place. Gazing at the star-filled heavens, Abram sees and suddenly understands. The stars are the future generations of a great nation stretched out before him; a great nation that *he* will father. Yahweh's patient and subtle instruction has helped Abram realize that he is part of something greater than himself, something that involves more than simply fathering a single child. Abram's brief but revelatory glimpse into the divine plan, coupled with his previous experiences with Yahweh, convince him—at least for the moment—that God will make good on his promise.

The exchange between Yahweh and Abram in Genesis 15:1-6 reflects a relationship that has clearly grown since their first encounter. They now share a comfortable yet volatile relationship that benefits both parties. On the one hand, Abram has the freedom to doubt God's intentions and to voice his misgivings without fear of punishment. On the other hand, Yahweh uses Abram's doubts to teach him the meaning of righteousness. The outcome of Abram's outburst bears this out, for in doubting Yahweh's intentions, Abram has gained a greater understanding of the divine plan and with that understanding a deepening trust in God. Doubt thus becomes an important catalyst for spiritual growth. Yahweh clearly shares this view, for it is only after resolving Abram's crisis of faith that God deems him righteous enough to enter into a covenant relation with him—but not without further assurances.

The Covenant with Abram

> Then he said to him, "I am the LORD who brought you from Ur of the Chaldeans, to give you this land to possess." But he said, "Oh Lord GOD, how am I to know that I shall possess it?" He said to him, "Bring me a heifer three years old, a female goat three years old, a ram three years old, a turtledove, and a young pigeon." He brought him all these and cut them in two, laying each half over against the other; but he did not cut the birds in two. And when birds of prey came down on the carcasses, Abram drove them away. (Gen 15:7-11)

As this passage indicates, Abram's righteousness is again characterized by doubt. To reassure Abram, Yahweh freely enters into a covenant relation that takes the form of a "self-curse." The cutting of the animals is part of an ancient tradition in Mesopotamia in which parties to a covenant would walk between the dismembered animals, announcing that a similar fate would await them if they violated the covenant requirements. In this case, Yahweh is promising Abram the land of Canaan without asking him for anything in return. The burden of keeping the covenant thus falls on God alone. The significance of this gesture cannot be overstated. The covenant is presented as a gift, a good faith offering to Abram that further demonstrates the trustworthiness of God.

If only Abram would be so accommodating! Instead, he and his wife, Sarai, attempt to speed up the divine plan through the use of a surrogate mother. Exchanging the barren Sarai for the slave girl, Hagar, was not such an outrageous idea, for the ancients believed the male seed housed the off-spring while the woman merely provided the fertile ground where the seed could grow. At Sarai's urging, Abram impregnates Hagar, but the mating has unintended consequences. Foolishly, Hagar shows disdain for her barren mistress and quickly becomes the target of a jealous Sarai. The girl soon runs away to escape Sarai's abuse. Facing certain death in the wilderness, Hagar is aided by an angel of the LORD, who convinces her to return to Abram's house. Shortly afterward, "Hagar bore Abram a son; and Abram names his son, whom Hagar bore, Ishmael. Abram was eighty-six years old when Hagar bore him Ishmael" (Gen 16:15). Oh the irony! While Abram is still capable of fathering a child, his efforts to circumvent God's plan only result in further delays.

Thirteen more years elapse before Yahweh appears to Abram again. During this time, Abram continues his seasonal journeys through the land of Canaan, pitching his tent, tending his sizeable flocks, and no doubt fulfilling his husbandly duties as he waits for the child of the promise. The lapse in communication is never explained, but the next exchange introduces substantive changes in the covenant relation.

> When Abram was ninety-nine years old, the LORD appeared to Abram, and said to him, "I am God Almighty; walk before me, and be blameless. And I will make my covenant between me and you, and will make you exceedingly numerous." Then Abram fell on his face; and God said to him, "As for me, this is my covenant with you: You shall be the ancestor of a multitude of nations. No longer shall your name be Abram, but your name shall be Abraham; for I have made you the ancestor of a multitude of nations. I will make you exceedingly fruitful; and I will make nations of you, and kings shall come from you. I will establish my covenant between me and you, and your offspring after you throughout their generations, for an everlasting covenant, to be God to you and to your offspring after you. And I will give to you, and to your offspring after you, the land where you are now an alien, all the land of Canaan, for a perpetual holding; and I will be their God." (Gen 17:1-8)

This passage, attributed to the Priestly writer, is designed to reinforce key events and religious themes in Israel's history. Writing during the Babylonian exile, the Priestly writer interprets the covenant relation from the perspective of a people who have endured the loss of the land, the monarchy, and the Jerusalem Temple. God's speech affirms Israel's history (Abram indeed fathered the kings of Israel) while extending the covenant blessings. The covenant is now eternal, providing the exiles with a much-needed message of hope as they await their deliverance.

As in Genesis 15, God reassures Abram that the earlier promises will be fulfilled, but this time Abram responds in perfect humility, prostrating himself before his divine benefactor. The name change is also significant. While both *Abram* and *Abraham* roughly mean "exalted father," God's pronouncement indicates that Abram is about to take on some of the burdens of the covenant relation. God then goes on to spell out the precise nature of the burden:

> God said to Abraham, "As for you, you shall keep my covenant, you and your offspring after you throughout their generations. This is my covenant, which you shall keep, between me and you and your offspring after you: Every male among you shall be circumcised. You shall circumcise the flesh of your foreskins, and it shall be a sign of the covenant between me and you. Throughout your generations every male among you shall be circumcised when he is eight days old, including the slave born in your house and the one bought with your money from any foreigner who is not of your offspring. Both the slave born in your house and the one bought with your money must be circumcised. So shall my covenant be in your flesh an everlasting covenant. Any uncircumcised male who is not circumcised in the flesh of his foreskin shall be cut off from his people; he has broken my covenant."(Gen 17:9-14)

Circumcision was an ancient ritual that may have been connected to marriage. The ancients believed that circumcision would ward off evil spirits that might interfere with fertility. For the Priestly writer, circumcision was an ethnic marker that distinguished the Judean exiles from their Babylonian captors. Because of the threat of cultural assimilation, the inclusion of the ritual in the Priestly version of the covenant was no doubt prompted by the priests' desire to preserve the people's cultural identity. They had lost the land, the monarchy, and the Temple; circumcision was the last visible sign of Israel's ongoing relationship with God.

In contrast to previous encounters with Abraham, God doesn't leave Sarai out of the loop. She, too, experiences a name change. God now calls her Sarah, meaning "princess," and says to her husband: "I will bless her, and moreover I will give you a son by her. I will bless her, and she shall give rise to nations; kings of peoples shall come from her" (Gen 17:16). True to form, Abraham's response reflects the tension within the divine-human relationship. As he did earlier in the scene, Abraham falls on his face before his divine benefactor—but this time it's from laughter.

> "Can a child be born to a man who is a hundred years old? Can Sarah, who is ninety years old, bear a child?" And Abraham said to God, "O that Ishmael might live in your sight!" God said, "No, but your wife Sarah shall bear you a son, and you shall name him Isaac. I will establish my covenant with him as an everlasting covenant for his offspring after him. As for Ishmael, I have heard you; I will bless him and make him fruitful and exceedingly numerous; he shall be the father of twelve princes, and I will make him a great nation. But my covenant I will es-

tablish with Isaac, whom Sarah shall bear to you at this season next year." And when he had finished talking with him, God went up from Abraham. (Gen 17:17-22)

The practicalities of giving birth at an advanced age certainly justify Abraham's doubts. With frustration and a tinge of bitterness, he pleads for Ishmael. Why not recognize a child that already exists? But Abraham's plan is not God's plan. Rejecting the "bird in the hand" approach, God patiently explains that Sarah is to be the mother of the promised child. To further appease Abraham, God extends his providential care to Ishmael, who was the product of Abraham and Sarah's impatience. Abraham immediately responds by circumcising himself and "every male among the men of [his] house" (Gen 17:23). Whether his response is prompted by renewed faith or resignation is unclear. What is clear is that, despite the tense and rocky nature of their relationship, neither God nor Abraham is ready or willing to give up on it—there is simply too much at stake. Their next encounter, however, raises the tension to the breaking point, with accusations and finger-pointing on both sides.

The Debate about Sodom and Gomorrah

Resuming the Yahwist narrative, Genesis 18 is a patchwork of oral and written traditions that reflect the Yahwist's brilliant editorial hand. The chapter begins with an unusual visitation.

> The LORD appeared to Abraham by the oaks of Mamre, as he sat at the entrance of his tent in the heat of the day. He looked up and saw three men standing near him. When he saw them, he ran from the tent entrance to meet them, and bowed down to the ground. He said, "My lord, if I find favor with you, do not pass by your servant. Let a little water be brought, and wash your feet, and rest yourselves under the tree. Let me bring a little bread, that you may refresh yourselves, and after that you may pass on—since you have come to your servant." So they said, "Do as you have said." (Gen 18:1-5)

On this occasion, Yahweh does not come to Abraham through speech or visions; instead, the theophany takes the form of three men, traditionally believed to be Yahweh and two angelic attendants. In attending to the visitors, Abraham is presented as an ideal host, running out to greet them, bowing to the ground as a sign of respect, and offering them rest, relaxation, and refreshment. His humble offer of a "little bread" quickly becomes a sumptuous feast of veal, curds, milk, and fresh-baked cakes. The strangers immediately accept Abraham's hospitality. After serving his guests, Abraham waits nearby under a tree while they eat, no doubt anxious to attend to their needs.

Although Abraham's behavior may seem exaggerated by contemporary standards, his actions and those of his guests are carefully choreographed to show their good intentions toward each other. In the ancient Near East, hospitality was a core value. Whether friends or strangers, visitors were always treated with the utmost care and respect, for in the merciless conditions of the desert, such consideration often meant the difference between life and death. The strangers' willingness to enter Abraham's tent and accept his hospitality indicate that they mean him no harm; they come in peace.

One purpose of the visit is revealed when Abraham's guests ask him about the whereabouts of Sarah.

> The one said, "I will surely return to you in due season, and your wife Sarah shall have a son." And Sarah was listening at the tent entrance behind him. Now Abraham and Sarah were old, advanced in age; it had ceased to be with Sarah after the manner of women. So Sarah laughed to herself, saying, "After I have grown old, and my husband is old, shall I have pleasure?" (Gen 18:10-12)

Clearly, Sarah shares Abraham's pessimism about parenthood. Yahweh once again reassures the couple, but reiterating the promise is not the only reason for the visit. As Abraham sees the visitors off (a host's final obligation) on their way to Sodom, Yahweh asks himself a startling question.

> The LORD said, "Shall I hide from Abraham what I am about to do, seeing that Abraham shall become a great and mighty nation, and all the nations of the earth shall be blessed in him? No, for I have chosen him, that he may charge his children and his household after him to keep the way of the LORD by doing righteousness and justice; so that the LORD may bring about for Abraham what he has promised him." Then the LORD said, "How great is the outcry against Sodom and Gomorrah and how very grave their sin! I must go down and see whether they have done altogether according to the outcry that has come to me; and if not, I will know." (Gen 18:17-21)

Here we see a very worried deity who is contemplating an action that he knows is questionable. At this point, the reader has no idea what God is contemplating, but it appears that he has already decided to punish Sodom and Gomorrah; hence the concern about Abraham's reaction. Could it be that the deity who demands that his chosen one be righteous and just is contemplating an act that compromises these ideals?

As with the Tower of Babel story, God travels quite a distance to investigate the reports about Sodom and Gomorrah. He's clearly not happy with what he sees and confides to Abraham his plan to wipe out the cities. What follows is a heated and somewhat comical exchange in which Abraham severely chides Yahweh, demanding that he treat the cities' inhabitants with justice and mercy.

So the men turned from there, and went toward Sodom, while Abraham remained standing before the LORD. Then Abraham came near and said, "Will you indeed sweep away the righteous with the wicked? Suppose there are fifty righteous within the city; will you then sweep away the place and not forgive it for the fifty righteous who are in it? Far be it from you to do such a thing, to slay the righteous with the wicked, so that the righteous fare as the wicked! Far be that from you! Shall not the Judge of all the earth do what is just?" (Gen 18:22-25)

Abraham's words are blunt and to the point, reflecting the candor and intimacy that has developed between him and God. The words also reflect the inability of human beings to understand the mysterious ways of God. How can Yahweh sweep away the righteous with the wicked? Such an act is neither fair nor just. Hearing Abraham's complaint, God reconsiders (or so it seems), telling him, "If I find at Sodom fifty righteous in the city, I will forgive the whole place for their sake" (Gen 18:26). Perhaps God's measured response brings Abraham to his senses. Whatever the reason, Abraham's righteous indignation is suddenly replaced with the realization that he's scolding a powerful deity who could blot him out in a heartbeat. His tone swiftly changes, becoming more conciliatory and respectful.

Abraham answered, "Let me take it upon myself to speak to the LORD, I who am but dust and ashes. Suppose five of the fifty righteous are lacking? Will you destroy the whole city for lack of five? And he said, "I will not destroy it if I find forty-five there." Again he spoke to him, "Suppose forty are found there." He answered, "For the sake of forty I will not do it." Then he said, "Oh do not let the LORD be angry if I speak. Suppose thirty are found there." He answered, "I will not do it, if I find thirty there." (Gen 18:27-30)

And so it goes. The bargaining continues until Yahweh agrees to spare Sodom for the sake of ten righteous people.

Abraham's debate with Yahweh is instructive, because it indicates that some progress has been made in Abraham's spiritual journey. Rather than taking matters into his own hands—which has been his modus operandi—Abraham hopes to influence the outcome by taking the high moral ground and convincing God that destroying Sodom and Gomorrah contradicts the dictates of divine justice. For a man who has used lies and deceit to great advantage, this is quite a breakthrough. But, in the end, Abraham's intercession merely postpones the inevitable, for ten righteous people cannot be found.

Poised to strike, Yahweh remembers his promise of protection to Abraham and his household—a promise that extends to his nephew, Lot, who now lives in Sodom with his wife and daughters. The two angelic attendants call out to Lot, instructing him to take his family out of the city, saying, "Flee for your life; do not look back or stop anywhere in the Plain; flee to the hills, or else you will be consumed" (Gen 19:17). Echoes of the flood story resound as Yahweh rains down death and destruction, only this time the cities are engulfed in a terrifying storm of fire and sulfur (Gen 19:15-26). In a classic and oft-quoted incident, Lot's wife meets a cruel fate. Disobeying God's instruction, she looks back at the cities he is destroying and is instantly turned into a pillar of salt. As in the case of Eve, Lot's wife's curiosity proves her undoing.

After the destruction of the cities, Abraham departs to the region of the Negeb, eventually settling in Gerar, a city that lies on the southern border of Canaan, near Gaza. The volatile relationship between Abraham and Yahweh continues. Chapter 20 presents the second sister-wife story that underscores Abraham's waffling faith. This time, Abraham dupes King Abimelech of Gerar. While there are substantive differences between the two sister-wife stories, the sequence of events and the results are basically the same: God intervenes to counter Abraham's meddling, a lecherous ruler is punished, Abraham and Sarah are spared, and they depart the ruler's household much wealthier than when they arrived. Immediately afterward, Yahweh fulfills the final condition of the covenant promise.

> The LORD dealt with Sarah as he had said, and the LORD did for Sarah as he had promised. Sarah conceived and bore Abraham a son in his old age, at the time of which God had spoken to him. Abraham gave the name Isaac to his son whom Sarah bore him. And Abraham circumcised his son Isaac when he was eight days old, as God had commanded him. Abraham was a hundred years old when his son Isaac was born to him. Now Sarah said, "God has brought laughter for me; everyone who hears will laugh with me." And she said, "Who would ever have said to Abraham that Sarah would nurse children? Yet I have borne him a son in his old age." (Gen 21:1-7)

The child of the promise is finally given to the once-barren couple. Abraham responds with perfect obedience. He calls the child Isaac and has the boy circumcised on the eighth day, according to the covenant requirement. Sarah's joy and relief are evident. No longer is laughter a sign of cruel derision or disbelief; now it takes the form of a blessed child's name.

At last, all the elements for a happy ending seem to be in place, but the time of celebration and feasting is short-lived, for Abraham will soon endure the greatest test of his faith. Two incidents from the Elohist source set the stage for this crucial event. The first incident occurs at Isaac's weaning ceremony, where the rivalry between Hagar and Sarah erupts with renewed venom.

> The child grew and was weaned; and Abraham made a great feast on the day that Isaac was weaned. But Sarah saw the son of Hagar the Egyptian, whom she had borne to Abraham, playing with her son Isaac. So she said to Abraham, "Cast out this slave woman with her son; for

the son of this slave woman shall not inherit along with my son Isaac."
(Gen 21:8-10)

Biblical commentators have long speculated on Sarah's harsh response
to Ishmael's behavior. The meaning of Isaac's name (Heb. *yishaq*, "he
laughs") and the Hebrew fondness for puns provide some clues. Sarah believes that in "playing" with Isaac, Ishmael is mimicking (or perhaps mocking) Isaac's name in an attempt to take his place as the legitimate heir. Sarah
will have none of it, insisting that Hagar and Ishmael be expelled from the
household. Sarah's determination to secure her son's rightful inheritance
makes quite an impression on God, who counsels Abraham to go along
with the plan (Gen 21:12-13). Nevertheless, God assures him that Ishmael
will not perish in the wilderness; instead, he will share in the inheritance,
fathering a great nation (traditionally believed to be the Bedouin Arabs).
With Isaac's inheritance rights thus secured, the second incident reaffirms
Abraham's right to the land.

In its oral form, the story of Abraham and King Abimelech was probably an etiology (a story of origins) that explains how the city of Beer-sheba
was named. Having had first-hand experience of Abraham's tactics and the
power of his God, Abimelech suggests that they enter into a covenant and
implores Abraham to "swear to me here by God that you will not deal
falsely with me or with my offspring or with my posterity, but as I have
dealt loyally with you, you will deal with me and with the land where you
have resided as an alien" (Gen 21:23-24). Abraham agrees to the covenant,
but it isn't long before a conflict arises.

> When Abraham complained to Abimelech about a well of water that
> Abimelech's servants had seized, Abimelech said, "I do not know who
> has done this; you did not tell me, and I have not heard of it until
> today." So Abraham took sheep and oxen and gave them to Abimelech,
> and the two men made a covenant. Abraham set apart seven ewe lambs
> of the flock. And Abimelech said to Abraham, "What is the meaning of
> these seven ewe lambs that you have set apart?" He said, "These seven
> ewe lambs you shall accept from my hand, in order that you may be a
> witness for me that I dug this well." Therefore that place was called
> Beer-sheba; because there both of them swore an oath. (Gen 21:25-31)

Although hearing Abraham complain is nothing new, his approach to
dealing with Abimelech is. He seems a changed man. While the oath to God
may have something to do with Abraham's sense of commitment, there is
another, more compelling reason for his transformation. In fulfilling all the
covenant requirements, God has taught Abraham what it means to be a
covenant partner, setting an example that Abraham now seems anxious to
emulate. The proof lies in his conduct toward Abimelech. Instead of deceiv-
ing the ruler, Abraham deals openly and fairly with him; instead of accepting

bribes, Abraham is the gift-giver, offering Abimelech valuable livestock to secure his goodwill.

God's patient instruction and generous example seems to be paying off. Abraham has indeed become a model of righteous conduct. The final story in the Elohist series, however, tests the conviction of the new Abraham.

The Binding of Isaac

Many scholars believe that, in its original oral form, the story of the binding of Isaac (Gen 22:1-19) was intended as an indictment against the Canaanite practice of child sacrifice. In the skillful editorial hands of the Priestly writer, however, the story is transformed into an exploration of religious consciousness that calls into question the very possibility of faith in God. The story begins on a positive note that quickly turns dark with foreboding.

> After these things God tested Abraham. He said to him, "Abraham!" And he said, "Here I am." He said, "Take your son, your only son Isaac, whom you love, and go to the land of Moriah, and offer him there as a burnt offering on one of the mountains that I will show you." (Gen 22:1-2)

As in Genesis 12, God calls and Abraham obediently responds, indicating that he is ready for whatever God requires. In a speech that seems almost sadistic, God pointedly reminds Abraham of his deep affection for his son—the only child of the promise—just before demanding that Abraham kill him. This is a stunning reversal, for now it is God, rather than Abraham, who seems to be jeopardizing the divine plan. Abraham's response to the divine command is every bit as stunning.

> So Abraham rose early in the morning, saddled his donkey, and took two of his young men with him, and his son Isaac; he cut the wood for the burnt offering, and set out and went to the place in the distance that God had shown him. On the third day Abraham looked up and saw the place far away. Then Abraham said to his young men, "Stay here with the donkey; the boy and I will go over there; we will worship, and then we will come back to you." (Gen 22:3-5)

In contrast to earlier encounters, Abraham does not complain, challenge, or debate with God; instead he obeys without question, even rising early to start on the dreaded journey. We can only imagine the thoughts that must have been swirling in Abraham's mind as he traveled those three long days to the land of Moriah. While father and son make their way toward the appointed place of sacrifice, their actions and dialogue are heavy with irony.

Abraham took the wood of the burnt offering and laid it on his son Isaac, and he himself carried the fire and the knife. So the two of them walked on together. Isaac said to his father Abraham, "Father!" And he said, "Here I am, my son." He said, "The fire and the wood are here, but where is the lamb for a burnt offering?" Abraham said, "God himself will provide the lamb for a burnt offering, my son." So the two of them walked on together. (Gen 22:6-8)

How excruciating it must have been for Abraham to place the wood on Isaac's shoulders, to look into his trusting eyes and answer him as any righteous father would. Rather than challenge God, Abraham's words reflect his dependence on God, acknowledging God's power to provide whatever is needed and to determine the outcome. There is no self-serving meddling here, only obedience to the divine will. As the time of sacrifice nears, words end and action suddenly quickens.

When they came to the place that God had shown him, Abraham built an altar there and laid the wood in order. He bound his son Isaac, and laid him on the altar, on top of the wood. Then Abraham reached out his hand and took the knife to kill his son. But the angel of the LORD called to him from heaven, and said, "Abraham, Abraham!" And he said, "Here I am." He said, "Do not lay your hand on the boy or do anything to him; for now I know that you fear God, since you have not withheld your son, your only son, from me." (Gen 22:9-12)

Isaac's trauma must have been intense as he watched his father raise the knife against him. No doubt Abraham's relief was equally intense when the angel commanded him to stop. In the eyes of God, the father's readiness to sacrifice the son is the moment of truth that ultimately saves the child. The chosen model of righteousness has indeed passed the greatest of tests, but the perennial question for readers of the story is: Why would God submit Abraham and Isaac to such a horrible (and, some would argue, immoral) ordeal? And why would Abraham agree to murder his beloved son? The answer to these questions is found in the angel's words to Abraham: "for now I know that you fear God, since you have not withheld your son, your only son, from me." Clearly, fear of God is an essential attribute of God's model of faith, one that Abraham has not adequately displayed thus far; hence the test. If Abraham was motivated by fear of the Lord, then it is crucial to understand the meaning of this phrase.

Fear of the Lord

At its most fundamental level, to fear God is to experience a profound sense of awe and reverence in the presence of the Wholly Other; yet embedded in the phrase are other meanings that are equally important and that are often overlooked by readers of the Bible. Marc Jolley offers a helpful definition.

While "fear of the Lord" can mean outright fear of God's presence, it also means to revere God, an idea most directly expressed in the Wisdom Literature (e.g., Prov 2:5). Fear of God is connected to keeping the law and commandments (Eccl 12:13) and is "the whole of wisdom" (Sir 19:20) and "the root of wisdom" (1:20). Most succinctly stated, "Truly, the fear of the Lord, that is wisdom; and to depart from evil is understanding" (Job 28:28).[3]

To fear God, then, is to be aware that we are in the presence of something greater than ourselves, a presence that evokes a disposition of humility (rather than arrogant control) and a desire to do God's will as expressed in the divine commandments. Yet Jolley's definition does not adequately explain Abraham's behavior at Moriah, for where is the wisdom in sacrificing the life of a child? Why would Abraham continue to worship a deity who would make such a horrible demand? The simple answer is that Abraham had faith, but it is a kind of faith that can be understood only within the context of his covenant relationship with God.

The Development and Content of Abraham's Faith

As noted in chapter 1, faith is a personal commitment that is based on a person's experience and knowledge of the object of faith. The kinds of faith commitments a person has will influence and shape his or her character and behavior. In the case of Abraham, his covenant relationship with Yahweh resulted in a gradual shift in his religious consciousness, from an initial state of fear and awe of God (Gen 12) to a profound sense of reverence based on understanding and trusting God's providential power (Gen 22). This shift in religious consciousness suggests that fear of the Lord is a form of wisdom that can be acquired only over time and with experience.

Throughout his long and turbulent relationship with God, Abraham learns a great deal about God. He discovers, for example, that no matter how often he doubts the divine will or jeopardizes the divine plan, God remains steadfast, providing the means for Abraham to survive the experience, overcome his doubts, and even prosper. Abraham responds to this knowledge positively, eventually emulating divine generosity in his treatment of Abimelech. Through God's instruction and example, Abraham learns that true righteousness requires that he give to others as he has received, without expecting something in return. Similarly, Abraham's willingness to sacrifice Isaac is based on the firm conviction that if God demands his son as a sacrifice, God will provide another means to fulfill the covenant promise. This central insight is reflected in the final verses of the story, when Abraham renames the place of sacrifice.

And Abraham looked up and saw a ram, caught in the thicket by its horns. Abraham went and took the ram and offered it up as a burnt offering instead of his son. So Abraham called the place "The LORD will provide"; as it is said to this day, "On the mount of the LORD it shall be provided." (Gen 22:13-14)

The faith, obedience, and worship Abraham displays here make his previous behavior in Genesis 12 seem simplistic and almost superficial. While the actions are the same, Abraham's character has changed. His obedience is not prompted by self-interest or an unreflective assent to authority. On the contrary, it is prompted by a genuine respect for the will of God. He has learned that being dependent upon God poses no hardship because God *always* provides. Abraham may not always be happy or satisfied with what God provides, or with the timing of the gifts, but the fact remains that God never fails him. This knowledge eliminates the doubts that have plagued Abraham's mind and heart throughout the saga. The fitting response to this new outlook is worship.

With the test at Moriah, Abraham's transformation is complete. Acknowledging the quality of Abraham's faith, the angel of the Lord calls out to him a second time, reassuring him that, "Because you have done this, and have not withheld your son, your only son, I will indeed bless you, and I will make your offspring as numerous as the stars of heaven and as the sand that is on the seashore. And your offspring shall possess the gate of their enemies, and by your offspring shall all the nations of the earth gain blessing for themselves, because you have obeyed my voice" (Gen 22:16-19). After leaving Moriah, Abraham and his family return to Beer-sheba, where they live and continue to prosper.

Abraham and Isaac's ordeal at Moriah is the last major story in the Abraham saga. God never speaks directly or indirectly to Abraham again. The remainder of the Abraham narrative (Gen 23–25) sets the stage for the stories of Isaac and Jacob. Sarah dies, thus necessitating the purchase of a family plot; Abraham remarries and helps Isaac find a suitable wife so that their offspring may fulfill the divine plan. Soon afterward, Abraham "breathed his last and died in a good old age, an old man and full of years, and was gathered to his people" (Gen 25:8). In both word and deed, Abraham's life embodied what it means to fear the Lord, to live a righteous life in its truest and most complete sense.

Conclusion

Instead of focusing on single stories within the Abraham saga, this chapter has followed the many twists and turns of Abraham's life to discover the characteristics that make him a model of righteousness and the father of faith. In observing the development of Abraham's religious consciousness, we have discovered surprising aspects of his relationship with God that challenge traditional understandings of righteousness and the nature of the divine-human relation.

The most obvious surprise is God's selection of Abraham to be a model of righteousness. Despite his status as successor to Adam, Abraham is hardly a paragon of virtue. On the contrary, Abraham is depicted as a deeply flawed, flesh-and-blood human being who struggles in his relationship with God. Yet the stories establish that it is Abraham's imperfections, specifically, his doubts about God, that ultimately make him righteous, for they act as a catalyst for spiritual growth, helping him grasp the true meaning of faith, obedience, worship, and service to others. Abraham's story is exemplary, not because he is perfect but because his mistakes and missteps reflect our own relationship with God. We see ourselves in Abraham. His struggle is our struggle; his spiritual and moral growth offer us hope for our own.

Equally surprising is Yahweh's response to Abraham's moral failings. God welcomes the struggle, teaching Abraham what it means to be righteous through ongoing dialogue and debate and by setting a good example. When Abraham overreaches himself, God doesn't punish him. Instead he practices restraint, reinforcing his teachings and offering reassurances and rewards when Abraham demonstrates progress. Divine intervention is used only as a last resort and is never harsh or excessive. The Abraham stories thus present a mentoring model that doesn't demand unquestioned obedience to divine imperatives; rather, they present a deity who teaches his chosen model how to be righteous through active and sustained pedagogy and by setting a good example. Abraham's remarkable transformation establishes the effectiveness of this approach. Yet as the biblical narrative continues, we'll discover that God can't afford to dispense with imperatives completely. The book of Exodus offers a different covenant model that introduces the Ten Commandments—the world's most famous set of divine imperatives. But why the sudden switch? In helping the Hebrew slaves escape Egyptian bondage, Yahweh quickly discovers that changing circumstances often require changes in tactics and pedagogy.

Questions for Reflection and Discussion

1. Consider the story of Abraham. How did his "religious consciousness" develop over the course of his relationship with God? What events contributed to this development? What events (both positive and negative) do you think have influenced the development of your own sense of the sacred? How is your experience similar to and different from Abraham's?

2. Abraham's test at Mount Moriah highlights the conflict between the faith commitment and society. If Abraham had actually sacrificed Isaac, society would have condemned him as a murderer; instead, he is praised as an obedient servant of God worthy of admiration and emulation. In your view, when (if ever) does our faith commitment trump the laws and morals of society? What criteria should be used in making this judgment? What would happen if everyone acted as you suggest?

3. Reflecting on the story of Abraham, Sarah, and Hagar, why do you think the biblical writers would include such an unflattering story about Abraham and Sarah? In other words, what purpose did the story serve?

4. One of the central messages in the Abraham story is that human beings can have faith in God because God always provides. But what happens when God's providential activity does not meet our expectations? Reflecting on your own story, what unexpected (and perhaps unwelcome) "gifts" has God provided over the years and how have they changed your life? Did you perceive them as gifts at the time? How do you view them now?

Recommended Reading

Alter, Robert. *Genesis*. New York: W.W. Norton & Company, 1996. An insightful and carefully researched commentary on the book of Genesis.

Birch, Bruce C., et al. *A Theological Introduction to the Old Testament*. Nashville: Abingdon Press, 1999. Focuses on the historical contexts and theologies of the Old Testament writers and how the texts have been used by the synagogue and the church.

Coogan, Michael D., ed. *The Oxford History of the Biblical World*. New York: Oxford University Press, 1998. An invaluable collection of essays from noted scholars on the history of Israel and the early Christian communities.

Freedman, David Noel., ed. *Eerdmans Dictionary of the Bible*. Grand Rapids: William B. Eerdmans Publishing Company, 2000. An essential resource for biblical studies.

4

THE GIFT OF THE LAW AT SINAI

*Institutionalizing the Path toward Spiritual
and Moral Maturity*

As the second book in the Pentateuch, Exodus marks the transition from the mythical stories of Israel's primordial ancestors to the historical events surrounding the people's deliverance from Egyptian bondage, their birth as a nation, and their journey to the Promised Land of Canaan. The patchwork nature of scripture is clearly evident in the book, which blends stories, myths, songs, legal codes, and other literary materials to present an inspiring story of Israel's faith, liberation, and survival. Consensus among biblical scholars is that in its final form the book reflects the artistry and editorial hand of the Yahwist (J), the Elohist (E), and the Priestly writer (P).

While the narrative depicts seminal events in Israel's history, the saga in Exodus should not be considered history in the traditional sense. This is not to suggest that the exodus did not occur. It simply means that the biblical writers understood (far better than we) that historical facts are not always conducive to religious truth. Carol A. Redmount offers a good description of the biblical approach to history and theological meaning.

> The biblical Exodus account was never intended to function or to be understood as history in the present-day sense of the word. Traditional history, with its stress on objectivity and verifiable, detailed facts as the building blocks of historical understanding, is a modern obsession. Not that the ancients were incapable of bald, factual rendering if they deemed it appropriate—they, too, had accurate tax records. But for most occasions and especially for documents that expressed deeper truths and fundamental values, facts as such were not always valued, consistency was not always a virtue, and specific historical particulars were often irrelevant and therefore variable. In the end, it was necessary that the theologically informed events of the Exodus epic relate to history, in the sense that a true historical heart to the narrative exist, but not that these events be bound to history. Particular, individual details were superfluous.[1]

In short, the writer-redactors of the exodus narrative refused to let the facts of history get in the way of a good story, especially when there were important theological and ethical points to be made. Following their lead, this chapter will focus primarily on the story of the exodus—rather than its historicity—and examine the relationships that develop between Yahweh, Moses, and the Hebrew slaves. A close reading of selected passages in Exodus will reveal some surprising tensions between the main characters as they struggle for loyalty, liberation, and nationhood. At Mount Sinai, these tensions will prompt Yahweh to offer yet another covenant model that combines a rule-centered ethic of obedience (established with Adam, Eve, and Noah) with a more flexible, incremental program of character development (introduced with Abraham). Ultimately, it is God's shift in pedagogical strategy that enables the Israelites to transform themselves from a group of frightened and often cantankerous slaves to a unified nation under God.

Setting the Stage for the Exodus

Setting the context for the book of Exodus requires some literary backtracking. Recall that in Genesis, the God of Israel had promised Abraham the land of Canaan, numerous offspring, and divine protection (Gen 15:1-21). After Abraham's death, the covenant promises are restated and reaffirmed with Isaac and Jacob (Gen 26–35). Of the three patriarchs, Jacob is particularly blessed, producing twelve sons who vie for his affection. The machinations and familial conflicts of the house of Jacob dominate the remainder of Genesis (Gen 37–50). The primary cause for the infighting stems from the actions of Jacob and his youngest son, Joseph.

> Now Israel [Jacob] loved Joseph more than any other of his children, because he was the son of his old age; and he had made him a long robe with sleeves. But when his brothers saw that their father loved him more than all his brothers, they hated him, and could not speak peaceably to him. Once Joseph had a dream, and when he told it to his brothers they hated him even more. He said to them, "Listen to this dream that I dreamed. There we were, binding sheaves in the field. Suddenly my sheaf rose and stood upright; then your sheaves gathered around it, and bowed down to my sheaf." His brothers said to him, "Are you indeed to reign over us? Are you indeed to have dominion over us?" So they hated him even more because of his dreams and his words. (Gen 37:3-8)

A younger son usurping the place of the older son is a theme that occurs again and again in the Pentateuch. In each case, the message is clear: God's chosen ones will inherit, they will lead, they will further the divine plan, regardless of their initial station in life. For the brothers, Jacob's preference for Joseph is bad enough; having the obnoxious little cuss rub their noses in it is simply too much to bear. The brothers quickly hatch a plot to eliminate their rival. They first consider murder, but then decide to sell Joseph into slavery. To explain Joseph's disappearance, they dip his robe in goat's blood, which convinces their grief-stricken father that Joseph was killed by wild beasts (Gen 37:18-36).

Although Yahweh is noticeably absent throughout the narrative, the covenant blessings are clearly at work, for Joseph not only survives the ordeal but thrives, becoming a prominent figure in Pharaoh's court (Gen 40–41). When Jacob learns that Joseph is not dead, but is living in Egypt, he immediately prepares to join him. Jacob's decision to leave Canaan is highly significant. According to the Abrahamic covenant, the people of Israel are supposed to reside in the land of Canaan, not Egypt. Nevertheless, Jacob packs up his sizeable household (seventy persons in all, including eleven sons, numerous wives, children, and slaves) and sets out to join Joseph there. Upon reaching Beer-sheba, Jacob stops to worship Yahweh, perhaps hoping his sacrifices will appease God. Yahweh's response to Jacob's gesture is magnanimous and foreshadows the events depicted in Exodus.

> God spoke to Israel in visions of the night, and said, "Jacob, Jacob." And he said, "Here I am." Then he said, "I am God, the God of your father; do not be afraid to go down to Egypt, for I will make of you a great nation there. I myself will go down with you to Egypt, and I will also bring you up again; and Joseph's own hand shall close your eyes." (Gen 46:1-5)

Father and son are soon reunited with great rejoicing. Jacob's household settles in the region of Goshen, where the people live in peace and prosperity for many years.

Israel in Chains

As the book of Exodus opens, the Israelites have "multiplied and [grown] exceedingly strong, so that the land [is] filled with them" (Ex 1:7). Given God's promises to Abraham and Jacob, the sojourn of Joseph and his brothers in Egypt raises an obvious question that drives the plotline of Exodus, namely: How will Yahweh bring the Israelites back to the Promised Land of Canaan? Adding to the drama is the Egyptian pharaoh, who feels threatened by the Hebrews, principally for political reasons.

> [Pharaoh] said to his people, "Look, the Israelite people are more numerous and more powerful than we. Come, let us deal shrewdly with them, or they will increase and, in the event of war, join our enemies and fight against us and escape from the land." Therefore, they set taskmasters over them to oppress them with forced labor. They built supply cities, Pithom and Rameses, for Pharaoh. But the more they were oppressed, the more they multiplied and spread, so that the Egyptians came to dread the Israelites. The Egyptians became ruthless in imposing tasks on the Israelites, and made their lives bitter with hard service in mortar and brick and in every kind of field labor. They were ruthless in all the tasks that they imposed on them. (Ex 1:9-14)

It seems that Yahweh has his work cut out for him, but Pharaoh's shifting policies also reveal God's subtle ability to influence events. Pharaoh's forced labor is thus quickly countered by the divine gift of fertility. When sheer exhaustion fails to curb the Hebrew population, Pharaoh resorts to genocide, ordering the murder of all male babies (Ex 1:16). Yahweh indirectly foils his plan through the Hebrew midwives. The text pointedly states that "the midwives feared God" (Ex 1:17), and so they devise a clever excuse, telling Pharaoh that, unlike Egyptian women, Hebrew women "are vigorous and give birth before the midwife comes to them" (Ex 1:19). Their reverence for Yahweh and their ingenuity are rewarded: Yahweh "dealt well with the midwives; and the people multiplied and became very strong" (Ex 1:20).

Utterly frustrated, Pharaoh next orders his own people to throw all Hebrew male newborns into the Nile, but once again God's subtle hand influences the outcome.

> Now a man from the house of Levi went and married a Levite woman. The woman conceived and bore a son; and when she saw that he was a fine baby, she hid him three months. When she could hide him no longer she got a papyrus basket for him, and plastered it with bitumen and pitch; she put the child in it and placed it among the reeds on the bank of the river. (Ex 2:1-3)

The boat imagery is hardly coincidental. As with Noah, Yahweh saves his chosen one for future work in the divine plan. Ironically, it is Pharaoh's daughter who finds the child among the reeds, a reference to the future rescue of the Hebrews at the Red Sea or "Sea of Reeds."[2] She adopts the child and names him, Moses (Heb. *Mosheh*, "he who draws out"), a name befitting his future role. Thus, in one stroke, Yahweh has managed to ensure the safety of Moses while placing Israel's future liberator close to the seat of Egyptian power. Clearly, Pharaoh is no match for the God of Israel.

In the next scene, Yahweh is nowhere to be found; instead, we are introduced to Moses as a young man. His initial encounter with his kinsmen reveals tensions that will mark the relationship between them: "One day, after Moses had grown up, he went out to his people and saw their forced labor. He saw an Egyptian beating a Hebrew; one of his kinsmen. He looked this way and that, and seeing no one he killed the Egyptian and hid him in the sand" (Ex 2:11-12).

Moses clearly feels an affinity for the Hebrews, despite his privileged upbringing. While we have no way of knowing whether Moses meant to kill the Egyptian, his swift and forceful intervention establishes him as a man of action, defending his people against Pharaoh's harsh policies. But does his action spring from a genuine desire for justice, regardless of the consequences? Or does he slay the Egyptian because he knows he won't be seen? Moses' hasty burial of the victim and the Hebrews' accusations against him are not promising signs; yet, a closer look at the verses shows that his actions are largely a response to the inaction of the Hebrew slaves.

In his classic study of the meaning of the exodus story, Michael Walzer explores the relationship between Moses and the Hebrew slaves. He notes that, rather than faulting Moses, Israel's rabbis have interpreted his actions as a call to arms:

> [W]hen Moses looked this way and that way, he was looking for an Israelite ready to intercede and defend the beaten slave; he was looking for a *real* man, a proud and rebellious spirit. And when he saw no sign of resistance, when he saw, according to a midrashic commentator, "that there was no one ready to champion the cause of the Holy One Blessed be He," he acted himself, hoping to arouse his people and to "straighten their backs." This interpretation is the source, we are told, of the maxim attributed to [the rabbi] Hillel: "Where there is no man, try to be one."[3]

Expanding upon the rabbi's interpretation, Walzer argues that the shortage of *real* men is the result of the Israelites' slave mentality. The exodus story describes a people who are "weighed down by oppression, crushed, frightened, subservient, despondent."[4] The years of brutal treatment have left the Israelites psychologically incapable of standing up to the Egyptian taskmaster. Moses, on the other hand, has lived the life of a young prince of Egypt and has a strong sense of self. He embodies the "proud and rebellious spirit" that champions God's justice. Unfortunately, the sharp contrast between the strength of Moses and the weakness of the Hebrew slaves generates feelings of resentment that have serious consequences for Moses.

> When he [Moses] went out the next day, he saw two Hebrews fighting; and he said to the one who was in the wrong, "Why do you strike your fellow Hebrew?" He answered, "Who made you ruler and judge over us? Do you mean to kill me as your killed the Egyptian?" Then Moses was afraid and thought, "Surely the thing is known." When Pharaoh heard of it, he sought to kill Moses. But Moses fled from Pharaoh. He settled in the land of Midian, and sat down by a well. (Ex 2:13-16)

The old adage, "No good deed goes unpunished," certainly applies here. In trying to help his people, Moses succeeds only in alienating them. He is a member of Pharaoh's house, and the Israelites perceive him (whether rightly or wrongly) as an outsider—and a self-righteous one at that. His talk of justice smacks of hypocrisy. To make matters worse, Moses' kinsmen feel no sense of blood loyalty to him. If a Hebrew slave had killed the Egyptian taskmaster, the identity of the killer would have been buried with the body. But instead of keeping quiet, the Israelites talk openly about the crime, ensuring Moses' arrest and execution. Moses has little choice but to run for his life. Sitting near the well in Midian, Moses probably thinks he is well out of a bad situation, but Yahweh is about to launch a campaign to free the Israelites that will send the young Hebrew back to his ungrateful kinsmen.

The Call of Moses

Thus far in the narrative, Yahweh's influence on human events has been subtle and indirect. The death of an old adversary, however, prompts God to change tactics.

> After a long time the king of Egypt died. The Israelites groaned under their slavery, and cried out. Out of the slavery their cry for help rose up to God. God heard their groaning, and God remembered his covenant with Abraham, Isaac, and Jacob. God looked upon the Israelites, and God took notice of them. (Ex 2:23-25)

Unfortunately for the Israelites, the change in rulers does not improve their situation. They cry out in agony and despair; but cry out to whom? There is no indication that the slaves are pleading directly to Yahweh for deliverance. Do they believe that God has abandoned or forgotten them? Perhaps they do. At the very least, the verses suggest a distance between the people and their God that is reminiscent of the Tower of Babel story, but with one crucial difference. Instead of disrupting the plans of human beings, Yahweh intends to honor his commitments to the patriarchs. But the God who calls out to Moses is very different from the God of Genesis.

> Moses was keeping the flock of his father-in-law Jethro, the priest of Midian; he led his flock beyond the wilderness, and came to Horeb, the mountain of God. There the angel of the LORD appeared to him in a flame of fire out of a bush; he looked, and the bush was blazing, yet it was not consumed. Then Moses said, "I must turn aside and look at this great sight, and see why the bush is not burned up." When the LORD saw that he had turned aside to see, God called to him out of the bush, "Moses, Moses!" And he said, "Here I am." Then he said, "Come no closer! Remove the sandals from your feet, for the place on which you are standing is holy ground." He said further, "I am the God of your father, the God of Abraham, the God of Isaac, and the God of Jacob." And Moses hid his face, for he was afraid to look at God. (Ex 3:1-6)

The first theophany at Horeb (the Elohist's name for Mount Sinai) is memorable, to say the least. Instead of speaking directly to Moses, Yahweh grabs his attention with a burning bush. In the ancient world, fire often symbolized the divine presence and (more ominously) divine judgment. On this occasion, however, Yahweh is making a substantive statement about the very nature of God. He instructs Moses to remove his sandals because he is in the presence of something *holy*. This is the first time the word appears in the Pentateuch and its appearance marks a significant change in divine expectations. As Timothy P. Jenney explains,

[t]he root idea of holiness is that of "separation" or "withdrawal." It is a divine quality, part of the intrinsic nature of God, but absent from a fallen world, perhaps best described as "alienness" in a religious or divine sense. The basic theological problem is that this holy God desires to have fellowship with sinful humans living in a fallen world. Since God cannot become less holy in order to fellowship with humans, they must become more holy ("sanctified"); once gained, holiness may be lessened or contaminated by contact with various proscribed substances ("uncleanness") and by feeling, thinking, or acting in ways that God has forbidden ("sinfulness").[5]

In revealing this divine attribute to Moses, Yahweh foreshadows what he will expect of the Hebrews once they are freed from Egyptian bondage. As Jenney's definition makes clear, holiness involves more than obedience to the will of God; it involves degrees of purity and perfection that will become an integral part of the Sinai covenant.

In the presence of such holiness, Moses can do little but shield his eyes—to do otherwise would bring instant death. His sense of awe and dread becomes even more acute when Yahweh tells him the reason for the visit.

Then the LORD said, "I have observed the misery of my people who are in Egypt; I have heard their cry on account of their taskmasters. Indeed, I know their sufferings, and I have come down to deliver them from the Egyptians, and to bring them up out of that land to a good and broad land, a land flowing with milk and honey, to the country of the Canaanites, the Hittites, the Amorites, the Perizzites, the Hivites, and the Jebusites. The cry of the Israelites has now come to me; I have also seen how the Egyptians oppress them. So come, I will send you to Pharaoh to bring my people, the Israelites, out of Egypt." (Ex 3:7-10)

While the transcendence of God is displayed in Yahweh's power over nature and in his holiness, these verses reveal the immanence of God. Yahweh is a deity who is close enough to his people to see their suffering, hear their cries, and be deeply affected by their plight. While the God of Genesis was close to his creatures, here a more intimate, emotional tie is forged. "I know their suffering" is not a simple statement of fact; it is a statement of genuine empathy. In witnessing the slaves' oppression, Yahweh empathizes with their suffering to such a degree that he feels compelled to send a deliverer to liberate them immediately. The theophany at Sinai not only establishes that Yahweh is a transcendent and immanent God; it also establishes that Yahweh is a compassionate God, one who acts in the face of injustice. The linkage between compassion and action will reappear at Sinai and will also become part of the covenant requirements with the Israelites.

Unfortunately, Yahweh's compassion is not shared by his chosen deliverer. Like Abraham before him, Moses is skeptical of the divine plan and has no qualms about voicing his concerns.

But Moses said to God, "Who am I that I should go to Pharaoh, and bring the Israelites out of Egypt?" He said, "I will be with you, and this shall be the sign for you that it is I who sent you: when you have brought the people out of Egypt, you shall worship God on this mountain." But Moses said to God, "If I come to the Israelites and say to them, 'The God of your ancestors has sent me to you,' and they ask me, 'What is his name?' what shall I say to them?" God said to Moses, "I AM WHO I AM." He said further, "Thus you shall say to the Israelites, 'I AM has sent me to you.'" God also said to Moses, "Thus you shall say to the Israelites, 'The LORD, the God of your ancestors, the God of Abraham, the God of Isaac, and the God of Jacob, has sent me to you': This is my name forever, and this my title for all generations." (Ex 3:11-15)

The narrative doesn't state how many years have elapsed since Moses left Egypt, but it is clear that Moses hasn't forgotten the circumstances surrounding his departure or the Israelites' deep resentment of him. Although Yahweh tries to reassure Moses, he knows his credibility with the Israelites is nonexistent. Moses needs more than grand pronouncements; he needs some convincing proof, which God quickly provides with the revelation of the divine name.

The English translations of the Hebrew ("*eyheh asher ehyeh*") are diverse (e.g., "I AM WHO I AM," "I shall be who I shall be," "He who causes to be"), yet none begin to capture the subtle complexity embedded in this verbal expression. What is of singular importance here is why Yahweh would reveal his name to Moses at all. What difference could it possibly make to Moses or to the Hebrews? John Courtney Murray offers a plausible explanation.

> The name of a person in Hebrew thought was not a mere appellation used only for purposes of designation. The name was, as it were, the definition of the person. Even more, it was the person himself in the form of an alter ego which represented him, exhibited him, was him. To know the name of another was to know who and what the other was— his identity, qualities, and character, or, perhaps more exactly...his power, role, function—what the other was entitled or empowered to do. To be "nameless" is to be "worthless" (Job 30:8), of no avail.... In the case of God, the Hebrew impulse was not to know his existence or essence; these were alien concepts. It was to know his Name, which was an operative entity in its own right. Knowledge of God's Name was empowering: one could address him as God, call on him, enter into community with him, make valid claims upon him. Similarly, for people to have the Name of God "put" upon them was to come into God's possession and under his protection.[6]

Thus, the giving of the divine name appears to be a good-faith gesture on God's part. It indicates that Yahweh is willing to come under the power of Moses and the Israelites to some degree.

God's willingness to become vulnerable to his creation is a startling development—the God of Genesis made no such offer. Yahweh was willing to undergo a self-curse in instituting the covenant with Abraham, but he never revealed himself to Abraham in such a direct way. Nevertheless, the revelation of the name doesn't seem to have the desired effect on Moses. He is still a reluctant liberator, even after God reveals how he will defeat Pharaoh, plunder the Egyptians, and deliver Moses' kinsmen back to Canaan (Ex 3:20-22). But for Moses, the power of Yahweh is not the issue. Given his own past history with the Israelites, Moses is clearly worried that they will not believe him or even listen to him—and then there's the whole public speaking issue. He confesses to God that "I have never been eloquent, neither in the past nor even now that you have spoken to your servant; but I am slow of speech and slow of tongue" (Ex 4:10). Yahweh tries to reassure Moses, telling him, "I will be with your mouth and teach you what you are to speak" (Ex 4:12). Yet Moses is still reluctant, begging God to "please send someone else" (Ex 4:13). Exasperated, God will have none of it, settling the matter with a flurry of observations and directives.

> Then the anger of the LORD was kindled against Moses and he said, "What of your brother Aaron the Levite? I know that he can speak fluently; even now he is coming out to meet you, and when he sees you his heart will be glad. You shall speak to him and put the words in his mouth; and I will be with your mouth and with his mouth, and will teach you what you shall do. He indeed shall speak for you to the people; he shall serve as a mouth for you, and you shall serve as God for him. Take in your hand this staff, with which you shall perform the signs." (Ex 4:14-17)

This is the first mention of Moses' brother, Aaron, who will later become the high priest of the Aaronic priesthood. Not daring to test God's patience further, Moses returns with Aaron to Egypt, where they assemble all the elders of Israel. Aaron tells them all the words Yahweh spoke to Moses and performs the signs in the sight of the people. Their response was more than Moses could have hoped for: "The people believed; and when they heard that the LORD had given heed to the Israelites and that he had seen their misery, they bowed down and worshiped" (Ex 4:31).

Liberating the Israelites

The promising start between Moses and the Israelites is short-lived, however. When Moses and Aaron meet with Pharaoh and demand that the people be freed, Pharaoh not only rejects the demand, he punishes the people more severely, forcing them to make bricks without straw. The Israelites understandably turn against Moses. In a speech reminiscent of

Abraham's sharp rebuke at Sodom, Moses bitterly complains to Yahweh: "O LORD, why have you mistreated this people? Why did you ever send me? Since I first came to Pharaoh to speak in your name, he has mistreated this people, and you have done nothing at all to deliver your people" (Ex 5:23). Unruffled by Moses' words, Yahweh tells him to return to the people and reiterate the covenant promises, but it does no good. The Israelites refuse to listen to Moses "because of their broken spirit and their cruel slavery" (Ex 6:9).

Moses is truly a man in the middle, but his insecurities and failures have little bearing on the success of the divine plan, for the book of Exodus is about the power of Yahweh, the warrior God of Israel. Moses is merely his chosen instrument, as God himself makes clear.

> The LORD said to Moses, "See, I have made you like God to Pharaoh, and your brother Aaron shall be your prophet. You shall speak all that I command you, and your brother Aaron shall tell Pharaoh to let the Israelites go out of his land. But I will harden Pharaoh's heart, and I will multiply my signs and wonders in the land of Egypt. When Pharaoh does not listen to you, I will lay my hand upon Egypt and bring my people the Israelites, company by company, out of the land of Egypt by great acts of judgment. The Egyptians shall know that I am the LORD, when I stretch out my hand against Egypt and bring the Israelites out from among them. Moses and Aaron did so; they did just as the LORD commanded them." (Ex 7:2-6)

As this passage indicates, Yahweh is more than a match for an earthly king, but does his power extend to dictating the inner workings of Pharaoh's heart? Commentators have debated this question for centuries. While the passage seems to suggest an all-controlling deity (Yahweh as puppet-master), there is another reading that doesn't compromise human freedom and autonomy. As with the curses in Genesis 3, the passage could be interpreted as a prediction of what will happen, based on Yahweh's experience of human nature. He knows that his demand to release the Israelites is a direct challenge to Pharaoh's power. He also knows that the ruler, because of his pride—an emotion God has observed with human beings on more than one occasion—will not capitulate. From this perspective, the statement "I will harden Pharaoh's heart" is not describing what Yahweh intends to do to Pharaoh; rather, it is describing the ruler's probable reaction to the divine demand. While Pharaoh is free to do otherwise, Yahweh is confident (human nature being what it is) that the ruler will reject the demand, and indeed he does. Pharaoh's stubborn refusal to free the captives triggers a series of plagues and miraculous events that ravage Egypt and that ultimately destroy Pharaoh's army at the Red Sea.

Throughout the campaign, Moses again acts as the middleman, but this time he acquits himself admirably, demonstrating the obedience, humility, and success that characterize God's chosen ones. Nevertheless, the text is very clear about who deserves the credit for Israel's glorious victory:

> As the Egyptians fled before it [the Red Sea], the LORD tossed the Egyptians into the sea. The waters returned and covered the chariots and the chariot drivers, the entire army of Pharaoh that had followed them into the sea; not one of them remained. But the Israelites walked on dry ground through the sea, the waters forming a wall for them on their right and on their left. Thus the LORD saved Israel that day from the Egyptians; and Israel saw the Egyptians dead on the seashore. Israel saw the great work that the LORD did against the Egyptians. So the people feared the LORD and believed in the LORD and in his servant Moses. (Ex 14:27-31)

The Murmurings in the Wilderness

Yahweh and Moses are indeed a formidable team, and yet the Israelites' faith in God and his servant soon dissolves into grumbling and rebellion. As they make their way toward Mount Sinai, the Israelites quickly discover that life in the wilderness is hard and provisions are scarce. In one particularly revealing passage, the entire assembly complains against Moses and his brother, Aaron: "The Israelites said to them, 'If only we had died by the hand of the LORD in the land of Egypt, when we sat by the fleshpots and ate our fill of bread; for you have brought us out into this wilderness to kill this whole assembly with hunger'" (Ex 16:3). Michael Walzer's interpretation of the passage offers some important insights into the mindset of the Hebrew slaves prior to their arrival at Mount Sinai.

Walzer explains that the "fleshpots" are not the property of the Israelites; they belong to their Egyptian masters and symbolize Egyptian prosperity and decadence. In the ancient Near East, meat was a luxury that few could afford. As slaves, the Israelites "sat by" the fleshpots—that's as close as they could get to such luxury. They consoled themselves by savoring the tantalizing aroma, eating their meager bread, and dreaming about the possibility of their own fleshpots someday. What is puzzling is the people's reference to Egypt. Given their newfound freedom, why would the Israelites reminisce about their days as Egyptian slaves? For Walzer, the people's inexplicable desire for Egypt is based on the fear and dependency that characterize their slave mentality.

> [The Israelites' complaints reflect] the normal anxiety of men and women faced with the difficulties of the march, the terrible austerity of the desert. God and Moses take the long view, see the promised land ahead, and think that no hardship is too great to endure for the sake of such an end. But the people, or many of them, were unsure of the end. ... Pharaoh at least fed his slaves, and he fed them, so they remembered or misremembered, abundantly.[7]

So, the slaves remember "the bad old days" and complain loudly about their present hardships in the wilderness. God quells the complaints through the miracle of manna and quails (Ex 16:12-36), but the people's nostalgia for Egypt and their murmuring against Moses continue, establishing a pattern of behavior that nearly drives their leader to distraction.

> The people quarreled with Moses, and said, "Give us water to drink." Moses said to them, "Why do you quarrel with me? Why do you test the LORD?" But the people thirsted there for water; and the people complained against Moses and said, "Why did you bring us out of Egypt, to kill us and our children and livestock with thirst?" So Moses cried out to the LORD, "What shall I do with this people? They are almost ready to stone me." (Ex 17:2-4)

What cheek! The Israelites clearly resent Moses and even threaten his life, yet they still expect *him* to provide water. For Walzer, such brazen behavior is the result of a skewed understanding of freedom.

> Indeed, there is a kind of freedom in bondage; it is one of the oldest themes in political thought, prominent especially in classical and neo-classical republicanism and in Calvinist Christianity, that tyranny and license go together. The irresponsible slave or subject is free in ways the republican citizen and Protestant saint can never be.[8]

Walzer's point here is that enslavement has inadvertently given the Israelites the freedom not to think, not to make decisions, not to accept obligations, not to be and act as responsible adults. But now that they're liberated, their embrace of negative freedom makes them incapable of governing themselves as a people—a fact not lost on either Yahweh or Moses. At this stage of the journey, Israel is nothing more than an assembly of cranky malcontents—hardly the "great nation" Yahweh envisioned with Abraham. Something must be done and done quickly. As the Israelites grumble their way toward the holy mountain, Yahweh's plan takes a new and innovative turn.

The Events at Mount Sinai

After three months on the road, Moses and the people finally arrive at God's mountain in the wilderness of Sinai. Their initial encounter with Yahweh lasts less than a week, and yet the people are changed (at least temporarily) by the experience. During this time, the Israelites are given a crash course in civics, virtue theory, and religious ethics that transforms them from a company of ungrateful, grumbling slaves to a unified nation under God. Yahweh and his trusted servant, Moses, accomplish this miracle in three incremental stages, with each stage forming the basis for the next.

Stage One: The Initial Offer

Arriving at Mount Sinai, Moses immediately climbs up the mountain (not for the last time) to confer with Yahweh.

> Then Moses went up to God; the LORD called to him from the mountain, saying, "Thus you shall say to the house of Jacob, and tell the Israelites: You have seen what I did to the Egyptians, and how I bore you on eagles' wings and brought you to myself. Now therefore, if you obey my voice and keep my covenant, you shall be my treasured possession out of all the peoples. Indeed, the whole earth is mine, but you shall be for me a priestly kingdom and a holy nation. These are the words that you shall speak to the Israelites." (Ex 19:3-6)

As is his habit, Yahweh first reminds his creatures of what he has done for them. In this case, Yahweh reminds the Israelites that he vanquished their Egyptian oppressors and brought them to Sinai, as he told them he would. The message is clear: Yahweh is a God who is worthy of allegiance and loyalty because Yahweh keeps his promises. Establishing Yahweh's credibility paves the way for the conditional, if-then statement. If the people obey the covenant (the nature and content of which is yet to be presented), then Yahweh will greatly favor them and raise them to the status of a "priestly kingdom and a holy nation." The people are thus presented with an ideal vision of what Israel might be like. All they have to do is obey the covenant requirements and a "new Eden" will be realized. How hard can that be? After years of brutal oppression, the people's response to Yahweh's generous offer is immediate, predictable, and yet surprising.

> So Moses came, summoned the elders of the people, and set before them all these words that the LORD had commanded him. The people all answered as one: "Everything that the LORD has spoken we will do." Moses reported the words of the people to the LORD. Then the LORD said to Moses, "I am going to come to you in a dense cloud, in order that the people may hear when I speak with you and so trust you ever after." (Ex 19:7-10)

Self-interest is obviously the prime motivator here; after all, the Israelites have nothing to lose and everything to gain by this alliance. What is surprising, however, is how they respond. Although the elders are summoned to hear Yahweh's offer, it is the people themselves who affirm their intention to uphold the covenant. This is a promising sign, because it indicates that each member of the assembly is willing to accept responsibility for the covenant. Yahweh is pleased by their action, but not by their appearance. After three long and dusty months on the road, the Israelites hardly embody the purity and perfection that characterize a priestly kingdom. Yahweh thus instructs Moses: "Go to the people and consecrate them today and tomorrow. Have them wash their clothes and prepare for the third day, because on the third day the LORD will come down upon Mount Sinai in the sight of all the people."

After three days of ritual purification, the people are ready to meet their divine Benefactor.

> Moses brought the people out of the camp to meet God. They took their stand at the foot of the mountain. Now Mount Sinai was wrapped in smoke, because the LORD had descended upon it in fire; the smoke went up like the smoke of a kiln, while the whole mountain shook violently. As the blast of the trumpet grew louder and louder, Moses would speak and God would answer him in thunder. (Ex 19:17-19)

For the original audience of Exodus, the pyrotechnics and trumpet blasts were expected features of a theophany. The ancients wanted their gods to be more powerful than gods from neighboring regions. Yahweh's appearance on the mountain has the desired effect: the people are terrified but attentive (much like Moses was during his first encounter). They are now ready to begin the next stage in their transformation.

Stage Two: The Fine Print

Yahweh's initial offer of the covenant was long on vision but short on specifics, which may explain why the Israelites responded so quickly and boldly. But do they really understand what they're getting themselves into? At this point, the people have agreed to the rewards of the covenant without knowing what they must do to receive them. Given their childish behavior on the road, Yahweh is understandably concerned about the depth of their commitment and their capacity to govern themselves. He thus presents to the people the Decalogue and the Book of the Covenant, which outlines the legal, moral, and religious obligations of the covenant. If the people still agree to the covenant after hearing all the details, then some progress will indeed have been made.

The Decalogue is often called Israel's constitution, and with good reason. The ten prescriptions establish the priorities, values, and principles that will govern the priestly kingdom. The first three commandments focus on the people's responsibilities to God. Once again, Yahweh begins with a review of what he has done for his people.

> Then God spoke all these words: I am the LORD your God, who brought you out of the land of Egypt, out of the house of slavery; you shall have no other gods before me. You shall not make for yourself an idol, whether in the form of anything that is in heaven above, or that is on the earth beneath, or that is in the water under the earth. You shall not bow down to them or worship them; for I the LORD your God am a jealous God, punishing children for the iniquity of parents, to the

third and the fourth generation of those who reject me, but showing steadfast love to the thousandth generation of those who love me and keep my commandments. (Ex 20:1-6)

God's commandment to the Israelites that they shall "have no other gods before me" reflects the common belief that there were indeed many gods in the universe, each with its own nature and function. The ancients worshiped a variety of gods for health, prosperity, fertility, and other blessings. While an acknowledgment of the existence of other gods may surprise modern readers, for the Israelites the surprise is Yahweh's demand that they worship *only* him. Accepting the covenant means they cannot turn to Egyptian, Canaanite, or other regional gods for assistance or protection; to do so would be to invite disaster. Equally surprising is Yahweh's candor. He freely admits that he is a jealous God, suggesting a degree of vulnerability (and even weakness) that is striking. Gods in the ancient world rarely made such confessions, especially to human beings.

The second and third commandments reinforce and elaborate upon the first. The people are not to "make wrongful use of the name of the LORD your God" and they must "Remember the sabbath day, and keep it holy." With the obligations of the divine-human relationship established, the rest of the commandments focus on social norms:

Honor your father and your mother, so that your days may be long in the land that the LORD your God is giving you. You shall not murder. You shall not commit adultery. You shall not steal. You shall not bear false witness against your neighbor. You shall not covet your neighbor's house, you shall not covet your neighbor's wife, or male or female slave, or ox, or donkey, or anything that belongs to your neighbor. (Ex 20:12-16)

For a group of fugitive slaves who have little experience in self-rule, the commandments offer a blueprint for family and community relations. In presenting the commandments, Yahweh's words and tactics are reminiscent of Eden. Once again God desires to be in relationship with human beings and offers them many blessings, as well as a rule-centered ethic of obedience. Yet, upon hearing God's words, the people show the first sign of hesitation.

When all the people witnessed the thunder and lightning, the sound of the trumpet, and the mountain smoking, they were afraid and trembled and stood at a distance, and said to Moses, "You speak to us, and we will listen; but do not let God speak to us or we will die." Moses said to the people, "Do not be afraid; for God has come only to test you and to put the fear of him upon you so that you do not sin." Then the people stood at a distance while Moses drew near to the thick darkness where God was. (Ex 20:18-21)

The people are clearly overwhelmed by God's holy presence and divine imperatives. They had witnessed his power in Egypt, but it had been channeled through Moses, a kinsman they tolerated but deeply resented. The theophany at Sinai changes their opinion of Moses—at least for the moment. In the swirl of thunder, lightning, and trumpet blasts, Moses suddenly appears a safe haven. He is God's chosen instrument, and his words not only reassure the terrified Israelites, but they also reveal important clues about Yahweh's intentions for Israel.

Yahweh's theophany is indeed a test. The people must understand that they are about to enter into a covenant with a powerful and holy deity who is not to be trifled with. The overwhelming presence of God sets the stage for the covenant demands, because the people must know the specifics of the covenant before deciding whether they will fully commit themselves to it. The intensity of the theophany also serves to instill fear of the Lord into the people, but the fear Moses speaks of is not simply the Israelites' fear of annihilation—although that is very real. It is also the recognition that human beings are wholly dependent upon this deity for their very existence and continued survival. The point Moses is making is that if the people fear Yahweh (i.e., if they acknowledge their dependence upon God), then they will not be tempted to take matters into their own hands for their own selfish ends. The theophany is thus meant to teach the Israelites the simple yet profound truth that Abraham learned so well at Mount Moriah: the Lord always provides, so there is no need to meddle or rebel.

Speaking directly to Moses (for the people are still too frightened), Yahweh reveals the Book of the Covenant (Ex 20:22–23:19). The book is a collection of legislation that covers a wide range of topics including the rights of slaves, property rights, personal injury, regulations for worship, and social and religious commands. The laws are specific, colorful, and often shocking. For example,

> When a man seduces a virgin who is not engaged to be married, and lies with her, he shall give the bride-price for her and make her his wife. But if her father refuses to give her to him, he shall pay an amount equal to the bride-price for virgins. You shall not permit a female sorcerer to live. Whoever lies with an animal shall be put to death. Whoever sacrifices to any god, other than the LORD alone, shall be devoted to destruction. (Ex 22:16-20)

Modern readers are often struck by such passages. Did God really make laws regarding virgins, female sorcerers, and bestiality? The simple answer is no. Most biblical scholars agree that the collection is very similar in style and substance to other legal codes in the ancient Near East. The laws probably existed apart from the book's literary sources (J, E, P) and were incorporated into the exodus narrative during the exilic and postexilic periods. For the Priestly redactors, having Yahweh present the legislation at Mount

Sinai provided divine authority and sanction to laws that had guided Israel for centuries.

The Social Justice Command

Almost lost among the many rules and regulations contained in the collection is a command that could arguably be considered the Eleventh Commandment: "You shall not wrong or oppress a resident alien, for you were aliens in the land of Egypt. You shall not abuse any widow or orphan. If you do abuse them, when they cry out to me, I will surely heed their cry; my wrath will burn, and I will kill you with the sword, and your wives shall become widows and your children orphans" (Ex 22:21-24).

From a literary perspective, these verses introduce the Israelites to three figures that represent the most vulnerable persons in their society. In the ancient Near East, public assistance was nonexistent and travel was difficult and dangerous. The widow and orphan are particularly vulnerable because they have no family to protect or provide for them; likewise, the stranger is vulnerable because he or she has no kinsmen nearby to offer protection and support. God thus demands that the Israelites practice social justice, namely, to see to it that everyone in the community is treated fairly and receives a just share. What is interesting and enlightening is how he constructs the command.

While the prescription takes the form of a command ("You shall not..."), it is immediately tempered with an appeal to the emotions. The Israelites must not oppress the vulnerable *because they remember what it was like to be oppressed.* They remember the humiliation and powerlessness of slavery, feelings shared by all oppressed and vulnerable people. In connecting the command with the collective memory of Israel, Yahweh is moving beyond the obedience model introduced in Genesis. As he did with Abraham, Yahweh's focus is shifting from the demand for strict and unreflective obedience to the cultivation of character. With the command for justice, Yahweh intends that the Israelites' obedience spring not only from fear of the Lord, but from genuine empathy and compassion for others.

Although Yahweh once again alters his pedagogical strategy, he is not as tolerant of mistakes as he was with Abraham. The verses also present a graphic picture of what will happen if the people do not obey the command. Even though Yahweh favors the Israelites, he is a just God who listens to all those who cry out to him—a subtle reminder of their own desperate condition in Egypt. God's justice demands retribution, regardless of the perpetrator. If the Israelites follow the ways of their Egyptian oppressors (i.e., if they lack empathy and compassion), then they will suffer a similar fate, and their wives and children will experience the pain and suffering so callously inflicted by them on others.

Yahweh's next revelation to Moses is a vision of the future conquest of Canaan that reinforces the Israelites' favored status while reiterating the prohibition against idolatry. Yahweh knows full well that the gods of Canaan will be a temptation to the people. He thus demands that "You shall make no covenant with them and their gods. They shall not live in your land, or they will make you sin against me; for if you worship their gods, it will surely be a snare to you" (Ex 23:32-33). Having revealed the specifics of the covenant and a promising (yet subtly foreboding) vision of the future conquest of Canaan, Yahweh awaits an answer from the people. After Moses tells the people all God's words and ordinances, "the people answered with one voice, and said, 'All the words that the LORD has spoken we will do.' And Moses wrote down all the words of the LORD" (Ex 24:3). Thus, after hearing all details of the covenant and reviewing the fine print, the people freely commit themselves to its requirements.

The Israelites have indeed made progress on their journey toward spiritual and moral maturity, but there is one final stage. The people must be willing to recommit themselves publicly in a formal ceremony.

Stage Three: The Public Ceremony

Moses coordinates the ritual, which is like a marriage ceremony.

> He [Moses] rose early in the morning, and built an altar at the foot of the mountain, and set up twelve pillars, corresponding to the twelve tribes of Israel. He sent young men of the people of Israel, who offered burnt offerings and sacrificed oxen as offerings of well-being to the LORD. Moses took half of the blood and put it in the basins, and half of the blood he dashed against the altar. Then he took the book of the covenant, and read it in the hearing of the people; and they said, "All that the LORD has spoken we will do, and we will be obedient." Moses took the blood and dashed it on the people, and said, "See the blood of the covenant that the LORD has made with you in accordance with all these words." (Ex 24:4-8)

The people are represented by the twelve pillars; God's presence is represented by the altar. Moses once again acts as an intermediary (and priest), uniting the parties in a series of symbolic actions. The use of blood is significant. It is an ancient symbol of life and was often used as an expression of worship for the Giver of life (and death). In this ritual, the blood symbolizes both the covenant as a living relationship and the fate of all those who break it. Thus, as he did with Abraham in Genesis 15, Yahweh freely enters into a covenant relation that takes the form of a self-curse. The dashing of blood against the altar affirms Yahweh's commitment to this relationship.

For contemporary readers, the idea of Yahweh's death may seem farfetched and even a little ridiculous. How can the God of the universe die? This is an understandable question for those who ascribe to a strict monotheism, but in the ancient world, most people believed in many gods. God's command that "you shall have no other gods before me" acknowledges the existence of other gods (polytheism), yet demands that the Israelites worship only him (henotheism). For the ancients, loyalty to a particular god was largely determined by the god's effectiveness. Did the god protect crops, ensure fertility, or ward off sickness? If not, the god would be abandoned and another more effective god would take its place. Abandonment was the fate of inferior gods—a fate that was just as horrific and as permanent as death. Yahweh's willingness to enter the covenant, therefore, has genuine consequences for the deity. If he does not deliver on his promises, he risks abandonment by his "treasured possession."

The people are also willing to bind themselves to Yahweh, but before they can agree, Moses must read the Book of the Covenant one final time, reiterating all the benefits and burdens of the relationship. Only after they hear it all again and publicly affirm their commitment before witnesses and before God does Moses dash the blood on them, sealing the covenant relation.

The True Meaning of Obedience

The people's response to the covenant offer warrants a closer look because it reveals a genuine turning point for the Israelites. In the two previous responses, the people proclaim that "All that the LORD has spoken we will do." Obedience is clearly implied in these words, so why do they add the phrase "and we will be obedient" to the response? A plausible answer is found if we consider the nature of Abraham's transformation. As we discussed in chapter three, Abraham undergoes a process of spiritual and moral growth that changes his character and his behavior. His obedience to God's will is prompted not by fear or an unreflective assent to authority, but by a genuine respect for and faith in Yahweh that he had acquired over a long and turbulent relationship with him. Although the Israelites' relationship with Yahweh is not nearly as long as Abraham's, it is no less turbulent or transformative. Like Abraham, the Israelites have progressed from an initial state of fear and awe of God to a profound sense of reverence based on understanding of and trust in God's providential power. The catalyst for this transformation is the gift of the Law. When the people tell Yahweh "All that the LORD has spoken we will do, and we will be obedient," they are reassuring him that they recognize and respect the authority and validity of the Law because they understand its true purpose. They know that Yahweh has given them the gift of the Law to promote and sustain their relationship with him, to provide them with a collective identity and with a blueprint for their continued welfare as a people and as a nation. With this affirmation, the people's education and transformation are complete. In these few fateful and event-filled days, they have changed from a band of childish and irresponsible slaves to a unified nation under God. The metamorphosis is marked by a final theophany and a ceremony among Israel's leaders.

> Then Moses and Aaron, Nadab, and Abihu, and seventy of the elders of Israel went up, and they saw the God of Israel. Under his feet there

was something like a pavement of sapphire stone, like the very heaven for clearness. God did not lay his hand on the chief men of the people of Israel; also they beheld God, and they ate and drank. (Ex 24:9-11)

Moses, the leaders of the Aaronic priesthood, and the elders are permitted to see Yahweh and live—another indication of the importance of the occasion and the special status of Israel. The ceremonial meal provides a joyous contrast to the bitter herbs and unleavened bread they ate on the night of the Passover. After the meal, God instructs Moses to join him on the mountain, where he will receive "tablets of stone, with the law and the commandment, which I have written for their instruction" (Ex 24:12).

Chapters 25 through 31 present detailed instructions regarding the tabernacle (a portable shrine) and its furnishings, the building of the Ark of the Covenant (a container for the covenant tablets), the vestments of the priests, priestly ordination, and other matters of worship. Then Moses is presented with two tablets of stone, "written with the finger of God." After working out the details for forty days and nights, Yahweh and Moses are finally ready to lead the people to the Promised Land. But in their absence, the people's resolve has withered, prompting a fall from grace that will sorely test Yahweh's new covenant model.

The Golden Calf Incident

With their leader gone (and for a long time, too), the Israelites become frightened and restless. They turn to Aaron for a possible solution for their collective insecurity.

When the people saw that Moses delayed to come down from the mountain, the people gathered around Aaron, and said to him, "Come make gods for us, who shall go before us; as for this Moses, the man who brought us up out of the land of Egypt, we do not know what has become of him." Aaron said to them, "Take off the gold rings that are on the ears of your wives, your sons, and your daughters, and bring them to me." So all the people took off the gold rings from their ears, and brought them to Aaron. He took the gold from them, formed it in a mold and cast an image of a calf; and they said, "These are your gods, O Israel, who brought you up out of the land of Egypt!" When Aaron saw this, he built an altar and said, "Tomorrow shall be a festival to the LORD." They rose early the next day, and offered burnt offerings and brought sacrifices of well-being; and the people sat down to eat and drink, and rose up to revel. (Ex 32:1-6)

Ironically, the people's fear of abandonment prompts them to abandon the Sinai covenant. Moses is no longer their trusted leader, but simply "the man who brought us out of the land of Egypt." They make no mention of

Yahweh, but connect their request for gods with the loss of Moses—a human leader. Equally disturbing is Aaron's response. The high priest doesn't try to reassure the people or challenge their demand. He immediately starts making a calf from the gold taken from Egypt. Richard Elliott Friedman offers an interesting explanation for Aaron's behavior.

> The text does not reveal what Aaron has in mind when he makes the golden calf: does he mean it as a throne platform for such pagan deities, or as a throne platform for YHWH?! All we know is that, after he sees the people associating it with gods and claiming that these gods brought them out of Egypt, he declares that the worship that is to take place is "A festival to YHWH!" ... Aaron is not completely innocent in the matter of the golden calf, as we can see from the defense he offers to Moses afterward (32:24); but it may be that he is to be credited as a person who recognizes that he has made a dangerous mistake and tries to turn it to something good.[9]

Regardless of Aaron's about-face, Yahweh is not happy with what has happened. The construction of the calf and the altar, and the people's eating, drinking, and reveling make a mockery of the covenant ceremony. The pain and anger in Yahweh's words express the depths of the betrayal.

> The LORD said to Moses, "Go down at once! Your people, whom you brought up out of the land of Egypt, have acted perversely; they have been quick to turn aside from the way that I commanded them; they have cast for themselves an image of a calf, and have worshiped it and sacrificed to it, and said, "These are your gods, O Israel, who brought you up out of the land of Egypt!" The LORD said to Moses, "I have seen this people, how stiff-necked they are. Now let me alone, so that my wrath may burn hot against them and I may consume them; and of you I will make a great nation." (Ex 32:7-10)

Yahweh's rejection of the people is so complete that he credits *Moses* with their liberation from Egypt—quite a reversal! Ironically, in his anger, God also seems to be reverting to former ways. Yahweh's threat to destroy the people and start again echoes the flood story in Genesis. Likewise, Moses' response to Yahweh's plan is reminiscent of Abraham's accusation at Sodom.

> But Moses implored the LORD his God, and said, "O LORD, why does your wrath burn hot against your people, whom you brought out of the land of Egypt with great power and with a mighty hand? Why should the Egyptians say, "It was with evil intent that he brought them out to kill them in the mountains, and to consume them from the face of the earth"? Turn from your fierce wrath; change your mind and do not bring disaster on your people. Remember Abraham, Isaac, and Israel,

your servants, how you swore to them by your own self, saying to them, "I will multiply your descendants like the stars of heaven, and all this land that I have promised I will give to your descendants, and they shall inherit it forever." And the LORD changed his mind about the disaster that he planned to bring on the people. (Ex 32:11-14)

Moses quickly turns the tables by reminding God that it was he, not Moses, who liberated the Hebrew slaves. They are Yahweh's people and Yahweh's responsibility, but destruction is not the answer. Moses' pointed reference to the Egyptians and his restatement of the covenant promises are designed to appeal to God's vanity and sense of justice. Fortunately for the Israelites, the strategy works, but the cost of their folly is high: human beings have once again lost their Eden. Given the time and attention Yahweh lavished upon the Israelites, why would the Israelites be so foolish? Friedman offers a plausible explanation.

How could they have committed the golden calf sin so soon after the revelation—within forty days after actually hearing God speak from the sky? It is when God is *closest* that humans commit the greatest sin. Similarly in the story of Eden, where God walks among humans, they violate a direct command. Similarly through the wilderness period to come, in which the people see miracles daily (manna, column of cloud and fire), they are repeatedly rebellious. It appears that close proximity to divinity—to an all-seeing, all-knowing divine parent who is always watching, commanding, and judging—is barely tolerable for human beings. Like adolescents who love and need their parents but who long for independence, humankind is pictured as longing to be out of the divine shadow.[10]

The people's longing for independence and their blasphemous behavior cannot go unpunished. Moses is so angry at the sight of their revelry that he throws the stone tablets against the foot of the mountain, smashing them to bits. He then takes the calf, melts it down with fire, grinds it into powder, scatters it on the water, and forces the Israelites to drink it (Ex 32:20). But that is only the beginning of their punishment. As he did with the Egyptian taskmaster, Moses' retaliatory actions against the people are swift and merciless.

When Moses saw that the people were running wild (for Aaron had let them run wild, to the derision of their enemies), then Moses stood in the gate of the camp, and said, "Who is on the LORD's side? Come to me!" And all the sons of Levi gathered around him. He said to them, "Thus says the LORD, the God of Israel, 'Put your sword on your side, each of you! Go back and forth from gate to gate throughout the camp, and each of you kill your brother, your friend, and your neighbor.'" The sons of Levi did as Moses commanded, and about three thousand of the people fell on that day. Moses said, "Today you have ordained yourselves for the service of the LORD, each one at the cost of a son or a brother, and so have brought a blessing on yourselves this day." (Ex 32:25-29)

The crime of idolatry was indeed serious, but the bloodshed seems extreme, even by biblical standards. Yet even more startling is the demand that the people themselves act as executioners. Why would God and Moses command the murder of family, friends, and neighbors? Michael Walzer explains the political calculation behind the bloody purge.

> The pedagogy of the desert is not only slow, it is uneven; some people or some groups of people learn more quickly than others. Some of them [the people] commit themselves more wholeheartedly to the covenant, shape themselves to the new model of the chosen people, internalize the law at a time when for others the law is still an external command, a threat to their Egyptian habits. Moses' call "Who is on the LORD's side?" draws these new-modeled men to *his* side, divides the community, creates a subgroup—we might call it a vanguard—whose members anticipate, at least in their own minds, the "free people" of the future. In fact, they become the magistrates of the future, the priests and bureaucrats. And meanwhile, in the present, they rule by force; they are the enemies of "graciousness" and gradualism.[11]

Having the Israelites choose sides and participate in the purge signal (both literally and symbolically) the death of the old ways. The blood of the golden calf idolaters forever binds the executioners to the new model—there is no turning back now. Yet despite this costly sacrifice, the purge does not diffuse God's wrath. He sends a plague upon the people and punishes them further by refusing to be present among them. Ironically, it was Yahweh's absence that had prompted the golden calf incident in the first place; nevertheless, he keeps his distance, speaking only to Moses in the tent of meeting "as one speaks to a friend" (Ex 33:11).

The breach in the relationship is a serious one, but Moses once again intercedes on the Israelites' behalf, persuading Yahweh to be present with them as they make their way to the Promised Land of Canaan. Yahweh agrees, but insists that the Israelites receive further instruction in righteousness. The remainder of the exodus narrative recounts the renewal of the covenant (with another version of the Decalogue) and the construction of the portable tabernacle. As the book ends, Moses resumes the role of priest, presiding over the goodwill offerings made by a chastened and grateful people. Resplendent in his glorious tabernacle, Yahweh dictates the progress of their journey in true storm-god fashion.

> Then the cloud covered the tent of meeting, and the glory of the LORD filled the tabernacle. Moses was not able to enter the tent of meeting because the cloud settled upon it, and the glory of the LORD filled the

tabernacle. Whenever the cloud was taken up from the tabernacle, the Israelites would set out on each stage of their journey; but if the cloud was not taken up, then they did not set out until the day that it was taken up. For the cloud of the LORD was on the tabernacle by day, and fire was in the cloud by night, before the eyes of all the house of Israel at each stage of their journey. (Ex 40:34-38)

The book of Exodus thus ends on a hopeful note: God is with his people, the Israelites have stopped their grumbling and their idolatry (at least for the moment), and Moses enjoys the unparalleled status of being the friend of God and leader of his people.

WHY A GOLDEN CALF?

The golden calf incident in Exodus 32 shows us what the wrath of God truly means. The construction of the golden calf and altar and the people's eating, drinking, and reveling so enraged Moses and God that they launched a bloody purge against the idolaters, killing thousands. While they were clearly upset with the people's descent into idolatry, their anger also reflects the religious rivalry that existed between Yahwism and Canaanite religion, which was practiced to some degree by many of Israel's ancient ancestors. The golden calf was associated with the Canaanite deity El, father of the gods, and his son Baal, god of storms. In recent years, archaeologists have uncovered calf and bull statuettes in northern Samaria and in the ancient settlement of Ashkelon in Israel. The appearance of calf-bull imagery indicates the people's reluctance to eliminate their Canaanite gods altogether and worship Yahweh alone.

The temptation to idolatry and the competition between the religions occur repeatedly in the biblical narrative. For example, the great contest between Elijah and the prophets of Baal (1 Kings 18) is designed to show the superior power of Yahweh over Baal. The biblical editors condemn King Jeroboam of Israel for building a calf shrine in Israel (1 Kings 12:25–13:33) and Hosea condemns the people for worshiping the Samarian calf rather than Yahweh (Hos 8:5, 10:5-6). In the New Testament, Stephen cites the golden calf incident in his indictment of the Jews (Acts 7:39-51). In all these cases, condemnation of and violence against "the other" was sanctioned for the sake of religious survival.

Can you think of some contemporary examples of this phenomenon? How might these conflicts be resolved without resorting to exclusion, condemnation, or violence?

Conclusion

For the original audience of Exodus, the climax of the story completes the answer to the central question of the book. Yahweh has indeed fulfilled the covenant promises by destroying the Egyptian oppressors and sending his chosen one, Moses, to orchestrate the liberation of Israel. Together they will watch over the Israelites as they make their way back to Canaan. Yet, from an ethics perspective, the question involves more than considering the "how" of liberation. We must also consider the effects of the liberative process on all the actors in the drama.

As mentioned above, the primary character in the book of Exodus is the God of Israel. In Exodus, the justice and holiness of Yahweh are emphasized. Here is a deity who acts in the face of human suffering and who demands that his creatures uphold divine standards of justice and righteousness. This is not to suggest that Yahweh hadn't made such demands earlier—Genesis is filled with divine imperatives—but in Exodus, God presents his creatures with the gift of the Mosaic Law, which offers explicit and comprehensive instructions for righteous living.

The giving of the Law highlights a central feature of Yahweh's pedagogical strategy. As he did with Adam, Eve, Noah, and Abraham, God now presents an ideal (e.g., Eden, a new creation, a great nation) and then provides the practical program to realize it. Moreover, Yahweh is flexible enough to adjust the program to accommodate human failings. For example, with Adam, Eve, Noah, and Noah's offspring, Yahweh's program required strict and unquestioning obedience to divine imperatives. Unfortunately, the results were mixed. With Abraham, Yahweh introduced a more flexible covenant model that emphasized character development. Although the results were promising, the Israelites posed new and different challenges that required further refinements.

The Lord's ideal for the Israelites is indeed lofty. They are to become a "priestly kingdom" and a "holy nation." The practical program to realize this ideal is the gift of the Law. Yet the slave mentality of the people prevents them from fully understanding and embracing the Sinai covenant and its laws. God thus initiates three progressive stages that transform the consciousness of the people and elicit their promise to be obedient in the truest sense of the word. Ultimately, Yahweh's willingness to adapt to changing circumstances is as critical to the liberation of the Israelites as is his power to destroy the Egyptians.

Yahweh's flexibility is also evident in his relationship with Moses. As he did with Abraham, Yahweh selects a less than perfect hero, but he is willing to groom Moses for the work ahead and to provide whatever is necessary to ease his concerns. The revelation of the divine name to Moses also indicates Yahweh's willingness to change his tactics. For the sake of the covenant relationship, God is willing to be less of a mystery to human beings. As Bruce C. Birch explains,

[f]or God to be so intensely present with Israel is a new divine experience. This move seems to be for God's sake as much as for the people's. God desires such a "home" among the people! No more mountain hideaways; no more palace precincts. This enhances the intimacy of the relationship with the people whom God loves. At the same time, it makes for greater vulnerability; God can be more easily hurt by advantages assumed and presumptions advanced. That God does this in the wake of the golden calf debacle indicates something of the risk God is willing to take for closeness.[12]

The God of the Pentateuch is thus an evolving deity—not in divine essence, but in divine character. His ongoing struggle with human beings has made changes in the divine-human relation necessary and even welcome.

The process of liberation also has a profound effect on Moses. Like Abraham before him, Moses has a turbulent relationship with Yahweh, one that transforms Moses from a reluctant and often inept liberator to a strong and able leader who persists in his mission, despite the behavior of the Israelites. As he takes on the mantle of leadership, his feelings toward God also change, for he understands that they are genuine partners in a glorious experiment. His sense of fear and awe and initial reluctance soon give way to a deep and abiding affection for God. Moses' loyalty and single-minded devotion to Yahweh is so great that he is willing to put his own people to the sword to realize God's ideal. Perhaps this is why Yahweh often visits Moses and speaks to him "face to face, as one speaks to a friend" (Ex 33:11). God's chosen one is the only creature who understands and shares his vision. Whatever the case, Moses stands alone among all the figures in the Old Testament for his integrity, his sense of justice, and his unwavering devotion to Yahweh.

For the Israelites, the physical departure from Egypt is the most obvious effect of liberation. The people are free, and yet they are still enslaved by a mentality that prevents them from accepting the leadership of Moses and becoming fully responsible adults. Although their journey through the wilderness and their schooling on the mountain help them reach a level of moral maturity, their rapid fall from grace reveals an important ethical truth, namely, that genuine moral growth requires training, constant reinforcement, vigilance, and time. It is fortunate for the Israelites that Yahweh and Moses appear willing to provide them with all of these. Yet despite such positive developments, the story is tinged throughout with foreboding. Yahweh's stern warning against the gods of Canaan and the golden calf incident are reminders that human beings are insecure, rebellious creatures who are capable of willful disobedience and idolatry.

This fundamental truth about the human condition is borne out in the remainder of the Pentateuch. In the book of Numbers, for example, the Israelites' lack of faith and their fearful refusal to enter Canaan—despite the pleas and assurances of Moses, Aaron, and Joshua—bring further punishment. In a fit of anger and disgust, Yahweh condemns the Israelites to wander forty years until "the last of your dead bodies lies in the wilderness" (Num 14:33). Only after all the faithless rebels are dead can the new generation of Israelites enter the Promised Land.

Conflict, willful rebellion, and divine punishment also drive the historical books, which recount the conquest of Canaan, the rise of the monarchy, the split of Israel into the two smaller kingdoms of Israel and Judah, and their eventual destruction at the hands of the Assyrians and Babylonians. As the next chapter will make clear, these tumultuous events raise the tension between Yahweh and Israel to the breaking point, prompting God to offer yet another gift—the gift of the prophets. Following the example of Moses, the prophets will attempt to lead the people back to the spiritual and moral Eden articulated at Mount Sinai before God's righteous wrath consumes them.

Questions for Reflection and Discussion

1. Reflecting on the story of Moses, how would you describe Moses and his leadership style? Which characteristics do you find most admirable? Which do you find most troubling? What does his experience reveal about the nature of leadership?

2. The golden calf incident was a crisis that threatened to destroy the covenant community. What was the nature of the crisis? Why were God and Moses so angry? How was the crisis resolved? What does the golden calf incident teach us about the development of new social and/or religious movements? What does it teach us about the psychology of worship and idolatry? What "idols" are prevalent in today's society? How are they a threat?

3. The exodus is a biblical story that makes truth claims about the human condition. What are some of these truth claims? How do you see them reflected in your own life and in the world today?

Recommended Reading

Falk, Ze'ev W. *Hebrew Law in Biblical Times*. Provo: Brigham Young University Press, 2001. An informative introduction to the development of Hebrew law in ancient Israel within the tribe, the monarchy, and the state, and how it was administered.

King, Philip J., and Lawrence E. Stager. *Life in Biblical Israel*. Louisville: Westminster John Knox Press, 2001. A fascinating study of daily life in biblical Israel, containing a wealth of illustrations, photographs, and archaeological data.

Walzer, Michael. *Exodus and Revolution*. New York: Basic Books, 1985. A classic study of the meaning of the exodus story as a political document and its use in the history of political and revolutionary thought.

5
THE GIFT OF THE PROPHETS
Mediating Tradition, Innovation, and Divine Mystery

In the ancient world, where the constant threat of starvation, disease, war, and sudden death shadowed every waking moment, seers, diviners, prophets, and other visionaries were indispensable figures, functioning as intermediaries between the gods and a wary and frightened populace. In their role as intermediaries, these spiritually gifted men and women would discern the will of the gods through a variety of methods. Some would search for divine messages in the entrails of animals or in the movements of the stars, while others received more direct communication through visions, dreams, and ecstatic trances. The ancients consulted these visionaries with one purpose in mind: to learn the will of the gods so that they might receive their blessing. With the gods on their side, health, prosperity, and peace were assured or at least possible for a time.

In ancient Israel, prophets were the primary intermediaries between the people and Yahweh, inaugurating a fascinating and colorful chapter in the people's history. In the Bible, prophets are traditionally classified into two main groups: the Former Prophets, whose exploits are depicted in the historical books, and the Latter Prophets, whose speeches and oracles were written down and preserved in books under their individual names. Lawrence Boadt summarizes the differences between the two groups.

> [T]he early forms of prophecy in Israel leaned more to the discovery of the divine will for specific occasions and for specific individuals. The prophetic personnel were marked by great psychic gifts of seeing the future and by powers of divination. Some of these prophets were members of organized groups that favored ecstatic behavior rather than "messages" to be delivered.... This role contrasts sharply with the concerns of the writing prophets who speak to the whole nation and who see their primary task as challenging popular but false values while exhorting the people to rediscover the covenant and to reverse their evil ways.[1]

As designated messengers of Yahweh, the writing prophets were consummate wordsmiths, using poetry, prose, and song to proclaim God's word in public venues and in the royal court. As Boadt makes clear, their mission was to remind the people of their obligations to the covenant, often through frightening images of judgment and punishment, interspersed with urgent calls for repentance and reform and idyllic visions of a future God-fearing kingdom.

The writings of the biblical prophets cover a period of several hundred years and were composed in different geographic locations within the region. Micah, for example, was a southern prophet who condemned the leadership of Jerusalem during the late eighth century BCE. Amos preached against the excesses of the Northern Kingdom of Israel in the first half of the eighth century BCE, and Jeremiah was active in the Southern Kingdom of Judah during the late seventh and early sixth centuries BCE. Despite differences in time and place, the central purpose of the prophets was the same: to bring the people back to the covenant so that they could become the "priestly kingdom and a holy nation" Yahweh had envisioned at Sinai.

The consistency in theological message between the prophetic writings and the Pentateuch is not particularly surprising. The authors of the Old Testament all affirm that the God of Israel is a jealous God who demands loyalty and obedience from his chosen people. What is surprising, however, is the consistency in Yahweh's pedagogical approach, which appears throughout the biblical corpus. One of the most striking examples of this intertextual phenomenon is found in the book of Isaiah.

Isaiah is one of the largest books in the Bible, fifth in line behind Psalms, Jeremiah, Ezekiel, and Genesis. Debates continue about the authorship and structure of Isaiah.[2] Tradition held that Isaiah of Jerusalem wrote the book, but with the rise of modern biblical criticism, a consensus formed that the book contained two or more independent collections that were written at different times and places. One generally accepted theory holds that First Isaiah (1–39) was written by Isaiah of Jerusalem during the latter half of the eighth century BCE; Second Isaiah (40–55) was written by a disciple of the prophet during the exilic period of the sixth century BCE; Third Isaiah (56–66) was written by another disciple during the postexilic period when the people were returning to Jerusalem from Babylon. In recent years, the theory of independent collections has been challenged by scholars who believe the book is actually the product of a final redactor (much like the Priestly writer in the Pentateuch), who gathered, edited, and shaped the prophetic materials of Isaiah and his followers to form a unified, literary whole.

While these debates are interesting and important for biblical scholarship, the historical authorship of Isaiah is not as important to our study as the meaning of the book for spiritual and moral guidance. Read as a literary whole, the historical chronology, prophetic messages, and common themes in Isaiah generate an overarching narrative structure that recounts the rise, fall, restoration, and future redemption of the people of Israel. When considered individually and collectively, the writings not only mirror the basic plotline of the Pentateuch, but also confirm patterns in Yahweh's pedagogical activity first established in Genesis and Exodus.

To reveal these intertextual dynamics, our reading of Isaiah will adopt a historical-literary perspective that focuses on context and meaning; in other words, we shall first review the history surrounding each prophet and then examine his work in some detail, noting textual inconsistencies and relevant editorial points. This approach assumes at the outset that the book contains three separate collections that were produced at different times and places, and that a final, unknown redactor illuminated and enhanced the revelation embedded in the writings.

As we make our way through the collections, we shall once again encounter a deity who upholds key components of his pedagogical program while introducing innovative changes that address the specific situations and needs of his people. Collectively, the writings of the three Isaiahs—whether they existed as historical individuals or not—present a progressive program for human development that is designed to transform the people of Israel from demoralized victims of war to a nation of humble servants who are given a central role in God's redemptive plan. Our journey begins with an overview of the events that prompted First Isaiah's mission to Israel.

The Historical Background

The Rise of the Monarchy in Israel

The historical books of the Old Testament (Joshua, Judges, 1 and 2 Samuel, and 1 and 2 Kings) detail the story of the conquest of Canaan and the rise and fall of Israel's monarchy. While scholars still debate the historical accuracy of the books, the general consensus is that after the people settled in Canaan, they formed loose tribal federations that were united in their worship of Yahweh and in their mutual struggle for survival. Tribal leaders would meet periodically at central sanctuaries (for example, Shechem and Shiloh) to renew their religious and tribal loyalties and settle disputes, chiefly over land, water, and trade. But the continued growth and expansion of Israelite settlements and the increasing threat of the Philistines (the quintessential "bad guys" of the narrative) prompted tribal leaders to form a more centralized state. While the biblical writers looked upon kingship as a mixed blessing (as witnessed in the short and tragic reign of Saul), there is no question that the tribes benefited from a strong central government, which offered the people protection from military threats as well as greater social stability, and reliable access to necessary resources.

The kingdom reached its zenith during the reigns of David and Solomon in the tenth century BCE. David was a warrior king who unified the nation, established Jerusalem as the capital, and made Israel a military power to be reckoned with. Solomon, who was known for his great wisdom (1 Kings 4:29-34), negotiated treaties and trade agreements with neighboring kingdoms, thus bringing peace and prosperity to Israel for many years. Solomon's palace and the Temple complex in Jerusalem were glorious signs of Israel's success. But after Solomon died, his son, Rehoboam (922–915 BCE), made a costly diplomatic blunder in his initial meeting with the tribes. Rather than rescind his father's policies of heavy taxation and forced labor (which had made the king's glorious building projects possible), the young king callously informed the people of his intention to increase their burdens. Their reaction was swift and predictable: "When King Rehoboam sent Adoram, who was taskmaster over the forced labor, all Israel stoned him to death. King Rehoboam then hurriedly mounted his chariot to flee to Jerusalem" (1 Kings 12:18). With the king's hasty retreat, the tribes felt emboldened enough to withdraw from the Davidic monarchy altogether, forming the independent state of Israel (often called "Ephraim"), with the city of Samaria as the capital. The remaining tribes of Judah and Benjamin formed the Southern Kingdom of Judah, retaining Jerusalem as their capital and the Temple as the central shrine of Yahweh's cult.

Over the next two centuries, the rivalry between Israel and Judah was intense and not always peaceful. Skirmishes over disputed border lands were frequent and often deadly. The rivalry between the two kingdoms also extended to religion. Determined to develop their own religious identity (and keep pious Israelites at home), the northern kings established numerous shrines (e.g., Bethel and Dan) to compete with the Jerusalem Temple. To that end, northern priests and prophets developed their own interpretations of Israel's past to suit their anti-establishment outlook, producing materials that would eventually become the Elohist source. Despite these ongoing tensions and periodic wars with neighboring kingdoms (chiefly Moab, Edom, and Aram-Damascus), Israel and Judah survived in relative prosperity, but in a much weakened state from the glory days of the Davidic house. Their unsteady peace would end, however, with the expansionist plans of the Assyrian Empire.

The Destruction of the Northern Kingdom of Israel

Assyria had been an unwelcome predator in the region for much of the ninth century BCE, conquering small states in Syria-Palestine and applying pressure on neighboring ones, but the threat was sporadic and largely determined by the strength of each particular Assyrian king. By the eighth century, the region had experienced a welcome lull in Assyrian activity. However, when the Assyrian general, Tiglath-pileser III (745–727 BCE), seized power in a military coup, he immediately launched a series of highly successful campaigns of conquest that gobbled up much of the ancient Near East, including Babylonia and Syria-Palestine. John Bright explains why Tiglath-pileser was so successful and so greatly feared.

> The campaigns of Tiglath-pileser differed from those of his predecessors in that they were not tribute-gathering expeditions, but permanent conquests. In order to consolidate his gains, Tiglath-pileser adopted a policy which, although not wholly novel, had never been applied with such consistency before. Instead of contenting himself with receiving tribute from native princes and punishing rebellion with brutal reprisals, Tiglath-pileser, when rebellion occurred, habitually

deported the offenders and incorporated their lands as provinces of the empire, hoping in this way to quench all patriotic sentiment capable of nurturing resistance. This policy, consistently followed by Tiglath-pileser and copied by all his successors, was one of which Israel would in turn learn the meaning.[3]

The Northern Kingdom's unhappy education began with the miscalculations of King Pekah (737–732), who conspired with King Rezin (750–732) of Aram-Damascus to fight the Assyrians. The two kings tried to persuade Judah's king, Jotham (742–735), to join their coalition, but when Jotham refused, they allied their forces against the Southern Kingdom, intent on destroying the potential enemy at their rear.

The Syro-Ephraimite War (734 BCE), as it has been called, was a bloody conflict, indeed. As described in the Old Testament, coalition forces plundered Jerusalem, slaughtered thousands of Judeans, and brought thousands more back to Damascus as captives (2 Kings 16:5-9; 2 Chr 28:5-7). The invasions prompted Jotham's successor, King Ahaz (735–715), to take the prudent but risky move of appealing to Tiglath-pileser for help. The Assyrian general moved swiftly against the conspirators, putting his policy to work with ruthless efficiency. His armies overran the northern territories, destroying numerous cities, deporting large portions of the population (primarily the ruling and intellectual elites of Israel), and dividing the captured territories into Assyrian provinces. All that remained of Israel was a small territory around the capital city of Samaria. The rebel kings were shown no mercy. King Pekah was assassinated by Hoshea (who became the next king of Israel), and King Rezin was executed by Tiglath-pileser (2 Kings 15:30; 16:9). Although King Ahaz and the people of Judah escaped Israel's brutal fate, the appeal to the Assyrians was costly, for after the victory, Tiglath-pileser declared Judah a vassal state, demanding loyalty and heavy tribute from the Judeans.

Amazing as it may seem, the conquest of Israel did nothing to quash the people's desire for national autonomy, and it wasn't long before the ruling remnants of the Northern Kingdom began to regroup and plot against the Assyrian oppressor. The death of Tiglath-pileser in 727 BCE seemed like a golden opportunity to break free. Shortly after Shalmaneser V (727–722) took the Assyrian throne, King Hoshea (732–724) made his move, refusing to pay further tribute and appealing to Egypt for military support. Unfortunately, after years of warfare Egypt was in no position to help, and in 724 Shalmaneser attacked. The Assyrians quickly regained control of the lands surrounding Samaria, but the capital city refused to surrender, holding out for three years before the next Assyrian king, Sargon II (721–705) destroyed it in 722–721 BCE. With the fall of Samaria, the state of Israel effectively ceased to exist. Most survivors of the carnage, which numbered over 27,000 by Assyrian count, were exiled to other regions of the empire.[4] Others fled south, seeking refuge among their kinsmen in Judah.

The Subjugation of Judah

The successor to King Ahaz was his son, Hezekiah (715–687). Like his counterpart in the Northern Kingdom, King Hezekiah was determined to break free from the Assyrian yoke. In 705 BCE, Sargon II died on the battlefield, triggering a revolt among vassal states throughout the empire. Seizing the moment, Hezekiah joined the rebellion, refusing to pay further tribute to Assyria. In preparation for the war he knew would come, the young king fortified Jerusalem and other Judean cities while forging military alliances with Egypt, Babylon Tyre, and other vassal states in Syria-Palestine (2 Kings 18:21; 20:12-15). Meanwhile, Sargon's successor, King Sennacherib (704–681) was on the march. He spent several years securing rebellious territories in the east before turning his attention to Syria-Palestine. The invading armies crushed the opposition, executing and deporting rebels by the thousands. Bright offers a chilling description of Sennacherib's treatment of Judah.

> [In his own account of the invasion, Sennacherib] tells us that he reduced forty-six of Judah's fortified cities and deported their population, while shutting Hezekiah and the remnant of his troops up in Jerusalem "like a bird in a cage." The slaughter must have been fearful. Excavations at Lachish, which Sennacherib stormed, reveal, along with evidence of destruction, a huge pit into which the remains of some 1,500 bodies had been dumped and covered with pig bones and other debris—presumably the garbage of the Assyrian army.[5]

With thousands dead and nearly every Judean city in flames, King Hezekiah had little choice but to sue for peace. Sennacherib's terms of surrender were harsh. Sizeable tracts of Judean lands were turned over to Assyrian loyalists and the amount of tribute was substantially increased, so much so that Hezekiah had to strip the Jerusalem Temple and the royal treasury to pay it. As recorded in 2 Kings 18:14-16, "The king of Assyria demanded of King Hezekiah of Judah three hundred talents [about eleven tons] of silver and thirty talents [one ton] of gold." The city of Jerusalem was spared, but Judah was decimated, bankrupt, and still under the thumb of Assyria.

Sennacherib's decisive victories against Judah did not deter the people's rebellious spirit, however, and in 688 BCE he found it necessary to return to Syria-Palestine for a second campaign.[6] The invading force quickly captured fortified towns and cities and laid siege to Jerusalem, but this time the Assyrians were defeated, and not by any force of arms. Although historians still debate the exact cause, Sennacherib's army fell victim to some kind of epidemic that killed thousands of his troops.[7] The Assyrian king had no choice but to withdraw, leaving Jerusalem relatively unscathed. While many Judeans (including First Isaiah) attributed the city's deliverance to the hand of God (2 Kings 20:32-36; Isa 36–37), Judah remained an Assyrian vassal. It was during this time of political intrigue, war, and subjugation that First Isaiah lived and worked.

WHO WERE THE PROPHETS?

With the rise of the monarchy came the prophets of Israel. Prophets were not fortune tellers or clairvoyants but were spiritually motivated social critics adept at reading the "signs of the time." The prophets were influential in the ancient world because they were considered authoritative messengers of God who communicated God's will to kings and common folk alike. Some were on the royal payroll, providing monarchs with counsel and advice, particularly in times of crisis. In the Bible, prophets are often cast as God's prosecutors, delivering oracles of judgment and imminent destruction to the king and the people for failing to uphold a covenant. The basic message of the prophets is one of repentance, reform, and care for the vulnerable and powerless (represented by the widow and the orphan). Isaiah, Amos, Hosea, and Jeremiah are biblical prophets who reflect this pattern.

As judges and social critics, the prophets were central to the self-understanding of the people of Israel; they helped them realize (not always in time) that the ethical dimension of the covenant was just as important as the worship of Yahweh. They also reinforced a fundamental truth, first expressed in the "curses" of Genesis 3:14-19, that actions indeed have consequences.

Every age needs and has its prophets. Where do you think we might find them today? What is the nature and content of their message? How do they communicate it? If you were to create a prophetic message, what might it be?

The Life and Mission of First Isaiah

Isaiah (which means "Yahweh has saved") was active in the Southern Kingdom of Judah between 740 and 700 BCE. Little is known of the prophet except what can be gleaned from his writings. He was the son of Amoz and was married to a prophetess who bore him two sons (Isa 7:3; 8:3). Although he never specifically mentions his family's status, his access to Kings Ahaz and Hezekiah, his familiarity with the liturgy of the Jerusalem Temple, and his presence in the Temple during his inaugural vision suggest that he was a member of the Judean ruling classes.

The event that launched Isaiah's career as a prophet was his vision of Yahweh's heavenly throne room, which revealed the awesome holiness of Israel's God (Isa 6). From the moment he volunteered to be Yahweh's appointed messenger, Isaiah found himself increasingly at odds with Judah's kings and the Judean aristocracy, who were anything but holy— at least by the prophet's standards. For nearly fifty years he voiced his criticisms of their politics and religious practices in the harshest possible terms. Although there is no historical evidence to substantiate the claim, tradition holds that Isaiah's mission ended abruptly when he met a martyr's death during the reign of Hezekiah's successor, the much despised King Manasseh (686–642 BCE).[8]

Isaiah's writings are an excellent example of the dynamic development of revelation. As noted in chapter 1, the content of revelation doesn't simply drop from the sky as a fully formed message. Human beings experience the divine and then try to make sense of it through a process of reflection, articulation, revision, and so on until there is insight, or "revelation." In experiencing and reflecting upon the turmoil and tragedy of his time, Isaiah's revelation reflected a major shift in Israel's religious consciousness.

Israel's Shift in Religious Consciousness

The shift was gradual and most likely began when the people of Israel moved from tribal federations to a unified monarchy. Although scholars still debate the extent of this unity, the kings of the Davidic house established an organized administration, negotiated treaties and trade agreements with neighboring states, supported a standing army, fought wars, and participated in the power politics of the region. The monarchy's success thrust the people of Israel onto the world stage for the first time in their history. With this positive change in worldly status came a more global perspective and a new understanding of their God. Yahweh was no longer perceived as a local tribal god who focused solely on the welfare of the Israelites in Canaan. He was now a cosmic deity who favored Israel out of all the nations of the world and whose awesome power determined the course of world events. This is the God we encounter in Isaiah. The prophet, who was so close to the seat of Judean power, was in a perfect position to grasp the shift and articulate its meaning for the people of Israel. But his revelations were a double-edged sword, for Isaiah challenged the notion that the fates of the two kingdoms were simply the result of losing the game of power politics; instead, Isaiah explained the losses in theological terms, forging a causal link between the religious and moral failings of Israel and Judah and Yahweh's power to make the nations of the world instruments of divine wrath and retribution.

First Isaiah as a Prophet of Doom and Hope

Isaiah's writings combine prose narrative with prophetic oracles. Written in the first person, Isaiah's oracles are direct messages from God to the prophet that take the form of accusations or judgments against the people of Judah and Israel—and just about everybody else who was living at the time. The collection found in First Isaiah is commonly divided into four sections:

Chapters 1–12	Oracles condemning Judah and Jerusalem (1–5); Isaiah's inaugural vision and political activism (6–10); visions of universal peace (11–12)
Chapters 13–27	Oracles against foreign nations (13–23); the "Little Apocalypse" presenting eschatological visions of cosmic judgment and restoration (24–27)
Chapters 28–35	Oracles about Israel and Judah (28), additional oracles of judgment and blessing (29–35)
Chapters 36–39	Prose excerpts from 2 Kings 18–19 detailing Sennacherib's invasion of Judah

Biblical scholars disagree about which materials were written by the prophet and which were later additions by his disciples. Whatever the case, the collection offers alternating visions of doom and hope that reflect the turbulent period of the two kingdoms and Isaiah's prophetic mission to Judah.

Reading Isaiah can be daunting, not only because of the poetic forms that are used but also because the order of the writings does not follow the chronology of events (hence the debates about sources and editorial hands). Oracles about Sennacherib's invasion of Judah (701 BCE), for example, precede oracles about the Syro-Ephraimite War (734 BCE). The narrative thread is also intermittent, appearing for the first time in chapter 6, which presents Isaiah's vision of the heavenly throne room and his call from God. For the sake of clarity, we shall begin our exegetical analysis here. As a prophet of doom and hope, Isaiah offers specific reasons why the Sinai program was lost, the consequences for God's chosen people, and the obvious remedy. His writings thus follow the pattern established in the Pentateuch, for just as Genesis provided the necessary context for Sinai, the oracles in First Isaiah provide the necessary context for the writings of the Second and Third Isaiah, which outline God's program for Israel's rehabilitation.

The Call of Isaiah

The God that appears in the heavenly throne room is very different from the deity we encountered in Genesis and Exodus. He doesn't take leisurely walks in the garden or debate with human beings or appear in a burning bush. This God is a God of monarchs, with all the accoutrements and responsibilities befitting a king. In Isaiah's vision, the Lord is seated "on a throne, high and lofty; and the hem of his robe filled the temple" (Isa 6:1). In attendance are winged seraphim (the "burning ones") who continually call out to one another, "Holy, holy, holy is the LORD of hosts; the whole earth is full of his glory" (Isa 6:3). Yahweh's cosmic aspect is represented by his very size (he is massive) and the extent of his realm (he is everywhere).

In true Sinai fashion, God's presence shakes the thresholds of the throne room and fills it with smoke. Awestruck by the theophany, Isaiah cries out "Woe is me! I am lost, for I am a man of unclean lips, and I live among a people of unclean lips; yet my eyes have seen the King, the LORD of hosts!" (Isa 6:5). Like so many biblical figures before him, Isaiah feels inadequate for God's mission, but his "unclean" status is quickly rectified by one of the seraphs, who touches his lips with a hot coal, cleansing him from guilt and sin. In a highly stylized and very public ceremony reminiscent of Sinai, Yahweh initiates Isaiah's call, asking the entire divine assembly, "Whom shall I send, and who will go for us?" To which Isaiah immediately replies, "Here am I, send me!" (Isa 6:8). Unlike Moses, Isaiah is most anxious to serve, yet no sooner has he accepted the mission than he learns that it will be a futile undertaking. Paradoxically, God calls upon Isaiah to warn a people who will not listen or understand his words. When Isaiah asks how long he must persist in this thankless job, Yahweh tells him: "[U]ntil cities lie waste, without inhabitant, and houses without people, and the land is utterly desolate; until the LORD sends everyone far away, and vast is the emptiness in the midst of the land" (Isa 6:11-12). Several oracles in the beginning of the collection, which condemn Judah and Jerusalem, provide reasons why Isaiah's mission is doomed to fail.

The Sins of Israel

Using the legal language of the courts (a reflection of Judah's well-established judiciary), Yahweh assumes the role of cosmic prosecutor and judge, calling upon heaven and earth to hear the evidence against Judah. The first oracle offers a stinging indictment against his chosen people:

> Hear, O heavens, and listen, O earth,
>   for the LORD has spoken:
> I reared children and brought them up,
>   but they have rebelled against me.
> The ox knows its owner,
>   and the donkey its master's crib;
> but Israel does not know,
>   my people do not understand.
> Ah, sinful nation,
>   people laden with iniquity,
> offspring who do evil,
>   children who deal corruptly,
> who have forsaken the LORD,
>   who have despised the Holy One of Israel,
>   who are utterly estranged! (Isa 1:2-4)

In this passage, Yahweh accuses the people not only of failing to acknowledge their relationship with him ("the ox knows its owner"), but also of rejecting God's Law through their evil and corrupt practices. God's pain at their betrayal is evident. Their willful disobedience has resulted in estrangement from him, but that is not the only negative consequence.

Your country lies desolate,
    your cities are burned with fire;
in your very presence
    aliens devour your land;
    it is desolate, as overthrown by foreigners.
And daughter Zion is left
    like a booth in a vineyard,
like a shelter in a cucumber field,
    like a besieged city.
If the LORD of hosts
    had not left us a few survivors,
we would have been like Sodom,
    and become like Gomorrah. (Isa 1:7-9)

Most scholars agree that this first oracle refers to Sennacherib's invasion of Judah in 701 BCE. What is striking here is the assumption that Yahweh permitted the Assyrians to destroy Judean cities. "If the LORD of hosts had not left us a few survivors" suggests that Yahweh had a hand in Judah's destruction, as well as its continued survival. But what did the people do to warrant such harsh punishment? As divine prosecutor and judge, Yahweh offers damning evidence of the people's corruption.

One of their most grievous sins is false worship: "What to me is the multitude of your sacrifices? says the LORD. I have had enough of burnt offerings of rams and the fat of fed beasts; I do not delight in the blood of bulls or of lambs, or of goats" (Isa 1:11). The people's actions are hollow and meaningless before God because they are divorced from social justice. God's disgust at the people's hypocrisy becomes a painful lament of what has been lost:

How the faithful city
    has become a whore!
    She that was full of justice,
righteousness lodged in her—
    but now murderers!
Your silver has become dross,
    your wine is mixed with water.
Your princes are rebels,
    and companions of thieves.
Everyone loves a bribe
    and runs after gifts.
They do not defend the orphan,
    and the widow's cause does not come before them. (Isa 1:21-23)

In describing the moral corruption of Judah, Yahweh makes direct reference to his teachings at Sinai. In the Book of the Covenant the people were commanded not to "abuse any widow or orphan" (Ex 22:22), but with their emerging status as a regional power and their increasing wealth and prosperity, they have forgotten (or rejected) God's teachings.

The false worship of the Judean citizenry is only part of the evidence. In another oracle, God takes aim at the smug complacency and greed of Judah's leaders.

> The LORD rises to argue his case;
>   he stands to judge the peoples.
> The LORD enters into judgment
>   with the elders and princes of his people:
> It is you who have devoured the vineyard;
>   the spoil of the poor is in your houses.
> What do you mean by crushing my people,
>   by grinding the face of the poor?
>   says the Lord GOD of hosts. (Isa 3:13-15)

Instead of joining Judah's elders and princes in judgment of the people, Yahweh turns the tables on the rascals, condemning their exploitation of the people through forced labor and the confiscation of their lands.

The failure in leadership is exacerbated further by the unwillingness of Judah's kings to depend on God alone for survival. The most obvious example is King Ahaz, who displays a distressing lack of faith when Judah is threatened by Israel and Aram-Damascus. In a narrative section, Isaiah recalls that when the Southern Kingdom learned of the northern alliance "the heart of Ahaz and the heart of his people shook as the trees of the forest shake before the wind" (Isa 7:2). Speaking through the prophet, Yahweh tries to reassure Ahaz, telling him: "Take heed, be quiet, do not fear, and do not let your heart be faint" (Isa 7:4). The message is clear: do not turn to Tiglath-pileser for aid because Israel and Aram-Damascus will not prevail. A later oracle in the collection describes their fate:

> See, Damascus will cease to be a city,
>   and will become a heap of ruins.
> Her towns will be deserted forever,
>   they will be places for flocks,
>   which will lie down, and no one will make them afraid.
> The fortress will disappear from Ephraim [the Northern Kingdom],
>   and the kingdom from Damascus;
> and the remnant of Aram will be
>   like the glory of children of Israel,
>   says the LORD of hosts. (Isa 17:1-3)

Unfortunately, the reality of the political and military situation overwhelms Ahaz and, like many before him, his faith in God wavers.

The tug of war between the king's faith and his fear is voiced in an important exchange between God and Ahaz. Speaking through the prophet,

Yahweh takes the unusual step of pleading with the king to ask for a sign to prove his presence—quite a concession for an all-powerful cosmic God. In fact, God almost dares Ahaz to test his power, telling him that the sign can be as "deep as Sheol [the underworld] or high as heaven" (Isa 7:11). Too shrewd or perhaps too frightened to reject the offer outright, Ahaz navigates the theo-political minefield with a display of false humility, telling Isaiah, "I will not ask, and I will not put the LORD to the test" (Isa 7:12). The prophet sees through the ploy and proclaims the advent of a divine sign that will ultimately become a source of hope for Jews and Christians alike.

> Then Isaiah said: "Hear then, O house of David! Is it too little for you to weary mortals, that you weary my God also? Therefore the LORD himself will give you a sign. Look, the young woman is with child and shall bear a son, and shall name him Immanuel. He shall eat curds and honey by the time he knows how to refuse the evil and choose the good. For before the child knows how to refuse the evil and choose the good, the land before whose two kings you are in dread will be deserted. The LORD will bring on you and on your people and on your ancestral house such days as have not come since the day that Ephraim departed from Judah—the king of Assyria." (Isa 7:13-17)

The young woman has been identified variously as the wife of Isaiah or the mother of King Hezekiah.[9] Later Christian interpreters believed the woman was the mother of Jesus, but the Christian reading does not consider the historical situation of the prophet. For Isaiah, the birth of the child, Immanuel ("God with us"), symbolizes God's presence among the people during the crisis of the Syro-Ephraimite War. The Immanuel figure has other meanings that will be discussed presently. In this context, the birth of the child offers King Ahaz reassurance that God is with Judah and that Israel and Aram-Damascus will soon be destroyed. The word of hope is tempered, however, by a thinly veiled threat: disloyalty to Yahweh will result in Assyrian domination.

Yahweh's demand for justice and his cosmic reach are evident in these texts and are reinforced further in the oracles that describe the sins and the destruction of the Northern Kingdom.

The Consequences of Sin

The reasons for God's wrath against the Northern Kingdom echo his indictments against Judah. Instead of embracing the laws and instructions of the Sinai covenant, the Israelites are unfaithful, idolatrous, greedy, and unjust (Isa 2:5-9). Some of Yahweh's harshest words are reserved for Israel's judicial system, particularly its judges, who "make iniquitous decrees, who write oppressive statutes, to turn aside the needy from justice and to rob the poor of my people of their right, that widows may be your spoil, and that you may make the orphans your prey!" (Isa 10:1-2). According to the Mosaic Law, such behavior warrants death, but Yahweh is merciful, warning the people through the prophets.

> The LORD sent a word against Jacob,
>   and it fell on Israel
> and all the people knew it—
>   Ephraim and the inhabitants of Samaria—
>   but in pride and arrogance of heart they said:
> "The bricks have fallen
>   but we will build them with dressed stones;
> the sycamores have been cut down,
>   but we will put cedars in their place."
> So the LORD raised adversaries against them,
>   and stirred up their enemies,
> the Arameans on the east and the Philistines on the west,
>   and they devoured Israel with open mouth.
> For all this his anger has not turned away;
>   his hand is stretched out still. (Isa 9:8-12)

God's warnings through the words of the prophets (probably Amos and Hosea) and the earthquake (a common attention-getter for deities) are ignored. After bruising battles with regional enemies (yet another sign of God's displeasure), the Israelites still don't take the hint; instead, they resolve to rebuild their cities and resume their rebellious ways. But their actions are futile because Yahweh is a deity who controls pagan nations, using them to inflict further punishment on Israel. Tiglath-pileser's army delivers Yahweh's final word: "Ah, Assyria, the rod of my anger—the club in their hands is my fury! Against a godless nation I send him, and against the people of my wrath I command him, to take spoil and seize plunder, and to tread them down like the mire of the streets" (Isa 10:5-6).

Unfortunately, the destruction of the Northern Kingdom and Isaiah's repeated warnings do little to reform their Judean kinsmen. They continue to ignore the covenant requirements, indulging themselves in every possible vanity. Yahweh has particular contempt for the ladies of Jerusalem's court, who "walk with outstretched necks, glancing wantonly with their eyes, mincing along as they go, tinkling with their feet" (Isa 3:16). The punishment for such vanity and material excess echoes the warning and punishment of the social justice command (Ex 22:21-24):

> Instead of perfume there will be a stench;
>   and instead of a sash, a rope;
> and instead of well-set hair, baldness;
>   and instead of a rich robe a binding of sackcloth;
>   instead of beauty, shame.
> Your men shall fall by the sword
>   and your warriors in battle.

And her gates shall lament and mourn;
>   ravaged, she shall sit upon the ground. (Isa 3:24-26)

The once proud women of the Judean court are reduced to wailing widows, sitting among the dust and ashes of Jerusalem, their husbands slain because of their own corruption and lack of mercy.

Together, these passages offer theological rather than political reasons for the devastation of Israel and Judah. Isaiah's writings claim that behind the Assyrian's lust for territory and their ruthless military campaigns is the righteous wrath of the Holy One. Nowhere is the image of this cosmic God more powerfully displayed than in chapters 24–27, which are called Isaiah's "Little Apocalypse."

The Little Apocalypse

The apocalyptic genre was a later development in Jewish eschatology that will be explored in the next chapter. Suffice it to say that although these apocalyptic additions were probably written during the postexilic period, they serve their intended purpose here, which is to reinforce the notion of Yahweh's universal rule. In these oracles, the Lord of hosts holds up all the nations (including Assyria) for judgment and punishment. Images of waste and devastation, as well as the terrors of God's hellish pit, swirl before the terrified inhabitants of heaven and earth.

On that day the LORD will punish
>   the host of heaven in heaven,
>   and on earth the kings of the earth.
They will be gathered together
>   like prisoners in a pit;
they will be shut up in a prison,
>   and after many days they will be punished.
Then the moon will be abashed,
>   and the sun ashamed,
for the LORD of hosts will reign
>   on Mount Zion and in Jerusalem,
and before his elders he will manifest his glory. (Isa 24:21-23)

Despite the frightening images and portents, Isaiah's message is not completely negative. One of the most hopeful images in Isaiah is the "righteous remnant," which symbolizes all those who remain faithful to God and who will be spared during the dreadful days of judgment. In prose commentary, Isaiah tells the people that on the coming days of destruction,

[T]he survivors of the house of Jacob will no more lean on the one who struck them [Assyria], but will lean on the LORD, the Holy One of Israel, in truth. A remnant will return, the remnant of Jacob, to the mighty God. For though your people Israel were like the sand of the

sea, only a remnant of them will return. Destruction is decreed, over-
flowing with righteousness. For the Lord GOD of hosts will make a full
end, as decreed, in all the earth. (Isa 10:20-23)

Thus, while Yahweh's justice demands that the people suffer for their
numerous sins, he offers the righteous remnant liberation from their suffering and, just as he did with the slaves at Mount Sinai, God presents the survivors with an ideal that they can strive for in the years ahead, an ideal
articulated in one of the most famous passages in the Bible.

> In the days to come
>   the mountain of the LORD's house
> shall be established as the highest of the mountains,
>   and shall be raised above the hills;
> all the nations shall stream to it.
>   Many peoples shall come and say,
> "Come, let us go up to the mountain of the LORD,
>   to the house of the God of Jacob,
> that he may teach us his ways
>   and that we may walk in his paths."
> For out of Zion shall go forth instruction
>   and the word of the LORD from Jerusalem.
> He shall judge between the nations,
>   and shall arbitrate for many peoples;
> they shall beat their swords into plowshares,
>   and their spears into pruning hooks;
> nation shall not lift up sword against nation,
>   neither shall they learn war any more. (Isa 2:2-4)

The cosmic reach of Yahweh is once again affirmed. As at Sinai, the revelation centers on a mountain, but God's teachings are no longer restricted
to the Israelites. They are now offered to all people, as is the promise of
peace. The center for this global movement is Jerusalem—*Zion*, a biblical
name used variously to designate a fortress, the people of Israel, the city of
Jerusalem and its environs, or the whole country.[10] Within this context, it
seems likely that Zion refers to the Temple compound in Jerusalem where it
is believed Yahweh dwells and where his teachings are promulgated.

In the new Jerusalem, the leadership of Israel will be also be transformed. As a southern prophet and staunch supporter of the Davidic house,
Isaiah connects the vision of the new Jerusalem with the Immanuel figure:

> For a child has been born for us,
>   a son given to us;
> authority rests upon his shoulders;
>   and he is named

Wonderful Counselor, Mighty God,
>   Everlasting Father, Prince of Peace.
His authority shall grow continually,
>   and there shall be endless peace
for the throne of David and his kingdom.
He will establish and uphold it
with justice and with righteousness
>   from this time onward and forevermore.
The zeal of the LORD of hosts will do this. (Isa 9:6-7)

While the date and circumstances of the poem are debated by scholars (some believe Isaiah wrote it; others believe it is postexilic), the theological message is clear. The Immanuel figure—the Messiah (or "anointed one")—will come from David's family tree and will possess all the attributes the current leaders lack. The poem thus establishes the centrality of Jerusalem and the Davidic house for the future of Israel. Stephen L. Harris and Robert L. Platzner explain the sweeping and enduring significance of this linkage for the people of Judah and for future generations.

> Although Israel and other nearby states were crushed by Assyria, this coronation hymn for the new Davidic ruler predicts a flourishing Judah, secure because of God's pact with David (9:2-21). So forceful is Isaiah's Immanuel prophecy, with its optimism for Judah's divinely appointed monarchy, that—after the Davidic throne had been permanently over-thrown—later generations viewed it as a messianic prediction. A term meaning "anointed" and applied to all Davidic kings, *messiah* later be-came identified with a future heir of David who would restore David's kingdom and vindicate YHWH's people. In the Christian New Testa-ment, Jesus of Nazareth is portrayed as the royal figure whom Isaiah foretold, although the historical Jesus did not reestablish the Davidic monarchy or free the covenant community from its political oppressors.[11]

As mentioned above, many scholars believe that Isaiah's Immanuel prophecy refers to King Hezekiah. Unlike his father, Ahaz, Hezekiah listens to Isaiah's counsel, although his rebel alliance with Egypt against the Assyrians draws a sharp rebuke from God (Isa 30:1-7). The last chapters of First Isaiah recount Hezekiah's struggle to protect his shrinking kingdom from the Assyrians while remaining loyal to Yahweh (Isa 36–39)—not an easy task by any means. Although shaky at times, his faithfulness is rewarded. Jerusalem is spared from Sennacherib's siege by the divine plague (Isa 37:6), and Hezekiah's prayers to Yahweh save him from a life-threatening illness (Isa 38). But these acts of grace are only temporary remedies. While Hezekiah may be a noble king, the ideal of the new Jerusalem will not be realized during his reign. Given Israel's past behavior, Yahweh decides that the righteous remnant must endure further suffering before they are ready to establish the new Jerusalem. Their fate is foreshadowed in a prediction at the end of the collection. Scholars believe the prediction is part of a historical appendix (probably taken from 2 Kings 20) that was added long after the time of the prophet and that serves as a transition to Second Isaiah.[12] The prophet tells Hezekiah that his wealth and his descendants will be carried away, and that some of his sons will serve as eunuchs "in the palace of the king of Babylon" (Isa 39:6-7).

The reasons for extending the people's suffering are a central part of Yahweh's pedagogical plan and are detailed in the writings of Second Isaiah. But before exploring the prophet's work, we must first review the events leading up to Judah's exile to Babylon.

The Historical Context of Second Isaiah

The Assyrian army's retreat from Jerusalem in 687 BCE was a momentary respite from Assyrian aggression. The Assyrian king was not so lucky. In 680 BCE Sennacherib was assassinated by his own sons (2 Kings 19:37), but his murder did not result in freedom for Judah. On the contrary, Hezekiah's successor, King Manassah, was hauled in chains before King Asshurbanapal (668–627) and held captive until he pledged his loyalty to the Assyrian throne (2 Chr 33). Manassah was quick to comply. So eager was he to appease his overlords that the young king had altars to Assyrian gods built in the Jerusalem Temple (an abomination that did not endear him to the biblical writers.). But like all predatory nations, Assyria's grip on power would slip. Years of political intrigue and corruption, constant warfare, and assassinations sapped the empire's resources, leaving it vulnerable to its neighbors. Between 626 and 612 BCE, the once formidable Assyrian army was defeated in a series of battles with the Medes and Babylonians that left Assyria's capital city of Nineveh in ruins. By 610 BCE the empire was finished and the kingdoms of Babylonia and Egypt were fighting for control of Assyria's western territories. Judah was suddenly caught in the middle of a major power struggle, pledging loyalty to each kingdom in turn while plotting for independence. The Egyptians were finally driven from the region by the Babylonian armies of King Nebuchadnezzar in 605, but Judah did not remain a compliant vassal for long. In 599, King Jehoiakim refused to pay further tribute, prompting Nebuchadnezzar to send an invading force to surround Jerusalem. After a short siege, the city surrendered in the spring of 598. Nebuchadnezzar, weary of Judah's recalcitrance, began a systematic campaign of destruction and deportation. Lawrence Boadt describes the last tragic years of Judah's existence under King Zedekiah (597–587).

> The twelve years between the first fall of the city of Jerusalem in 598 and its final destruction in 586 was a troubled time with many people still hoping for victory over Babylon and complete independence.

[King] Zedekiah . . . proved to be a weak and uncertain man who first leaned one way and then another. But finally he too broke with Babylon about 589 B.C. under the prodding of the new Egyptian pharaoh, Hophra. Nebuchadnezzar moved quickly to deal with the rebellion because he feared Egyptian designs on Palestine. He captured all the cities of Judah, surrounded Jerusalem and for two years starved the people into defeat. When all was lost, Zedekiah tried to flee at night to safety but the Babylonian army caught him near Jericho and he had to watch while his sons were executed before his eyes, then have his own eyes put out and finally be led away to die a captive in a Babylonian prison. Nebuchadnezzar took more people into exile, this time leaving only a remnant . . . to make some kind of a living in the land. He tore down the city walls and leveled the temple to the ground so that Jerusalem would no longer serve as a center for Jewish hopes. But despite his efforts, many still waited for the day when God would restore the city.[13]

Some of the survivors who were not deported to Babylon migrated to Egypt, the Arabian Peninsula, and other lands. Thus began the Jewish Diaspora (or dispersion) of the Jewish people throughout the world. The Babylonian exile would not end until 539 BCE, when the Persian king, Cyrus (558–530 BCE), conquered Babylon and permitted all subject peoples to return to their homelands. Second Isaiah was Israel's voice of hope in the dark years between the exile and the second exodus.

The Life and Mission of Second Isaiah

The identity and life of the author of Second Isaiah are shrouded in mystery. Unlike Isaiah of Jerusalem, Second Isaiah does not offer any autobiographical information in his writings. Some scholars speculate that he was a disciple who adopted the theology and literary style of the original prophet. Others suggest that the "he" may, in fact, be a "she"—not such a far-fetched claim, given that women served as prophets in ancient Israel.[14] Whatever the case, many scholars agree that the author of Isaiah 40–55 lived in Babylon during the exile and may even have witnessed the Persian army as it entered the city in triumph.[15]

The second collection is called the Book of Consolation, and with good reason, for in contrast to the harsh judgments and graphic images of First Isaiah, the prophet offers only words of comfort and hope to the exiles. The switch in tone was desperately needed. After the overwhelming loss of the monarchy, the Jerusalem Temple, and the land, the exiles naturally began to wonder whether Yahweh was as powerful as the Babylonian gods (particularly Marduk, the warrior god who ruled the Babylonian pantheon). The people needed some reassurance that Yahweh was still an effective deity and that he had not forsaken them. Isaiah of Babylon accomplishes this through writings that offer the exiles a new understanding of Yahweh and a renewed sense of their place and purpose in the world. From an intertextual perspective, Second Isaiah's work also introduces the central components of God's new and improved program for his people.

The book is divided into two main sections: chapters 40–48 are prophecies concerning the liberation of Israel from Babylon by the Persian king, Cyrus; chapters 49–55 are prophecies concerning the return and restoration of Jerusalem-Zion. Unlike First Isaiah, this book contains no narrative portions. The poems in the first section reinforce some of the major themes presented in First Isaiah while introducing others that complement or amend those themes.

Second Isaiah as a Prophet of Comfort and Hope

The book begins with members of the divine council announcing God's intention toward his people. God has had a change of heart. Using the juridical language so prominent in First Isaiah, the council offers words of consolation to the "prisoners" of Babylon:

> Comfort, O comfort my people,
> > says your God.
> Speak tenderly to Jerusalem,
> > and cry to her
> that she has served her term,
> > that her penalty is paid,
> that she has received from the LORD's hand
> > double for all her sins.
> A voice cries out:
> "In the wilderness prepare the way of the LORD,
> > make straight in the desert a highway for our God.
> Every valley shall be lifted up,
> > and every mountain and hill be made low;
> the uneven ground shall become level,
> > and the rough places a plain.
> Then the glory of the LORD shall be revealed,
> > and all people shall see it together,
> > for the mouth of the LORD has spoken." (Isa 40:1-5)

The words are indeed comforting. The God of Israel has not forsaken his people. Like the golden calf idolaters, the people have paid dearly for their sins and will soon be free to journey to the homeland, but that is not the only good news. The poem also announces the dawning of a new age for all the peoples of the earth. It is an age in which the "uneven ground" of ignorance, inequality, and injustice will be leveled, and all people will be united and illumined in the glory of God. This radical proclamation echoes the idyllic vision of Jerusalem presented in First Isaiah. In announcing the new age, Yahweh challenges the legitimacy of the Babylonian gods (despite the reality of the exile), as well as the power of the nations to dictate world events. It is Yahweh alone who has that power. Returning to the courtroom, God throws down the gauntlet to the gods of other nations:

> Set forth your case, says the LORD;
>> bring your proofs, says the King of Jacob.
> Let them bring them, and tell us
>> what is to happen.
> Tell us the former things, what they are,
>> so that we may consider them,
> and that we may know their outcome;
>> or declare to us the things to come.
> Tell us what is to come hereafter,
>> that we may know that you are gods;
> do good, or do harm,
>> that we may be afraid and terrified.
> You, indeed, are nothing
>> and your work is nothing at all;
> whoever chooses you is an abomination. (Isa 41:21-24)

In challenging these gods, Yahweh makes the point that the "former things" (the earlier prophecies) that he proclaimed through the prophets have indeed come to pass—the two kingdoms were destroyed and the people were sent into exile for their sins. Can the Babylonian gods, or any gods for that matter, say the same? And are they powerful enough to control the leaders of other nations? Yahweh boasts that the success of Cyrus, who at this point has conquered much of Asia Minor, is the direct result of his intervention and direction.

> Who has roused a victor from the east,
>> summoned him to his service?
> He delivers up nations to him,
>> and tramples kings under foot;
> he makes them like dust with his sword,
>> like driven stubble with his bow.
> He pursues them and passes on safely,
>> scarcely touching the path with his feet.
> Who has performed and done this,
>> calling the generations from the beginning?
> I, the LORD, am first,
>> and will be the last. (Isa 41:2-4)

Unlike First Isaiah, Second Isaiah does not look to an heir of the Davidic house to ensure the survival of the Israelites—given the fate of King Zedekiah and his sons, why would he? Instead, the prophet names Cyrus— a pagan ruler—as the new Messiah who will fulfill God's plan to free the captives. In proclaiming his intentions in the Cyrus oracle, Yahweh makes an even bolder claim:

> For the sake of my servant Jacob,
>   and Israel my chosen,
> I call you [Cyrus] by your name,
>   I surname you, though you do not know me.
> I am the LORD, and there is no other;
>   besides me there is no god.
> I arm you, though you do not know me,
> so that they may know, from the rising of the sun
>   and from the west, that there is no one besides me;
>   I am the LORD, and there is no other.
> I form light and create darkness,
>   I make weal and create woe;
>   I the LORD do all these things. (Isa 45:4-7)

> I made the earth,
>   and created humankind upon it;
> it was my hands that stretched out the heavens,
>   and I commanded all their host.
> I have aroused Cyrus in righteousness,
>   and I will make all his paths straight;
> he shall build my city
>   and set my exiles free,
> not for price or reward,
>   says the LORD of hosts. (Isa 45:12-13)

In these verses are present the seeds of change, from henotheism (loyalty to one god among many) to monotheism (the worship of the one and only God). In a stroke of genius (and revelation), the prophet proclaims that the gods of other nations will no longer be a temptation to the exiles, because Yahweh's incomparable power not only challenges their effectiveness but also calls into question their very existence. In an ironic twist of fate, Yahweh mocks the Babylonian gods as their followers flee Cyrus's armies: "Bel [another name for Marduk] bows down, Nebo [his son] stoops, their idols are on beasts and cattle; these things you carry are loaded as burdens on weary animals. They stoop, they bow down together; they cannot save the burden but themselves go into captivity" (46:1-2).

This sad parade is in stark contrast to the Babylonians' New Year's festival in which the people would proudly parade their gods through the city streets.[16] Now, before the mighty power of Yahweh, the gods are nothing but useless idols that cannot save the faithful or themselves from destruction. Their humiliating defeat confirms that Yahweh is the sole power in the universe and Israel's true redeemer. Alluding to the exodus from Egypt, Yahweh reassures the exiles:

Thus says the LORD,
    your Redeemer, the Holy One of Israel:
For your sake I will send to Babylon
    and break down all the bars,
    and the shouting of the Chaldeans will be turned to lamentation.
I am the LORD, your Holy One,
    the creator of Israel, your King.
Thus says the LORD,
    who makes a way in the sea,
    a path in the mighty waters,
who brings out chariot and horse,
    army and warrior;
they lie down, they cannot rise,
    they are extinguished, quenched like a wick:
Do not remember the former things,
    or consider the things of old.
I am about to do a new thing;
    now it springs forth, do you not perceive it?
I will make a way in the wilderness
    and rivers in the desert. (Isa 43:14-17)

As this passage makes clear, Israel's redemption requires that a "new thing" be introduced. But what is this new thing? Yahweh's activity offers many possible options. It could refer to the anticipated liberation from Babylon (the second exodus) or to God's designation of Cyrus as the Immanuel figure—the elevation of a pagan to such a role is a radical departure from the plan outlined in First Isaiah. The new thing could also refer to the servant, a central figure that is introduced in Isaiah's celebrated "Servant Songs."

The concept of servanthood is a new thing that redefines the people's place and purpose in the world. With the defeat of the Babylonians, the exiles are poised to return to the world stage, but not as the selfish and sinful nation of the Davidic house. They will return as God's servant, which Isaiah claims was their destiny from the very beginning. Yahweh explains that his decision to liberate the exiles was prompted in part by their special status as his servant.

But you, Israel, my servant,
    Jacob, whom I have chosen,
    the offspring of Abraham, my friend;
you whom I took from the ends of the earth,
    and called from its farthest corners,
saying to you, "You are my servant,
    I have chosen you and not cast you off";
do not fear, for I am with you,
    do not be afraid, for I am your God;
I will strengthen you, I will help you,
    I will uphold you with my victorious right hand." (Isa 41:8-10)

Following this proclamation are four Servant Songs (Isa 42:1-9; 49:1-6; 50:4-9; 52:13–53:12) that describe the role of the servant in the divine plan. While God designates Israel as his servant, some commentators suggest that the servant could also be a single person (such as Moses or Jeremiah) who embodies the ideals of Israel. A brief examination of several passages will show these dual images and detail the servant's role in establishing the new Jerusalem.

Israel as Servant of God

The first Servant Song presents the mission of the servant.

> Here is my servant, whom I uphold,
>   my chosen, in whom my soul delights;
> I have put my spirit upon him;
>   he will bring forth justice to the nations.
> He will not cry or lift up his voice,
>   or make it heard in the street;
> a bruised reed he will not break,
>   and a dimly burning wick he will not quench;
>   he will faithfully bring forth justice.
> He will not grow faint or be crushed
>   until he has established justice in the earth;
>   and the coastlands wait for his teaching. (Isa 42:1-4)

In this song, the vision of a new world order is affirmed, as well as the need for innovation in response to changing circumstances. God's chosen servant will bring justice to the world in a new way. Instead of the "might makes right" credo embraced by the region's predatory nations, the servant will bring justice through gentle persuasion, an approach so humble, quiet, and unassuming that he will not quench a burning wick or break a brittle reed as he passes by. The servant will also persist in his mission. His work will not be completed until the coastlands (in other words, the pagan nations) have heard his teaching. The servant's mission to the nations is thus the first step in God's plan to level the "uneven ground" of ignorance, inequality, and injustice so that all people will be united and illumined in the glory of God.

In the second Servant Song (Isa 49:1-6), the servant speaks in the first person, offering insight into his life and destiny. He calls out to the pagan nations,

> Listen to me, O coastlands,
>   pay attention, you peoples from far away!
> The LORD called me before I was born,
>   while I was in my mother's womb he named me.
> He made my mouth like a sharp sword,
>   in the shadow of his hand he hid me;

> he made me a polished arrow,
>> in his quiver he hid me away.
> And he said to me, "You are my servant,
>> Israel, in whom I will be glorified." (Isa 49:1-3)

The passage affirms that Yahweh is indeed a cosmic God whose plans are not revealed until the proper time. The servant is one of God's many instruments, predestined to fulfill God's mission but hidden away until needed. The "sharp sword" and the "polished arrow" conjure up images of friction, heat, effort, and time, symbolizing Israel's suffering at the hands of the Assyrians and Babylonians. Ironically, the "sword" of the servant is his gentle teaching, which has been sharpened (i.e., made wise) through his experience of suffering and hardship. This subtle allusion to the servant's suffering is made more explicit in the next song.

In bringing the servant out of hiding, the Lord offers him "as a light to the nations, that my salvation may reach to the end of the earth" (Isa 49:6). Yet the mission to the nations will not be an easy one. The third song (Isa 50:4-9) describes the servant's role as that of a teacher who is met with rejection. Speaking in the first person, the servant acknowledges that "I gave my back to those who struck me, and my cheeks to those who pulled out the beard; I did not hide my face from insult and spitting" (50:6). Although the violence is undeserved, it increases in intensity. The fourth song (52:13–53:12) dramatically describes the rejection and death of the servant.

> Surely he has borne our infirmities
>> and carried our diseases;
> yet we accounted him stricken,
>> struck down by God, and afflicted.
> But he was wounded for our transgressions,
>> crushed for our iniquities;
> upon him was the punishment that made us whole,
>> and by his bruises we are healed.
> All we like sheep have gone astray;
>> we have all turned to our own way,
> and the LORD has laid on him
>> the iniquity of us all.
> He was oppressed, and he was afflicted,
>> yet he did not open his mouth;
> like a lamb that is led to the slaughter,
>> and like a sheep that before its shearers is silent,
>> so he did not open his mouth.
> By a perversion of justice he was taken away.
>> Who could have imagined his future?
> For he was cut off from the land of the living,
>> stricken for the transgression of my people.

> They made his grave with the wicked
>   and his tomb with the rich,
> although he had done no violence,
>   and there was no deceit in his mouth. (Isa 53:4-9)

In this passage, the prophet introduces the concept of redemptive suffering. The mission of the servant is not only to teach the nations, but to suffer on their behalf. The punishment and death of the servant is wholly undeserved; in fact, it is a perversion of justice, and yet the servant willingly accepts his fate ("he did not open his mouth") so that the guilty may be redeemed.

While the servant's gesture is extraordinary, it is not without precedent. Each year on the Day of Atonement, the Israelites would participate in a "scapegoat" ritual in which their sins would be transferred onto the animal. After the ceremony, the goat would be led out to die in the wilderness, thus ensuring that the sins would not return to the people (Lev 16:20-22). The Servant Song radicalizes this atoning ritual, not only because it involves human sacrifice, but because "it was the will of the LORD to crush him with pain" (Isa 53:10). In a striking reversal, it is Yahweh rather than the people who initiates the sacrifice, making it a necessary condition for redeeming the world. The servant's willingness to accept his fate is another necessary condition (in other words, it must be a freewill offering) that does not go unrewarded. Yahweh will allot to the servant "a portion with the great, and he shall divide the spoil with the strong; because he poured out himself to death, and was numbered with the transgressors, yet he bore the sin of many, and made intercession for the transgressors" (53:12).

Christian commentators have long identified the suffering servant with Jesus Christ, but the Isaiah of Babylon did not compose the songs with Jesus in mind. He was addressing his own situation, and so we return to the question: Who is the servant? Is he the nation of Israel or a humble man who embodies the ideals of Sinai? The passages would seem to support both interpretations. On the one hand, the servant could symbolize Israel in exile. The people's suffering was necessary to cleanse them of their sins and prepare them for their work in the new Jerusalem. On the other hand, the servant could symbolize past prophets and leaders or even individual survivors who experienced first-hand the horrors of the Babylonian invasion and its aftermath and who constitute Israel's righteous remnant. In either case, the death of the servant symbolizes the death of the old life and the start of a new one in Jerusalem.

Ultimately, the identity of the servant is not as important as the meaning of his life and death for the exiles. The Servant Songs offered the Judean exiles a new understanding of themselves and an important psychological victory when they needed it most. Individually and collectively the people had survived the destruction and loss of their homeland and the degradation of captivity. The songs helped them realize that their suffering was not in vain; it had a reason and a purpose. Their ordeal prepared them to become God's servant, "a light to the nations." Now, Yahweh was announcing a second exodus. They would again be freed to return to the Promised Land, where they would have the opportunity to fulfill their new role as the servant who teaches all the peoples of the earth the ways of God. This joyous message is affirmed in the final poem of the collection, in which Yahweh enjoins nature itself to celebrate the return of the exiles.

> For you [the exiles] shall go out in joy,
>   and be led back in peace;
> the mountains and the hills before you
>   shall burst into song,
>   and all the trees of the field shall clap their hands.
> Instead of the thorn shall come up the cypress;
>   instead of the brier shall come up the myrtle;
> and it shall be to the LORD for a memorial,
>   for an everlasting sign that shall not be cut off. (Isa 55:12-13)

The idealism and hope that permeate this passage are quickly tempered, however, by the sobering words of Third Isaiah, an unknown prophet who lived and worked during the postexilic period.

The Postexilic Period in Judah

Shortly after Cyrus defeated the Babylonians and entered the capital city, he issued a decree that permitted the exiles to return to Jerusalem and rebuild the Temple at state expense. Despite his generosity, the response from the people was mixed. Several generations of Judeans had lived in Babylon and many "Jews" (or Judean Yahweh worshipers) now considered it their home. While many of them were naturally hesitant to pull up stakes and move to a land they knew only through nostalgic stories and the traditions of their parents and grandparents, some of them did feel the tug of the homeland and made the trek back to Judah. Nevertheless, their lofty dreams and hopes for a new Jerusalem were quickly dashed by the harsh realities of the homeland.

The city and its environs were underdeveloped and sparsely populated and the Temple was still in ruins. Moreover, the returning exiles faced unexpected difficulties from the local residents (principally non-exiled Judeans and Samaritans) who practiced their own form of Yahwism and who deeply resented the newcomers. John Bright summarizes the challenges:

> The newcomers faced years of hardship, privation, and insecurity. They had to make a fresh start in a strange land—in itself a task of staggering difficulty. They were dogged by a succession of poor seasons and partial crop failures (Hag. 1:9-11; 2:15-17), which left many of them destitute, without adequate food and clothing (ch. 1:6). Their neighbors, especially the aristocracy of Samaria, who had regarded Judah as part of their territory and resented any limitation of their prerogatives

there, were openly hostile. How and when the hostility first expressed itself cannot be said, but it was surely present from the beginning. Nor is it likely that Jews resident in the land in every case welcomed the influx of immigrants with enthusiasm. They had regarded the land as theirs (Ezek 33:24) and presumably still did; they would scarcely have been eager to give place to the newcomers and acquiesce in their claims to ancestral holdings. The fact that the returning exiles considered themselves the true Israel and tended to draw apart both from Samaritans and their less orthodox brethren as from men unclean (cf. Hag. 2:10-14) surely heightened the tension.[17]

The Yahwism practiced by many of the non-exiled Judeans incorporated Canaanite religious practices that included sexually explicit fertility rituals, the sacrifice of unclean animals, and other questionable activities. Given the long-standing and contentious competition between Yahweh and the gods of Canaan, the returning exiles found these practices extremely offensive. The tension was heightened further by an internal power struggle over the control and rebuilding of the Jerusalem Temple. Some scholars believe Third Isaiah was right in the middle of the conflict.

The stakes were indeed high. With the loss of the monarchy, the office of high priest became increasingly important, with that individual assuming many of the responsibilities once reserved for the king. In addition to his religious duties, the high priest would represent the Jewish people before the ruling authorities, assume responsibility for maintaining the peace, and administer the collection of taxes.[18] Needless to say, whoever controlled the rebuilding and administration of the Temple wielded a great deal of power.

Prior to the exile, the Temple had been dominated by the Zadokites, a priestly class that had ascended to power under King Solomon. In returning to Jerusalem, the Zadokites naturally assumed they would control the office of high priest and administer the central shrine. The rebuilding of the Temple had barely begun when they were challenged by another priestly group—probably Levites—that embraced the religious idealism of Second Isaiah. In their view, the Zadokites were unfit to administer the Temple because of their willingness to cooperate with foreign occupation forces (in this case, the Persians), and to accept non-Yahwistic ritual practices. They believed that the Zadokites' accommodation to pagan influences not only contaminated Yahwism, but threatened further judgment and punishment from God. Although Third Isaiah never identifies himself, his writings indicate that he was very concerned about the issues surrounding this power struggle.

Who Was Third Isaiah?

The identity of the prophet remains a mystery. Some scholars contend that Second Isaiah wrote the third collection. Others argue that the writings were the product of several postexilic prophets. Still others suggest the prophet was most likely a member of the dissident group that questioned the legitimacy of the Zadokites.[19] Debates about sources, identity, and theological stance aside, the writings in the third collection address specific problems that jeopardized the survival of the Restoration community. In addition to the prophet's fears about priestly accommodation, he was clearly worried about the low morale of the exiles and their tendency to forget the teachings of the covenant. Third Isaiah thus presents readers with an interesting religious hybrid—a prophet who was also concerned about ritual observances. In addressing these problems, the Isaiah of the Restoration crafts a theological message that combines the fierce judgment of First Isaiah with the idealism and hope proclaimed in Second Isaiah.

The collection is divided into three sections: Chapters 56–59 alternate oracles of judgment with songs of consolation; chapters 60–62 present a utopian vision of the destiny of Jerusalem-Zion; chapters 63–66 offer poems of lamentation and wisdom, followed by apocalyptic visions of a final judgment. In combining the work of his predecessors with his own theological insights, Third Isaiah offers a message of cautious hope, reminding the Judeans of their past mistakes while encouraging them to have faith in the future.

Third Isaiah as the Prophet of a Chastened and Humble People

Expanding upon the central theme of Yahweh's universal rule, the prophet begins the collection with God calling all the people—both Judean and foreigner alike—to embrace the covenant and uphold its requirements of justice, honest worship, and loyalty to the one true God.

> And the foreigners who join themselves to the LORD,
> > to minister to him, to love the name of the LORD,
> > and to be his servants,
> all who keep the sabbath, and do not profane it,
> > and hold fast my covenant—
> these I will bring to my holy mountain,
> > and make them joyful in my house of prayer;
> their burnt offerings and their sacrifices
> > will be accepted on my altar;
> for my house shall be called a house of prayer
> > for all peoples.
> Thus says the Lord GOD,
> > who gathers the outcasts of Israel,
> I will gather others to them
> > besides those already gathered. (Isa 56:6-9)

The "foreigners" are not aliens, but potential converts to Yahwism. The "others" probably refer to Judean exiles who have not made the journey back to Jerusalem. As the passage indicates, inclusion in the Restoration community requires that the people "hold fast" to the covenant. This means that they must reject the idolatrous practices (57:4-13) and false worship (58:1-5) that precipitated their downfall and that now threaten to splinter the new community. Continuing with the reformist theme, the prophet offers words of consolation that promise blessings, but with an important condition attached.

> If you remove the yoke from among you,
>   the pointing of the finger, the speaking of evil,
> if you offer your food to the hungry
>   and satisfy the needs of the afflicted,
> then your light shall rise in the darkness
>   and your gloom be like the noonday.
> The LORD will guide you continually,
>   and satisfy your needs in parched places,
>   and make your bones strong;
> and you shall be like a watered garden,
>   like a spring of water,
>   whose waters never fail.
> Your ancient ruins shall be rebuilt;
>   you shall raise up the foundations of many generations;
> you shall be called the repairer of the breach,
>   the restorer of streets to live in. (Isa 58:9-12)

The tone of the poem and its references to "parched places," "ancient ruins," and broken streets no doubt reflect the conditions the exiles first encountered when they entered Jerusalem, as well as their ongoing struggle to rebuild the Temple. Yahweh promises that these obstacles will be overcome, but only if the people change their ways and take up the work of social justice.

The prophet's call to reform is immediately followed by a response from the exiles, which takes the form of a communal confession of sin. The verses articulate a consciousness of guilt that contrasts sharply with the arrogance and selfishness the people displayed in First and Second Isaiah. Clearly, Yahweh's carrot-and-stick approach has had its intended effect. In this revealing confession, the people fully acknowledge their culpability.

> . . . justice is far from us,
>   and righteousness does not reach us;
> we wait for light, and lo! there is darkness;
>   and for brightness, but we walk in gloom.
> We grope like the blind along a wall,
>   groping like those who have no eyes;
> we stumble at noon as in the twilight,
>   among the vigorous as though we were dead.
> We all growl like bears;
>   like doves we moan mournfully.
> We wait for justice, but there is none;
>   for salvation, but it is far from us.

For our transgressions before you are many,
>   and our sins testify against us.
Our transgressions indeed are with us,
>   and we know our iniquities;
transgressing, and denying the LORD,
>   and turning away from following our God,
talking oppression and revolt,
>   conceiving lying words and uttering them from the heart.
>   (Isa 59:9-13)

These verses express the shame, fear, and painful soul-searching that characterize genuine remorse. The bitter experience of Babylon and the disillusionment of Jerusalem have made the exiles a chastened and humble people who fully understand the seriousness of their offenses. Their confession of guilt is a turning point in their personal journey that sets the stage for chapters 60–62, which proclaim the glory and destiny of Jerusalem-Zion. In this section, the prophet reassures the returning exiles that despite their present troubles their deliverance is at hand, for Yahweh has placed Jerusalem-Zion and its inhabitants at the very center of his plan to redeem the world.

The Destiny of Jerusalem-Zion

Reaffirming the utopian visions of his predecessors, the prophet calls out to Jerusalem, "Arise, shine; for your light has come, and the glory of the LORD has risen upon you. For darkness shall cover the earth, and thick darkness the peoples; but the LORD will arise upon you, and his glory will appear over you" (Isa 60:1-2). In the surrounding darkness of Persian rule (the Judeans still longed for independence), people from all corners of the earth will be drawn to God's light and gather to pay tribute and homage to Jerusalem-Zion. Extending the vision of First Isaiah, Yahweh declares that in this new age, "The descendants of those who oppressed you shall come bending low to you, and all who despised you shall bow down at your feet; they shall call you the City of the LORD, the Zion of the Holy One of Israel. Whereas you have been forsaken and hated, with no one passing through, I will make you majestic forever, a joy from age to age" (Isa 60:14-15). Yet in contrast to First and Second Isaiah, the prophet does not attribute the exiles' deliverance to a ruler of the Davidic house, or a pagan Messiah, or the Lord's servant. Yahweh, the Holy One of Israel, is the liberator who will rule the nation directly.

I will appoint Peace as your overseer
>   and Righteousness as your taskmaster.
Violence shall no more be heard in your land,
>   devastation or destruction within your borders;
you shall call your walls Salvation
>   and your gates Praise.

The sun shall no longer be
	your light by day
nor for brightness shall the moon
	give light to you by night;
but the LORD will be your everlasting light,
	and your God will be your glory.
Your sun shall no more go down
	or your moon withdraw itself;
for the LORD will be your everlasting light
	and your days of mourning shall be ended.
Your people shall all be righteous;
	they shall possess the land forever.
They are the shoot that I planted, the work of my hands,
	so that I might be glorified.
The least of them shall become a clan,
	and the smallest one a mighty nation;
I am the LORD;
	in its time I will accomplish it quickly. (Isa 60:17-19)

The light signifies Yahweh's presence and power in Jerusalem-Zion, a light so brilliant that the sun and the moon are blotted out. God as everlasting light is a recurring theme in the Bible, particularly in the apocalyptic literature. There are striking parallels, for example, with Third Isaiah's description of Jerusalem-Zion and John's depiction in the book of Revelation (21:22, 22:5). The point here is that Jerusalem-Zion will soon be transformed by the will of God, who desires that the city's residents experience peace, righteousness, praise, prosperity, and salvation, both now and in the future.

Yet Yahweh is not without some assistance in his plan. An unidentified speaker comes forward, declaring that he must fulfill an important mission for God. Scholars debate the speaker's identity. It could be the prophet, or Jerusalem-Zion (the ancients often portrayed cities as persons), or it could be a continuation of the servant figure in Second Isaiah. The verses clearly resemble the Servant Songs in both content and form, but, whoever the speaker is, there is little doubt that Yahweh greatly favors him.

The spirit of the Lord GOD is upon me,
	because the LORD has anointed me;
he has sent me to bring good news to the oppressed,
	to bind up the brokenhearted,
to proclaim liberty to the captives,
	and release to the prisoners;
to proclaim the year of the LORD's favor,
	and the day of vengeance of our God;
	to comfort all who mourn;
to provide for those who mourn in Zion—
	to give them a garland instead of ashes,

the oil of gladness instead of mourning,
  the mantle of praise instead of a faint spirit. (Isa 61:1-3)

In the new Jerusalem, the speaker's "good news" is realized in concrete actions that promote peace, unity, and prosperity. The people will "repair the ruined cities" while foreigners from other nations tend their flocks and vineyards. Judeans will be appointed priests to the Gentiles to show them the ways of the Lord and they will receive a "double portion" in compensation for their years of suffering and deprivation (Isa 61:4-7). Like the servant figure, the speaker is persistent in his work, not resting "until her [Jerusalem's] vindication shines out like the dawn, and her salvation like a burning torch" (Isa 62:1). In the final speech of the section, Yahweh affirms the speaker's mission, impatiently directing his people to prepare the way for the citizens of the restored Jerusalem.

Go through, go through the gates,
  prepare the way for the people;
build up, build up the highway,
    clear it of stones,
    lift up an ensign over the peoples.
The LORD has proclaimed
    to the end of the earth:
Say to daughter Zion,
  "See your salvation comes;
his reward is with him,
    and his recompense before him."
They shall be called, "The Holy People,
    The Redeemed of the LORD";
and you shall be called, "Sought Out,
    A City Not Forsaken." (Isa 62:10-12)

In this new age, it is the citizenry of Jerusalem-Zion, not the Babylonians, who proudly march through the streets, welcoming fellow exiles and praising their God. But before the people can become too sure of their renewed status (always a dangerous sign), the prophet switches gears. He inserts a communal lament (probably composed during the Babylonian conquest) to remind the people of what could happen if they turn away from Yahweh and his teachings. Once again the people respond in the first person and the mood is just as dark. They plead with Yahweh:

Do not be exceedingly angry, O LORD;
    and do not remember iniquity forever.
    Now consider, we are all your people.
Your holy cities have become a wilderness,
    Zion has become a wilderness,
    Jerusalem a desolation.

Our holy and beautiful house,
    where our ancestors praised you,
has been burned by fire,
    and all our pleasant places have become ruins.
After all this, will you restrain yourself, O LORD?
    Will you keep silent, and punish us so severely? (Isa 64:9-12)

Acknowledging their many sins, the people nevertheless ask questions that are tinged with accusation against Yahweh: Are you satisfied now? Isn't the destruction of everything we have enough for you? How long will you continue the silent treatment? In a powerful and utterly heartbreaking response, Yahweh explains his actions.

I was ready to be sought out by those who did not ask,
    to be found by those who did not seek me.
I said, "Here I am, here I am,"
    to a nation that did not call on my name.
I held out my hands all day long
    to a rebellious people,
who walk in a way that is not good,
    following their own devices;
a people who provoke me
    to my face continually,
sacrificing in gardens
    and offering incense on bricks;
who sit inside tombs,
    and spend the night in secret places;
who eat swine's flesh
    with broth of abominable things in their vessels;
who say, "Keep to yourself,
    do not come near me, for I am too holy for you."
These are a smoke in my nostrils,
    a fire that burns all day long.
See, it is written before me:
    I will not keep silent, but I will repay;
I will indeed repay into their laps
their iniquities and their ancestors' iniquities together,
says the LORD;
because they offered incense on the mountains
    and reviled me on the hills,
I will measure into their laps
    full payment for their actions. (Isa 65:1-7)

In a stunning role reversal, Yahweh portrays himself as a humble servant. "Here I am, here I am" are the very words of Abraham and Moses as they answered God's call, but Yahweh never receives his call. He waits patiently, like a long-suffering parent, hands outstretched, ready to do his children's bidding, but they never call—cruel treatment for such a proud and gracious deity! Ironically, it is the people, not God, who are silent, and by turning away from Yahweh, they become vulnerable to their own selfish desires and to the false allure of pagan religions. The references to outdoor rituals, secret nocturnal ceremonies, and unclean foods reflect the religious conflict within the postexilic community. For God and for his prophet, no accommodation is possible. To drive home the point, God compares the destiny of his faithful servants with that of those who engage in pagan practices.

> Thus says the LORD:
> As the wine is found in the cluster,
>> and they say, "Do not destroy it,
>> for there is a blessing in it,"
> so I will do for my servants' sake,
>> and not destroy them all.
> I will bring forth descendants from Jacob
>> and from Judah inheritors of my mountains;
> my chosen shall inherit it,
>> and my servants shall settle there.
> Sharon shall become a pasture for flocks,
>> and the Valley of Achor a place for herds to lie down,
>> for my people who have sought me.
> But you who forsake the LORD,
>> who forget my holy mountain,
> who set a table for Fortune
>> and fill cups of mixed wine for Destiny;
> I will destine you to the sword,
>> and all of you shall bow down to the slaughter;
> because, when I called, you did not answer,
>> when I spoke, you did not listen,
> but you did what was evil in my sight,
>> and chose what I did not delight in.
> Therefore, thus says the Lord GOD:
> My servants shall eat,
>> but you shall be hungry;
> my servants shall drink,
>> but you shall be thirsty;
> my servants shall rejoice,
>> but you shall be put to shame;
> my servants shall sing for gladness of heart,
>> but you shall cry out for pain of heart
>> and shall wail for anguish of spirit. (Isa 65:8-14)

The prophet's reference to the righteous remnant (the "inheritors of my mountains") sharpens the contrast between God's faithful servant and the reprobate. Eschatological images of reward and punishment continue as the prophet proclaims Yahweh's intention to redeem the world and make Jerusalem-Zion its spiritual center. In the conclusion of the book, Yahweh makes a promise and utters a warning to all the people, whether faithful servant or reprobate, Judean or non-Judean:

> For as the new heavens and the new earth,
>   which I will make,
> shall remain before me, says the LORD;
>   so shall your descendants and your name remain.
> From new moon to new moon,
>   and from sabbath to sabbath,
> all flesh shall come to worship before me,
> says the LORD.
> And they shall go out and look at the dead bodies of the people who
> have rebelled against me; for their worm shall not die, their fire shall
> not be quenched, and they shall be an abhorrence to all flesh.
> (Isa 66:22-24)

Sadly, Third Isaiah never witnessed the divine intervention he so vividly describes, nor did any of his contemporaries. As the years passed, the Restoration community continued to experience political and social oppression and religious conflict. After the Persian occupation, the Judeans were ruled by the Greeks (fourth century BCE) and later the Romans (first century BCE). Moreover, by the second century BCE, the bitter divisions regarding the character of Yahwism (later "Judaism") splintered the faith into sects and parties that fought for influence and control. Despite these many problems, the prophet's message of cautious hope continued to resonate among the people, helping fuel their unwavering belief in the ultimate triumph of God's rule and the fulfillment of God's promises to Israel.

The Unity of Isaiah

While there is no way of knowing whether the final editor of Isaiah was Third Isaiah or another postexilic prophet, the overall structure of the book shows a clear editorial hand that constructs a complex and progressively unfolding message about God's intentions toward Israel and the world. In this scheme, First Isaiah is the quintessential prophet of doom, offering harsh judgment against the idolatry and injustice of the people of Israel and Judah. In contrast, Second Isaiah's message is one of comfort and hope for a demoralized people who have lost everything, except their desire and need to believe in God and the future. Third Isaiah's message combines elements of doom, hope, and wisdom, urging the people to remember their past and current sins so that they might escape the fate of the two kingdoms and start again. Differences in content, form, and historical context are tempered by the editor's integration of central themes that unify the work. For example, all three Isaiahs acknowledge Yahweh as a powerful, cosmic deity who demands justice, controls pagan nations, and determines world events. They emphasize Jerusalem-Zion as the spiritual and moral center of God's plan for redeeming and ruling the world. They also establish a sharp division between the faithful and the damned, and they all emphasize (to a greater or lesser degree) an anointed ruler, or servant, who will help restore Israel to its former glory.

The unifying themes that thread through Isaiah are critical for grasping the ethical intention of the book, because when they are combined with the different historical circumstances and messages of the prophets, they construct a progressive program for spiritual and moral development that mirrors the program Yahweh introduced with Abraham and amended at Sinai. Each of the Isaiahs represents an important stage in this transformative process.

Stage One: Punishment and Possible Renewal

First Isaiah establishes the central goals of the program. Initially, he urges the people to repent for their sins and reform their conduct or face the righteous wrath of the Holy One. But, as Yahweh predicted, the pride, greed, and ignorance of the people prevent them from listening or attempting any genuine change. Given their response, Yahweh has little choice but to punish them—to do otherwise would compromise God's justice. Echoing the curses articulated in Genesis 3, the prophet explains in graphic images and emotionally charged language the inevitable consequences of the people's rebellion against God: the two kingdoms will be destroyed and the people will be exiled. Like Adam and Eve, they, too, will be cast out of their garden. Yet the prophet's message of doom also contains a seed of hope, for God proclaims Jerusalem-Zion as a future ideal for the righteous remnant that survives the disaster. The practical program for realizing this ideal is the Mosaic Law, which was given to their ancestors at Sinai. The faithful few who return to the covenant will become the priestly kingdom and holy nation Yahweh envisioned so long ago at Sinai.

But the ideal described in First Isaiah contains a crucial difference. The God of Israel—who is now perceived as a cosmic deity—intends to redeem the entire world. The people's transformation, therefore, is not only for the future survival of Israel, but for all the nations. With so much at stake, God cannot simply reintroduce the people to the Law and hope they will obey—their track record is far too dismal for that. Instead, Yahweh sends each of the kingdoms into an extended period of exile (replicating the Israelites' forty years in the wilderness) so that they may reflect and learn from their mistakes and prepare themselves for their new, more expansive role. The writings of Second Isaiah outline the particulars of this training program.

Stage Two: The New and Improved Program

Much like the giving of the Law at Sinai, the writings of Second Isaiah introduce theological and ethical concepts that structure and guide the people's rehabilitation. The prophet's writings speak to a people whose situation is strikingly similar to that of the Israelites in Egypt. Both are held captive and deprived of their homeland and both experience a process of transformation that restores their identity and their sense of place and purpose in the world. What is different is the reason for their captivity and the timing of their liberation. In Exodus, Yahweh frees the Hebrew slaves after years of brutal oppression by the Egyptians and then instructs them (through Moses and the Law) on how to become an ideal nation. After their schooling at the mountain, the people are ready to assume their new role as they make their way to the Promised Land. In contrast, Yahweh frees the Judeans only *after* they have endured the consequences of forgetting the Law. Ironically, God's exile of the people is intended to liberate them from the self-inflicted slavery of idolatry and narcissism.

For a humbled and demoralized people, Second Isaiah's message of comfort and hope offers a blueprint for the future. In returning to the Law, the people are given the ethical and religious foundations for the new Jerusalem. In addition, the Servant Songs provide them with a role model for developing the proper character for their new role. Like Abraham before him, the servant figure demonstrates what it means to fear the Lord. By emulating the servant, the people can move away from selfishness and sin to a life of true obedience, humble service, and redemptive sacrifice. While the teachings of Second Isaiah make no mention of public declarations or ceremonies, the final images of a restored Jerusalem symbolize a righteous people's ongoing commitment to the covenant, to servanthood, and to God's redemptive plan. The public aspect of this transformation is witnessed in the celebration of all the nations—and even the earth itself—for the restoration of Israel (Isa 55).

Stage Three: Recommitment and Realism

Third Isaiah introduces a new and final stage in Yahweh's educational program, namely, the wisdom that comes with painful experience. Recall that one of the primary goals at Mount Sinai was to make sure that in accepting the covenant the Hebrew slaves knew what they were getting themselves into; hence the three declarations. But the idealism and naive optimism displayed on the mountain and in the glory days of Israel's monarchy were quickly compromised by the failings of the golden calf incident and the excesses that led to the destruction of the two kingdoms. While the book of Isaiah follows the Sinai model of incremental stages (each prophet elaborating on the nature of the new Jerusalem and the role of the people in God's ever-expanding plan), Third Isaiah introduces a level of realism lacking at Sinai. The destruction of the Northern Kingdom and the Babylonian exile were indeed cruel teachers. The prophet's words of cautious hope serve as a "reality check" and a warning that if the new Jerusalem is to become a reality, the people must never forget the lessons of experience—a warning alluded to in the social justice command (Ex 22:2-

24) and in Moses' farewell address to the people (Deut 31:9-22), both of which were quickly forgotten. Centuries later, experience has shown the exiles how easily they turn away from God and fall into the traps of idolatry, arrogance, and injustice. The communal lament at the end of the collection suggests that they have reached levels of moral and spiritual maturity that were lacking at Mount Sinai and that are crucial for the future survival of the postexilic community and the furtherance of Yahweh's redemptive plan. Like the experience of Abraham at Moriah, their experience too reaffirms the biblical truth that the road to spiritual and moral growth is indeed a long and painful one.

Yahweh as a Mysterious, Cosmic Deity

The intertextual connections between the Pentateuch and Isaiah and the evolving nature of the divine-human relation are not limited to Yahweh's training program; they are also evident in the book's depiction of Yahweh. The prophets' experience of God parallels the experience of many central characters in the Pentateuch. They also experience God as a powerful, providential deity who is just and merciful and who displays an amazing degree of patience in his relationships with human beings. The God of Isaiah is also a flexible deity, changing his strategy when the occasion calls for it. While Yahweh's penchant for innovation is nothing new, the book of Isaiah takes this inclination to a new level. As a cosmic deity, the God of Isaiah expands the scope of his activity, including all nations in his salvific plan and introducing "new things" to accomplish it. Yahweh's use of pagan nations as instruments of his justice, his elevation of Cyrus to the role of Messiah, the introduction of the servant figure, whose redemptive suffering makes the new Jerusalem possible—all of these innovations challenge traditional assumptions about God's intentions and his activity.

The challenge is heightened further by Third Isaiah's dark assessment of human nature. The mystery and unpredictability of God and the reality of human weakness introduce a subversive element into the narrative that pulls the rug out from under the human need for and obsession with certainty. The God of Isaiah affirms the fundamental truth that human beings can never assume they know God or the ways of God or take for granted that he is on their side. They are simply too broken and corrupt to see things clearly and too limited to presume to know the mind of God. As creatures and servants of God, the exiles' task is to make an honest effort to live according to God's will (made known through scripture and the prophets) and to trust in God's intentions for his creation. By embracing the examples of Abraham, Moses, and the suffering servant, the people can live in hope instead of despair, because God always provides—their liberation from Babylon and return to Jerusalem are concrete proof of that.

Conclusion

Given the pedagogical patterns and intertextual connections in Isaiah, we can thus conclude that the ethical intention of the book is to transform the people of Israel from demoralized victims of war to a nation of humble servants who will make the new Jerusalem a reality for all the nations of the earth. To realize this ideal, Yahweh instructs his people in a program of religious and moral reform that (1) balances tradition and innovation, (2) combines a rule-centered ethics of obedience with a more flexible mentoring model that emphasizes character development, and (3) entails listening to and practicing the wisdom born of suffering and uncertainty. All of these components are necessary to address the complexities of the human condition and the needs of the human heart.

The intertextual relation between the Pentateuch and Isaiah is only one example of this phenomenon. There are many others. The subversive element introduced in Isaiah, for example, is explicated further in the wisdom tradition, particularly in the books of Job and Ecclesiastes. Both texts challenge traditional understandings of God and the nature of the divine-human relation. In the New Testament, Yahweh's emphasis on character development, the balance between tradition and innovation, and the model of the servant are central features of the life and teachings of Jesus of Nazareth. To further demonstrate this point, we shall explore how these intertextual connections influence and shape the depiction of Jesus in Matthew's gospel. But before we begin, we must first establish the proper context for our reading by exploring the troubled history between the two Testaments, a history that prompts God to introduce his most daring innovation.

Questions for Reflection and Discussion

1. Abraham, Moses, and Isaiah were called by God for certain missions. Describe their lives prior to God's call. What was the manner of God's call? What were their missions and how did they respond? When viewed together, what do the experiences of Abraham, Moses, and Isaiah suggest about the nature of the divine call and the human response?

2. The God who emerges in Genesis, Exodus, and Isaiah is a complex and multi-faceted deity. Given the different historical contexts of the biblical writers and the biblical books, what divine personality traits remain constant? Which traits do you find most surprising or revelatory in respect to God's nature?

3. The book of Isaiah interprets historical events through the theological lens of the prophets. Their central claim is that the two kingdoms didn't fall because of bad politics but as a result of the people's disloyalty and selfish refusal to abide by the covenant requirements. How do you think the three Isaiahs would assess some contemporary issues, such as global warm-

ing, the war in Iraq, HIV and AIDS, the growing gap between rich and poor, or any other national or local issue you care to discuss? How does a theological perspective enhance, challenge, or skew our perception of these issues? How does it illuminate possible solutions?

Recommended Reading

Berlin, Adele, and Marc Zvi Brettler, eds. *The Jerusalem Study Bible*. Oxford: Oxford University Press, 2004. An excellent translation of the Bible from the Jewish Publication Society that offers insightful annotations, informative essays, and other educational materials.

Bright, John. *A History of Israel*. 3rd ed. Philadelphia: Westminster Press, 1981. Essential reading for the researcher, student, or adult learner who wants to understand the rise of prophecy in Israel.

Sheppard, Gerald T. "Isaiah." In *The HarperCollins Bible Commentary*, edited by James L. May, 489–97. San Francisco: HarperSanFrancisco, Inc., 2000. Provides a helpful summary of scholarly attempts to determine the authorship and structure of Isaiah.

6

BETWEEN THE TESTAMENTS

Understanding the Roots of Jewish-Christian Animus

Moving from the Old Testament to the New Testament involves considering important historical and theological shifts before turning to Matthew's gospel. Historically, the biblical narrative jumps from the Jewish Restoration community (sixth century BCE) to the early Christian communities of Palestine (first century CE)—a gap of nearly six hundred years. Theologically, we find that the God of Israel virtually disappears from the biblical narrative, replaced by Jesus of Nazareth, who becomes the main character and central object of worship. This shift in theological emphasis has made Christianity a very *christocentric* ("Christ-centered") religion, but a closer reading reveals that God's disappearing act is only an illusion, for his presence is witnessed throughout the New Testament.

Yahweh's most direct appearance occurs at the baptism of Jesus, when he calls out from heaven, "You are my Son, the Beloved; with you I am well pleased" (Mt 1:11). God is also the central focus of the ministry of Jesus, a focus that grounds his proclamation of the coming kingdom and his teachings in the Sermon on the Mount. God's more traditional "fire and brimstone" persona is displayed to great effect in the book of Revelation, but by far the most stunning evidence of God's presence is the resurrection. In raising Jesus from the dead, Yahweh transforms him from a prophet and itinerant preacher to a messianic Savior whose death and resurrection signal still another step in God's salvific plan. Yet the presence of Israel's God in the New Testament has done little to bridge the religious chasm that exists between the two Testaments. Something happened during those six centuries that caused a schism within Judaism so bitter and decisive that it would lead to the birth of Christianity and to the systematic demonization of the Jewish people.

Ample evidence of anti-Jewish bias can be found in the New Testament (e.g., Mt 15:1-9; 23:13-39; Mk 14:55-65; Acts 2:36; 3:14-15; Jn 8:43-49; 1 Thess 2:14-16; Rev 2:9), but it is polemical and sporadic and offers little insight into the root causes of the conflict. One of the most infamous and oft-quoted verses is found in Matthew's passion narrative. In the heated emotions of the trial scene, the gospel writer has the Jews convict themselves of Jesus' death, crying out to Pilate, "His blood be on us and on our children!" (27:25).

The anti-Jewish intent of this verse and other biblical passages cannot be overlooked or minimized because they provided the foundation for the destructive teachings of Christian supersessionism. In its simplest terms, supersessionism (sometimes called "replacement theology") is the belief that with the coming of Jesus Christ, the Christian Church supersedes or replaces Israel in God's plan. Some early Christian writers argued that because the Jews had rejected and killed Jesus, God had essentially disinherited them. This meant that the biblical promises Yahweh had made to his "chosen people" were now transferred allegorically to the Christian Church, which became the "new Israel." Within this Christian triumphalist scheme, the old covenant of the Jews and the Law of Moses were replaced with the new and superior covenant of Jesus Christ; hence the division of the canonical scriptures into the "Old" and "New" Testaments. For some Christian hardliners, this meant that Jews had to either convert to Christianity or suffer God's just punishment for the unspeakable crime of deicide. In the crucial decades following the death of Jesus, supersessionist thinking would take root in the early church, providing the theological rationale for Christian anti-Semitism, with its shameful history of discrimination and abuse.[1]

While supersessionism has been criticized and discredited in recent years by Christian denominations, lay groups, and individual theologians, many Christians continue to embrace it in one form or another, thus extending and perpetuating the old animosity. Today supersessionist thinking can be found in the hate-filled ravings of the Christian Identity Movement, in Christian evangelical "Jesus Camps" and "Hell Houses," in the political rhetoric of the Christian Right, and in the careful reasoning of Cardinal Ratzinger (Pope Benedict XVI) in *Dominus Iesus*. Paula Fredriksen and Adele Reinhartz offer a plausible explanation of why anti-Jewish traditions like supersessionism persist in Christian thought.

> Anti-Jewish traditions run deep in church teachings in large part because they rest on particular readings of Christianity's core canon, namely, the four Gospels and the Letters of Paul. Throughout the long centuries that stood between the earliest followers of Jesus and ourselves, these readings have come to have the force and weight of historical descriptions: what these particular traditions teach has come to be seen as what Jesus and Paul themselves taught. Unless we can distinguish between Paul and his interpreters, gauge the distance that separates Jesus' words and acts from the Gospels' renditions of his teachings, or measure the gap between the Gospels and their subsequent interpretations, we have little hope of overcoming Christian anti-Judaism.[2]

The persistence of anti-Jewish traditions in Christianity is one reason why contemporary Christians must accept the challenge and the responsibility that attend biblical interpretation. Thus, before engaging New Testament texts, we must first consider the historical events that fueled

Jewish-Christian animus and how they influenced the formation and content of early Christian writings.

To that end, this chapter will explore the development of Palestinian Judaism during the Persian, Greek, and Roman occupations, the life of Jesus,
the emergence of the Jesus movement, the Jewish war with Rome, and the
breakdown of Jewish-Christian relations during this period. While we cannot undertake an in-depth analysis, a general survey of the events and the
issues at stake will enable us to recognize and hopefully look beyond the
anti-Jewish bias of the New Testament and the Christian interpretative tradition, and discern God's intentions in the life and work of Jesus of
Nazareth.

The Development of Palestinian Judaism

Uncovering the roots of Jewish-Christian animus requires that we travel
back in time to the Restoration community in Judah. Recall that in 540 BCE,
the Persian king Cyrus issued an edict permitting the exiles to return to
Jerusalem and rebuild their homeland and their Temple. Unfortunately, the
optimism and hope that had carried them back to Jerusalem were quickly
dashed by the harsh realities of postexilic Judah. A lack of economic opportunity, the mistrust and intolerance of the native populations, and a series
of poor growing seasons threatened their very survival. The Jewish leaders
realized that the rebuilding of the Temple, which grounded and sustained
Jewish identity, had to be completed, but the exiles had neither the will nor
the financial resources necessary to take on the project in any serious way
(it's difficult to think about rebuilding the Temple when your children are
starving). The result was that nearly twenty years after reconstruction
began, only the foundation stones were in place. The prophets of the
Restoration community—most notably Haggai and Zechariah—pushed for
completion of the project, warning that Yahweh would not bless the people, reestablish the Davidic monarchy, or bring about the universal rule of
Zion while his house lay in ruins (Hag 1:1-11; Zech 4:6-10; 9:9-11). After
numerous delays and much prodding, the Temple was finally completed in
515 BCE, but the Second Temple, as it came to be known, was not nearly as
grand as the original, nor did it bring about the expected results. Yahweh
didn't come to relieve the exiles' hardships or establish his universal kingdom. To make matters worse, the community was experiencing mounting
harassment from Samaritans, Edomites, and other regional neighbors who
feared the power of a restored Judah. John Bright describes the exiles' reaction to these conditions.

> Disappointment had led to disillusionment and this, in turn, to religious
> and moral laxity. The words of Malachi and the slightly later Ne-
> hemiah memoirs illustrate this clearly. Priests, bored by their duties,
> saw nothing wrong in offering sick and injured animals to Yahweh
> (Mal 1:6-14), while their partiality in handling the law had debased

their sacred office in the eyes of the people (Mal 2:1-9). The Sabbath was neglected and given over to business (Neh 13:15-22).

Nonpayment of tithes (Mal 3:7-10) forced Levites to abandon their duties in order to make a living (Neh 3:10f.). The feeling, withal, had taken root that there was no profit in being loyal to the faith (Mal 2:13-16). Unhampered by principles, men cheated their employees of their wages and took advantage of their weaker brethren (Mal 3:5). The poor, having mortgaged their fields in time of drought, or to raise taxes, found themselves foreclosed and, together with their children, reduced to servitude (Neh 5:1-5). Even more serious in the long view, the lines separating Jews from their pagan environment were beginning to break down. Intermarriage with Gentiles was apparently common (Mal 2:11f.) and, as the offspring of such unions grew more numerous, this became increasingly a serious threat to the community integrity (Neh 13:23-27).[3]

The situation was indeed dire, but Israel was blessed by Ezra and Nehemiah, two strong leaders who would galvanize and reorganize the Jewish community. Although there is some debate about the exact dates and order of their careers (scholars are unsure which leader arrived on the scene first), there is no doubt about their accomplishments.

The Leadership of Ezra and Nehemiah

To ease tensions in the region, as well as honor Cyrus' edict, the Persian king Artaxerxes (465–424 BCE) sent Ezra, a high-born priest and scribe, to restore the foundations of Yahwism (the early form of Judaism). His task was to reestablish the sacrificial and juridical systems in Jerusalem, thus ensuring that the Temple and the requirements of the Law would be properly honored and obeyed. Arriving in Jerusalem in 458 BCE, Ezra appointed magistrates and judges to teach and administer the Law. Nevertheless, as recounted in the book of Ezra, the priest grew increasingly distressed by the people's lack of progress, particularly in respect to the scandal of mixed marriages. While the Law's proscription of relations with local populations was unambiguous (Deut 7:1-5), some of the exiles married "foreigners" and refused to separate themselves or renounce their marriages. In a dramatic display of moral outrage, Ezra throws himself on the ground before the Temple, weeping loudly to Yahweh over the people's many sins (Ezra 9:5-15). His demonstration attracts a large crowd of exiles who are quickly shamed by the priest's emotional confession. After a night of fasting and mourning, Ezra calls a great assembly in which the people acknowledge their guilt and make a solemn pledge.

> "We have broken faith with our God and have married foreign women from the peoples of the land, but even now there is hope for Israel in spite of this. So now let us make a covenant with our God to send away all these wives and their children according to the counsel of my lord

and of those who tremble at the commandment of our God; and let it be done according to the law. Take action, for it is your duty, and we are with you; be strong, and do it." Then Ezra stood up and made the leading priests, the Levites, and all Israel swear that they would do as had been said. So they swore. (Ezra 10:2-4)

This would not be the last time the pagan world would tempt the exiles.

Nehemiah's mission was more political. As a cupbearer and advisor to Artaxerxes, he persuaded the king to appoint him governor of Judah, which he ruled from 445 to 433 BCE. Upon his arrival, he acted swiftly to secure the province from the harassment of its neighbors. He fortified the walls around Jerusalem and placed armed guards at the city gates. With the city secured, he instituted much-needed economic reforms. Admonishing wealthy Jews who exploited their own people, he secured their pledges to eliminate usury, cancel debt, and restore property to the poor (Neh 5:1-13). In a scene reminiscent of Sinai, the people gather before Nehemiah and Ezra in a second great assembly to hear a reading of the Book of the Covenant and to recommit themselves to the covenant.

When the seventh month came—the people of Israel being settled in their towns—all the people gathered together into the square before the Water Gate. They told the scribe Ezra to bring the book of the law of Moses, which the LORD had given to Israel. Accordingly, the priest Ezra brought the law before the assembly, both men and women and all who could hear with understanding. This was on the first day of the seventh month. He read from it facing the square before the Water Gate from early morning until midday, in the presence of the men and the women and those who could understand; and the ears of all the people were attentive to the book of the law. (Neh 8:1-3)

Scholars believe that the text Ezra read on that day was an early version of the Pentateuch, which had been compiled and edited during the exilic and postexilic periods. The people now had a record—a written constitution—to guide them in fulfilling the covenant requirements. Although this new theocracy would be plagued by backsliding in the years ahead, the governor and the priest brought political and social stability and spiritual renewal to the people of Judah. They also helped the people embrace a new identity, one that was inextricably linked to the Mosaic Law. As Bright explains, with their renewed commitment to the Law,

Israel's transition from a nation to a law community had been made. As such she [Israel] would thenceforth exist, and this she could do without statehood and even though scattered all over the world. The distinguishing mark of a Jew would not be political nationality, nor primarily ethnic background, nor even regular participation in the Temple cult (impossible for Jews of the Diaspora), but adherence to the law of

Moses. The great watershed of Israel's history had been crossed, and her future secured for all time to come.[4]

The distinguishing mark of Jewish identity would prove costly, however, when the Greeks came on the scene.

The Greek Occupation

The relationship between the Persians and the Greeks had been a turbulent one. During the fifth century BCE, the Persians had tried to conquer Greece twice, but had been unsuccessful, finally resorting to political intrigue and bribery to keep the Greek city-states in line. In 338 BCE Philip of Macedonia (a region north of Greece) ended this arrangement, defeating the Greeks in battle and forcing them to accept him as their leader. Two years later, Philip cast a hungry eye toward Persia. While making final preparations for an invasion, Philip was assassinated by a disgruntled bodyguard, leaving his young son, Alexander, to take over the reins of power. A student of the Greek philosopher, Aristotle, Alexander was a lover of Greek culture and a brilliant general who managed to conquer the Persians and just about everybody else over a period of thirteen years, but his success was short-lived. In 323 BCE he died suddenly after a fever (some say by poison; others by riotous living) at the age of thirty-three.

One of the most interesting and significant directives in Alexander's empire building was his program of Hellenization, which was the systematic (and sometimes forced) imposition of Greek culture on the people of the conquered territories. Alexander's dream was to foster unity among all the peoples of the world, but his dream wasn't completely altruistic. One culture, one people, one language would be easier to control both militarily and politically. To get the ball rolling, Alexander married a number of foreign women from conquered territories and arranged for mass marriages between his troops and local women.[5] He also established Greek colonies throughout his vast empire. The systematic exportation of Greek politics, law, literature, philosophy, and religion began in earnest after Alexander's death, but the results were mixed. While most of the common folk remained loyal to their local gods, customs, and ways of life, some from the elite groups embraced all things Greek, and with good reason. They had more to gain—and to lose if they didn't go along with the practices of their Greek overlords.

After Alexander's death, his empire, which included Greece, Macedonia, and the Persian Empire, was split roughly into four regions, which were divided up among his most loyal generals. Two of them have significance for the history of Palestine. Ptolemy, a Macedonian Greek and founder of the last Egyptian dynasty, was given control over Egypt and Judea (the Greek term for Judah), while Syria and the eastern territories were given to Seleucus. For a century the Ptolemies dominated the region, but were later challenged by the Seleucid kings. After a number of battles between the rival kingdoms, the Seleucids prevailed in 200 BCE under the leadership of

Antiochus the Great (223–187 BCE). Initially he was welcomed by the Jews, especially since he gave special favors to the priests and other Jewish leaders. He also issued a decree that permitted the Jews to live according to their own law. Unfortunately, the sons who succeeded him were not so generous, often raiding the Jerusalem Temple to finance their campaigns against the Ptolemies. The most notorious of these sons—at least in Jewish history— was Antiochus IV Epiphanes ("God is Manifest"), so named because he believed that he was the earthly manifestation of the Greek god Zeus. Antiochus ruled from 175 to 164 BCE and was an active promoter of Hellenization. His lack of respect and tolerance for Jewish customs and religious practices generated divisions within Judaism between those who embraced the new order and those who fought against it. Bright describes the extent of the tension in a dispute about Jewish involvement with the Jerusalem gymnasium.

> A gymnasium was established in Jerusalem and young men enrolled in it; all sorts of Greek sports were fostered, as were Greek fashions of dress. Young priests neglected their duties to compete in the games. Embarrassed by their circumcision, since sports were participated in naked (cf. Jub. 3:31), many Jews submitted to surgery to disguise it. Conservative Jews, profoundly shocked, regarded all this as outright apostasy. Nor were they wrong. The gymnasium was not a mere sporting club, nor did its opponents object merely to what they considered immodest and indecent behaviors. The status of Jewish religion was in question. The gymnasium seems actually to have been a separate corporation of Hellenized Jews, with definite legal and civic rights, set up within the city of Jerusalem. Since Greek sports were inseparable from the cult of Heracles (2 Macc 4:18-20), or of Hermes, or of the royal house, membership in the gymnasium inevitably involved some degree of recognition of the gods who were its protectors. The presence of such an institution in Jerusalem meant that the decree of Antiochus III granting Jews the right to live solely in accordance with their own law had been abrogated—and with Jewish connivance.[6]

As opposition to his program mounted, Antiochus IV resorted to more extreme measures. In fact, he seemed determined to destroy the Jewish cult altogether. In his zeal he not only stripped the Jerusalem Temple of its precious objects, but he built an altar to Zeus in the Temple and had a pig slaughtered there (1 Macc 1:20-64). We can only imagine the people's outrage, but Antiochus didn't stop there. He also prohibited Jews from observing the sabbath, practicing circumcision, reading and studying the Torah, and worshiping at the Temple. Many Jews who refused to keep the prohibitions were executed. Descendants of these brave souls, called the *Hasidim* ("the pious ones"), would later become the Pharisees—the much maligned opponents of Jesus in the gospels.

THE SEPTUAGINT (LXX)

Alexander's conquest of much of the ancient Near East and his program of Hellenization had a tremendous influence on the formation and use of the Bible. The Old Testament was originally written in Hebrew, but with the Ptolemies installed in Egypt, a *koine* (common) Greek translation was produced in Alexandria. The Septuagint ("the work of the seventy") was the product of a long and painstaking process of translation. Beginning around 250 BCE, scholars in Alexandria translated the Torah and then over a period of many years translated the prophets and the writings, completing the task by the first century BCE. As a completed work, the Septuagint contains the thirty-nine books of the Old Testament canon. In the Christian canon, the Septuagint also includes apocryphal books (such as Tobit, Judith, 1 and 2 Maccabees, and Wisdom of Solomon).

Because many Diaspora Jews and Christians lived far from Palestine and didn't speak or read Hebrew, the Septuagint became the standard text for many synagogues and early Christian communities. It was also used for citing scripture by the writers of the New Testament and for developing other textual translations (such as St. Jerome's Latin Vulgate). But by the second century CE, rabbis discouraged its use, preferring their own translations of the canon.

The Maccabean Revolt

The callous brutality of Antiochus IV sparked the Maccabean Revolt (167–164 BCE), which is recounted in the books of the Maccabees. The leaders of the revolt were the priest, Mattathias, and his five sons, who were known collectively as the Hasmoneans.

According to 1 Maccabees 2:1-48, the trouble begins when a representative of Antiochus comes to the village of Modein to enforce Hellenization decrees. He requests that Mattathias set an example for the people by sacrificing to Zeus. Instead, Mattathias kills the king's officer and flees into the Judean wilderness with his sons. Mattathias dies shortly afterward, but his son, Judas Maccabeus (known as "The Hammer") assumes leadership of the revolt. He and his brothers are soon joined by the Hasidim and the revolt quickly spreads among the towns and villages of Judea.

The guerilla tactics of the rebels proved very effective against the Syrian army. By 164 BCE, they had recaptured the Jerusalem Temple after years of defilement by the cult of Zeus. The jubilant rebels cleansed and rededicated the Temple, an event commemorated in the yearly feast of Hanukkah (the "Festival of Lights"). As for Antiochus, he died somewhere in the east during the time of the Temple rededication. Like Egypt's Pharaoh, Antiochus IV Epiphanes was no match for the God of Israel.

Reclaiming the Temple did not end the fighting, however. Judas was killed in battle in 160 BCE and was succeeded by his brother, Jonathan. As the recognized leader of the Jews, Jonathan negotiated a fragile truce with the Seleucids and eventually assumed the role of high priest in 152 BCE. Lured into a trap by a Seleucid regent, he was held for ransom but then murdered, despite the payment of ransom by his brother, Simon.[7] After Jonathan's death, Simon rallied the people, leading them to independence from the Seleucids. In 142 BCE, Simon was proclaimed king, high priest, and commander of the Jewish army, thus establishing the Hasmonean Dynasty. For the first time in over four centuries there existed an autonomous Jewish state, but it wouldn't last long. Hasmonean rule (140–40 BCE) was plagued by political intrigue, treachery, and infighting among members of the Jewish aristocracy and emerging Jewish factions (Sadducees, Pharisees, and Essenes). Their grip on power ended in 63 BCE when the Hasmoneans made what could facetiously be called "The Big Mistake." They were foolish enough to ask the Roman general, Pompey, for help in settling a dispute between John Hyrcanus II and his younger brother Aristobulus II over the throne. Because Rome had been a frequent ally of the Hasmoneans against the Seleucids, the request was not unreasonable, and Pompey was more than happy to oblige. Upon his arrival in Damascus (he was in the midst of a Syrian campaign), Pompey summoned ambassadors from the feuding brothers to hear their claims but deferred a final decision. When he ruled in favor of Hyrcanus, Aristobulus refused to cooperate. Pompey moved quickly to settle the matter once and for all, and to Rome's advantage. He had Aristobulus arrested, but some of his die-hard supporters refused to submit to Roman authority and barricaded themselves on the Temple Mount. Interpreting this maneuver as an act of aggression, Pompey sent his legions to attack Jerusalem. After a three-month siege, his forces took control of the city and the Temple complex, thus ending Jewish independence. Although Pompey installed John Hyrcanus as high priest and ruling "ethnarch of the Jews" (63–40 BCE), the period of Roman occupation had begun.

The Roman Occupation

Rome's late entry into our historical survey is somewhat misleading. By the end of the second century BCE, Rome had become a formidable power. It had conquered Macedonia (148 BCE) and Greece (146 BCE) before moving on to Syria (64 BCE), and, finally, Egypt (31 BCE). In the first years of the occupation of Judea, the Herodians of Idumea (formerly ancient Edom) gained favor with Roman authorities. After outwitting the Hasmoneans in a final power play, their political dreams were realized in 40 BCE when the Roman Senate appointed the first Herodian king, Herod the Great, to rule all of Judea, which included Galilee, Samaria, Perea, Idumea, and most of the Mediterranean coast.

Contrary to the gospel accounts, Herod was a cruel but competent ruler. His most famous achievement was the renovation and expansion of the Second Temple, where Jesus would have his fateful encounter with the money changers (Mt 21:12-13; Mk 11:15-19; Lk 19:45-48). In addition to numerous building projects (which included cities, palaces, memorials, and needed infrastructure), Herod also managed to find the time to have hundreds of his political opponents executed, including members of his own family. His ruthlessness and paranoia were immortalized in Matthew's account of the killing of Bethlehem's firstborn (Mt 2:16-17). The northern region of Galilee, where Jesus conducted much of his ministry, was ruled by Herod Antipas (4 BCE–39 CE), a puppet king of lower rank who survived the machinations of his murderous father and whose major claim to fame (or infamy, from a biblical perspective) was the beheading of John the Baptist (Mt 14:1-12; Mk 6:14-29). The southern district of Judea where Jerusalem was located was ruled by the procurator, Pontius Pilate (26–36 CE), an incompetent and corrupt bureaucrat who ordered the execution of Jesus and many other innocent Jews before he was finally removed from office.

As these brief descriptions indicate, life under Roman rule was harsh and unpredictable and, not surprisingly, it carried a heavy financial burden. Dennis C. Duling and Norman Perrin describe the Roman system of taxation:

> The chief responsibilities of the various Roman governors were civil order, the administration of justice, including the judicial right of capital punishment, and the collection of various taxes and tolls. This system was enforced by a police force. Client kings carried out similar responsibilities, though their right to inflict capital punishment was often restricted. Taxes on individuals and land were normally collected by the agents of Rome and local client kings. Tolls, however, were "farmed out" to the highest bidders. Their income was whatever they collected in excess of the amount due Rome. Greedy toll collectors abused this system. In addition, client kings such as Herod the Great, who had ambitious building projects, added their own taxes. There were also religious taxes, such as the Jewish half-shekel Temple tax for Jewish men, due once a year.[8]

The crushing tax burden resulted in horrible living conditions for the vast majority of people. With no social safety net, most families were barely able to survive. The ever-widening gap between the rich and the poor, the inability of most people to move up the social ladder, and the Roman habit of confiscating Temple funds fueled a seething resentment among the Jews that would ultimately lead to armed insurrection.

While the Jewish people suffered greatly under Roman rule, their leaders were able to negotiate some concessions. For example, Jews were exempt from military service and they did not have to worship the emperor (a requirement for most conquered peoples). Moreover, the mint in Judea, which was under Roman administration, did not have to produce coinage with the emperor's image—an idolatrous practice that was strictly forbidden in the Torah (Ex 20:2). These concessions could be rescinded at any time and were contingent upon the people's cooperation with Rome. The fragile relations between Rome and the Jewish people were made even more tenuous by the religious divisions within Judaism itself.

Religious Divisions within Judaism

The history of world religions attests to the fact that all religions experience internal tensions that threaten the solidarity of the faith community. Disputes about doctrine, ritual observances, the function of priests and laypersons, the interpretation of sacred texts, and similar issues often result in the formation of factions or sects that vie for power and influence. Judaism was no exception to this rule. Of the groups that existed during the Greek and Roman occupations, the Sadducees, the Pharisees, the Zealots, the Sicarii, and the Essenes are particularly relevant to our study. Each had a distinctive religious outlook, as well as differing attitudes toward the Romans.

The Sadducees were members of the Jewish aristocracy and functioned as priests and Temple administrators. The origins of the group are unclear. Some scholars associate them with the Boethusians, an Egyptian priestly family that came into power with Herod the Great.[9] Others believe they were descended from the Zadokite priesthood, which had dominated the Jerusalem Temple and the office of high priest for centuries. When the Hasmoneans took control of the Temple, some Sadducees remained, preferring to accept a non-Zadokite high priest than lose the power and privilege of their priestly offices. As administrators of the Temple cult, the Sadducees were also leaders of the Sanhedrin, the ruling council in Jerusalem that held executive, legislative, and judicial responsibilities. Their strategy toward Rome was one of political accommodation, working with the Romans to maintain peace and influence Judean policy. In practical terms, their accommodationist stance was understandable. Keeping their Roman overlords happy ensured their own survival as the ruling elite—particularly since the Romans appointed the high priest! Theologically, they were very conservative, accepting only the Pentateuch as authentic scripture. They also denied the resurrection of the dead and a final judgment, which were theological imports from Persian Zoroastrianism.

In contrast to the Sadducees, the Pharisees (the "separated ones") were not priests or aristocrats, but laypersons and scholars of the Law who served as teachers and who often acted as intermediaries between the Jewish aristocracy and the people. Their attitude toward Rome differed slightly from that of the Sadducees. During the postexilic period, they were politically active, gaining and losing power and influence in the Hasmonean court. But after the Romans came and installed puppet regimes, the Pharisees retreated from politics, preferring to maintain a low profile with the Roman authorities. Their real power lay with their teaching role and their interpretation of the Law, which covered nearly every aspect of Jewish life. Amy-Jill Levine summarizes their basic religious beliefs and pedagogical goals:

> This confederation of like-minded individuals valued both the Torah and their own elaboration of its contents to fit new questions and circumstances of the changing world. Josephus [a Jewish historian] notes that they "handed down to the people certain regulations from the ancestral succession and not recorded in the laws of Moses" (*Antiquities* 13.10.6). This tradition of interpretation, which came to be known as the "oral law," thus took its place alongside the "written law," the Torah. The Pharisees extended the holiness of the Temple and its functionaries to domestic life: for them the home became a focal point for religious practice, and the household table matched the Temple altar in sanctity. Doctrinally expanding beyond scripture, the Pharisees also promoted such non-Pentateuchal concepts as the resurrection of the dead, and they coupled belief in free will with an acknowledgment of divine omnipotence.[10]

Their oral teachings on the Torah were extensive, establishing guidelines for almsgiving, fasting, sabbath observance, prayer, table fellowship, and other aspects of daily life. As their name implies, the Pharisees' emphasis on strict adherence to the Law and ritual purity "separated" them from many Jews, who did not study it or obey it as scrupulously as they did; yet they were popular among the common people, who considered them authoritative interpreters of the Law. Although the Pharisees' quest for holiness and ritual purity would become major issues for Jesus and Paul, their flexibility in interpreting the Torah in changing circumstances and their prudent attitude toward Roman rule would prove crucial for the later survival of Judaism.

In contrast to the Sadducees and Pharisees, the Zealots and the Sicarii (Lat. *sicarius*, meaning "dagger") were two radical Jewish groups that preferred to fight the Roman occupation through banditry, kidnapping, urban terrorism, and political assassination. Their goals were ambitious. Not only did they want to rid the region of the Romans, but they also wanted to instigate an uprising against the large Greek population in Palestine and eliminate the Jewish aristocracy as well. The Sicarii were particularly adept at assassinating priests and aristocrats who they believed collaborated with the enemy and exploited the poor. The first-century Jewish historian Josephus describes their tactics and their impact on the populace.

The Sicarii committed murders in broad daylight in the heart of Jerusalem. The holy days were their special seasons when they would mingle with the crowd carrying short daggers concealed under their clothing with which they stabbed their enemies. Thus, when they fell, the murderers joined in cries of indignation, and through this plausible behavior, were never discovered. The first assassinated was Jonathan, the high-priest. After his death there were numerous daily murders. The panic created was more alarming than the calamity itself; everyone, as on the battlefield, hourly expected death. Men kept watch at a distance on their enemies and would not trust even their friends when they approached.[11]

Theologically, many Zealots and Sicarii embraced an apocalyptic worldview that fueled their political and nationalistic ambitions. While scholars still debate the origins and development of apocalyptic in Israel, the general consensus is that the genre emerged in Israel during the late Second Temple period (200 BCE–70 CE), with antecedents in the eschatological writings of the prophetic and wisdom traditions and in mythologies of the ancient Near East (e.g., Babylon and Persia).[12]

Jewish Apocalyptic Eschatology

Eschatology (Gr. *eschatos*, "last," and *logos*, "study") is the study of the events of the eschaton (end time), which could refer to the end of an age, the close of history, or the end of the world itself. Jewish eschatology was grounded in the belief that Yahweh was a providential deity who acted and would continue to act in history. The belief was not unfounded. Time and time again Yahweh had called leaders and prophets to care for his people and to further their nationalistic ambitions, but as the turbulent and tragic events of Israel's history unfolded, the people's confidence and optimism were badly shaken. Had Yahweh abandoned them to their enemies? The prophets and wisdom writers responded to this crisis of faith through eschatological visions that offered the people liberal doses of both judgment and hope. The "Day of the Lord," for example, was a term prophets often used during the Monarchic period (1000–587 BCE) to signify God's coming judgment and doom for faithless people and corrupt nations (Ezek 30:1-4; Amos 5:18-24; Zeph 1:7-18). In contrast, First Isaiah's Immanuel prophecies (Isa 9:2-21, 11:1-5) offered the hope that Yahweh would liberate his people through a warrior-Messiah of the Davidic line. As the "anointed one" of God, the Messiah would destroy the oppressors (whoever they were at the time) and reestablish the Davidic house, which would rule Jew and Gentile alike with justice and mercy.

The Messiah figure is articulated in a number of places in the Old Testament, including Psalms (Pss 2, 89, 132), Ezekiel (Ezek 34:23-24, 37:24-28), and Jeremiah (Jer 23:5-7, 33:14-22). But the loss of the Davidic monarchy during the exile and the unlikelihood of its restoration prompted some postexilic prophets to minimize the royal connection. They believed that God would intervene directly to destroy Israel's enemies and restore the people to their land. The prophet Joel, who was writing during the Persian period (531–331 BCE), offers one such vision:

> The LORD roars from Zion, and utters his voice from Jerusalem, and the heavens and the earth shake. But the LORD is a refuge for his people, a stronghold for the people of Israel. So you shall know that I, the LORD your God, dwell in Zion, my holy mountain, and Jerusalem shall be holy, and strangers shall never again pass through it. In that day the mountains shall drip sweet wine, the hills shall flow with milk, and all the stream beds of Judah shall flow with water; a fountain shall come forth from the house of the LORD and water the Wadi Shittim. Egypt shall become a desolation and Edom a desolate wilderness, because of the violence done to the people of Judah, in whose land they have shed innocent blood. But Judah shall be inhabited forever, and Jerusalem to all generations. I will avenge their blood, and I will not clear the guilty, for the LORD dwells in Zion. (Joel 3:16-21)

Unfortunately, Joel's optimistic vision (and those of many other postexilic prophets) did not materialize. As the harsh realities of the Restoration dragged on and Greek and Roman oppression intensified, the people began to question whether God would ever save them from the predatory nations of the earth. As a result, by the late Second Temple period (200 BCE–70 CE), Jewish eschatology took on a darker, apocalyptic aspect that interpreted the end time from a cosmic, otherworldly perspective.

Apocalyptic derives its name from the Greek *apokalypsis*, which means "uncovering" or "revelation." Whereas Jewish eschatology interpreted God's activity in relation to particular historical events or periods, Jewish apocalyptic eschatology was more global in scope and was grounded in the belief that God was driving history toward a final culmination in accordance with the divine plan—a plan that was hidden from human beings. Moving beyond the confines of history and Israel's national interests, Israel's visionaries used fantastic images, symbolic numbers, demonic creatures, angelic emissaries, and scenarios of cosmic destruction to reveal secret information about God's plan and the ultimate destiny of the world. Masking the information in this way not only intensified the message, but it minimized the chances of detection if the writings fell into the wrong hands.[13]

The drama of Jewish apocalyptic played out within a dualistic worldview (another Zoroastrian import), where the powers of good and evil, God and Satan, were in constant tension, often erupting into periods of upheaval and crisis. The message of Israel's visionaries was simple: In the present evil age, Satan's power had so thoroughly corrupted the world that it could not be redeemed through the conventional means of divine-human cooperation. At some point in the future (no one knew precisely when), Yahweh would engage in a great cosmic battle in which he would defeat Satan and his minions, punish the wicked, save the faithful, and bring a dramatic and fitting end to the world. In its place God would fashion a new heaven and a new earth that would herald a glorious new age of righteousness and justice for all peoples and nations of the earth. Proto-apocalyptic depictions of a final conflict and its resolution are found in Ezekiel (Ezek 37–39) and Isaiah (Isa 65:17-25; 66:22-23); however, the only full-blown example of Jewish apocalyptic in the Old Testament is the book of Daniel. Written during the terrible persecutions of Antiochus IV (about 168 BCE), the anonymous author (or authors) combined entertaining folktales and apocalyptic revelations to craft a message of encouragement and hope for the Jewish people.

In contrast to the apocalyptic visions found in Ezekiel and Isaiah, Daniel 7–12 offers an extended and very specific depiction of events leading up to the eschaton, including the destruction of Israel's enemies, the downfall and death of the evil king (Antiochus IV), the resurrection of the dead, the final judgment, and the afterlife. One of the central figures in Daniel's triumphant scenario is the "Son of Man." In a famous passage from the book, the young exile describes the heavenly throne room, the judgment of nations, and the emergence of the messianic hero who is destined to rule in the coming age:

> As I watched, thrones were set in place, and an Ancient One took his throne, his clothing was white as snow, and the hair of his head like pure wool; his throne was fiery flames, and its wheels were burning fire. A stream of fire issued and flowed out from his presence. A thousand thousands served him, and ten thousand times ten thousand stood attending him. The court sat in judgment and the books were opened. I watched then because of the noise of the arrogant words that the horn [Antiochus IV] was speaking. And as I watched, the beast [the Seleucid kingdom] was put to death, and its body destroyed and given over to be burned with fire. As for the rest of the beasts [the kingdoms of Babylon, Media, and Persia], their dominion was taken away, but their lives were prolonged for a season and a time. As I watched in the night visions, I saw one like a human being [the Son of Man] coming with the clouds of heaven. And he came to the Ancient One and was presented before him. To him was given dominion and glory and kingship, that all people, nations, and languages should serve him. His dominion is an everlasting dominion that shall not pass away, and his kingship is one that shall never be destroyed. (Dan 7:9-14)

The identity of the Son of Man is disputed. Some commentators believe he is the angel, Michael, who is Israel's guardian in battle. Others suggest he is Judas Maccabeus or even Daniel himself. Whatever the case, similar conceptions of a redeemer figure are found in apocryphal and pseudepigraphal writings (e.g., Psalms of Solomon 17, 4 Ezra, 1 Enoch). 1 Enoch 46:1-7 reveals striking parallels with Daniel and warrants citing in full.

And there I saw One who had a head of days, and His head was white like wool, and with Him was another being whose countenance had the appearance of a man, and his face was full of graciousness, like one of the holy angels. And I asked the angel who went with me and showed me all the hidden things, concerning that Son of Man, who he was, and whence he was, (and) why he went with the Head of Days? And he answered and said unto me: This is the Son of Man who hath righteousness, with whom dwelleth righteousness, and who revealeth all the treasures of that which is hidden, because the Lord of Spirits hath chosen him, and whose lot hath the pre-eminence before the Lord of Spirits in uprightness for ever. And this Son of Man whom thou hast seen shall raise up the kings and the mighty from their seats, [And the strong from their thrones] and shall loosen the reins of the strong, and break the teeth of the sinners. [And he shall put down the kings from their thrones and kingdoms] because they do not extol and praise Him, nor humbly acknowledge whence the kingdom was bestowed upon them. And he shall put down the countenance of the strong, and shall fill them with shame. And darkness shall be their dwelling, and worms shall be their bed, and they shall have no hope of rising from their beds, because they do not extol the name of the Lord of Spirits.[14]

Despite the diversity in tone and imagery, collectively these writings reflect the Jewish belief in a final judgment and in a powerful redeemer figure who was often (but not always) connected to the Davidic line. Unlike later Christian interpretations, the messianic figure in postexilic Israel was not divine, nor was he a suffering servant. He was usually depicted as a flesh-and-blood (albeit superhuman) being who would vanquish Israel's enemies and rule over God's kingdom. The Zealots, the Sicarii, and many other Jews embraced an apocalyptic eschatology during the Greek and Roman occupations, and for good reason: its triumphant vision offered a vanquished and beleaguered people a source of hope and the will to resist their oppressors.

The Essenes and the Dead Sea Scrolls

By far the most mysterious and fascinating proponents of this view were the Essenes ("pious ones"), an ascetic Jewish sect that is credited with compiling and preserving the Dead Sea Scrolls. Most scholars believe the Essenes were a disenfranchised priestly class (probably Zadokites) that wanted nothing to do with the Romans or the Jewish leadership, specifically, the Hasmoneans, who had taken control of the Jerusalem Temple after the Maccabean Revolt.[15] Unlike the Sadducees, the Essenes refused to make peace with the Hasmonean rulers. In their view, the Maccabean priests had corrupted Judaism and the Temple and were unworthy of their priestly offices. Prior to the Roman occupation, some of the Essenes abandoned Jerusalem for Qumran, where they established a monastic community near the northwest shore of the Dead Sea.

The bitterness the Essenes felt toward their Jewish brethren is evident in their eschatological writings. In contrast to the Zealots and the Sicarii, the Essenes interpreted the end time in spiritual rather than political terms, envisioning a decisive battle between the "Children of Light" (God's righteous remnant) and the "Children of Darkness" (Hasmonean priests, apostate Jews, and Gentiles). The Essenes were convinced that God would soon intervene to destroy the polluters of his Temple, condemn the wicked to everlasting damnation, and redeem the elect. Among the Dead Sea Scrolls are Essene documents that add an interesting twist to the apocalyptic scheme. Although scholars are still debating the issue, textual evidence suggests that the Essenes believed in the arrival of *two* Messiahs: a Priestly Messiah descended from Aaron, and a Royal Messiah descended from David. Not surprisingly, the Essenes gave the Priestly Messiah a higher status than the Davidic one, but there was no rivalry between them because they served different functions: The Priestly Messiah would restore the Temple, purify the faithful, and reestablish proper worship of God; the Royal Messiah would command the armies in the final conflict. The following passage from the "Community Rule" document describes the governance structure of the new covenant community (the *Yahad*) and the expected arrival of the two Messiahs:

> At that time the men of the *Yahad* shall withdraw, the holy house of Aaron uniting as a Holy of Holies, and the synagogue of Israel as those who walk blamelessly. The sons of Aaron alone shall have authority in judicial and financial matters. They shall decide on governing precepts for the men of the *Yahad* and on money matters for the holy men who walk blamelessly. Their wealth is not to be admixed with that of rebellious men, who have failed to cleanse their path by separating from perversity and walking blamelessly. They shall deviate from none of the teachings of the Law, whereby they would walk in their willful heart completely. They shall govern themselves using the original precepts by which the men of the *Yahad* began to be instructed, doing so until there come the Prophet and the Messiahs of Aaron and Israel.[16]

In their compound at Qumran, the Essenes lived, worked, worshiped, and waited in fervent hope for the final battle to begin.

Although these different Jewish groups revealed the fault lines within Judaism, they still shared a number of commonly held beliefs that kept them from veering toward outright schism. As John Bright explains,

> [e]xcept for the careless and the apostate, all Jews gave allegiance to the law; and, with the exception of the worldly-minded Sadducees, all had eschatological expectations and nationalistic aspirations. The differences lay in the interpretation of the law, in the degree of stress laid upon eschatology, and in the way in which it was thought that the future hope of the nation would be brought to pass.... [Nevertheless, the

divisions] are an index of the fact that Jews were not agreed regarding what Israel should be and what course her future ought to take.[17]

Jesus of Nazareth was one of these conflicted Jews. The brutal oppression and tragic hope that fueled eschatological expectations, as well as differences regarding the application of the Mosaic Law, would also influence his life and work.

Jesus and the Jesus Movement

Over the years, a host of scholars and other experts have examined biblical and non-biblical sources and have drawn some general conclusions about the life of Jesus. Most historians place his birth between 6 and 4 BCE, during the reign of Augustus and before the death of Herod the Great. Jesus was born into a poor family that lived in the small village of Nazareth in Galilee. Like most Jews of his time, Jesus spoke Aramaic (a Hebrew dialect) and was probably literate. In his youth he worked as a carpenter. He associated with and was baptized by John the Baptist, the leader of a small sectarian group in Judea. Shortly after his baptism, Jesus began a public ministry in the towns and villages of Galilee. His ministry was brief and controversial, but quite successful, attracting a number of disciples (both male and female) and generating a sizeable following among people from different classes and ethnic groups. His teachings, laced with apocalyptic images of final judgment and inspiring visions of the kingdom of God, proclaimed the joys of God's rule in both heaven and earth. Major sources of controversy were Jesus' claims to authority, his teachings on the Law, his healings on the sabbath, and his close association with ritually unclean persons, such as non-observant Jews, tax collectors, prostitutes, and other persons of low standing. Jewish leaders eventually accused him of blasphemy because he claimed the authority to ease the requirements of the Law (Mk 2:23-28; Mt 12:1-8; Lk 6:1-5) and to forgive sins (Mk 2:1-12; Mt 9:1-8; Lk 5:17-26)—actions that were reserved for God alone.

Around 30 CE, Jesus traveled to Jerusalem for Passover. While in Jerusalem, he created a major disturbance by expelling the money changers and sellers of sacrificial animals from the Temple, claiming that such blatant commercial practices defiled the sanctity of God's house (Mk 11:15-19; Mt 21:12-13; Lk 19:45-46). Jesus' public protest against the greed of the Temple administrators and priests immediately caught the attention of the Jewish authorities. After a meal with his disciples, Jesus was arrested and interrogated by members of the Sanhedrin. To avoid possible Roman intervention, the Jewish authorities quickly condemned Jesus and went to the Roman procurator, Pontius Pilate, demanding that the young rabbi be executed for fomenting rebellion and committing blasphemy. The last thing Pilate wanted or needed was a religious agitator stirring up trouble. He ordered Jesus crucified with other criminals, who were probably Zealots. After his execution, Jesus was buried in a tomb donated by a wealthy patron. Three days later, female disciples reported that the tomb was empty and that Jesus had been resurrected, thus defeating Satan's destructive power. His followers further claimed that, after making numerous appearances and instructing his disciples on their mission, Jesus ascended into heaven. This fueled the hope that he would soon return to establish God's kingdom.

From these brute facts the Jesus movement was born. Initially, the movement was a Jewish sect that was based in Jerusalem under the leadership of Peter, John, and James, the brother of Jesus; however, it wasn't long before other followers of Jesus took to the road, some preaching the good news in the towns and villages of Galilee, southern Judea, and Samaria while others moved on to urban areas in Egypt, Syria, and Asia Minor. As the book of Acts attests, Peter's conversion of a Gentile, Cornelius (Acts 10:1-28), and Paul's mission to the Gentiles in Greece and Asia Minor (49–59 CE) transformed the Jesus movement into a more inclusive faith, one that accepted converts from different religious backgrounds and social strata.

It is virtually impossible to determine precisely when the Jesus movement formed an independent identity because in these early years, Jews and Jewish "Christians" were virtually indistinguishable. The first followers of Jesus were Jews and, in their minds, the Jesus movement did not conflict with their tradition. On the contrary, they believed that Jesus was fulfilling God's promises to Israel. As pious Jews, they continued to study at the synagogues, offer sacrifices at the Temple, and follow the requirements of the Law with little opposition from their Jewish brethren. Initially, the few Gentile converts to the movement joined their Jewish Christian brethren in the synagogues. The inclusion of pagan God-fearers (Gr. *theosobeis*) in Jewish religious practice was a common occurrence in Jewish communities. Paula Fredriksen explains:

> Pagan culture itself was pluralistic. Ancient peoples typically worshiped their own ancestral gods—in antiquity, religion ran in the blood—and these gods formed aggregates of larger pantheons as politics required. ...Further, simple courtesy and common sense encouraged showing respect to gods as they were encountered. Pagan interest in the Jewish god was thus one particular instance of the general pagan interest in any divinity. And Jews, a minority wherever they lived in the Diaspora, encouraged this sympathetic interest in their own God, while making no demands on the volunteer. Thus, in the innumerable synagogues scattered throughout the Empire, Jews made room for pagans, as pagans, to worship the God of Israel just as in Jerusalem's great Temple ...the largest court was set aside for pagans to worship the Jewish God.[18]

The acceptance of non-Jews in the Temple and synagogues was more than just good public relations for a minority people; it was also an effective strategy for bringing potential converts to the Jewish faith. While most scholars agree that Jews were not active missionaries in the traditional sense, their willingness to engage Gentiles in the Temple, the synagogues, and the marketplace resulted in a substantial increase in conversions to the faith and a substantial number of God-fearers, who adopted Jewish practices to some degree.[19] But as the theological implications of the Christian witness became clear, and the situation with Rome deteriorated, the peaceful coexistence between Jews and their Christian brethren would dissolve into mutual suspicion and rejection.

Sources of Jewish-Christian Animus

The cause of tensions between Jews and Christians was not so much about the teachings of Jesus; after all, disagreements about the interpretation and application of the Law were common among Jewish groups. The stumbling block was the claim that Jesus was the Messiah. Most Jews rejected the claim, and with good reason—he didn't fulfill the expected role of the Messiah. He wasn't the powerful military leader described in the Old Testament, he didn't destroy the Romans, and he didn't usher in a new age of peace and justice. Instead he was executed by the Romans and in a manner that immediately disqualified him as Messiah. According to the Torah "anyone hung on a tree is under God's curse" (Deut 21:22). The very notion that God's chosen deliverer would be crucified was unthinkable. How could the followers of Jesus be so deluded and so mistaken? From a contemporary perspective, the answer is found in the historical process of revelation.

As was the case with the writings of Isaiah, the claims about Jesus emerged from the lived experience of God within the faith community. Jesus' early followers participated in a dynamic and ongoing process of reflection, articulation, dialogue, and refining reflection that revealed Jesus of Nazareth as the Christ (Gr. "Messiah"). "Who do people say that I am?" is the question Jesus asks in three of the four gospels. In answering this question, the biblical writers followed the creative path of Isaiah, introducing a shift in religious consciousness that revolutionized the concept of Messiah. Whereas the image of a crucified Christ scandalized most Jews, it offered joy and hope to the followers of Jesus, the Christ. For these early Christians, the Messiah was not the warrior figure of Jewish apocalyptic (although Jesus would later take on that persona in the book of Revelation). In their eyes, the Messiah was Isaiah's suffering servant. Stephen L. Harris explains the significance of this reinterpretation.

> For those living in the protracted interval between Jesus' ascension to heaven and his return to earth, New Testament writers emphasize the spiritual significance of Jesus' innovative messiahship. Instead of coming to earth to conquer political enemies and forcibly establish a theocratic monarchy, Jesus is seen as having appeared primarily to conquer less

tangible but more formidable foes—human sin, evil, and death. After his sacrificial death, paying the ultimate penalty to redeem humankind, Jesus then ascends to the celestial throne room, standing at God's "right hand" (a position symbolic of his unity with God) (Acts 8:55-56; cf. Rev. 1:11-20, etc.). In thus being portrayed as God's co-regent, an immortal being of cosmic stature, the ascended Jesus becomes infinitely more powerful than a Davidic Messiah, ruling invisibly but eternally over human minds and hearts (Phil 2:6-11). In Christian reinterpretation, traditional expectations of a renewed Davidic kingdom are transformed into the concept of a heavenly messianic reign, one in which believers—joined by sacrament and spirit—can participate.[20]

The divine-human nature of the "immortal being" who served as God's co-regent would not be clarified until the First Council of Nicaea (325 CE), but for these early Christians the resurrection of Jesus was a divine sign that vindicated his unique person and work and validated their radical reinterpretation of Jewish tradition. But the Jews didn't see it that way. From their perspective, the Christian reinterpretation was completely unacceptable because it introduced a new salvation scheme in which the Mosaic covenant was superseded by the covenant of Christ. In shifting salvation from Torah observance to faith in Jesus as God's true Messiah, the Christians were quite literally excluding from God's family all Jews who followed the Mosaic covenant and reducing Judaism to little more than a prophetic predictor of the new and greater revelation in Jesus Christ. The indignation and anger generated by this turned to violence in the marketplace, where Jews and Christians not only exchanged goods and services with the pagans but also presented conflicting (and often competing) visions of the Jewish faith and its God. The martyrdom of Stephen is a dramatic (albeit biblically biased) episode in the early days of this religious rift.

The Martyrdom of Stephen

As recounted in Acts, Peter, John, and Stephen are quite successful in persuading the Jews of Jerusalem that Jesus is the Messiah and that the Easter event has indeed occurred. As a result, "The word of God continued to spread; the number of the disciples increased greatly in Jerusalem, and a great many of the priests became obedient to the faith" (Acts 6:7). Whether Luke's assessment is pure hyperbole or a true picture of Christian inroads in Jerusalem is anyone's guess, but Stephen's dynamic preaching and his many "signs and wonders among the people" bring a swift response from members of the synagogue and other Diaspora Jews who pointedly argue with him (Acts 6:8-9). Unable to best Stephen rhetorically, they secretly persuade some fellow Jews to accuse him publicly of making blasphemous statements against Moses and God. The agitated crowd seizes Stephen and hauls him before the council. Instead of defending himself against the false accusations, Stephen launches into a powerful but highly critical sermon that presents a Christianized version of Jewish history (Acts 7:2-53). The sermon recounts God's covenant promises to Abraham, the people's repeated rejection of Moses as God's appointed leader, and their idolatry with the golden calf. In the climax of the sermon, Stephen fearlessly accuses the Jews of purposely obstructing God's plan by killing the prophets and God's Messiah.

> "You stiff-necked people, uncircumcised in heart and ears, you are forever opposing the Holy Spirit, just as your ancestors used to do. Which of the prophets did your ancestors not persecute? They killed those who foretold the coming of the Righteous One, and now you have become his betrayers and murderers. You are the ones that received the law as ordained by angels, and yet you have not kept it." (Acts 7:51-53)

Outraged, the "stiff-necked people" suddenly become a murderous mob, dragging him out of the city and stoning him to death (the prescribed punishment for blasphemy), thus making Stephen the first Christian martyr (Acts 7:58-60). Afterward, a severe persecution begins against the church in Jerusalem, prompting many Christians to flee the city. Paul (or Saul) of Tarsus, who was present at Stephen's execution, is conspicuous among the early persecutors, "ravaging the church by entering house after house," dragging hapless men and women off to prison (Acts 8:3). In one of the great ironies of history, Paul would soon become one of Christianity's greatest champions, devoting the remainder of his life to spreading the gospel to Gentile populations, suffering persecution, imprisonment, and eventual martyrdom.

While scholars debate the extent of Jewish persecution of the Christian sect during these early years, the religious differences between Christians and other Jews and their hostile and accusatory rhetoric were clearly driving a wedge between the emerging church and the synagogue. Their religious rift would soon be eclipsed, however, by unfolding events that would overwhelm them all, hurtling them toward revolt, further division, and war.

The Jewish Revolt

During the roughly thirty-five years between the crucifixion of Jesus (30–33 CE) and the completion of the Gospel of Mark (66–70 CE), the situation in Judea had deteriorated to such an extent that a Jewish revolt was inevitable. The Roman emperors who succeeded Augustus were neither as wise nor as competent as he had been. The reign of Gaius Caligula (37–41 CE) was particularly notorious. Unlike Augustus, who commanded that perpetual sacrifices be made to the God of the Jews, Caligula demanded that all his subjects worship him as a god. When the Jews resisted, he ordered that a statue of himself be erected in the Jerusalem Temple. Fortunately, cooler heads prevailed and Caligula was persuaded to abandon his plan, but not before berating the Jewish delegation that had come to plead their case.[21] In 54 CE Nero became emperor, but he was more interested in music, games, extravagant parties, and debauchery than in ruling an empire. His appointed officials were no better. Instead of administering the provinces, they ruthlessly plundered them. Amy-Jill Levine describes the extent of the corruption and its toll on the people of Judea.

> Albinus [governor of Judea] (62–64), together with the last governor prior to the revolt, Gessius Florus (64–66), confirmed for much of the local populace that independence from Rome was essential. Each took bribes, looted treasuries, and served only himself. Simmering hatred of the governors reached the boiling point in 66 C.E., heated by growing nationalism, religious enthusiasm, increasing strife between Jews and Gentiles in various areas of the country, major economic problems caused by droughts and famines as well as by taxation, massive unemployment in Jerusalem in the early 60's occasioned by the completion of Herod's Temple, the inability of the upper classes either to provide leadership or to evoke popular support, and a series of local incidents. Adding even more heat were the diverse interest of peasants from the rural areas of Galilee and urban merchants from the cosmopolitan centers, of those who expected divine intervention and those who relied on their own skill with weapons, of those who hated the Romans and those who hated the rich.[22]

The Christians had their own problems with Roman rule. As more Gentiles joined the movement, Christians became more conspicuous and more vulnerable to attack by their neighbors, who were suspicious of their refusal to worship Roman gods—an exemption generally reserved for Jews alone. Nero's first widespread persecution of Christians began in 64 CE with the great fire of Rome. The conflagration raged for days and destroyed major portions of the city, including Nero's palace. While scholars still debate who actually started the fire (Christians, Jews, and Nero have all been named as prime suspects), Nero blamed the Christians and the consequences were extreme. Writing years later, the Roman historian, Tacitus, describes how Nero tried to divert suspicion away from himself to the hapless Christians. In this passage, we find the first reference to "Christians" outside of the New Testament.

> But all human efforts, all the lavish gifts of the emperor, and the propitiations of the gods, did not banish the sinister belief that the conflagration was the result of an order. Consequently, to get rid of the report, Nero fastened the guilt and inflicted the most exquisite tortures on a class hated for their abominations, called Christians by the populace. Christus, from whom the name had its origin, suffered the extreme penalty during the reign of Tiberius at the hands of one of our procurators, Pontius Pilatus, and a most mischievous superstition, thus checked for the moment, again broke out not only in Judaea, the first source of the evil, but even in Rome, where all things hideous and

shameful from every part of the world find their centre and become popular. Accordingly, an arrest was first made of all who pleaded guilty; then, upon their information, an immense multitude was convicted, not so much of the crime of firing the city, as of hatred against mankind. Mockery of every sort was added to their deaths. Covered with the skins of beasts, they were torn by dogs and perished, or were nailed to crosses, or were doomed to the flames and burnt, to serve as a nightly illumination, when daylight had expired.... Hence, even for criminals who deserved extreme and exemplary punishment, there arose a feeling of compassion; for it was not, as it seemed, for the public good, but to glut one man's cruelty, that they were being destroyed.[23]

It was during this horrific period of persecution that Paul and Peter are believed to have been martyred.

By 66 CE, Judea was a powder keg waiting to explode. The spark was provided by Nero, who ordered the much-despised governor Florus to confiscate a substantial quantity of silver from the Temple. Florus, who had never been a master of public relations, turned a fairly routine practice into a riot, forcing him to flee to Caesarea and leaving only a small garrison in Jerusalem. With the authorities gone, the riot quickly turned to armed rebellion. Firmly convinced that God was on their side, the Zealots and Sicarii slaughtered the soldiers of the Jerusalem garrison, captured the Temple Mount and the fortresses of Masada and Antonia, plundered palaces, destroyed debt and tax records, and murdered members of the Jewish aristocracy.[24] Although Christians had suffered many abuses at the hands of the Romans, they refused to participate in the rebellion and fled to Pella, a Decapolis city located east of the Jordan River. Some Jews interpreted this move as an act of national betrayal, furthering the tensions and violence between the two groups. The Zealots, for example, went so far as to hold illegal trials and execute fellow Jews and Christians who did not demonstrate their commitment to the rebellion.[25]

Within a year, the revolt had spread beyond the confines of Judea to include Samaria and Galilee. Upon hearing of the uprising, Nero quickly sent a seasoned military commander, Vespasian, to crush the revolt. Ably assisted by his son, Titus, Vespasian coordinated his armies and embarked on a successful campaign against the rebels in the towns and villages of Galilee, working his way south along the coast toward Jerusalem. Rather than form alliances against the Romans, Jewish groups fought among themselves. By 67 CE Jerusalem had spiraled into civil war, with Zealots, priests, Pharisees, and other rebel factions vying for control. Content to let the enemies of Rome destroy themselves (which they did in great numbers), Vespasian delayed his attack, securing nearby cities while preparing for the final assault against Jerusalem. Before he could proceed, however, he learned that Nero had committed suicide (68 CE). The power struggle following Nero's death resulted in a quick succession of emperors, concluding with the claimant Vitellius, a general who had little support, even from his own troops. Sensing an opportunity, Vespasian postponed the assault again, and with strong military backing proclaimed himself emperor in 69 CE. After hearing of Vitellius's assassination, Vespasian journeyed to Rome to assume his new role. Titus remained behind in Judea and in the spring of 70 CE began his assault against Jerusalem.

The brutality of the campaign is legendary. With an overwhelming force of over sixty thousand soldiers, Titus constructed elaborate siege works around the city. The siege lasted six months. Duling and Perrin describe the carnage and its aftermath:

> While the Jews fought valiantly, Titus' armies surrounded the city. Hunger and thirst began to take their toll. Gradually the walled sections of the city fell, one by one, and the fortress of Antonia was retaken. The Temple was ravaged by fire. The Jews refused to surrender. Women, children, and the elderly, were butchered, and the city and most of its walls were destroyed. The major battle over, Titus set sail for Rome with 700 handsome prisoners for the victory parade through Rome, later commemorated by the arch of Titus, still to be seen in the Roman Forum.[26]

After the siege, the Romans secured the remaining rebel strongholds, but only after several more years of bloodshed. When Roman soldiers finally breached the walls of the fortress Masada in 73 CE, they discovered only a few frightened survivors. Having realizing that the battle was lost, many Jewish defenders and their families (approximately 960 persons) had killed themselves rather than live under Roman rule. With this final act of defiance, the war with Rome was over.

For the Palestinian Jews, the war not only took a terrible human toll, but it also radically transformed the political and religious landscape. Most of the Zealots and Sicarii were either imprisoned, or exiled, or dead, and with the Temple gone, the priests and the Sadducees no longer had a power base and soon disappeared from history. The Essenes met a similar fate. Perhaps they believed the Jewish Revolt was the beginning of the eschaton—we can only speculate. What we do know is that they hid their precious manuscripts in the caves around Qumran before being wiped out by Vespasian's troops. The few that escaped fled to Masada, where they joined their doomed kinsmen. The Pharisees (who had prudently cautioned against war with Rome) quickly stepped in to fill the power vacuum, restructuring Judaism along Pharisaic lines and offering the survivors a way of life that would help them cope with the latest disaster.

The Council of Yavneh

The transition to rabbinic Judaism began with the prominent Pharisee, Yohanan ben Zakkai (1–80 CE), who was granted permission from Vespasian to establish a rabbinical school in the coastal city of Yavneh (or Jamnia). The school became the acknowledged replacement for the Sanhedrin and had a tremendous influence on the subsequent development of Judaism. The central goal of the academy was to overcome religious factionalism and nurture social and spiritual unity under Pharisaic leadership. Between 75 and 100 CE, a council of rabbis engaged in debates about the canonical status of some books included in the Jewish canon and other matters of communal worship and practice. With the Temple gone, the rabbis institutionalized public prayer as a replacement for the sacrificial system. To that end, they collected and formulated a number of prayers called the *Eighteen Benedictions* (Heb. *Shemoneh Esreh*), which included prayers of praise and thanksgiving, petitions for aid and comfort, and blessings of God. Pious Jews recited these prayers three times a day (usually in the morning, afternoon, and evening) while facing their beloved city of Jerusalem.[27]

The twelfth benediction (the *Birkath ha-Minim*) is a prayer against heretics that has been the source of much controversy and debate among scholars because of its apparent reference to Christians. Tradition holds that Rabbi Gamaliel instructed Samuel the Small to compose a prayer aimed at Jewish heretics and sectarians who the Yavneh rabbis feared would further disrupt and divide the Diaspora community. Sometime between 85 and 95 CE, Samuel completed the prayer. One translation reads: "For the apostates may there be no hope unless they return to your Torah. As for the [*Nozrim* and the] *Minim*, may they perish immediately. Speedily may they be erased from the Book of the Life and may they not be registered among the righteous. Blessed are You, O Lord, who subdue the wicked."[28]

Nozrim is bracketed in the passage because it appears in some but not all formulations of the prayer. The word refers to Nazarenes (the Jewish term for followers of Jesus of Nazareth), while *Minim* refers to Jewish apostates. The wording appears simple, straightforward, and damning, but many scholars question the origin, form, and intent of the malediction. Steven T. Katz has studied the various theories, as well as the sketchy historical evidence, and offers the most persuasive explanation for the purpose and meaning of the prayer and its textual variations. He contends that the prayer was directed against all types of Jewish heretics and that the reference to Nazarenes was added to the malediction years later after the Bar Kochba Revolt (132–135 CE), when Jewish-Christian tensions were at their height.[29] The original purpose of the prayer was to encourage conformity among Diaspora Jews by making them sensitive to heresies and possible heretics in their midst. The threat was designed to frighten heretics back into the fold or justly condemn them if they proved stubborn. Katz contends that, given the stress and pressures of the time, the Jewish Christians' personal sense of outrage at the prayer was the unfortunate result of "selective hearing."

> The Jewish leadership directed its malediction against all heretics, while the Jewish Christians, who knew of the animosity against them and of the feeling that they were heretics, "heard" the *Birkath ha-Minim* as particularly aimed at them. This was a perfectly natural response. Thus

John [the gospel writer] and other later second-century Christian sources could well speak of Jews cursing Christians in the synagogue, when in fact the malediction was against *minim* in general. Had we relevant Gnostic sources from this same period—late first and second century C.E.—we might well find the same angry denunciations against Jews "cursing" them. The incompleteness of the complex historical evidence and the perspectival subjectivity account for the narrowness of vision.[30]

Katz's explanation has the commonsense ring of truth to it, but the malediction was not the only charge Christians leveled against the Yavneh rabbis. According to Edward H. Flannery,

[a]t this same time, letters were sent by the Sanhedrin at Jabne [Yavneh] to the Diaspora concerning the new malediction and the attitude to be adopted *vis à vis* Christianity. Three of the [church] Fathers—St. Justin, Eusebius, and St. Jerome—give an inkling of the content of the letters, which to some extent may be reconstructed: Jesus, a charlatan, was killed by the Jews, but his disciples stole his body and preached his Resurrection, calling him the Son of God; Jews should have no dealings with his followers.[31]

While Katz acknowledges that Yavneh sages probably spread anti-Christian gossip among Diaspora Jews, he disputes the existence of "official" letters, primarily because there is no clear reference to Jesus or Jewish Christianity in any of the major rabbinic sources—a glaring omission for rabbis intent on stamping out this heretical movement. Nevertheless, their use of the *Birkath ha-Minim* (in whatever form) and the spread of negative gossip about Jesus (whether official or not) resulted in the expulsion and voluntary exclusion of Jewish Christians from some of the synagogues (Jn 9:22, 16:2). But, as Shaye J. D. Cohen points out, these actions did not mean that all Jews followed suit.

Synagogues were not beholden to any central body; every community ran its synagogue in its own way. Even if the rabbis wished to expel Christians from all the synagogues of the empire, they lacked the power and the authority to do so. Furthermore, although by the fourth century the "benediction against heretics" was directed against Christians or some Jewish-Christian sects, its original version was a generic denunciation of all heretics. The intent was not to single out Christians or any other specific group, but to proclaim the end to sectarianism.[32]

In other words, the rabbis were more than willing to listen to and debate different points of view (including those of Jews who accepted Jesus as the Christ), but they would not permit factions, which many of them believed had precipitated the war with Rome. Be that as it may, the ongoing tensions between Jews and Jewish Christians in the synagogues and sporadic expulsions prompted a harsh response from the Christian side.

As noted at the beginning of the chapter, the New Testament writings were an early source for anti-Jewish invective, but early Christian writers also generated sermons, dialogues, treatises, and other texts that were not included in the canon. In the book of Barnabas (130 CE), for example, the author argues that the Jews were so sinful that they permanently lost their covenant with God (4:6-8). Disgusted with their idolatry and wickedness, God transferred the promises he made to Abraham to Christians through the suffering Messiah—an event foreshadowed in the Old Testament through the words and deeds of Moses and the prophets (Barn 7–10, 15).

In the Gospel of Peter (written between 70 and 160 CE), the pseudonymous author has the Jews condemn themselves for killing Jesus, claiming that after the crucifixion "the Jews, the elders, and the priests realized how much evil they had done to themselves and began beating their breast, saying 'Woe to us because of our sins. The judgment and the end of Jerusalem are near'" (v. 25).[33] This gospel voices the common Christian belief that God permitted the Romans to destroy Jerusalem and the Temple as fitting punishments for deicide.

Returning to the New Testament, the Gospel of John (90–120 CE) is even more provocative because it brings Jesus into the fight. When Jewish leaders affirm that they are descendants of Abraham and thus already have God's truth, Jesus rejects them, claiming that their murderous intentions toward him make them children of Satan.

> They answered him, "Abraham is our father." Jesus said to them, "If you were Abraham's children, you would be doing what Abraham did, but now you are trying to kill me, a man who has told you the truth that I heard from God. This is not what Abraham did. You are indeed doing what your father does." They said to him, "We are not illegitimate children; we have one father, God himself." Jesus said to them, "If God were your Father, you would love me, for I came from God and now I am here. I did not come on my own, but he sent me. Why do you not understand what I say? It is because you cannot accept my word. You are from your father the devil, and you choose to do your father's desires. He was a murderer from the beginning and does not stand in the truth, because there is no truth in him. When he lies, he speaks according to his lies. But because I tell the truth, you do not believe me. Which of you convicts me of sin? If I tell the truth, why do you not believe me? Whoever is from God hears the words of God. The reason you do not hear them is that you are not from God." (Jn 8:39-47)

The "Christ-killer" accusation voiced in these and other early Christian writings are considered by many scholars to be the turning point in the conflict between Christians and Jews. As Thomas A. Idinopulos and Roy Bowen Ward explain, [the Christ-killer accusation] signals the later, more destructive stage of the church's mission: not merely to refute the theological claims of the synagogue, but to drive out and punish all those who resist the message of Jesus Christ and continue to practice Jewish religion.... The "seed of contempt" planted in the later first century took root during two hundred years of church-synagogue rivalry and came to poisonous flower during the fourth century when the essentially anti-Semitic view that the Jewish people are forever cursed by God for their crime of deicide was widely propagated. But, as we see it, neither the early anti-Judaic polemic, nor its later anti-Semitic turn...appears to be in this three hundred years' development, some sort of necessary, negative translation of the church's confession of the Messiahship of Jesus. What we discern in the evidence is that with the deicide charge the church introduced a new, more potent weapon in its ongoing, increasingly bloody struggle with the synagogue.[34]

The authors are clearly attempting to counter the charge that Christian claims about Jesus are inherently anti-Semitic; nevertheless, they also acknowledge that as the first centuries passed, "anti-Judaism was converted into a sword against Jewish communities,"[35] forming the basis for anti-Jewish legislation (both in the church and in the Roman state), and for Christian anti-Semitism, the effects of which continue to poison Jewish-Christian relations today.

Conclusion

Tracing the history between the two Testaments is a grim but necessary journey because it helps us understand the development of Palestinian Judaism, the reasons for Jewish-Christian animus, and its subsequent influence on the Jesus movement and on early Christian writers. It is important, for example, to understand and appreciate the formidable obstacles the Jewish people faced upon their return to Jerusalem and how their faith sustained them in their ongoing struggle for survival. Rather than compromise or renounce their beliefs, many Jews endured humiliation, excruciating torture, and death at the hands of the Greeks and Romans. Central to their faith was the Mosaic Law, which grounded their national identity and structured the Jewish way of life. As Judaism developed, the people increasingly understood themselves as a community that was committed to the proper interpretation and application of God's Law.

The people's sense of identity and whole-hearted commitment to the Law ultimately led to the emergence of different factions within Judaism. As is often the case with internal conflicts, each group believed it was following the "true" Judaism and was highly critical of other interpretations and points of view. Despite their disagreements, most Jewish leaders were men of deep faith who were determined to maintain and protect their Jewish heritage—even from their fellow Jews! Although they were portrayed as hypocritical villains in the gospels, we can understand now why the Pharisees, the Sadducees, and the scribes were so strongly opposed to Jesus. In their eyes, his blasphemous claims to authority and his unorthodox ministry challenged traditional teachings and practice. We can also understand why the Jewish leadership would reject the disciples' claim that the crucified Jesus was their long-awaited Messiah. In the view of these leaders, such a radical reinterpretation of the Messiah figure was a literal negation of their religion.

On the other hand, we can also see that Jesus' ministry was responding to a serious problem within Judaism. Among the different "Judaisms" that appeared in first-century Palestine, there was something about this young man's teaching that struck a chord among the people. The success of his ministry and the missionary inroads of the early church suggest that many ordinary Jews were feeling alienated from their leaders and unfulfilled in their faith and were searching for some form of spiritual renewal.

Understanding the history between the Testaments also illuminates the anti-Jewish bias of early Christian writings, which were produced with specific purposes in mind; namely, to persuade both Jews and Gentiles that Jesus of Nazareth was the Christ and to articulate the significance of his life, death, and resurrection for their salvation. To make their case, Christian writers not only reinterpreted central concepts in Jewish theology but also vilified Jews and their leaders who opposed Jesus on religious grounds. This "no-holds-barred" approach was unjust and tragic, but these early Christians clearly believed it was theologically justified and necessary for the survival and growth of their fledgling faith. From a biblical perspective, it could be argued that both Christians and Jews were following the harsh example set by Moses against the golden calf idolaters and by Israel's prophets against Canaanite religious practices. In all these cases, the exclusion of and violence against "the other" was sanctioned for the sake of communal survival.

Ultimately, the fear and misunderstanding that led to synagogue expulsions, the Christ-killer accusation, and countless other abuses are the sinful products of a religious family feud that has alienated and harmed countless generations and that shows no signs of letting up. The next two chapters will offer a tentative step toward resolution—or at least peaceful co-existence—through a theocentric reading of Matthew's gospel, Paul's letter to the Galatians, and key passages in Romans. These readings will not only challenge some of the claims that stoked Jewish-Christian hatred, but will illuminate established pedagogical patterns that affirm God's ethical intentions for all human beings, thus offering important guidance for the interpretation and use of the Bible as a spiritual and moral source and for furthering interfaith dialogue.

Questions for Reflection and Discussion

1. For religious traditions to thrive there must be a creative tension and balance between innovation and tradition. If the tension breaks to one side or the other, the result can be the formation of factions, a schism, or a dead

tradition. Schism is eventually what happened within Judaism when God introduced the prophet-Messiah to his people. In your view, did God have schism in mind or did human beings misinterpret the divine intention? Does God think in "either-or" terms or is that an all-too-human tendency? How might Jews and Christians overcome the destructive effects of the break without compromising their own religious identities?

2. In conquering Judah, the Babylonian strategy was one of cultural assimilation. The Babylonians believed the exiles would eventually adopt Babylonian culture and worship Babylonian gods. The Greeks followed a similar strategy, but their program of Hellenization was even more effective and more brutal in its implementation. Consider examples of cultural assimilation in the modern world. In times of war or peace, is imposing one culture on another ever justified? How should different cultures engage each other, particularly in respect to religion?

3. The New Testament texts focus almost exclusively on the person, work, and mission of Jesus of Nazareth, making Christianity a christocentric religion. How might a more theocentric perspective alleviate the tensions between Judaism and Christianity? Would a God-centered Christianity alter or compromise Christian understandings of Jesus Christ?

Recommended Reading

Duling, Dennis C., and Norman Perrin. *The New Testament: Proclamation and Parenesis, Myth and History.* 3rd ed. Fort Worth: Harcourt Brace & Company, 1994. A scholarly introduction to the New Testament that offers detailed historical and exegetical analyses of New Testament texts.

Flannery, Edward H. *The Anguish of the Jews: Twenty-three Centuries of Antisemitism.* New York/Mahwah, NJ: Paulist Press, 1985. A concise treatment of the roots of Christian anti-Jewish bias and anti-Semitism, the anti-Jewish writings of the church fathers, and the systematic abuse of the Jews over the centuries.

Fredriksen, Paula, and Adele Reinhartz, eds. *Jesus, Judaism, and Christian Anti-Judaism: Reading the New Testament after the Holocaust.* Louisville: Westminster John Knox Press, 2002. An informative collection of essays that explore anti-Judaism in the early church and New Testament texts.

7

THE GIFT OF THE GOSPEL
Who Do People Say That I Am?

W ho do people say that I am?" is the central question Jesus of
Nazareth poses in the gospels. The answer to the question depends upon the religious perspective of the respondent. For the
majority of first-century Palestinian Jews who actually knew about Jesus,
he was a disgraced prophet and itinerant preacher executed by the Romans
for his blasphemous statements and unorthodox behavior. For his early
followers, Jesus was the suffering Messiah and Savior, whose death and
resurrection marked a new and definitive stage in God's divine plan. The
differences in perception could not be more stark or the consequences
more tragic, for, whether by accident or design, the figure of Jesus drew a
theological line in the sand that both groups dared not cross. And how
could they? Jews could no more surrender their religious heritage and identity for a dead Messiah than Christians could deny the revelation and reality of the empty tomb. As noted in the previous chapter, the expulsion of
Jewish Christians from some synagogues and the Christ-killer accusation
were just two of the unfortunate products of this fearful and divisive either-
or thinking.

Nearly two thousand years later, "Who do people say that I am?" is a
question that still haunts Jewish-Christian relations, perpetuating an animus between two traditions that profess to worship the same God. Surely
this is not God's intention, yet both sides seem determined to remain within
their own theological constructions, unwilling or unable to break the impasse. But what if the response developed by first-century Jews and Christians was partial or perhaps even flawed? What if their theological biases
blinded them to the possibility that God's salvific initiative in Jesus might
take multiple forms; that is to say, at one moment in time God would call
the prophet, Jesus, to show his chosen people the path to true righteousness
under the Mosaic Law, then, at another moment in time, God would raise
his dead prophet and transform him into a concrete symbol of universal salvation—an initiative first introduced in Isaiah and extended in the
prophetic mission and sacrificial death of Jesus. In this configuration, the
dual roles of Jewish prophet and Christian Messiah are held in tension, extending their salvific power to both groups, without privileging one over the
other. The "either-or" of the Jewish-Christian impasse is overcome by the
"both-and" of God's prophet-Messiah.

The next two chapters of this book will make the case for such a possibility through a reading of Matthew's gospel, Paul's letter to the Galatians,
and some key passages in Romans. Tracing God's activities within these
texts will reveal intertextual connections and patterns between the Old and
New Testaments that establish the multivalent character of God's intentions
in Jesus. This chapter will focus on Jesus as God's prophet in Matthew's
gospel; the next chapter will explore Jesus as Messiah in Paul's writings.

Jesus as Jewish Prophet in the Gospel of Matthew

Clarifying the role of Jesus as Jewish prophet is important not only theologically but ethically as well. Jesus' teachings in the Sermon on the Mount (Mt
5:1–7:27) are acknowledged by most Christians as the ethical centerpiece of
his ministry. Among the sermon's most distinctive and oft-quoted features
are the "hard sayings" in which Jesus commands his disciples to "turn the
other cheek," and to "love your enemies and pray for those who persecute
you" (Mt 5:44). For many Christian theologians, ethicists, and laypersons,
such teachings are a blueprint for a new morality that supersedes the alleged
legalism of the Torah and that distinguishes Christian ethics from moral philosophy and from other forms of religious ethics. While proponents of this
view seek to establish and protect the distinctiveness of Christian ethics—
which is a legitimate and worthy goal—the exclusivist tendencies of this
reading also reinforce the either-or thinking that continues to divide the Jewish and Christian traditions.[1] A theocentric reading, which focuses on God's
pedagogical intention in the life and work of Jesus, opens up new possibilities for Jewish-Christian dialogue because it presumes that the Galilean
prophet and teacher has something vitally important to say to both Jews and
Christians without any supersessionist strings attached.

The validity of our reading rests to a great extent on whether we can distinguish the intentions of the Jesus of history (the Galilean prophet) from the
Christ of faith (the Messiah and Savior)—a tricky bit of business, since the
anti-Jewish bias of the gospels tends to downplay his prophetic identity in
favor of his messianic role. Since the gospels of Matthew, Mark, and Luke
share similar sources, it is important that we first consider how the gospels
were formed, what sources were used, and what biblical scholars have learned
about the mission of the historical Jesus. We shall then explore the historical
background and situation of the writer of Matthew and consider what issues
influenced and shaped his attitude toward the Jews and his depiction of Jesus.

Once the parameters for our exegetical analysis are established, we
shall read through major portions of the gospel from a theocentric perspective, examining Yahweh's activities in the narrative and his relationship
with the Galilean prophet. Attention will focus on Jesus' early ministry and
his teachings in the Sermon on the Mount, the Transfiguration, and his final
commission to the disciples. Finally, the chapter will revisit Jesus' question
regarding his identity, offering insights from our study that could be used to
help overcome the impasse between Jews and Christians.

The Formation of the Christian Gospels

Like the Old Testament, the Christian gospels are a patchwork of sources written at different times and places and using various literary styles. Isolating the prophet Jesus from within any of the gospels is notoriously difficult because the texts combine historical events with liberal doses of theology and literary artistry. The mixed nature of the gospels is the result of a revelatory process that began with Jesus' death and continued on for decades afterward. Michael J. McClymond describes the likely process by which his followers transformed the Jesus of history into the Christ of faith.

> To understand the Gospels it may be helpful to envision the immediate aftermath of the crucifixion. After Jesus' death his followers fled or hid, but their hopes were renewed when they had a vision of him alive again. Convinced that the kingdom Jesus predicted would soon arrive in full force, they waited in Jerusalem and sought to convince others that Jesus was the promised Messiah. Given their situation, it is unlikely that they sat down together at this early stage, collectively ransacked their memories, and in this sort of deliberate fashion composed a biography of Jesus. Since they expected that he would soon be among them, the question of how best to preserve the knowledge of his life for future generations was probably not in their minds. Yet, even at this earliest stage, while trying to communicate their own convictions regarding Jesus to others, they must have often told stories of Jesus' actions and words. It is likely that these stories were not initially written down, but circulated for some time in oral form. Thus the sayings and doings of Jesus were preserved, though perhaps in a somewhat different context than that of Jesus' own life, namely, in the context of the teaching and practice of the earliest Christian communities. As time passed, and as Jesus' expected return did not occur, the traditions about Jesus were then put into written form.[2]

Like all oral stories, the traditions about Jesus evolved in the telling, with each storyteller editing and no doubt embellishing the accounts to entertain, inspire, and challenge his (or her) audience. Eventually, the many stories about Jesus were written down, collected, and crafted into chronological narratives that would later bear the names of Matthew, Mark, and Luke. While the Gospel of John no doubt followed a similar process, it is the quintessential odd duck of the group; its origins and formation are so unique that it is always considered separately.

The first gospel presented in the New Testament is the Gospel of Matthew, but despite its pride of place, it was not the first written. Most scholars agree that Mark's gospel was the first. An anonymous author completed the work between 66 and 70 CE, during the Jewish Revolt against Rome. While Mark may have been the first Christian writer to craft a gospel, he did not invent the word. The term "gospel" is the translation of the Greek *euangelion*, meaning "good news." Stephen L. Harris explains its origin:

> In the Greek-speaking world of New Testament times, *euangelion* commonly was used to denote public proclamations about the Roman emperor. The "good news" of the emperor's military victories, welfare policies, or elevation to the status of a god were typical examples of Roman political "evangelizing." Paul uses *euangelion* to describe his message about salvation through Jesus Christ. Matthew also employs it to denote Jesus' oral teaching (Mt 4:23; 9:35; 24:14; 26:13). Mark, however, is apparently the first to use *euangelion* to describe a written work about Jesus' life.[3]

Given the many stories about Jesus that were circulating among the faith communities, the obvious question is, Why did Mark find it necessary to construct a gospel of Jesus' life? As McClymond notes, one of the primary reasons was practical. Jesus was executed by the Romans in the early 30s CE. As the years passed and Jesus did not return to inaugurate God's kingdom, there was a move among the faithful to preserve the traditions. This move was not only for the sake of future generations but for accuracy's sake as well. The apostles and disciples who had known and worked with Jesus were either dead or dying off. Soon there would be no one left with first-hand knowledge to verify the authenticity of the many stories about Jesus that were circulating among the faithful.

Another reason for composing a gospel was to address the situation in the early faith communities. Initially, the Jesus movement was very small and its membership was almost exclusively Jewish, but Paul's missionary journeys to the Gentiles (45–58 CE) quickly brought non-Jews into the fold in significant numbers. Since they had no official meeting place (the synagogues were increasingly off-limits), they met in members' homes. These early "house churches," which were modeled after the synagogues, offered the faithful a place to gather, commune, and worship. Typically they would repeat oral traditions about Jesus or read aloud from written traditions about him. They would also share a communal meal, baptize new converts, read and discuss scripture, sing hymns, receive lessons in the faith, and participate in other cultic practices. During this time, the only common text most communities had was the Septuagint, a Greek translation of the Old Testament. The New Testament we know today was decades away from composition and centuries away from canonization, so the faithful had little to guide them in their understanding of the life and work of Jesus. Even if they were fortunate enough to have access to copies of Paul's letters, which were written between 50 and 60 CE, they would find that the apostle rarely mentioned Jesus' earthly ministry. He was more concerned with articulating the significance of Jesus' death and resurrection for salvation. Consequently, the people's understanding of Jesus was fragmentary at best. Their "Jesus" was defined largely by the materials they had managed to collect, preserve, and study. Moreover, as new converts joined the movement, they were understandably curious about Jesus. Where was he born? Did he have a family? Why did he suffer? What events led to his death? Mark's gospel provided much-needed answers to these questions, offering the faithful a detailed portrait of Jesus that revealed the theological significance of his entire life, from baptism to resurrection.

The Synoptic Gospels and Their Sources

Together the gospels of Mark (66–70 CE), Matthew (85–90 CE), and Luke (85–90 CE) are called the synoptic gospels (Gr. *synoptikos*, "seen together") because when placed side-by-side, they show striking similarities, as well as substantive differences. For example, all three gospels present seed parables (Mk 4:30-32; Mt 13:31-32; Lk 13:18-19) and miraculous healings (Mk 3:1-6; Mt 12:9-14; Lk 6:6-11) that are nearly identical in phrasing. In contrast, only Matthew and Luke have infancy narratives, and they bear little resemblance to each other.

Over the years biblical scholars have offered a variety of theories to explain the interrelationships among the three. Our study will adopt the Two-Source Theory, which has been and continues to be the prevailing explanation. Proponents of the theory argue that Mark's gospel was written first and that the authors of Matthew and Luke used Mark as a primary source and model for their gospels. In addition to Mark, they also used their own materials ("Special M" and "Special L") and another source called the "Q" document (shorthand for *Quelle*, the German word for "source"). Although there are no extant copies of Q, biblical scholars have discerned, through painstaking textual analysis, the document's probable date and content. Written between 50 and 70 CE, Q was a sayings gospel that emphasized Jesus' teachings and his continuity with Israel's prophetic tradition. The Beatitudes, the "hard sayings" in the Sermon on the Mount, and the Lord's Prayer, for example, are materials not found in Mark but present with some variation in both Matthew and Luke. Scholars attribute these materials to Q.[4]

While the "theological biographies" of Mark, Matthew, and Luke share many of the same traditions about Jesus, each of the gospel writers shaped the materials to produce a unique gospel that addressed the issues and concerns of his own particular community. The result is a series of complex and varied portraits of Jesus that are several steps removed from the Galilean prophet who lived, worked, and died in first-century Judea.

The Search for the Historical Jesus

The patchwork nature of the gospels complicates our attempt to isolate the Galilean prophet within Matthew's gospel because there is much disagreement among scholars about what Jesus actually said and did. The search for the historical Jesus is a fascinating and complex academic odyssey that first came to the world's attention with the publication of Albert Schweitzer's

Quest of the Historical Jesus in 1906. A review of the scholarship—which is considerable—cannot detain us here; suffice it to say that over the last several decades biblical exegetes and other specialists have debated over which biblical materials originated with the historical Jesus and which were later additions introduced by his followers and shaped by the creative genius of the gospel writers.[5] While the debates continue, some progress has been made. Harris offers an excellent summary of how many scholars understand the Galilean prophet, particularly in relation to his depiction in the gospels.

> Scholars in large part agree that the historical Jesus taught about God's kingdom (whatever his precise meaning by the phrase), but most question the belief that he taught about himself. Although he seems to have perceived the world and his mission from the vantage point of someone who holds a peculiarly close relationship to God, he is not believed to have called himself Christ, Son of God, or the Holy One of Israel. All these honorific titles, scholars believe, were bestowed on him posthumously by a community that—in retrospect—recognized him as Israel's Messiah and God's chief agent, the means by which the Deity reconciles humanity to himself. In telling Jesus' story so that readers could understand his true significance, it was natural for Gospel writers to apply titles such as Christ and Son of God to the historical figure. In the Evangelists' view, they could not write the truth about who Jesus was unless they presented him in the light of his resurrection and glorification. The Galilean prophet and teacher who had challenged the world's norms in the name of a radical egalitarianism for all God's children was—by his continuing life in the believing community—vindicated as divine, the Wisdom and love of God made flesh.[6]

As Harris notes, most scholars agree that the kingdom was one of the central teachings of Jesus. His understanding of the kingdom was influenced to some extent by his early association with John the Baptist, a Jewish prophet and leader of a sectarian baptizing movement that was active in the wilderness of Judea and at the Jordan River. For both prophets, the kingdom of God served as a theological paradigm and organizing principle for their ministries.

The Kingdom of God

One question that continues to intrigue scholars is what John and Jesus meant by the kingdom. Was it a place or an idea? Was it a present reality or a future one? Was it an apocalyptic term or a spiritual one? Did it represent an escape from the suffering of the present life or did it denote a transformation of the material world? As a theological concept, the kingdom of God had its roots in Jewish apocalyptic eschatology.

As detailed in the previous chapter, many first-century Jews ascribed to the belief that Yahweh would again intervene in human history in a direct, dramatic, and final way. At the eschaton, God and his angelic armies (often aided by a warrior Messiah) would destroy Satan and his forces, vindicate the faithful, and establish a new heaven and a new earth. John's "fire and brimstone" brand of preaching reflected this belief. For the Baptist, the kingdom was a future reality that would soon break in and overthrow the sin and corruption of the present age. His urgent and repeated calls for repentance and baptismal cleansing promised the people forgiveness and the hope of inclusion in God's future kingdom—as long as their repentance and conversion were genuine.

While Jesus agreed with John's basic eschatological message of repentance and reform, he had a different conception of God's kingdom. He envisioned the kingdom as a timeless, all-encompassing reality with both present and future dimensions. For Jesus, the presence of the kingdom was revealed in his mission and in the work of his disciples, yet their efforts were only a hint of what was to come, for the kingdom would soon achieve its fullest and most complete expression at the eschaton, when God's mighty rule would transform both heaven and earth. Jesus' teachings on the nature of the kingdom (Mk 4:1-34; Mt 13:44-50; Lk 16:19-31), his instruction on obedience to God's will (Mk 7:1-23; Mt 5:17-48; Lk 16:16-18, 17:7-10), the radical demands of discipleship (Mk 10:17-31; Mt 6:19-34, 10:16-31; Lk 12:13-21, 14:25-33) and his warnings of coming judgment (Mk 13:14-37; Mt 11:20-25; Lk 13:22-30, 17:11-37), acquired their meaning and significance within this overarching kingdom theology.

The kingdom theologies of John and Jesus are not without some mention of a redeemer figure. In all three gospels, John proclaims the coming of a deliverer: "The one who is more powerful than I is coming after me; I am not worthy to stoop down and untie the thong of his sandals" (Mk 1:7; Mt 3:11; Lk 3:16). Jesus also makes frequent reference to the "Son of Man," an eschatological figure found in the book of Daniel (Dan 7:14), as well as in Ezekiel (Ezek 2:1), Job (Job 25:6), and other Jewish apocalyptic literature (1 Enoch 69; 4 Ezra 13:1-11).

His use of the title is perplexing and has generated much debate among scholars. In some passages, Jesus refers to the Son of Man as a future cosmic judge who will soon act on God's behalf to punish the wicked and gather the elect (Mk 13:26-27; Mt 24:30-31; Lk 21:25-36). In other passages, he identifies himself as this redeemer figure, telling his disciples that the Son of Man must suffer and die before attaining power and glory (Mk 8:31, 14:62; Mt 17:12; Lk 9:22). While most scholars agree that Jesus probably used the title in his preaching, they continue to debate its use in the gospels. Did Jesus actually use the title as a self-designation or did the early church change the usage to link the Son of Man to the crucified and risen Christ? Whatever the case, it seems likely that, as a prophet of God, Jesus understood the Son of Man figure as a potent symbol of God's coming kingdom—a symbol that was recognized and eagerly embraced by his Jewish audience.

Although Jesus never specifies when the kingdom will come, the urgency of his preaching suggests that he believed it would arrive during his lifetime. As E. P. Sanders explains,

[i]n Jesus' view, the kingdom of God existed in heaven, and individuals would enter it on death (e.g., Mk 9:47). God's power was in some respects omni-present, and Jesus may have seen "the kingdom" in the sense of God's presence as especially evident in his own words and deeds. But Jesus was an eschatologist: in the future, the kingdom would *come to earth* in its full power and glory, at which time God's will would be done "on earth as it is in heaven" (Mt 6:10). Jesus died before this expectation was fulfilled, and this, coupled with the resurrection appearances, led his followers to expect his return in the near future, bringing in the kingdom and ruling in God's stead. The fact that the early Christian movement expected the kingdom to arrive in the very near future is one of the strongest indications that this had been Jesus' own expectation during his lifetime.[7]

Given all the available evidence, it thus seems likely that the historical Jesus understood himself as a Jewish prophet and teacher whose mission was to announce the coming of God's kingdom and to call his people back to God and their covenant obligations, thus setting the stage for the eschaton and the full realization of the kingdom. The historical Jesus, as God's chosen prophet, was wholly committed to this practical and very earthly task. As McClymond, Harris, and Saunders all note, the Christ of faith would emerge only *after* the Easter event, after his followers had had the time to reflect on all that had happened and to express the meaning of the events for themselves and for their faith communities. This blending of historical and theological elements is clearly at work in Matthew's gospel.

Matthew, the Matthean Community, and the Jews

Matthew's gospel is the only one to use the term "church" (Gk. *ekklesia*), or to have Jesus found the church during his earthly ministry (16:13-20). These unique characteristics may well account for Matthew's placement as the first gospel in the New Testament canon. Whatever the case, the scholarly consensus is that the unknown author of the gospel (whom we shall continue to call "Matthew" for simplicity's sake) was an educated Jewish Christian who had a thorough knowledge of the Old Testament.[8] Most scholars believe he composed his gospel in or around the city of Antioch in Syria between 85 and 90 CE.

Antioch was a thriving commercial and cultural center of the Greco-Roman world, strategically located on the trade routes between Asia Minor and Syria-Palestine. In the first century, the city's population numbered from 150,000 to 200,000, with a large and prosperous Jewish population that welcomed non-Jews into their religious ceremonies. The church in Antioch, which was founded in the late 30s CE, was a small, mixed Jewish-Gentile community (Gentiles were definitely in the minority) that was experiencing a number of external and internal pressures. After the horrors of the Jewish Revolt (66–70 CE), the church found itself increasingly at odds with the local synagogues, which were influenced by the Yavneh rabbis' reformulation of Judaism (although it should be noted that the gospel was written before the institution of the *Birkath ha-Minim*). Matthew's harsh criticism of the Jewish leadership and the people (Mt 3:7-10, 6:1-6, 15:1-9, 23, 28:11-15) reflects a community at odds with many of the Jews of Antioch, who rejected Christian claims about Jesus. One of the most infamous attacks takes place in the trial scene with Pontius Pilate: "So when Pilate saw that he could do nothing, but rather that a riot was beginning, he took some water and washed his hands before the crowd, saying, 'I am innocent of this man's blood; see to it yourselves.' Then the people as a whole answered, 'His blood be on us and on our children!' So he released Barabbas for them; and after flogging Jesus, he handed him over to be crucified" (Mt 27:24-26).

This is strong stuff. Pilate's hand-washing is a Matthean addition to Mark's account that appears to shift the blame for Jesus' death from the Romans to the Jews and to all their descendants.[9] The "blood guilt" of future generations is a punishment not found in the other gospels, although all of them blame the Jews for the death of Jesus (Mk 15:11-15; Lk 23:1-25; 18:28-40).

In some instances, the invective is voiced by Jesus himself, as in one of the gospel's famous "woes":

> Woe to you scribes and Pharisees, hypocrites! For you clean the outside of the cup and of the plate, but inside they are full of greed and self-indulgence. You blind Pharisee! First clean the inside of the cup so that the outside also may become clean. Woe to you, scribes and Pharisees, hypocrites! For you are like whitewashed tombs, which on the outside look beautiful, but inside they are full of the bones of the dead and of all kinds of filth. So you also on the outside look righteous to others, but inside you are full of hypocrisy and lawlessness." (Mt 23:25-28)

The number and intensity of these kinds of attacks are an indication of just how strained Jewish-Christian relations had become in Antioch, but Warren Carter makes the important point that the conflict reflected in Matthew's gospel was not between Jews and Gentile Christians; rather, it was among the Jews of Antioch, some of whom confessed Jesus as the Messiah.

> Crucial to understanding the situation of Matthew's (largely) Jewish community committed to Jesus, is the recognition that it is involved in a local fight within a synagogue over its place in a common tradition. They share the same scriptural traditions. They share the same focus on divine presence, with knowing the divine will, with encountering divine favor and forgiveness, with worship, with living faithfully. Yet along with this common history, traditions, relationships, and practices is ground which divides—namely, the claims that Jesus occupies a central role in those traditions, that he interprets them definitively, and that he manifests God's saving presence and empire. The synagogue of origin

increasingly rejects these claims and practices and does not see any pre-eminent place for Jesus. Matthew's audience is thus a Jewish group in tension with a synagogue community yet shaped by and committed to shared Jewish traditions.[10]

This means that the anti-Jewish bias of Matthew's gospel was very local and very limited. The polemical nature of the attacks was never intended to condemn all Jews and Judaism per se; rather, it was intended to undercut the influence of other Jewish leaders and teachers in Antioch and to help Matthew's audience make sense of their past and future as a marginalized community within Judaism and the Roman Empire.

Within the church itself, the mixed Jewish-Gentile membership led to strong disagreements about the relevance of the Law for the community's way of life—an issue that had been dramatically debated in Antioch years earlier by Peter and Paul (Gal 2:11-14). Apparently, the issue had not been resolved to everyone's satisfaction. Gentile Christians still questioned the necessity of observance of the Mosaic Law, but Matthew clearly believed the Jesus movement was an authentic Jewish movement and that the teachings of Jesus were the natural outgrowth of Torah Judaism. Stephen L. Harris summarizes Matthew's response to the conflict:

> Some Jewish Christians demanded that all Gentile converts to the new faith keep the entire Mosaic Law or at least undergo circumcisions (Acts 15:1-6; Gal 6:11-16). Matthew does not mention circumcision, but he insists that the Mosaic Torah is binding on believers (5:17-20). In his view, Christian are to continue such Jewish practices as fasting (6:16-18), regular prayer (6:5-6), charitable giving (6:2), and formal sacrifices (5:23). His account also implies that Mosaic purity laws, forbidding certain foods, apply to his community.[11]

Matthew's emphasis on observance of the Mosaic Law indicates his desire to maintain a strong connection with Judaism; however, his silence on the issue of circumcision—a notoriously touchy subject for potential Gentile converts—may suggest an attempt at compromise between Jewish Christians who demanded obedience to the entire Mosaic Law and Gentile Christians who were disinclined to follow it at all.

Given these external and internal pressures, the need for ecclesial guidance was critical. Several decades had passed since the death of Jesus and the Messiah was nowhere in sight. The continued survival of the church depended upon establishing doctrines, institutional structures, and religious and ethical norms that could be maintained over time. Matthew's gospel provided all of these things and more.

Central to Matthew's ecclesial project was establishing Jesus as Israel's true Messiah and authoritative interpreter and teacher of the Mosaic Law. Matthew believed that Jesus was the new revelation of God and that Jesus' teachings and instructions to the disciples should serve as the standard for the new community's belief and practice. To make his case, Matthew followed the basic narrative structure of Mark but added materials from Q and Special M to bolster his claims about the person and mission of Jesus. Matthew also shaped the gospel to coincide with his understanding of salvation history, dividing the narrative into two distinct epochs. Jack Dean Kingsbury explains:

> There is the "time of Israel," which is preparatory to and prophetic of the coming of the Messiah; and there is the "time of Jesus (Messiah, Lord, and son of Man)," in which the time of Israel finds its fulfillment and which, from the vantage point of Matthew's day, extends from the beginning of the ministry of John and of Jesus (past) through post-Easter times (present) to the coming consummation of the age (future). In Mt's scheme of history, one does not, strictly speaking, find any such epoch as the "time of the Church," for this "time" is subsumed under the "last days" inaugurated by John and Jesus.[12]

Within this overarching structure, Matthew integrates fives major discourses, which introduce the revelation of a new Torah. As a literary whole, the gospel thus takes the following form:

Chapters 1–2	Prologue: Infancy Narrative
Chapters 3–4	Narrative: Baptism by John; temptation by Satan; beginning of Galilean ministry
Chapters 5–7	*First Discourse:* Sermon on the Mount
Chapters 8–9	Narrative: Acts of power (ten miracle stories)
Chapter 10	*Second Discourse:* Mission of the Twelve
Chapters 11–12	Narrative: Jesus and John the Baptist; growing opposition from Jewish authorities
Chapter 13	*Third Discourse:* Teaching in Parables
Chapters 14–17	Narrative: Miracle stories; rejection in Nazareth; death of John the Baptist; conflicts with Jewish authorities; Peter's confession at Caesarea Philippi; the Transfiguration
Chapter 18	*Fourth Discourse:* Instructions on Community Order in the Church
Chapters 19–23	Narrative: Journey to Jerusalem; confrontation in the Temple; debates with Jewish leaders
Chapters 24–25	*Fifth Discourse:* Warnings of Final Judgment
Chapters 26–27	Narrative: Passion story
Chapter 28	Epilogue: The Resurrection; the Great Commission

While some scholars disagree with the five-book structure, it is a persuasive reading, particularly given Matthew's historical situation and his ecclesial and theological agendas.

Dennis C. Duling and Norman Perrin have made the observation that for Matthew, "the new revelation fulfills, yet supersedes, the old. Perhaps he imagines that, as Moses was thought to have taught the old Torah, Jesus is thought to have taught the new Torah. In any case, this structure emphasizes Jesus as *the* teacher."[13] Given Matthew's affinity for the Torah and his linear understanding of salvation history, these statements may very well reflect his thinking, but in pitting the new revelation against the old, and in having the Jewish people condemn themselves for killing the Christ, Matthew's fight with the Jews of Antioch would soon move beyond the borders of Syria, providing ample ammunition for early supersessionists who were determined to place Judaism and all Jews in a subservient position, both theologically and socially.

Whether Matthew shared such goals is anyone's guess, but we should not assume that because he made anti-Jewish statements against local leaders his gospel is inherently and irredeemably corrupt. On the contrary, a theocentric reading of Matthew's gospel may well provide the ground for a possible rapprochement between Jews and Christians because it presumes that Jesus—who was Yahweh's prophet before he was recognized as the Christ—offers something vitally important to both groups.

Our search for common ground will focus on God's activity in the narrative and his relationship with his prophet, Jesus of Nazareth. Reading the gospel through the "big picture" of the canon will help us see beyond the anti-Jewish bias of Matthew's gospel and discover how the teachings of the prophet contribute to the pedagogical program that God established in the Old Testament and extend into the New Testament.

Matthew's Theocentric Gospel of the Church

While the narrative gap between the two Testaments is not fatal to the story, it does raise questions about Yahweh's activity that require some reasonable speculation. What was God doing during the years between the reading of the Pentateuch by the priest, Ezra (fifth century BCE) and the birth of Jesus (4–6 CE)? The noticeable lack of divine intervention (at least in the Christian canonical books) suggests that God was relatively satisfied with (or at least not seriously alarmed about) the people's religious and ethical progress. Ezra had succeeded in restoring the foundations of Yahwism in Judea. Under his strict guidance, the old temptation of pagan cults was effectively eliminated and the Law had become the motive force and normative standard for every aspect of Jewish life. As John Bright explains,

> [t]he canonizing of the law gave to Judaism a norm far more absolute and tangible than anything old Israel had known. Since God's commandments were stated in the law once and for all, with eternal valid-

ity, his will for every situation was to be determined from it; other means to that end were overlaid or suppressed. This doubtless explains why prophecy gradually ceased, for the law had, in fact, usurped its function and rendered it superfluous. Though the prophets of old were revered, and their words accorded authority, the law actually left no place for a free prophetic statement of the divine will. What prophecy there still was would take the form of pseudepigrapha (i.e., prophecies issued under the names of heroes of the distant past). Though Jews might hope for the time when prophets would appear once more (1 Macc 4:46; 14:41), they were keenly aware that the age of prophecy had ended...to learn the divine will one must consult the Book of the Law.[14]

The Mosaic Law had indeed enabled the Jews to maintain their cultural and religious identity and survive the cruel assaults of Antiochus IV, the many abuses of Rome, and the splintering of Judaism into competing factions. Nevertheless, something happened in those intervening years that prompted Yahweh to send other prophets to act as his intermediaries and proclaimers of his word. These prophets, of course, were John the Baptist and Jesus of Nazareth. As pious Jews, they felt compelled to speak out in God's name, but why were their missions necessary? What had changed within Judaism that required these strong prophetic voices? Matthew provides some clues in the introductory chapters of the gospel.

The first two chapters constitute a prologue that establishes Jesus' messianic credentials. Using his own materials (Special M), Matthew opens with a genealogy (a time-honored biblical tactic) that traces Jesus' connection to Abraham (the recipient of God's promises) and David (progenitor of the royal line). Immediately following is an infancy narrative that incorporates a number of passages from the book of Isaiah (Isa 7:14; 9:6-7; 11:1-3) to show that the birth of Jesus fulfills Isaiah's messianic prophecies. In the infancy narrative, God is present through an angel of the Lord (another time-honored biblical tactic), who visits Joseph on several occasions to protect Mary and her newborn son from harm (Mt 1:20-21; 2:13, 19). Matthew clearly wants to emphasize that divine providence is at work in the child's life. Picking up Mark's narrative thread, Matthew next introduces John the Baptist, who presents us with the first indications of trouble.

In those days John the Baptist appeared in the wilderness of Judea, proclaiming, "Repent, for the kingdom of heaven has come near." This is the one of whom the prophet Isaiah spoke when he said, "The voice of one crying out in the wilderness: 'Prepare the way of the Lord, make his paths straight.'" Now John wore clothing of camel's hair with a leather belt around his waist, and his food was locusts and wild honey. Then the people of Jerusalem and all Judea were going out to him, and all the region along the Jordan, and they were baptized by him in the river Jordan, confessing their sins. (Mt 3:1-6)

The phrase, "kingdom of heaven," is unique to Matthew; the other gospels use the phrase "kingdom of God." Scholars believe that Matthew followed the common Jewish practice of avoiding names for God, because using a name for God was thought to be presumptuous. In proclaiming the reality of the kingdom and the coming of the promised Messiah, the Baptist's words generate a sense of expectation. Where is the kingdom and who is the Messiah? Interestingly, John's reference to the kingdom is absent in the other gospels, yet, after John's arrest, Matthew has Jesus repeat the Baptist's words verbatim, using it to launch his own public ministry.

Scholars have long debated the nature of the relationship between John the Baptist and Jesus. Some believe John was a mentor to Jesus, while others believe he was a friendly competitor. Whatever the case, in Matthew's gospel, God's kingdom is a central feature in both ministries and both prophets contend that repentance is needed to establish it. The noted differences in their understanding of the kingdom will become apparent as we examine the texts.

The spatial location of the kingdom (it's near but not here yet) and John's call for repentance are the first clues that something is amiss. The size of the crowds is another indicator. Clearly John's message is hitting a nerve among the people—they know something is amiss and they want to do something about it before it's too late. Baptism in the river is the means through which they will be cleansed of their sins. McClymond explains the ritual's significance:

> While John's baptism bears some analogy to the water lustrations and ritual cleansings at Qumran in the desert, there is a decisive difference. This water ritual does not seem to be administered more than once, and so it does not fit into the pattern of the Levitical laws that specified that ritual washing was to occur whenever a person became ceremonially unclean. Instead John's baptism seems to mark a once-for-all transition into a new religious state or identity.[15]

But what is the nature of the kingdom for which the people are preparing? The Baptist's words suggest an apocalyptic vision akin to that of the Essenes, who believed God would ultimately destroy the world and fashion a new one. Further evidence is found in his encounter with a group of Sadducees and Pharisees who make the mistake of coming to him for baptism.

> But when he saw many Pharisees and Sadducees coming for baptism, he said to them, "You brood of vipers! Who warned you to flee from the wrath to come? Bear fruit worthy of repentance. Do not presume to say to yourselves, 'We have Abraham as our ancestor'; for I tell you, God is able from these stones to raise up children to Abraham. Even now the ax is lying at the root of the trees; every tree therefore that does not bear good fruit is cut down and thrown into the fire." (Mt 3:7-10)

The scene is not present in Mark, but Matthew inserts it to introduce the "villains" of the story and to highlight the nature of the conflicts they will have with Jesus. John's fiery speech contains many apocalyptic themes. The ax "lying at the root of the trees" indicates that the end is near and it will be swift and deadly. God's wrath and judgment will consume sinners in the fires of damnation. In singling out the Pharisees and the Sadducees, John seems a bit distressed that they may escape the merciless flames—someone warned them and he's not too happy about it. Although the two groups were hardly compatriots, Matthew lumps them together here to "kill two birds with one stone." In effect, Matthew accuses the entire Jewish leadership of the sin of pride born of privilege. As Jews, they are proud of their possession of the Mosaic Law and their status as God's chosen people. They assume that as descendants of Abraham they are part of God's covenant and are thus shielded from divine judgment and wrath. But John warns them that without the proper attitude and the proper works (the "good fruit"), their "privilege" will be useless on the Day of Judgment.

On its face, the appearance of the Sadducees and Pharisees at the river is puzzling. Why would members of the Jewish elite want to be baptized by a crazed wilderness preacher who calls them nasty names and publicly humiliates them? The text is silent on their motivation. Perhaps like the common folk they also feared God's wrath and wanted to confess their sins, but it's more likely a clever literary device to introduce the second accusation. The Baptist proceeds with their baptism, giving them a warning that reveals their sin: "I baptize you with water for repentance, but one who is more powerful than I is coming after me; I am not worthy to carry his sandals. He will baptize you with the Holy Spirit and fire. His winnowing fork is in his hand, and he will clear his threshing floor and will gather his wheat into the granary; but the chaff he will burn with unquenchable fire" (Mt 3:11-12).

John is not fooled by their sudden and very public appearance. Although he baptizes them, his speech also warns them that appealing to the crowds through public displays of piety (a time-honored political tactic) will not save them. They must humbly acknowledge their sins and make a genuine effort to reform their conduct; otherwise, when the Messiah comes he will inflict another kind of baptism that fits their hypocrisy.

As these passages indicate, John's function in the narrative is to prepare the way for the Messiah by announcing his coming, calling the people to repentance, performing baptisms, and explaining why God's intervention is necessary. Just as it was in the Old Testament, divine intervention is prompted by the people's religious and moral lapses. Matthew uses John's encounter with the Sadducees and Pharisees to make the point that their pride and hypocrisy have broken the crucial connection between the act and the intention behind the act, thus making them—and the people they are obliged to teach and guide—incapable of fulfilling God's Law. The Baptist's harsh criticism of the Jewish leadership thus sets the stage for the appearance of Jesus, who is much more than a prophetic intermediary between

God and the people. In Matthew's gospel, he is portrayed as the great teacher and authoritative interpreter of the Mosaic Law whose words and deeds will guide the faithful on the path of true righteousness before the final Day of Judgment. The authority of Jesus to fulfill this mission is given by the God of Israel at Jesus' baptism—a scene that contrasts sharply with John's earlier baptism of the Sadducees and Pharisees.

> Then Jesus came from Galilee to John at the Jordan, to be baptized by him. John would have prevented him, saying, "I need to be baptized by you, and do you come to me?" But Jesus answered him, "Let it be so now; for it is proper for us in this way to fulfill all righteousness." Then he consented. And when Jesus had been baptized, just as he came up from the water, suddenly the heavens were opened to him and he saw the Spirit of God descending like a dove and alighting on him. And a voice from heaven said, "This is my Son, the Beloved, with whom I am well pleased." (Mt 3:13-17)

Commentators have observed that John's words of protest are not found in the other gospels and may reflect an early conflict between his followers and those of Jesus. The gospel writer clearly wants to establish the superiority of Jesus to John. Whatever the case, the exchange makes a sharp distinction between the behavior of the Jewish leaders and that of Jesus, who seeks out the Baptist for a more private baptism. Rather than appeal to the crowds in a public display of piety, Jesus shies away from the spotlight, demonstrating attitudes of humility and obedience and a genuine desire to serve God. Through word and deed—through the union of intention and action—Jesus is the exemplar of what it means "to fulfill all righteousness" (i.e., to be in right relationship with God). God's declaration reflects the pride and love of any father who sees his son performing well. In response God bestows upon the young man the gift of the Spirit, a legacy that will serve him throughout his earthly ministry. The presence of the dove harkens back to the blessings of peace, reconciliation, and hope given to Noah after the devastation of the flood (Gen 8:6-12).

The close relationship between Yahweh and Jesus and God's gift of the Spirit are characteristic of biblical prophecy (Deut 34:10; Num 11:25-26; Isa 42:1, 61:1). God's designation of Jesus as "my Son, the Beloved, with whom I am well pleased" confirms the divine parentage Matthew established in the infancy narrative and reveals the unique nature of the Father-Son relationship. Yahweh loves his Son deeply and Jesus' desire to please his Father in every way reflects the level of intimacy between them. God's phrasing also links Jesus to the Servant Song in Isaiah 42, which depicts God's servant as one who will "faithfully bring forth justice" in a new way that is quiet, gentle, and persistent—an approach radically different from that of the warrior Messiah of Jewish tradition.

Following his baptism, Jesus endures the temptations of the devil and remains faithful to the Father's will (Mt 4:1-11), passing another crucial test.

John's arrest, which follows immediately afterward, signals the beginning of Jesus' ministry. He first establishes a home in Capernaum and then travels along the Sea of Galilee (fulfilling the prophecy of Isaiah 9:1-2), proclaiming, "Repent, for the kingdom of heaven has come near" (Mt 4:17). The first public act of his ministry is the calling of disciples. Like his Father before him, Jesus is the one who initiates contact with human beings. He encounters two local fishermen, Simon (called Peter) and James, and instructs them to "Follow me, and I will make you fish for people" (Mt 4:19). The men respond as Abraham did, with unquestioned obedience, dropping their nets without a word and following the young teacher as he continues his travels. The scene is repeated when Jesus calls two more brothers, James and John. To say that Jesus had charisma is an understatement! The impact of his ministry on the region is immediate and impressive: "Jesus went throughout Galilee, teaching in their synagogues and proclaiming the good news of the kingdom and curing every disease and every sickness among the people. So his fame spread throughout all Syria, and they brought to him all the sick, those who were afflicted with various diseases and pains, demoniacs, epileptics, and paralytics, and he cured them. And great crowds followed him from Galilee, the Decapolis, Jerusalem, Judea, and from beyond the Jordan" (Mt 4:23-25). Matthew's reference to "their" synagogues hints at the tensions between Jews and Jewish Christians in Antioch. During Jesus' lifetime, however, the synagogue was a recognized center of Torah study and theological debate and was the natural place for Jesus to present his teachings.

In describing Jesus' early ministry, Matthew presents two important contrasts. While John proclaimed the kingdom of heaven as a future reality, Jesus' power to heal (a power given and sanctioned by God) is a sign that the kingdom is also a present reality that human beings can experience in the here and now. Moreover, the power of this Messiah is not in armies and weaponry but in his compassion and mercy and in his ability to instill hope in those around him through his healing, teaching, and preaching.

In the opening chapters of Matthew, God's activity has established the identity, mission, and authority of Jesus, and God has given him the gift of the Spirit, which he uses to reveal the nearness of the kingdom through his words and deeds. In chapters 5 through 7 Matthew presents the Sermon on the Mount, the first major discourse of the gospel. His considerable editorial skill gives the impression that the sermon is a spontaneous moment in Jesus' ministry and that Jesus is the primary source for the teachings, but the growing consensus among biblical scholars is that the sermon is a creative synthesis of the sayings of Jesus preserved in Q and materials from Special M.[16] The diversity of sources does not compromise the revelatory content of the sermon, however. In crafting these materials, Matthew uses the authoritative figure of Jesus to communicate a number of theological claims and ethical prescriptions that reflect the collective wisdom of the early Jesus movement, a movement that was influenced and shaped by Judaism and by Jesus himself. Moreover, a theocentric reading of the sermon is less concerned with the number of sources and the historicity of the teachings and more concerned with how the sermon reflects and extends God's efforts to redeem the creation in light of the canonical narrative as a whole. As Jesus' first major discourse, the sermon offers a blueprint for the realization of God's kingdom on earth until the eschaton. The question we shall consider is whether Jesus is introducing a radically new morality—as some Christians claim—or whether he is clarifying how ethics should be developed within the Judaic tradition.

The Sermon on the Mount

Chapter 5 opens with Jesus surveying the crowds. Like Moses before him, Jesus "went up the mountain, and after he sat down, his disciples came to him. Then he began to speak, and taught them..." (Mt 5:1). And, as the Father did at his Son's baptism, Jesus bestows upon his disciples a priceless gift; he gives them the gift of his teachings, which they will transmit to the crowds (the future church). His begins with the Beatitudes, or blessings, which read:

> Blessed are the poor in spirit, for theirs is the kingdom of heaven. Blessed are those who mourn, for they will be comforted. Blessed are the meek, for they will inherit the earth. Blessed are those who hunger and thirst for righteousness, for they will be filled. Blessed are the merciful, for they will receive mercy. Blessed are the pure in heart, for they will see God. Blessed are the peacemakers, for they will be called children of God. Blessed are those who are persecuted for righteousness' sake, for theirs is the kingdom of heaven. Blessed are you when people revile you and persecute you and utter all kinds of evil against you falsely on my account. Rejoice and be glad, for your reward is great in heaven, for in the same way they persecuted the prophets who were before you. (Mt 5:1-12)

As statements of congratulations and praise, the Beatitudes have several important functions. First, they provide a vision of life within the kingdom—an ideal vision of hope, love, and justice that ultimately serves as a foundation for the sermon. Second, the Beatitudes function as statements of definition. They describe the dynamic realities of the human condition—the great contrasts of poverty and wealth, mourning and comfort, satisfaction and want, hypocrisy and purity of heart—and they define the task that all the disciples of Jesus are called upon to take up. They are to become the peacemakers, the humble, the patient, and so on. The Beatitudes also indicate that discipleship in the earthly kingdom will not be easy. References to persecution and slander no doubt reflect the conflict between Antioch's Jweish leadership and the Matthean community after the death of Jesus.

The sermon continues with a description of the disciples' new mode of being within the kingdom.

> You are the salt of the earth; but if salt has lost its taste, how can its saltiness be restored? It is no longer good for anything, but is thrown out

and trampled under foot. You are the light of the world. A city built on a hill cannot be hid. No one after lighting a lamp puts it under the bushel basket, but on the lampstand, and it gives light to all in the house. In the same way, let your light shine before others, so that they may see your good works and give glory to your Father in heaven. (Mt 5:13-16)

Describing disciples as the "salt of the earth" has multiple meanings. Salt is both a preservative and a welcome seasoning. In conveying the teachings of Jesus to others, the disciples will preserve the traditions that will preserve the faith community. As a seasoning, the disciples' mission is to make things better, but a point that is often lost in commentary is the amount of salt that is needed. As all good cooks know, too much salt will ruin a dish. The salt metaphor suggests that the disciples do not have to hold lofty positions (like the Pharisees and Sadducees), embark on grandiose schemes to change the world, or achieve sainthood. They can make things better in humble ways, in day-to-day activities that seem insignificant but that nurture and reflect the reality of the kingdom. Common courtesy, an honest day's work, kindness to a neighbor—these are the "salty" activities of daily life, activities in which anyone can engage to make the kingdom a reality.

The city on the hill and the lamp and light metaphors harken back to the images of Jerusalem-Zion in Isaiah (Isa 2:1-4; 42:6-7; 60:1-3) and emphasize teaching through example. Just as Jesus did at his baptism, the disciples are to let their "light shine before others" so that they may see the "good works" that are a reflection of God's kingdom.

The sayings on discipleship convey an important point about the mission of Jesus. As the proclaimer of the kingdom and prophet of the God of Israel, Jesus is instructing his followers about their obligations as God's people—not as followers of Jesus. Matthew's emphasis on the identity of Jesus as Messiah and authoritative teacher, his conflict with the Jews of Antioch, and the formation and maintenance of the church were not concerns of Jesus. In his role as prophet, Jesus called disciples to join him in a reform movement within Judaism, a movement that focused on God's kingdom and on fulfilling God's Law. As a group, their first loyalty was to Yahweh and the kingdom, not to Jesus. While Matthew's concerns clearly shape the sermon, Jesus' prophetic message is evident in the next section of the sermon, which reveals the overall intention of his teaching.

Do not think I have come to abolish the law or the prophets; I have come not to abolish but to fulfill. For truly I tell you, until heaven and earth pass away, not one letter, not one stroke of a letter, will pass from the law until all is accomplished. Therefore, whoever breaks one of the least of these commandments, and teaches others to do the same, will be called least in the kingdom of heaven; but whoever does them and teaches them will be called great in the kingdom of heaven. For I tell you, unless your righteousness exceeds that of the scribes and Pharisees, you will never enter the kingdom of heaven. (Mt 5:17-20)

This passage is the first to mention the scribes, a class of scholars and authoritative interpreters of the Law. In making these statements, Jesus is not attempting to found a new religion or a new morality but to retrieve an understanding of the Mosaic Law that he believed had been lost over time by the Jewish leaders and the people. Like the prophets before him, Jesus was calling his people back to the Law and educating them about its meaning and function in their lives—something which he clearly believed the scribes, Pharisees, and Sadducees had failed to do. Their failure—at least in the eyes of Jesus—stemmed primarily from a shift in thinking about the Law.

As Judaism developed, some Jews fell into a common ethical trap. In fulfilling the Law, which gave them their sense of identity and pride as God's chosen people, some of them perceived the Mosaic Law as an assurance of God's favor rather than the proper response to God's grace—a charge John the Baptist leveled at the Jewish leadership. Once again, John Bright offers some valuable insight into the problem.

> Each Jew felt obligated to maintain the covenant by his personal loyalty to the law. But there also resulted a heightened stress upon man's obligation, with an inevitable lessening of stress upon divine grace. Although God's grace was never forgotten, and his mercy continually appealed to, religion in practice was a matter of fulfilling the law's requirements. This meant that Judaism was peculiarly liable to the danger of legalism: i.e., of becoming a religion in which a man's status before God is determined entirely by his works. Though it is unlikely that any thoughtful Jew would have boasted that he had kept the law perfectly..., righteousness through the law was believed a goal to be striven for, and attainable. It was felt, moreover, that God would reward with his favor those who were faithful in this regard.... The notion even emerged that good deeds accrued to one's credit with God and constituted a treasury of merit.[17]

Bright is not suggesting that *all* Jews adopted a legalistic approach to the Mosaic Law. On the contrary, he notes that "mechanical conformity was never the aim of the law's best teachers."[18] The point he's making here is that over time the people's personal sense of loyalty to the Law sometimes resulted in an "externalizing of righteousness" that stressed correct action without giving adequate consideration to the intention behind the act (i.e., the motive, one's response to God's gracious gifts). Whether Jesus believed all Jews fell into this trap is highly doubtful, but he clearly thought this tendency was widespread enough to challenge it in the sermon with his famous "antitheses."

> You have heard that it was said to those of ancient times, "You shall not murder"; and "whoever murders shall be liable to judgment." But I say to you that if you are angry with a brother or sister, you will be liable to judgment; and if you insult a brother or sister, you will be li-

able to the council; and if you say, "You fool," you will be liable to the hell of fire. So when you are offering your gift at the altar, if you remember that your brother or sister has something against you, leave your gift there before the altar and go; first be reconciled to your brother or sister, and then come and offer your gift. (Mt 5:21-24)

Jesus cites the Mosaic commandment against murder ("You have heard that it was said...") and then contrasts it with an antithesis ("But I say to you..."). His use of the authoritative "I" is unique to prophecy. "Thus says the Lord" was the common phrase prophets used to indicate who was really doing the talking. Some scholars argue that Jesus's self-reference is an assertion of his divinity and that the antitheses are subordinating the Mosaic Law to the new teaching, but it is also possible that Jesus is simply trying to drive home his point in a bold and effective way, which was not uncommon for the young prophet. In the gospels, the crowds often comment on his teaching style, noting that he taught as "one with authority" (Mk 1:22; Mt 7:29; Lk 4:32). His unique phrasing may be an attention-getter designed to help the disciples see beyond the "letter" of the law to the "Spirit," or divine intention, behind it. In Matthew, the teaching on murder introduces this strategy.

By contrasting the law against murder with the antithesis, Jesus is arguing that it is not enough simply to refrain from killing. Such restraint might be motivated by fear or self-interest; after all, no rational person wants to go to prison or face execution for killing someone. But obedience to the letter of the law (the external act) does nothing to address the sources of our murderous impulses (the motivation behind the act). The sad truth is there are many "law-abiding" citizens who would murder without batting an eye or shedding a tear if they thought they could get away with it. In presenting the antithesis to murder, Jesus teaches that if the kingdom is to become a reality, we must not limit ourselves to the prescriptive intent of the Law, but contend with and overcome the anger, jealousy, and sense of injustice that often spark violent acts. This is what Jesus means when he tells his disciples, "unless your righteousness exceeds that of the scribes and Pharisees, you will never enter the kingdom of heaven" (Mt 5:20).

Moreover, by focusing on the interior dispositions that inform motive, we not only address the source of violence, but we are more likely to obey the law for the right reasons; that is, not out of fear or self-interest but because we recognize and respect the values embedded in the law. In this case, God's commandment against murder is intended to protect the gift of life and to nurture unity and peace within the community—sacred goods that were first established in the Garden of Eden, commanded at Mount Sinai, and reaffirmed in the idyllic vision of the Beatitudes. The desire to promote and protect these goods is the "Spirit," or divine intention that prompted the Mosaic Law in the first place. By developing traits of character that minimize violence and promote peace and justice, we naturally obey God's Law in both letter and Spirit, thus practicing the level of righteousness that is needed to realize the ideal of the kingdom.

Jesus employs the same strategy in his teachings on adultery: "You have heard that it was said, 'You shall not commit adultery.' But I say to you that everyone who looks at another woman with lust has already committed adultery with her in his heart" (Mt 5:27-28). Once again, Jesus stresses the faults in character that motivate sinful actions. As the verse implies, the spouse is unfaithful in his heart long before the actual act of betrayal. If the kingdom is to become a reality, husbands and wives must overcome the moral corruption that produces adultery. This means not only refraining from adulterous acts, but also developing traits of character that promote and honor personal commitments and that see adultery for what it is—a serious betrayal of trust that erodes the very fabric of relationships between couples, as well as relations within the family and in the greater community.

As Jesus stated, his teachings on murder and adultery do not abolish the Law and the teachings of the prophets. On the contrary, they fulfill or complement them by illuminating the embedded values and the failures in human motivation that are often overlooked by legalistic interpretations but that are crucial for true obedience to God's Law. This pedagogical strategy becomes more subtle and complex when Jesus turns to what scholars call "the hard sayings":

> You have heard that it was said, "An eye for an eye and a tooth for a tooth. But I say to you, Do not resist an evildoer. But if anyone strikes you on the right cheek, turn the other also; and if anyone wants to sue you and take your coat, give your cloak as well; and if anyone forces you to go one mile, go also the second mile. Give to everyone who begs from you, and do not refuse anyone who wants to borrow from you. You have heard that it was said, "You shall love your neighbor and hate your enemy." But I say to you, Love your enemies and pray for those who persecute you, so that you may be children of your Father in heaven; for he makes his sun rise on the evil and on the good, and sends rain on the righteous and on the unrighteous. For if you love those who love you, what reward do you have? Do not even the tax collectors do the same? And if you greet only your brothers and sisters, what more are you doing than others? Do not even the Gentiles do the same? Be perfect, therefore, as your heavenly Father is perfect. (Mt 5:38-48)

The commands are aptly named "hard sayings"—turning the other cheek and loving our enemies are far from easy! But why would Jesus make such incredible (and some would say unrealistic and impractical) demands? To answer this question, we must first have some understanding of the legal context in which Jesus is working.[19]

Legal Justice and the Law

In keeping with his program of reform, Jesus affirms the legal tradition by citing the golden rule and the law of retribution (Lat. *lex talionis*), which are universally recognized as principles of justice. In their most basic form, these principles are designed to give to each person what he or she is due, whether it is a positive good (e.g., property rights), a shared burden (e.g., income taxes), or a corrective punishment (e.g., traffic fines). The chief aim of legal justice and individual laws is to secure and protect the common good, which are the shared values, interests, and objectives of the community as a whole.

Jesus cites the golden rule in a straightforward formulation that links it directly to the tradition of the Mosaic Law: "In everything do to others as you would have them do to you; for this is the law and the prophets" (Mt 7:12). By making this connection, Jesus makes it clear that the golden rule is something his teachings will not abolish. As a principle of justice, the golden rule promotes reciprocity (i.e., mutual exchange) and fundamental fairness in relationships. In contrast, the law of retribution is a legal sanction that aims to protect and restore this reciprocal relation. In Exodus, the law reads: "If any harm follows, then you shall give life for life, eye for eye, tooth for tooth, hand for hand, foot for foot, burn for burn, wound for wound, stripe for stripe" (Ex 21:23-25). A more detailed formulation is found in Leviticus: "Anyone who kills a human being shall be put to death. Anyone who kills an animal shall make restitution for it, life for life. Anyone who maims another shall suffer the same injury in return: fracture for fracture, eye for eye, tooth for tooth; the injury inflicted is the injury to be suffered" (Lev 24:17-20). The aim of these prescriptions is not to inflict an identical injury on the guilty party but to establish a proportionate punishment that curtails retaliatory acts of revenge. Modern readers are often struck by the brutality of these prescriptions, but in the ancient world, where there were few uniform judicial or penal systems, the *lex talionis* was a definite advance over vendettas, or blood feuds, which were common among Near Eastern peoples and tribes. Perceived slights or breeches in hospitality were enough to trigger escalating cycles of violence that could last for generations. By demanding that the punishment be proportionate to the crime, the *lex talionis* defused the tribal one-upsmanship that perpetuated these feuds.

The golden rule and the law of retribution are time-honored ethical principles that have informed many legal codes over the centuries. In citing them in the sermon, Jesus is affirming their legitimacy as legal instruments, but even the best principles and laws have limitations. Reviewing these limitations will show how Jesus uses the hard sayings to overcome them.

The Limits of the Law

One of the principal limitations of the golden rule and the law of retribution is their inability to address exceptional cases. As an instrument of public order, laws are meant to be universally applied. "No one is above the law" is a phrase we often use to make this point (especially when sentencing corrupt public officials or out-of-control celebrities). Yet we all recognize that there are some cases that are so unusual in nature that they must be treated differently. In fact we discover that in exceptional cases obedience to the law often results in a miscarriage of justice. Jesus makes this very argument in his confrontation with the Pharisees in the grain field (Mk 2:23-28; Mt 12:1-8; Lk 6:1-5). After the Pharisees condemn the disciples for picking grain on the sabbath, Jesus reminds them that "The sabbath was made for humankind, and not humankind for the sabbath" (Mk 2:28). His point is that God's laws are intended to help human beings, not make them suffer needlessly or punish them unfairly. Human beings must eat to survive and God would never intend to deprive them of this basic need, even on the sabbath! Exceptions, therefore, must be acknowledged if justice is to be fully realized. But what principle can we use in such cases? Exceptional cases by their very nature fall outside the parameters of the golden rule and the law of retribution, which are meant to be universally applied. The answer lies in the principle of equity, which is present in the dynamics of the hard sayings. Understanding how Jesus uses equity requires a brief analysis of the concept developed by Aristotle in the *Nicomachean Ethics*.

Equity and the Law

In Book V Aristotle defines equity as a form of justice that in some instances is *better* than justice because it addresses problems that arise because of the universal nature of the law. The following citation is lengthy, but necessary for understanding the relation of equity to the Law.

> [Aristotle argues that the] just and equitable are in fact identical (in genus), and, although both are morally good, the equitable is the better of the two. What causes the problem is that the equitable is not just in the legal sense of "just" but as a corrective of what is legally just. The reason is that all law is universal, but there are some things about which it is not possible to speak correctly in universal terms. Now, in situations where it is necessary to speak in universal terms but impossible to do so correctly, the law takes the majority of cases, fully realizing in what respect it misses the mark. The law itself is none the less correct. For the mistake lies neither in the law nor in the lawgiver, but in the nature of the case. For such is the material of which actions are made. So in a situation in which the law speaks universally, but the case at issue happens to fall outside the universal formula, it is correct to rectify the shortcoming, in other words, the omission and mistake of the lawgiver due to the generality of his statement. Such a rectification corresponds to what the lawgiver himself would have said if he were present, and what he would have enacted if he had known (of this particular case). That is why the equitable is both just and also better than the just in one sense. It is not better than the just in general, but better than the mistake due to the generality (of the law). And this is the very nature of the equitable, a rectification of law where law falls short by reason of its universality. (Book V, 1137b, 10–23)[20]

For Aristotle, equity is a form of justice that complements (fulfills or rectifies) legal justice because it addresses particular cases that do not fit the universal nature of the law. To apply the law in such cases would result in a "mistake" that would undercut the intention of the "lawgiver." The particularity of the case requires that flexibility rather than the strict reciprocity that characterizes legal justice be the rule. This is the reason for the incredible demands of the hard sayings and the point Jesus makes when he cites the *lex talionis*:

> You have heard that it was said, "An eye for an eye and a tooth for a tooth." But I say to you, Do not resist an evildoer. But if anyone strikes you on the right cheek, turn the other also; and if anyone wants to sue you and take your coat, give your cloak as well; and if anyone forces you to go one mile, go also the second mile. Give to everyone who begs from you, and do not refuse anyone who wants to borrow from you. (Mt 5:38-42)

In urging his disciples to turn the other cheek or go the extra mile, Jesus is attempting to educate them (and us) in the art of equity. In citing tradition he is acknowledging that ninety-nine times out of a hundred the law works just fine, but in introducing the antithesis he is also arguing that there will be times when reciprocity and retribution may not be what are needed or required. In describing his disciples as "the salt of the earth," he expects them (and us) to demonstrate a generosity of spirit that exceeds the norms of justice. This means that while all of us are entitled to reciprocity and fundamental fairness under the law, there may be times when it is *better* to give more than we receive, that in some cases exacting the retribution that legal justice demands and to which we are entitled does not always serve justice. In some instances, it may even corrupt it. The examples of the hard sayings teach us that if we are to fulfill the intentions of the Lawgiver, then we must be willing to look beyond the narrow confines of the law. A contemporary example will illustrate this point.

After a hard day's work, Mrs. Smith is walking to her car in a parking garage when a crazed young man with a knife jumps out from behind a vehicle, rips her bag from her shoulder, and knocks her to the ground, accidentally cutting her arm in the mad dash to get away. Hearing her screams, two male passersby tackle the boy and hold him down until the police arrive. Mrs. Smith learns from the district attorney that the mugger is a nineteen-year-old college dropout who has a serious drug problem. He's unemployed, suffers from depression, and is living at home. His parents are at their wits' end and plead with the district attorney to have him put on probation and sent to a rehabilitation center, where he can receive the treatment he needs. Mrs. Smith's husband is outraged by such a suggestion. He demands that justice be done and that the judge "throw the book at the punk!" The law of retribution is clearly on the husband's side. The crime is a serious one that calls for substantial jail time, even for a first-time offender. Although Mrs. Smith suffered a great deal of pain and suffering, she is troubled by the potential severity of the punishment. Should the boy be sent to prison as the law demands or would justice be better served if the court gave the boy a chance to straighten out his life and become a productive member of society? After thinking it over, talking with the young man's parents, and having a heated discussion with her husband, Mrs. Smith informs the district attorney that she would not object to supervised parole and a treatment program for the boy. In relinquishing her rightful claim of retribution, the woman has demonstrated a generosity of spirit that enables the district attorney (if he so chooses) to work out a more equitable sentence. Another victim might react differently and she would be well within her legal rights to do so, but Jesus teaches that as the "salt of the earth" disciples must be willing to temper justice with love, compassion, and mercy so that the kingdom envisioned in the Beatitudes may become a reality.

The Dark Side of the Golden Rule

Jesus also uses the hard sayings to rectify a limitation of the golden rule. While the principle promotes reciprocity, it is also vulnerable to self-serving interpretations that compromise its true intention. Within the rules of fair exchange, our decision to help others could be motivated by the selfish expectation that we'll receive something in return. Such an attitude can infect our motivation to such an extent that eventually our impulse to give is dominated by what we hope we can get out of it. The "what's in it for me" attitude is not only manipulative but also blunts true charity and limits the possibilities of help for needy people who can't always return the favor. This is why Jesus urges his disciples to "Give to everyone who begs from you, and do not refuse anyone who wants to borrow from you" (Mt 5:42). Contrary to popular belief, Jesus is not renouncing material wealth or suggesting that disciples give everything they have to others, but he is challenging the quid-pro-quo mentality that often corrupts our relations with others.

In emphasizing the needs of others over the needs of self, the hard sayings also overcome limitations triggered by personal hatred. Jesus may very well have had blood feuds in mind when citing another traditional teaching:

> You have heard that it was said, "You shall love your neighbor and hate your enemy." But I say to you, Love your enemies and pray for those who persecute you, so that you may be children of your Father in heaven; for he makes his sun rise on the evil and on the good, and sends rain on the righteous and on the unrighteous.... Be perfect, therefore, as your heavenly Father is perfect. (Mt 5:43-45, 48)

Commanding love is a radical step that is fraught with difficulties, the most obvious being the command itself. Is it possible to command love from human beings? We'll address this question presently. For now, suffice it to say that the practical goal of the command is to nurture a welcoming attitude toward others who may fall outside family or tribal relations, thus extending—or perhaps illuminating—the true scope of reciprocity.

It is important to note that while love of neighbor and accommodation to enemies is in the Torah (Lev 19:18; Ex 23:4-5), hatred of enemies is not.

Whatever the source of the traditional wisdom, its inclusion indicates that most Jews interpreted love of neighbor in a very narrow sense. Jesus is clearly troubled by this. In presenting the antithesis he argues that love of neighbor cannot be limited only to people we like because such minimalist behavior contradicts God's own actions ("he makes the sun rise on the evil and on the good"), as well as his general intentions toward humanity. Obedience to the command requires that we respect all persons, regardless of our personal feelings toward them, because they have an innate dignity and value as creatures of God.

Generosity and Justice

The conclusion to the hard sayings is particularly significant: "Be perfect, therefore, as your heavenly Father is perfect" (Mt 7:48). Once again, Jesus downplays his own position in favor of the Father. But what does he mean by "perfect"? Clearly, human beings are incapable of God's perfection, so why would Jesus make such an unrealistic demand? The answer lies in the meaning Jesus places on "perfection." Within the context of the sermon, the perfection of God refers to God's generosity. Paul Ricoeur has studied the dynamics of the hard sayings and cites God's generosity as the reason why God can command human beings to love their neighbor and their enemy. He believes that the obligation of the command arises from their experience of God's grace. Since God has given the gifts of life, love, peace, mercy, and forgiveness, disciples ought to give in turn. Thus, "According to this formula, and through the force of the 'since,' the gift turns out to be a source of obligation."[21] Another contemporary example will illustrate this point.

After a hard day's work, Mr. Smith (yes, the irate husband) stops at his neighborhood liquor store to pick up a bottle of wine for dinner. On a whim he decides to purchase a lottery ticket. He doesn't expect to win, but "what the heck, I have as much chance as anybody else." The next day he checks the numbers and discovers to his amazement that he's won the big prize. Suddenly he's ten million dollars richer! He can't believe his luck. He did absolutely nothing to deserve the money, but that's not going to stop him from claiming it. He jumps up and down, runs around the house, hugs his startled wife and kids, the family dog, the neighbor's dog, and any other moveable objects, then stays up all night thinking about all the things he can do with the money. Of course he'll pay off debts, quit his job, take a long vacation with the family, help his parents and in-laws, but he's so filled with joy that the first thing he wants to do is throw a big party to celebrate his good fortune. A guest list immediately starts forming in his mind. He'll invite all his friends, relatives, co-workers, and a few people he wants to make green with envy. As dawn breaks, Mr. Smith can hardly wait to start making phone calls and sending out e-mails.

The story illustrates how a gift can become a source of obligation. Often when we receive an unexpected and totally unmerited gift, one of our first impulses is to share it with others so that they can enjoy it, too. In fact, many of us feel *compelled* to share it. This generosity of spirit is the perfection God displays time and time again in his relations with human beings, from Adam and Eve and Abraham to Moses and the people of Israel. This generosity of spirit—what Ricoeur calls the "logic of superabundance"[22]—is the kind of perfection Jesus reveals in the hard sayings and the quality of character he wants disciples to emulate in their relationships with others.

The dynamics of the hard sayings thus follow the pattern of the other antitheses. They deepen our understanding of the Law and human motivation, and they illustrate through practical examples how the Law should be applied to fulfill God's intentions and to realize the kingdom. Rather than introducing a radical new morality, the hard sayings retrieve the true intention of the Lawgiver, as well as the true meaning of obedience to the Law. Before we leave this subject, however, Ricoeur makes another important observation about the hard sayings that bolsters the case against the "new morality" argument.

The Dialectic of Love and Justice

Let's suppose for a moment that the hard sayings were meant to be taken at face value. Ricoeur reasons that, given the extreme nature of the teachings, critics would have every right to ask, "What distribution of tasks, roles, advantages, obligations and duties would result from a commandment that seems to exclude the fundamental principle of reciprocity which makes justice possible?"[23] Wouldn't anarchy and chaos reign if the commandments to "love your enemies," "turn the other cheek," and "give your cloak as well" were followed by most people on a daily basis? For Ricoeur the answer is a resounding "Yes!" primarily because the radical command to love (which grounds the generosity of all the hard sayings) is not ethical but *supraethical*. That is to say, the love command is not meant to be practiced on its own but to be placed in a dialectical relation with the golden rule so that they enhance and rectify each other. Thus, within this encounter, the golden rule prevents the love command from veering into excess and social chaos while the love command opens up possibilities for achieving justice that are not limited to the golden rule or the law of retribution. In Ricoeur's view, the necessity of this dialectical or interactive relation "is the fundamental reason why the new commandment does not and cannot eliminate the golden rule or substitute for it. What is called 'Christian ethics,' or, as I would prefer to say, 'communal ethics in a religious perspective,' consists I believe in the tension between unilateral love and bilateral justice, and in the interpretation of each of these in terms of the other."[24] As with most situations, the "both-and" is a much more practical (and fair) solution than the "either-or."

Teachings on Piety and Prayer

The remainder of the sermon offers instruction and practical advice on matters of prayer (Mt 6:1-13), fasting (Mt 6:17-18), possessions (Mt 6:19-34), and community relations (Mt 7:1-23) in the present and in the future world to come. It is important to emphasize that Matthew's claims against the Jewish leadership are polemical and purposely exaggerated, reflecting the church's bitter conflict with the synagogues. On prayer, for example, Jesus instructs the disciples not to follow the practice of "the hypocrites," who "love to stand and pray in the synagogues and at the street corners, so that they may be seen by others." Instead, he says, "go into your room and shut the door and pray to your Father who is in secret; and your Father who sees in secret will reward you" (Mt 6:6). Similarly, disciples are not to fast like "the hypocrites," who make public displays of suffering; instead, they should fast in private "so that your fasting may be seen not by others but by your Father who is in secret; and your Father who sees in secret will reward you" (Mt 6:18).

For Matthew's community of disciples, the teachings hammer home the differences between the "hypocritical" practices of the Jewish leadership and the new righteousness of Jesus, which emphasizes purity of motives, humility, and true obedience to God's will. The contrast is further reinforced in the Lord's Prayer, which is notable for its reference to the present and future dimensions of the kingdom and for its affirmation of key themes within Jesus' kingdom theology. "Our Father in heaven, hallowed be your name. Your kingdom come, your will be done, on earth as it is in heaven. Give us this day our daily bread. And forgive us our debts, as we also have forgiven our debtors. And do not bring us to the time of trial, but rescue us from the evil one" (Mt 6:9-13).

This simple prayer acknowledges and affirms God's eternal rule and voices the fervent wish that God's kingdom will soon be realized on earth as it is in heaven. The humble pleas for bread and forgiveness link God's mercy and providential care to the moral obligations of the faith community. Whether the "debts" refer to financial matters or to sins (Lk 11:4), the point Jesus is making is that God's kingdom is present whenever and wherever the faithful emulate God's generous example. The prayer ends with a standard closing that asks God to spare the faithful from future trials and save them from the clutches of the evil one.

The sermon concludes with a fitting metaphor.

"Everyone then who hears these words of mine and acts on them will be like a wise man who built his house on rock. The rain fell, the floods came, and the winds blew and beat on that house, but it did not fall, because it had been founded on rock. And everyone who hears these words of mine and does not act on them will be like a foolish man who built his house on sand. The rain fell, and the floods came, and the winds blew and beat against that house, and it fell—and great was its fall!"

Now when Jesus had finished saying these things, the crowds were astonished at his teaching, for he taught them as one having authority, and not as their scribes. (Mt 7:24-29)

The teachings of the sermon are the rock, the spiritual and ethical foundations for the kingdom of God and for the church community. Like God,

Moses, and the prophets before him, Jesus emphasizes that disciples must *hear* the call of God, *respond* appropriately, and *persevere* in their faith, even in the face of adversity. The floods and winds symbolize the sporadic persecution of Christian missionaries by the Jews.

The end of the first discourse in Matthew affirms the authority of Jesus to teach. There is no mention of divinity here, only the prophet's extraordinary ability to reveal the nature of God's kingdom and the meaning of the Law, a meaning that had been lost during the endless years of exile, hardship, oppression, and war.

The rock metaphor appears again in Peter's confession at Caesarea Philippi. After Peter has publicly confessed Jesus as the Messiah, Jesus rewards the disciple's faith by telling him, "[Y]ou are Peter, and on this rock I will build my church, and the gates of Hades will not prevail against it" (Mt 16:18). Shortly after this scene, God makes his final speech at the Transfiguration (Mt 17:1-13) in which Jesus, Moses, and Elijah appear together before a terrified Peter, James, and John. As is often the case, the revelation takes place on a mountain and God's message is one of reassurance. Echoing the words used at the baptism, Yahweh proclaims: "This is my Son, the Beloved; with him I am well pleased; listen to him!" (Mt 17:5). God's admonition may be directed primarily to Peter, who earlier rebuked Jesus for speaking about his impending death on the cross (Mt 16:21-23). Peter's doubts are understandable and probably reflect the concerns of the early followers of Jesus, who were beginning to rethink the concept of Messiah with much fear and trembling.

After the Transfiguration, God disappears from the narrative until the resurrection scene. In God's final appearance, the transformation of Jesus from prophet to Messiah is complete.

> And suddenly there was a great earthquake; for an angel of the Lord, descending from heaven, came and rolled back the stone and sat on it. His appearance was like lightning, and his clothing white as snow. For fear of him the guards shook and became like dead men. But the angel said to the women, "Do not be afraid; I know that you are looking for Jesus who was crucified. He is not here; for he has been raised, as he said. Come, see the place where he lay. Then go quickly and tell his disciples, 'He has been raised from the dead, indeed he is going ahead of you to Galilee; there you will see him.' This is my message to you." So they left the tomb quickly with fear and great joy, and ran to tell his disciples. (Mt 28:2-8)

The passage reflects many literary elements from the Old Testament. The earthquake signals divine activity, just as the angel represents the divine presence. The angel's message is one of reassurance and hope, for just as Yahweh delivered the Hebrew slaves from Egypt and the exiles from Babylon, he has raised Jesus from the dead, thus liberating the faithful from the power of evil and death. But in raising Jesus, God permits the Son to become—at least for the church community—the central object of worship. The "Great Commission" at the end of Matthew's gospel establishes this relation.

> Now the eleven disciples went to Galilee, to the mountain to which Jesus had directed them. When they saw him, they worshiped him; but some doubted. And Jesus came and said to them, "All authority in heaven and on earth has been given to me. Go therefore and make disciples of all nations, baptizing them in the name of the Father and of the Son and of the Holy Spirit, and teaching them to obey everything that I have commanded you. And remember I am with you always, to the end of the age." (Mt 28:16-20)

Once again, an important event occurs on a mountain. After the resurrection, the disciples worship Jesus as the risen Christ; and yet, like Abraham and Moses before them, some of the disciples doubt. Perhaps they wonder about worshiping anyone other than Yahweh; after all, idolatry has been the bane of Israel's existence from the very beginning. How can they be sure they're doing the right thing? Following the example of the Father, Jesus reassures them with another reference to his authority, but it is important to note that Jesus acknowledges that his authority "has been given to me" by the Father. It is a gift that he now offers to his disciples. They are commissioned to use the gifts of the Spirit to "make disciples of all nations" and to further God's earthly kingdom until its final culmination at the eschaton.

It's interesting to speculate here about what Jesus means in his reference to disciples. Exactly whose disciples are they? Are all the nations to be disciples of God or of Jesus? The answer depends on whether the reader uses a theocentric or a christocentric lens, but whatever the case, the common ground that links these perspectives and the Jewish-Christian traditions together is found in the teachings, which are meant to be practiced by Jew and Gentile alike.

"Who Do People Say That I Am?"

Our theocentric reading of Matthew's gospel has attempted to look beyond the gospel writer's anti-Jewish bias and theological agenda and discover an answer to Jesus' question that mediates the impasse between Jews and Christians. Reviewing the results of our reading strongly suggests that Jesus is indeed Yahweh's prophet-Messiah who offers salvation to both Jews and Christians, but in multiple ways that do not privilege one tradition over the other.

Let us first consider the Jewish position. As detailed in chapter 6, for most Jews, the primary stumbling block to accepting Jesus is the claim that he is the Messiah, but if we suspend the messianic claim for a moment and focus solely on his credibility as a prophet, we discover some interesting parallels between the content and method of his teaching and the pedagogical strategies God employs in the Old Testament. The most striking example is found in the intertextual connections between the events at Mount Sinai and the Sermon on the Mount.

PARALLELS BETWEEN MOUNT SINAI AND THE SERMON ON THE MOUNT

Mount Sinai	*Sermon on the Mount*
Event takes place on a mountain	Event takes place on a mountain
Moses is a prophet of Israel	Jesus is a prophet of Israel
God expects that the Hebrews will become a kingdom of priests and a holy nation	Jesus expects that Jews will live the Beatitudes of the kingdom
God gives the gift of the law —the practical program to make the ideal possible	Jesus gives the gift of his teaching —the practical program to make the ideal possible
The law provides a "constitution" for the new nation of Israel	The teachings of Jesus provide a "constitution" for the new church

Recall that in the book of Exodus, the Hebrew slaves were brought to the mountain by God's prophet, Moses, whom they grudgingly accepted as their leader. Yahweh had high expectations for the Hebrews, pledging that he would make them a "priestly kingdom and a holy nation." To realize this ideal, God presented them with the gift of the Law, which served as a constitution and ethical guide for the new nation of Israel. This scene is essentially replayed in Matthew. At a mountaintop in Galilee, the prophet, Jesus, gathers his disciples and crowds of people and proclaims the ideal of the kingdom of God. The Beatitudes depict the kingdom as an idyllic place where the meek, the merciful, the needy, and other humble souls will dwell with their God in peace, security, and happiness. For Christians, Jesus' teachings serve as a constitution and ethical guide for the new church community until his expected return at the eschaton. In both of these seminal events, God acts through his prophets to present the people with an ideal to strive for and then provides them with a practical program to realize it. These parallels strongly suggest that Jesus is indeed a prophet of God whose teachings are worthy of serious consideration for Jews and Christians, for they are designed to bring God's chosen people back to the Law, as God intended.

Further proof is found in Jesus's kingdom theology, which also mirrors God's activity. As noted in previous chapters, Yahweh established a pattern of balancing traditional teachings with innovation, often introducing "new things" to help human beings achieve moral maturity and righteousness before God. Jesus' prophetic mission clearly reflects this dynamic relation. In proclaiming the kingdom, Jesus combines eschatology and Jewish apocalyptic to create a more hopeful and less judgmental scheme that grounds his teachings in the Torah. Moreover, in the sermon, Jesus affirms the legitimacy and authority of the Law while challenging legalistic interpretations that tend to minimize the connection between motive and act. Ironically, it is through his innovative teaching style that Jesus succeeds in retrieving the meaning and purpose of the Law as originally intended by God. Although God never explicitly states his intention in the biblical narrative, a review of some of the salient points of our study articulates what it might be.

Our readings in Genesis, Exodus, and Isaiah have shown that God's ethical intention for human beings is to educate them about the meaning and practical requirements of righteousness so that they might overcome the destructive effects of the fall, which corrupted the goods, values, and just relations that God established with the creation. One of the central claims of the biblical narrative is that true righteousness involves continuity between being and doing, between a person's interior motive and his or her external act. The stories of Noah, Abraham, and Moses, for example, reveal that righteousness before God is a mode of existence and relationship that acknowledges dependence upon God, embraces true obedience and justice, and emulates God's generosity toward all of creation. Humility, obedience, justice, and generosity are the attributes that ground Jesus' understanding of the kingdom, guide his own actions, and spur his efforts to retrieve and revitalize the meaning of the Law. As the sermon clearly demonstrates, a central part of his prophetic mission is to illuminate the dynamic relation between love and justice so that his fellow Jews can follow his example and fulfill the Law in the truest and most complete sense.

From an ethics perspective, this means that Jesus is not offering a blueprint for a distinctively Christian ethics. On the contrary, the message God reveals in and through Jesus is simple and inclusive: Like Jesus we are all human, we are all recipients of God's grace and are thus obligated to show the same degree of generosity toward others. This means all persons who worship Israel's God—whether Jew or Christian—can and should follow the example of Jesus and cultivate love of God and neighbor, embrace justice and true obedience, have faith in God's providential power, and use their God-given powers to serve rather than to exploit. In proclaiming the kingdom as a present reality, Jesus also establishes that salvation through the Law—as he preached and practiced it—is a valid path for all faithful Jews. Thus, from a theocentric perspective, Jesus is a righteous prophet whose words and deeds have real significance for understanding the relation between salvation and the Mosaic Law. While Jews may not agree with the Christian claim that Jesus is the Messiah, it should not compromise the validity of his role as God's prophet.

Now let us consider the Christian position. For many Christians, the major stumbling block for accepting Jews into God's family is a set of commonly shared beliefs about the Jews and their role in God's plan, beliefs that were introduced with the New Testament texts and developed further by Christians in subsequent interpretations. While the degree to which the New Testament writers were anti-Jewish continues to be debated, what we cannot ignore is how these texts were interpreted and used by Christians against the Jewish people. Amy-Jill Levine states the problem well in observing that, "The Gospels and Acts do not commend to their audiences the killing of Jews or forcing them into ghettos. The Synoptic authors would, I believe, be appalled at what has been done to Jewish communities in Jesus' name for close to two millennia. Nevertheless, these texts do plant seeds that, with certain types of fertilizer, yield an anti-Jewish growth."[25]

We found some of these seeds in Matthew's gospel. In addition to the Christ-killer accusation, the gospel claimed that the death and resurrection of Jesus marked a new and definitive step in the divine plan, a step that superseded or replaced all that had come before. In Matthew's gospel, the prophetic missions of John the Baptist and Jesus as God's prophet no longer had their own validity for Jewish salvation but were interpreted as preparing the way for the greater and more perfect revelation in Jesus as the Christian Messiah. In the centuries that followed, Christian tradition interpreted this to mean that to be part of the "new Israel," the Jews had to either convert to Christianity or be damned in the hellfires of the eschaton. For many Christians today this requirement remains in force, yet the theological rigidity and hubris that characterize this kind of supersessionist thinking are challenged by the canonical narrative itself. Our readings thus far have revealed the multivalent and mysterious nature of Israel's God, a God who reveals himself in many forms and who offers Jews and Gentiles the possibility of salvation through the dual initiatives of the prophet-Messiah. Thus, if we ever hope to overcome the impasse on the Christian side, we must remove the stumbling block of supersessionism by discrediting the claim that faith in Jesus Christ as Lord and Savior is the only path to salvation for human beings. The next chapter will attempt to do just that through an exegetical analysis of Paul's letter to the Galatians and some key passages in Romans.

Questions for Reflection and Discussion

1. Each of the gospel writers combined traditional materials with his own writings to produce a unique gospel that addressed the issues and concerns of his particular community. If you were a gospel writer working today, what portrait of Jesus would emerge from your community? What image of Jesus might emerge from a village in India or Peru or Jordan or the Australian outback? What do these varied portraits reveal about the nature of biblical revelation? What challenges do they present to biblical interpretation?

2. Matthew's anti-Judaism is not unique to the New Testament. How do you think anti-Jewish passages should be treated by contemporary interpreters? What does this phenomenon suggest about other biblical biases, such as sexism, homophobia, and intolerance of other faiths?

3. Jesus argues in the Sermon on the Mount that love of neighbor cannot be limited only to people we like because such minimalist behavior contradicts God's own actions ("he makes the sun rise on the evil and on the good"), as well as God's general intentions toward humanity. Obedience to the command requires that we respect all persons, regardless of our personal feelings toward them because they have an innate dignity and value as creatures of God. What is the source of this dignity and value? In other words, what characteristics do we share with God that command respect? What about non-human life? Are people and other creatures valuable because of what they can do for us or because they simply exist? Based on your discussion, do you think there are such things as human and animal rights that must be respected? What are they?

Recommended Reading

Brown, Raymond E. *An Introduction to New Testament Christology.* New York/Mahwah, NJ: Paulist Press, 1994. An accessible study of Jesus and how he was understood by the early church communities.

Ehrman, Bart D., ed. *The New Testament and Other Early Christian Writings: A Reader,* 2nd ed. New York: Oxford University Press, 2004.

Harris, Stephen L. *The New Testament: A Student's Introduction.* 4th ed. Boston: McGraw-Hill, 2002. Essential textbook for students of the New Testament that explores the history, content, and major themes of each book in the New Testament.

McClymond, Michael J. "Jesus." In *The Rivers of Paradise: Moses, Buddha, Confucius, Jesus, and Muhammad as Religious Founders,* edited by David Noel Freedman and Michael J. McClymond, 309–456. Grand Rapids: Wm B. Eerdmans Publishing Company, 2001. An excellent overview of the life and times of the historical Jesus and Jesus research.

Miller, Robert J., ed. *The Complete Gospels.* San Francisco: HarperSanFrancisco, 1994. Translations with commentary of all twenty of the known gospels from the early Christian period.

8

THE GIFT OF JESUS

The Promise of Salvation for All

Paul of Tarsus has often been called the co-founder of Christianity, and with good reason. After his encounter with the risen Christ on the Damascus road, he devoted the remainder of his life to preaching the gospel to the Gentiles and establishing Christian communities in Asia Minor and the Mediterranean region. Without his commitment and zeal, the Jesus movement would most likely have remained a small Jewish sect in Palestine, but Paul's tireless missionary work is not the only reason for his lofty status. His letters to his fledgling churches offer some of the earliest theological statements regarding the significance of Jesus for salvation, grounding the interpretive process that would ultimately transform the Jesus of history into the Christ of faith.

As discussed in previous chapters, the transformation began shortly after Jesus' execution. His humiliating death on the cross challenged his early followers to rethink the Jewish notion of a powerful military Messiah and to propose a new understanding that shifted the emphasis away from the destruction of Israel's enemies and the restoration of the Davidic monarchy toward more ultimate ends. In this new construction, Jesus' followers conceived the Messiah as a suffering servant whose death and resurrection defeated the universal afflictions of evil, sin, and death. At the eschaton, God would send Jesus to defeat Satan and his forces and to judge the living and the dead. The faithful would be spared God's righteous wrath and would dwell with God and Jesus in a glorious new Jerusalem. Paul's contribution to this Christianized version of the eschaton is considerable. His letters outline the first theological rationale for the Christ-event, as well as the ethical implications for the nascent church.

The message of the Christian salvation narrative is indeed a hopeful one, but it has a dark side as well, for early Christians used their reformulation—and the content of many of Paul's letters—to exclude Jews from the benefits of God's promise. This book has argued that the theological biases of Christians and Jews have blinded both groups to the possibility that God's salvific initiative in Jesus might take multiple forms without privileging one tradition over the other. While such an interpretation is controversial (and in some quarters it's absolutely blasphemous), it has substantial biblical backing. God's generosity, flexibility, and ingenuity are well-established patterns within the biblical corpus. Is it so far beyond the realm of possibility that the God of Israel would branch out and offer multiple gifts to address different people in different situations? Why should God's salvific activity be limited to a narrow, linear direction that divides and excludes so many human beings and that clearly contradicts all of God's previous efforts? A theocentric reading of Paul's letter to the Galatians will indeed confirm God's universal intentions.

The letter to the Galatians has been selected for two principal reasons. First, it offers a concise statement of Paul's theology (as opposed to the more detailed statement in Romans), and, second, it provides valuable insight into the theological claims and conflicts that fueled early supersessionist thinking.

This chapter will begin with a brief summary of Paul's life and work, his use of letters, and the crisis that prompted his letter to the Galatian churches. We shall then explore the letter in some detail, focusing on Paul's defense of his gospel, the doctrine of justification by faith, and the allegory of Hagar and Sarah, which was later used by Christian theologians (e.g., Tertullian, Origen, Augustine, and Luther) as a primary source for supersessionist thinking and anti-Jewish sentiments.[1] Analysis of the letter will show that, while some Christians have interpreted and continue to interpret Paul's theology as a warrant for excluding the Jews (and all non-Christians, for that matter), his use of the Old Testament in developing his doctrine of justification by faith and his ethical teachings introduce intertextual connections between Abraham and Jesus that refute the supersessionist claim that faith in the Christ-event is the only way of salvation. Reading key passages in Romans will confirm our reading and show that Paul himself was determined to set the record straight on this issue. The chapter will conclude with a reevaluation of the supersessionist position in light of Paul's theology and consider the contributions his work makes to God's progressive program for human development and to our understanding of Jesus as God's prophet-Messiah.

Paul of Tarsus

What little we know about Paul comes from his letters and the book of Acts. While Acts offers many interesting stories and biographical details about Paul's life, most biblical scholars consider Luke's account historically unreliable, principally because it was written decades after Paul's letters and often contradicts the apostle's version of events. Nevertheless, Acts is a valuable resource for our study because mixed in with Luke's great storytelling are traces of actual persons and events that provide insights into Paul's character and mission, his relationships with other church leaders, and the conflicts and controversies that prompted his letters.

Despite the sketchy historical evidence, there are some facts about Paul's life that are not in dispute. Paul was born a Jew in Tarsus, the capital city of Cilicia, which was located in Asia Minor (or modern-day Turkey). Although the exact year is unknown, Paul entered the world during the first decade of the Common Era. At that time Cilicia was a Roman province and Tarsus was a thriving port city and cultural center of the Greco-Roman world, attracting tradesmen, artisans, merchants, philosophers, and other enterprising souls from a variety of cultural and religious backgrounds. The cosmopolitan atmosphere of Tarsus was ideal for a young man like Paul, who possessed a sharp intellect and an inquisitive mind.

Paul's Jewish name was Saul, which Luke uses in Acts until the young apostle embarks on his mission to the Gentiles (13:9), no doubt to highlight Paul's radical transformation. Being born into a Jewish family, Paul naturally spoke Aramaic at home and in the synagogue, but scholars generally agree that his primary language was Greek and that his Bible was the Septuagint (the Greek translation of the Old Testament).[2] The content of Paul's letters, which demonstrate considerable rhetorical skill, reflects a formal Greek education, as well as familiarity with the philosophical schools that flourished in Tarsus. His use of the diatribe, his knowledge of natural law, and his frequent listing of virtues and vices reflect Stoic and Cynic influences. Paul's religious outlook, however, was thoroughly grounded in his Jewish heritage. In one of his speeches in Acts, Paul claims that he was brought to Jerusalem as a young man to be taught by the great Jewish rabbi Gamaliel (Acts 22:3-5). Whether he spent his formative years in Tarsus or in Jerusalem, there is little doubt that Paul valued both his Greek education and his Jewish roots. In his letter to the Philippians, he describes himself as "a member of the people of Israel, of the tribe of Benjamin, a Hebrew born of Hebrews; as to the law a Pharisee; as to zeal a persecutor of the church, as to righteousness under the law, blameless" (Phil 3:5-6).

As part of his Pharisaic training, Paul learned a trade, working as a tent maker and leatherworker to support himself (Acts 18:3). Whether Paul was married is still an open question. Marriage was expected for men of Paul's age and prospects. His first letter to the Corinthians hints at a possible marriage (1 Cor 7:8, 9:5), but he never mentions a wife by name—a conspicuous omission for a man who spoke quite candidly about his life.

As noted above, prior to his encounter with the risen Christ, Paul was a zealous persecutor of the early church. The book of Acts places him at the martyrdom of Stephen, who was stoned to death by a Jewish mob for his accusations against them (Acts 7:54–8:3). Paul's early animus toward Jewish Christians stemmed in part from the success of the Jesus movement. The apostles Peter and John as well as Stephen had persuaded many of Paul's fellow Jews that Jesus was the risen Messiah (Acts 4:1-4; 5:12-16; 6:7). The unwelcome competition and the blasphemous claims of these men were simply too much for the fiery young Pharisee to bear. In his view, they were making a mockery of the faith. F. F. Bruce offers a window into Paul's mind during this period.

The law and the customs, the ancestral traditions, and everything that was of value in Judaism, were imperiled by the disciples' activity and teaching. Here was a malignant growth which called for drastic surgery.

The defense of all that made life worth living for Paul was a cause which engaged all the zeal and energy of which he was capable. When the chief priests and their associates launched their attack on the disciples, Paul came forward as their eager lieutenant. Their motives may have been partly political, while his were entirely religious, but their action provided him with the occasion to protect the interests of the law. If the principal threat to those interests came from Stephen's party, then let that party be attacked and suppressed first of all; but the disciples of Jesus as a whole, however outwardly observant of the law they might be, undermined it by proclaiming their crucified master as Messiah.[3]

Paul's harassment of Jewish Christians was unrelenting until that fateful hour on the Damascus road. Acts reports that Paul had met with the high priest at the Jerusalem Temple to request extradition letters for the synagogues in Damascus (Acts 9:1-2). Paul's purpose was to hunt down disciples of Jesus who had fled Judea and bring them back to Jerusalem to stand trial before the Sanhedrin. What happened next would dramatically change his life and the course of the Jesus movement.

Now as he [Paul] was going along and approaching Damascus, suddenly a light from heaven flashed around him. He fell to the ground and heard a voice saying to him, "Saul, Saul, why do you persecute me?" He asked, "Who are you, Lord?" The reply came, "I am Jesus, whom you are persecuting. But get up and enter the city, and you will be told what you are to do." The men who were traveling with him stood speechless because they heard the voice but saw no one. Saul got up from the ground, and though his eyes were open, he could see nothing; so they led him by the hand and brought him into Damascus. For three days he was without sight, and neither ate nor drank. (Acts 9:3-9)

The passage displays the hyperbole that was common to ancient storytelling; nevertheless, it supports Paul's claim in his letter to the Galatians that he had verbal communication with the risen Lord—a claim that would prove crucial in his later battles with church leaders over his authority as an apostle.

Scholars have long debated the events of that day, which probably occurred sometime between 32 and 34 CE. Acts offers two similar accounts of the event (Acts 22:4-16; 26:9-18). Although the versions are consistent, no one knows for sure the precise nature of the event or whether Paul was actually blinded for a time. Paul himself refers only to his vision of the risen Christ and his words to him (Gal 1:11-12). Whatever the case, the consensus is that something extraordinary must have happened to Paul on the road.

After Paul's vision, his startled companions lead him to a house in Damascus, where he is visited by Ananias, a disciple sent by God to heal and baptize Paul into the faith (Acts 9:12-19). Shortly afterward, Paul enters the Damascus synagogues, "speaking boldly in the name of the Lord"

(Acts 9:28). Once again, Paul's own account challenges this version. In Galatians he states that he went to Arabia (the Nabatean kingdom) for an unspecified period before returning to Damascus (Gal 1:17-18).

Paul's radical transformation from a persecutor of the early church to its tireless champion naturally caused some suspicion and concern among the early followers of Jesus. This may explain why three years would pass before Paul would make the journey to Jerusalem to meet Peter and James (Gal 1:18-19). The visit lasted only two weeks and there is no record of their conversations. Evidence suggests, however, that their relationship was an uneasy one, for after the visit Paul traveled north into Syria and Cilicia where he worked for fourteen years, primarily in the mission city of Antioch and in his hometown of Tarsus.

As noted in the previous chapter, in the first century, Antioch was the prosperous Roman capital of Syria and the home of a thriving Jewish-Gentile church. According to Acts, Paul and his co-worker, Barnabas, are commissioned by the Holy Spirit to leave Antioch on their first missionary journey through Asia Minor (13:1-4). Paul first directs his activities to the Jews, but after they eject him from the synagogues, he turns his efforts to the Gentiles, who are much more receptive to his message.

Initially, Gentile converts to the Jesus movement were expected to adopt the rituals and practices of Judaism, which included strict dietary laws, rules about table fellowship, and circumcision. The requirements were understandable because the first followers of Jesus were Jews and, despite increased harassment by their Jewish brethren, they understood themselves as part of the diverse fabric of Judaism. But in light of the Christ-event, Paul and some of his followers began to question the necessity of these requirements. The apostles Peter, John, and James, who were the recognized leaders of the Jerusalem church, called a conference to address the issue. Paul attended the conference with Barnabas and Titus, a recent Gentile convert.

The Jerusalem Conference and Its Aftermath

The Jerusalem Conference (49 CE) was a seminal event in the history of Christianity. The purpose of the gathering was to determine whether Gentile converts should be required to uphold the Mosaic Law.

Paul and Barnabas arrive in Jerusalem and are welcomed by the apostles and other church leaders, who are thrilled to learn of Paul's success among the Gentiles. But despite their shared joy, a group of conservative Jewish Christians (which Luke refers to as "the sect of the Pharisees") insist that the new converts "be circumcised and ordered to keep the law of Moses" (Acts 15:5). After some extended discussion and debate, the conferees side with Paul, but in presenting the decision, James makes some concessions to the conservatives. He acknowledges that while Gentiles are not required to be circumcised, they are called upon for the sake of unity "to abstain only from things polluted by idols and from fornication and from whatever has been strangled and from blood" (Acts 15:20). Paul's account in Galatians makes no mention of the compromise. He claims that Peter,

James, and John only asked that he and his followers take up a collection for the Jerusalem poor (Gal 2:10). Such contradictions are indeed puzzling, but, as Stephen L. Harris explains,

> [s]ome historians believe that the apostolic decree involving dietary matters may have been issued at a later Jerusalem conference, one that Paul did not attend. In this view, Luke has combined the results of two separate meetings and reported them as a single event. Later in Acts, the author seems aware that Paul did not know about the Jerusalem church's decision regarding Torah-prohibited meats. During Paul's final Jerusalem visit, James is shown speaking about dietary restrictions as if they were news to Paul (21:25).[4]

While the compromise established a precedent for mediating future conflicts in the church, the breakdown in communication would come back to haunt them all when Peter visits Paul in his home base of Antioch. In the letter to the Galatians Paul presents his version of events:

> But when Cephas [Peter] came to Antioch, I opposed him to his face, because he stood self-condemned; for until certain people came from James, he used to eat with the Gentiles. But after they came, he drew back and kept himself separate for fear of the circumcision faction. And the other Jews joined him in this hypocrisy, so that even Barnabas was led astray by their hypocrisy. But when I saw that they were not acting consistently with the truth of the gospel, I said to Cephas before them all, "If you, though a Jew, live like a Gentile and not like a Jew, how can you compel the Gentiles to live like Jews?" (Gal 2:11-14)

"The Antioch incident," as it has come to be known, reveals some of the difficulties Peter faced as leader of the Jerusalem church. Negotiating deep doctrinal differences is never an easy task, but Paul made it nearly impossible for Peter by refusing to grant any concessions and by publicly forcing the issue. Paul's willingness to oppose a recognized pillar of the church—and Peter's willingness to endure Paul's rebuke—raises the important issue of Paul's authority as an apostle.

Paul's Authority as an Apostle

The origins of the title are unclear, but traditionally an apostle (Gr. *apostolos*, "one who is sent") was understood as a person who had seen the risen Christ and who was sent by Jesus to preach the gospel. Based on the gospel accounts, the disciples of Jesus were the only persons who qualified. For this Pharisee and former persecutor of Christians to insist that he had seen the risen Christ and that Jesus had commissioned him to preach the gospel to the Gentiles was an audacious claim, to say the least. Doubts about Paul's mission were understandable and may explain why conservative Jewish Christians often challenged his authority and his teachings on the Mosaic Law and why Paul took such pains to defend his authority in his letters.

Despite the unpleasantness of the Antioch incident, Paul remained loyal to the Jerusalem church, and church leaders remained supportive of him and his mission, although relations were somewhat strained. The request for the Jerusalem collection is a good case in point. While the recipients of the collection have never been identified, many scholars believe the church leaders requested the collection to assist the Jerusalem population after a severe famine in 46–48 CE. Paul's efforts to raise funds on their behalf and bring them to Jerusalem—at no small risk to himself—are mentioned in Acts 11:29-39 and in his letters (1 Cor 16:1-3; Gal 2:10). While Paul is grateful that the Jerusalem leadership recognizes his authority, his letters make it clear that he is no subordinate. In his view, the Jerusalem collection is a magnanimous gesture from one church leader to others who need assistance. Whether the Jerusalem leaders agreed with Paul's characterization is anyone's guess, but his letters indicate his determination to walk the fine line between church unity and ecclesiastical independence. Nevertheless, it is interesting to note that after the Antioch incident, Paul's missionary journeys moved westward into Asia Minor, away from Jerusalem and Palestine.

Paul's Missionary Journeys

Paul's authority may also have been challenged within his own mission. Acts reports that shortly after the Antioch incident, Paul and Barnabas have a heated quarrel over the commitment and loyalty of John (also called Mark) and the two abruptly part company (15:36-39). Enlisting the aid of Silas and Timothy, Paul embarks on a second missionary journey (49–52 CE). This time he travels throughout the northeastern Mediterranean region, focusing his efforts on major urban areas, such as Philippi, Thessalonica, Athens, and Corinth. Despite conflicts with local magistrates, "jealous" Jews, and assorted ruffians, Paul's efforts to establish churches in these cities are successful—with the notable exception of Athens (Acts 17:16-34).

Although Paul's churches blossomed, his missionary activities were not without their challenges and dangers. By his own accounting, Paul suffered many hardships on the road:

> Five times I have received from the Jews the forty lashes minus one. Three times I was beaten with rods. Once I received a stoning. Three times I was shipwrecked; for a night and a day I was adrift at sea; on frequent journeys, in danger from rivers, danger from bandits, danger from my own people, danger from Gentiles, danger in the city, danger in the wilderness, danger at sea, danger from false brothers and sisters; in toil and hardship, through many a sleepless night, hungry and thirsty, often without food, cold and naked. And, besides other things, I am under daily pressure because of my anxiety for all the churches. (2 Cor 11:24-28)

His anxiety may have prompted a third missionary journey (53–57 CE), which brought him back to established churches in Asia Minor and Greece. The fledgling church in Ephesus was a particular worry for Paul (Acts 19:1-20). He remained there for over two years, preaching the gospel in the synagogues and Greek lecture halls, where he boldly challenged Jewish exorcists and magicians. After completing his work in Ephesus, Paul turned his attention to Jerusalem and the delivery of the collection for the poor. Like Jesus before him, his journey to the holy city would mark the beginning of the end of his mission.

As presented in Luke's narrative, Paul's troubles begin shortly after he arrives in the city. To appease Jewish suspicions about his mission—and perhaps the sensibilities of conservative Jewish Christians—Paul agrees to participate in a Temple purification ritual, but the gesture backfires badly (Acts 21:17-31). Some Jews quickly spot the former Pharisee and accuse him of defiling the Temple by bringing Gentile converts into its holy precincts—a reflection of the increasing strain between Jews and Christians. Enraged Jews seize Paul, drag him out of the Temple, and begin beating him mercilessly. Fearing a full-scale riot, a Roman tribune places Paul under protective custody, but orders his troops to flog him to find out what he knows (Acts 22:24). Before the sentence can be carried out, however, the tribune learns that Paul is a Roman citizen—a surprising claim that continues to be debated among scholars today.[5] Whether he was a Roman citizen or not, the plot twist is a crucial one, for as a Roman citizen Paul was legally entitled to a trial before any punishment could be meted out. The next day the tribune sends Paul to the Sanhedrin for trial (Acts 22:30). Paul's claims of innocence sway some of the crowd, but when the tribune learns of further plots against Paul's life, he sends him under escort to the Roman governor. Paul's rhetorical skills serve him well before the officials. The Roman governor, Antonius Felix and his successor, Porcius Festus, absolve Paul of any guilt and grant him permission to plead his case to Rome (Acts 24–26).

Although Paul never mentions the trip to Rome, Acts presents an action-packed adventure story, complete with raging seas, a life-threatening shipwreck, and the apostle's miraculous encounter with a poisonous snake (Acts 27–28). After arriving in Rome, Paul is placed under house arrest, yet his captivity is relatively humane, by ancient standards. He lives the next two years in Rome at his own expense, welcoming visitors, "proclaiming the kingdom of God and teaching about the Lord Jesus Christ with all boldness and without hindrance" (Acts 28:30-31). The idyllic scene that closes the book is tempered by the sobering knowledge that Paul likely died a martyr's death at the hands of Nero during his first persecution of Christians (62–64 CE).

Luke's hyperbole aside, Paul's life was a difficult and courageous one, driven by the fierce conviction that Jesus was the risen Christ and that his death fundamentally changed the human path to salvation. His letters reflect the courage and conviction of the man and explain, in very explicit terms, why and how the change occurred and what that means for the Christian way of life.

The Letters of Paul

Paul's writings are the earliest in the New Testament, predating the gospels by at least a decade. Paul's urgent sense of mission prevented him from remaining in one location for too long, but he kept abreast of developments in his churches through oral and written reports from co-workers, delegations, and local church leaders. He responded to their reports in a number of letters that were copied (a common practice) and circulated among the churches. The importance of his letters for the survival of the early churches cannot be overstated, for they were used—both before and after Paul's death—as a foundation and guide for the development of Christian belief and practice, and for fostering a strong sense of Christian identity. Their central role in shaping and sustaining the early churches ensured their place in the Christian canon.

Modern scholarship has determined that Paul did not write all the letters attributed to him. Seven letters are considered authentic and include 1 Thessalonians, 1 and 2 Corinthians, Galatians, Philemon, Philippians, and Romans. The rest were written years later by Paul's followers in the style of the apostle (again, a common practice). Although we have no way of knowing how many letters he wrote, there is little doubt that he wrote more than we know about, for Paul was a conscientious pastor who was very concerned about the welfare of his churches. The content varied according to the issues and concerns within a particular church community; consequently, Paul's letters have an ad hoc quality that reflects the diversity and unique challenges of the early church communities. Nevertheless, the letters share some common literary and pedagogical characteristics.

AUTHENTIC LETTERS	PSEUDONYMOUS LETTERS	NON-PAULINE LETTERS
1 Thessalonians (50 CE)	2 Thessalonians (70–90 CE)	Hebrews (80–90 CE)
1 & 2 Corinthians (50s)	Colossians	
Philippians (from prison)	Ephesians	
Philemon (from prison)	1 & 2 Timothy (100–125 CE)	
Galatians		
Romans		

In writing to his churches, Paul followed the Greek letter form that we still use today. His letters typically begin with a general greeting or salutation, followed by the body of the letter, which addresses the central issues that prompted him to write, and a conclusion. In crafting his response, he often mixes autobiographical information with ethical teachings, explicit instructions about matters of worship and Christian piety, and strongly worded reminders of what is expected of the Christian way of life. He frequently uses his rhetorical skill to address and refute dissenters within his churches, suggesting what actions should be taken to reestablish peace and solidarity. Following common Pharisaic practice, Paul cites scripture to back up his arguments, often reinterpreting key texts to address new situations.

Although Paul followed Greek literary conventions, he wasn't afraid to take liberties, adding elements that gave his letters a distinctively Christian character. For example, he often enlarged the greeting to include offers of grace in Jesus Christ and in some cases to defend his own authority as an apostle. The conclusion frequently includes a wish for peace (a common Semitic feature), a prayer request, and a final benediction. These additions suggest that he knew the letters would be read aloud (which was the custom) and would thus serve several important functions. Calvin Roetzel explains the importance of the letter form in Paul's ministry.

> The letter perhaps more than a retelling of the gospel story proved to be an ideal vehicle for persuading doubters of the truth of his gospel, and it offered the most direct way of responding to rivals who thought his claim to apostleship spurious and his gospel outrageous. Moreover, the letter offered a way to be present with small house groups of converts to nurture, console, correct, cajole, exhort, remind, and instruct them in their life in Christ. In his ability to adopt and adapt the conventional form to serve his purposes Paul was ingenious and that ingenuity as well as the content he gave the form accounts for the continuing significance the letters had for the church.[6]

Paul's Theological Presuppositions

Unlike the gospels, which are theological interpretations of Jesus' life, Paul's letters are based in historical events, addressing specific issues and crises that occurred in his churches. Nevertheless, in crafting his responses, Paul relies on a number of theological presuppositions, three of which are crucial for understanding his argument in Galatians. The first is his theocentric worldview. As a Pharisaic Jew, Paul believed in the supremacy of the Holy God of Israel as creator, sovereign, judge, and redeemer. While in Paul's theology Jesus is central, his importance is based on his role as the crucified Christ—a role initiated by Yahweh in his ongoing efforts to redeem the world. But, as Leander E. Keck explains, Paul's belief that God intended to save Gentiles required some radical rethinking of traditional Jewish assumptions about God and the scope of God's activity in relation to sinners and Gentiles.

What . . . does it mean to believe that God rectifies the ungodly? First, God is not committed to vindicating clients, a group, party, nation, but to making right precisely everyone who is wrongly related to God. Because to be godly is to be like the God we image, each person or group regards God as the vindicator of its values. This makes God the opponent of those we oppose, the ultimate warrant of human power struggles, wars, acts of self-aggrandizement. God's moral integrity is therefore measured by the success of the clients. But if God is the rectifier of the ungodly, then God's moral integrity is measured solely by God's own character and commitments—"his ways are not our ways." If God rectifies the ungodly, then the persons who need rectification are not others, other groups, the outsiders, the enemy, but everyone whose relation to God is not right. If God rectifies the ungodly, then "God shows no partiality" (Rom 2:11), and is not the God of the Jews only or of any other group (Rom 3:29). God's wrath is against "*all* ungodliness and wickedness" (Rom 1:18).[7]

This position is radically different from the traditional view among the ancients, who understood their gods as intensely partisan. As has been noted, Jews took great pride in their status as the chosen people of God and in being the recipients of the Mosaic Law, but Paul believed that in initiating the Christ-event, Yahweh confirmed his independence as a deity and his character as a righteous God who does not exclude or favor one group over another. On the contrary, God's intention to save all the peoples of the earth is voiced repeatedly in the Old Testament (Jer 3:17, 31:33-34; Zech 2:11, 8:22, 14:9; Pss 9, 47, 67) and particularly in Isaiah (2:2-4, 25:6-9, 45:22-23, 52:10, 56:1-8, 66:18-21). Paul recognized—perhaps shortly after the encounter on the Damascus road—that the Christ-event embodied this divine intention.

The second presupposition follows from the first and, by ancient standards, is far less controversial. Paul had a cosmic conception of history that F. F. Bruce believes may also have been derived from his Pharisaic training. As Bruce explains,

[t]here was an ancient Jewish chronological scheme, probably going back beyond the time of Paul, which divided world history into three ages of two thousand years each—the age of chaos, the age of law (beginning with the revelation to Moses on Sinai) and the messianic age. These three ages would be followed by the eternal sabbath rest. Those who accepted this scheme might well have believed that the validity of the law was but temporary, lasting only to the dawn of the messianic age. If Paul had been brought up to accept it, then no doubt he would have expected the law to be superseded by a new order when Messiah came.[8]

The ancient scheme Bruce describes is a variant of Jewish eschatological schemes that were common during this period. Like many of his Jewish-Christian brethren, Paul believed that nothing happened by accident. Persons and events in the Bible, in history, and in his own life were interpreted through a linear chronology that promised a final culmination and return to God.

The third presupposition is closely aligned with the other two. The tone and imagery in Paul's letters indicate that he accepted Jewish apocalyptic eschatology to some degree. Like so many of his fellow Jews, he believed that Yahweh would intervene directly to fulfill the divine plan—a plan that was hidden from those who could not read the signs. As interpreted by Jewish Christians, Jesus of Nazareth was the promised Messiah whose death and resurrection signaled the start of the eschaton and the great cosmic battle that would soon decide the fate of the world. Paul was convinced that Jesus would return for the final judgment during his lifetime. Anticipation of the *parousia* (Gr. "coming," "advent") drove Paul's missionary activities, shaped his theology, and influenced his instructions to his churches. His teachings on marriage, celibacy, spiritual gifts, church relations, and other issues were designed with one goal in mind: to maintain peace and unity within the churches until the parousia. With so little time left, flexibility and innovation were often the rule, which helps explain why Paul's teachings sometimes appear inconsistent and even contradictory—a point we shall explore presently.

Paul's willingness to reinterpret the Old Testament, to adapt conventional forms to suit his purposes, and to innovate when the occasion called for it are clearly evident in his letter to the Galatians. One of the supreme ironies of the letter—and one of the fortunate mysteries of revelation—is that in reinterpreting the Mosaic Law within a Christianized chronology, Paul reveals the multivalent and universal character of God's initiative in Jesus Christ.

The Letter to the Galatians

While scholars disagree about the letter's date and place of composition, it was most likely written between 53 and 56 CE, while Paul was visiting the churches in Corinth or Ephesus. The location of the Galatian churches is also uncertain, because at the time there were two different regions in Asia Minor that were known as "Galatia": a northern plateau region populated by Celtic tribes of the "Galatian" kingdom, and a southern coastal province of Rome. While scholars continue to debate the question, the most likely location is the southern provincial cities of Iconium, Lystra, and Derbe, where Paul had established churches.[9]

The letter to the Galatians was prompted by the activities of a group of conservative Jewish Christians, known as "Judaizers." Whether they were members of the "sect of the Pharisees" or another conservative group is unclear, but their position on circumcision for Gentile converts was the same. Unbeknownst to Paul, they had visited the Galatian churches after he had left the area to persuade Gentile converts to abide by the requirements of the Mosaic Law. After learning of their activities, Paul was understandably furious, both with the Judaizers for undercutting his authority and with the Galatian Christians for being so gullible and weak in their faith. While his anger in the letter is apparent, he manages to muster enough self-control to present a brilliant and well-reasoned defense of his mission to the Gentiles and his understanding of the Law in light of the Christ-event. The letter unfolds in six parts:

Chapter 1:1-5	Opening Greeting
Chapters 1:6–2:14	An Autobiographical Defense of Paul's Apostolic Authority
Chapters 2:15–3:29	Paul's Gospel of Justification by Faith
Chapter 4:1-31	The Adoption of Christians as Abraham's Heirs
Chapters 5:1–6:10	The Meaning of Christian Freedom
Chapter 6:11-18	Conclusion

As in Matthew's gospel, God seldom appears as an acting "character" in the letter, yet Paul's many references to God make his presence palpable and provide Paul with the theological ground for attacking his opponents and for his ethical teachings.

Dispensing with his usual pleasantries and customary words of thanksgiving, Paul begins the letter with a direct assertion of his apostolic authority, an assertion that reflects his theocentric perspective:

> Paul an apostle—sent neither by human commission nor from human authorities, but through Jesus Christ and God the Father, who raised him from the dead—and all the members of God's family who are with me, To the churches of Galatia: Grace to you and peace from God our Father and the Lord Jesus Christ, who gave himself for our sins to set us free from the present evil age, according to the will of our God and Father, to whom be the glory forever and ever. Amen. (Gal 1:1-5)

Thus far the tone is strong, and assertive, yet congenial. Paul is quick to point out his divine credentials—his commission was not of human origin—and while repeating early creedal statements regarding Jesus' atoning death and resurrection, Paul wishes the Galatians the peace and blessings of God, the Father. His reference to Jesus Christ as Lord and liberator of the "present evil age" reflects his belief that the parousia is imminent, which explains his fierce defense against the Judaizers. For Paul, time is of the essence. The body of the letter thus begins with a blistering attack designed to shame his wayward flock and discredit the Judaizers.

> I am astonished that you are so quickly deserting the one who called you in the grace of Christ and are turning to a different gospel—not that there is another gospel, but there are some who are confusing you and want to pervert the gospel of Christ. But even if we or an angel

from heaven should proclaim to you a gospel contrary to what we proclaimed to you, let that one be accursed! As we have said before, so now I repeat, if anyone proclaims to you a gospel contrary to what you received, let that one be accursed! (Gal 1:6-10).

In referencing his opponents, Paul is clearly drawing a line in the sand. There can be no compromise with the Judaizers. No doubt the Judaizers feel the same way about him. The bitter impasse between them is unavoidable because both sides are convinced that the other side is perverting the gospel. The conflict revolves around their understandings of the role of the Mosaic Law in the faith community. For the Judaizers, the Jesus movement was a continuation of Judaism (Christianity was yet to emerge as a distinct faith), so it was expected that Gentile converts would adhere to Torah requirements (e.g., dietary laws and circumcision). But for Paul, God's salvific work in Christ (which offered salvation to all peoples) meant that Gentiles did not have to adopt Jewish customs and practices. For Judaizers to insist that Gentiles "become Jews" through Torah observance was to question God's grace and thwart God's universal intention. The stakes couldn't be higher, which is why Paul immediately follows his rebuke with a further defense of his authority as an apostle.

Repeating his earlier claim, he reminds the Galatian Christians "that the gospel that was proclaimed by me is not of human origin; for I did not receive it from a human source, nor was I taught it, but I received it through a revelation of Jesus Christ" (Gal 1:11-12). To further bolster his claim, Paul recounts his earlier life as a Pharisee and persecutor of the church and his fateful encounter with the risen Christ.

An Autobiographical Defense of Paul's Apostolic Authority

Paul's cosmic sense of history and his role in God's salvific plan are clearly in evidence here, for he maintains that God had "set me apart before I was born and called me through his grace" for the apostolic task, which is why it was not necessary for him to "confer with any human being" or "go up to Jerusalem to those who were already apostles before me" (Gal 1:15-17). His revelation required no instruction or consultation with the apostles, for he had been commissioned by God and Jesus himself. He also links his appearance at the Jerusalem conference to God's call, noting that he went up to Jerusalem "in response to a revelation" (Gal 2:1). The implication is clear: God was directing Paul's steps from the very beginning.

Paul's flair for the dramatic is also evident in his defense. Knowing that the letter would be read aloud to his churches, he recounts his meeting with the Jerusalem leaders and his enemies at the Jerusalem conference, building the verses to the dramatic moment when Peter, John, and James must acknowledge him as the apostle to the Gentiles.

Then I laid before them (though only in a private meeting with the acknowledged leaders) the gospel that I proclaim among the Gentiles, in order to make sure that I was not running, or had not run, in vain. But even Titus, who was with me, was not compelled to be circumcised, though he was a Greek. But because of false believers secretly brought in, who slipped in to spy on the freedom we have in Christ Jesus, so that they might enslave us—we did not submit to them even for a moment, so that the truth of the gospel might always remain with you. And from those who were supposed to be acknowledged leaders (what they actually were makes no difference to me; God shows no partiality)—those leaders contributed nothing to me. On the contrary, when they saw that I had been entrusted with the gospel for the uncircumcised, just as Peter had been entrusted with the gospel for the circumcised (for he who worked through Peter making him an apostle to the circumcised also worked through me in sending me to the Gentiles), and when James and Cephas [Peter] and John, who were acknowledged pillars, recognized the grace that had been given to me, they gave to Barnabas and me the right hand of fellowship, agreeing that we should go to the Gentiles and they to the circumcised. They asked only one thing, that we remember the poor, which was actually what I was eager to do. (Gal 2:4-10)

Using divine revelation—with a liberal dose of sarcasm—as a defense, Paul does a masterful job of discrediting his opponents while upholding his stand on circumcision. He also subtly establishes his equality with Peter by noting God's hand in both their callings. As mentioned above, Paul's reference to the Jerusalem collection is phrased to suggest that it is a discretionary request from the leaders rather than an order from ecclesiastical superiors.

Having established his equality with Peter, Paul immediately challenges the apostle's religious conviction by recounting the Antioch incident in which he accused Peter of hypocrisy because he refused to eat with Gentile Christians out of "fear of the circumcision faction" (Gal 2:12). Paul's public rebuke of Peter was a clever rhetorical move, for in shaming a respected leader of the church, Paul established the necessary context for presenting his gospel as the true one.

Paul's Gospel of Justification by Faith

In contrast to Peter's compromise, Paul lays out the basic principles of his gospel of justification by faith. He argues that neither Jewish nor Gentile Christians are justified (i.e., made righteous) before God through works of the Law, "but through faith in Jesus Christ" (Gal 2:15-16). But what does faith in Jesus Christ mean exactly? And how does faith justify the sinner? These questions are important ones because they pinpoint the central claim of early Christianity, a claim that is often confused—at least among many contemporary Christians—with belief in the divinity of Jesus. The gospel Paul preached to the Galatians has little to do with whether Jesus was the Son of God; in fact, Trinitarian theology was centuries away from creedal formulation. Paul's emphasis is on the divine-human relation—

specifically, how human beings relate to God and how the coming of the crucified Messiah changes that relationship.

At its very core, Paul's gospel is theocentric. The good news for Christians is that Jesus did not die the shameful death of a criminal, although, objectively speaking, it appears that way. On the contrary, to rectify the ungodly God raised Jesus, his chosen prophet-Messiah, and in that glorious moment a new age was inaugurated in which the efficacy of the Mosaic Law for salvation was radically altered by the Christ-event, an event that includes the cross and resurrection. For Paul, it is not the Law but faith in God's intentions, as realized and witnessed in the Christ-event that justifies human beings. Christians are made righteous before God because they *believe* that God raised Jesus and they have *faith* that God will raise them up on the last day, according to God's promises.

Paul's claim about God, Jesus Christ, and the Mosaic Law is the result of his simple but profound observation that "if justification comes through the law, then Christ died for nothing" (Gal 2:21). The observation is a crucial one, for once Jewish Christians accept a crucified Messiah—a plot twist that was not part of the original Jewish messianic scenario—they need to relinquish the primacy of the Torah for salvation as well. But old habits die hard and the Judaizers and other conservative Jewish Christians resist Paul's interpretation. While Paul is furious with their attempts at sabotage, he is just as upset with the Galatians for forgetting his gospel. After some paternal scolding, Paul attempts to bring them back to their senses by stating the obvious:

> You foolish Galatians! Who has bewitched you? It was before your eyes that Jesus Christ was publicly exhibited as crucified! The only thing I want to learn from you is this: Did you receive the Spirit by doing the works of the law or by believing what you heard? Are you so foolish? Having started with the Spirit, are you now ending with the flesh? Did you experience so much for nothing?—if it really was for nothing. Well then, does God supply you with the Spirit and work miracles among you by your doing the works of the law, or by your believing what you heard? (Gal 3:1-5)

Paul knows perfectly well who has "bewitched" the Galatians, but to counteract the spell of the Judaizers, Paul reminds his flock of their own experience of receiving the Spirit, which is the divine gift that comes with faith. The contrast Paul makes between the Spirit and the flesh is central to his gospel and warrants some attention.

The Spirit and the Flesh

Paul's understanding of the Spirit (Heb. *ruah*; Gk. *pneuma*) is rooted in the Old Testament. While the Spirit has a variety of meanings in the biblical texts, it most frequently denotes a divine force or power of being that emanates from God and that enables human beings to fulfill special tasks.

Throughout the biblical narrative God's Spirit descends upon shepherds, judges, prophets, and kings, giving them extraordinary powers of wisdom, prophecy, and other charismatic gifts that ensure their success—at least for a time. In the prophetic literature, God's Spirit also plays an active role at the final judgment. In an oft-quoted passage from the book of Joel, Yahweh declares that after delivering the faithful, "I will pour out my spirit on all flesh; your sons and your daughters shall prophesy, your old men shall dream dreams, and your young men shall see visions. Even on the male and female slaves in those days, I will pour out my spirit" (Joel 2:28-29). The Spirit is thus presented as a sacred power that enables human beings—regardless of social status—to play an active role in God's intentions for creation.

Paul clearly believes that the Galatian churches have received this generous outpouring because of their faith in what they heard in his gospel. The proof, according to Paul, lies in the many "miracles" that the life of the Spirit has brought them. But if that is true, how did the Judaizers gain a foothold in the churches? Paul believes the answer lies in the ongoing struggle between the flesh and the Spirit.

For Paul, the flesh is not the body, per se; rather, it is the material medium in which all existent beings operate.[10] In contrast to the Spirit, which is the eternal, empowering force of God in the universe, the flesh designates all that is transitory, vulnerable, and limited in the world, including physical bodies, political and social institutions, and cultural norms and values. Sin erupts when human beings set their hearts on matters of the flesh instead of the Spirit, focusing on the transitory instead of the eternal. In contrasting the Spirit and the flesh, Paul is accusing the Galatians of forgetting the faith that brought them the Spirit and turning themselves over to transitory practices—such as circumcision and other "works of the law"—that jeopardize their salvation; hence his pointed question about the source of the miracles. In asking the question, Paul is forcing the Galatians to reflect on their own experience in faith and to realize that the outpouring of God's Spirit and the attendant miracles will be lost if they follow the path of the Judaizers. The precise nature of these miracles is revealed in his ethical teachings, which will be discussed below.

Having established the source of the problem, Paul could have simply demanded that the Galatians stop following the Judaizers. As the founder of the churches, he certainly had the status and authority to make such a demand, but he wisely uses his rhetorical skill instead, developing an argument from scripture that forges vital links between the God of Israel, Abraham, the Christ-event, and the new Jewish-Gentile faith.

The Adoption of Christians as Abraham's Heirs

In a deft bit of exegesis, Paul interprets the Old Testament in light of the Christ-event, adapting the chronology of Judaism to support his gospel.

Just as Abraham "believed God, and it was reckoned to him as righteousness," so, you see, those who believe are the descendants of Abraham. And the scripture, foreseeing that God would justify the Gentiles by faith, declared the gospel beforehand to Abraham, saying, "All the Gentiles shall be blessed in you." For this reason, those who believe are blessed with Abraham who believed. (Gal 3:6-9)

Citing the Abraham story (Gen 5:6; 18:18; 22:18), Paul argues that faith, as practiced by Abraham, was the mechanism for salvation prior to the Mosaic Law. He was, after all, deemed righteous by God *before* he was circumcised (Gen 17:1-14). Proof for the primacy of faith is also found in God's words to Abraham, which indicate (in Pauline hindsight) that the plan to save the Gentiles through faith in the Christ-event was present in the Divine Mind from the very beginning; otherwise, why would God mention them to Abraham? Paul's reasoning must have resonated deeply with Jewish Christians—especially those who were still undecided about their relation to the Torah—and with Gentile Christians, who were no doubt relieved to learn that Paul's gospel was foreshadowed in the Old Testament, thus making circumcision (and other less painful requirements) unnecessary.

On its face, Paul's claim that the Age of Law has ended and the Messianic Age has begun supports a supersessionist construction, but does that mean that Jews are suddenly left out in the cold? Paul's teachings on the purpose of the Mosaic Law offer some important clues.

The Purpose of the Law

Paul's claim about the primacy of faith naturally raises the question about the need for the Mosaic Law. If faith is what saves human beings, why then the Law? Paul explains that the Law was added to the covenant "because of transgressions, until the offspring would come to whom the promise had been made" (Gal 3:19). Although the meaning of the phrase, "because of transgressions" is ambiguous, the most likely reading is that the Law was added to the covenant so that Jews would know what kinds of actions qualified as transgressions against the will of God. He offers further explanation in one of the most famous passages in the letter. Recalling his life as a pious Jew (hence the collective "we"), Paul first describes a life ruled by the Law: "Now before faith came, we were imprisoned and guarded under the law until faith could be revealed. Therefore the law was our disciplinarian until Christ came, so that we might be justified by faith" (Gal 3:23-24).

The Jews of the Galatian churches were well aware of what Paul meant when he said "the law was our disciplinarian until Christ came." Since the time of Ezra, the 613 dictates of the Mosaic Law had grounded Jewish identity and shaped Jewish piety. As a law community, Jews believed that their collective salvation depended upon upholding the Torah requirements. Consequently, the pressure to "get it right" was enormous, leaving conscientious Jews vulnerable to—but not inevitably guilty of—legalism and the sins of pride, corrupt motives, and hypocrisy.

But how can obedience to the Mosaic Law result in the imprisonment of the faithful? It seems antithetical to everything God and his prophets have said about the nature and purpose of the Law. Paul's answer, which is detailed in Romans 7:7-25, is rather paradoxical: As a standard or norm for human behavior, the Law can function as both a disciplinarian and a temptation to sin—a rather confusing claim to say the least. An example from contemporary life will illustrate how this happens.

George Steele is a successful businessman who earns a very comfortable living in the car business. The secret of his success is his honesty: "You'll always get a square deal with George Steele" is his dealership's motto. Like many fathers, George wants his son, Evan, to join the family business and Evan is more than happy to oblige. He is grateful for the opportunity to earn an honest living and make "George Steele & Son" a reality. After finishing high school, Evan joins his father's sales team, which has just hired some "new blood." Although he sells a respectable number of cars each month, his numbers are a bit low compared to those of the other new salesmen. Taking his son aside, George launches into one of his tried and true pep talks. Eager to please, Evan follows his father's advice to the letter, working twelve-hour days, six days a week, but despite his best efforts, his sales numbers don't improve. Evan feels inadequate and guilty for not living up to his father's standards. To make matters worse, George has just launched a year-end sales contest, telling his son that he expects him to "show the other guys how it's done!" Feeling even more panicky, Evan is determined to get ahead. As the days tick by with little improvement, he resorts to "dirty tricks" to sabotage his co-workers, but the strategy doesn't work. They're selling cars left and right, leaving Evan in the dust. George calls Evan into his office and upbraids him for not meeting his sales goals: "Look, Evan, there are only three weeks left and you're at least fifteen cars behind! It's time to get serious here!" Evan is so stressed and desperate to win the contest that he starts promising his customers incredible discounts, overly generous trade-ins, the moon and the stars—just about anything to make the sale and bump up his numbers. The strategy works only too well. Reading over his son's daily sales reports—which Evan has padded to hide some of his concessions—George is ecstatic. By the end of the third week, Evan has jumped ahead of the other salesmen, winning the contest by a comfortable margin. George and the car company's corporate executives are so impressed with Evan's sales record that they throw him a lavish party. Of course, George takes the opportunity to make a long-winded speech, praising Evan for his hard work and commitment to the company's values and goals. But the celebration is short-lived. Within days, "George Steele & Son" is confronted by a steady stream of irate customers who didn't get what Evan had promised them. Some threaten legal action and nearly all of them demand their money back. So much for the company motto! George makes good on all of Evan's promises, but it costs him a great deal of money, as well as his reputation in the community. To spare his father any further embarrassment or lost business, Evan quits his job and moves to another city until the scandal blows over.

This story illustrates how the Law can act as a both disciplinarian and a temptation to sin. In this case, George Steele set high standards of performance that Evan wanted to uphold but could never quite meet. As a result, the disciplinarian side of George stepped in, constantly reminding Evan of just how much he was falling short and urging him to work harder to get the results he wanted. But in constantly prodding his son, George inadvertently generated an opening for temptation. Evan's desire to win the contest—to meet his father's high standards—tempted him to act very badly, and like Adam, Eve, Cain, and countless others, he acted on his desire and both he and his father paid dearly for it.

As a former Pharisee, Paul understood better than most the power of this paradox. In Romans he confesses that "I can will what is right, but I cannot do it. For I do not do the good I want, but the evil I do not want is what I do" (Rom 7:19). Paul clearly believed that the Judaizers were steering the Galatian churches toward this same pitfall and he would have none of it. He thus attempts to bring the Galatians back from the brink by reminding them of the transformation effected by faith in Jesus Christ.

> But now that faith has come, we are no longer subject to a disciplinarian, for in Christ Jesus you are all children of God through faith. As many of you as were baptized into Christ have clothed yourselves with Christ. There is no longer Jew or Greek, there is no longer slave or free, there is no longer male and female; for all of you are one in Christ Jesus. And if you belong to Christ, then you are Abraham's offspring, heirs according to the promise. (Gal 3:25-29)

"Now that faith has come," marks the transition from the Age of Law to the Messianic Age, and for Paul this meant that those who have faith in the Christ-event—whether Jew or Gentile—are free from the Mosaic Law as the vehicle of salvation. His description of Christian baptism explains the transformative effects of faith on individual believers.

Baptism for purification and healing was practiced regularly among peoples of the ancient Near East, most notably the Egyptians, the Jews, and devotees of mystery religions that flourished at the time. With John the Baptist and other Jewish baptizers, the ritual was understood as a dramatic, one-time event that signified a believer's repentance and spiritual cleansing from sin. The early Christian communities extended and "Christianized" the ritual's meaning. As Paul explains, in Christian baptism, the faithful are "clothed" in Christ, which signifies his atoning intervention on their behalf. In that moment of spiritual rebirth, they receive the gift of the Spirit—just as Jesus did at his baptism—and are united with their fellow Christians in the body of Christ, which is the church. For Paul, the reception of the Spirit meant freedom from traditional divisions (i.e., fleshly limitations) of race, gender, and social status and the donning of new identities as Abraham's offspring and heirs to God's covenant promises.

Up to this point in the letter, Paul offers nothing to suggest that Jews are somehow disinherited from Abraham's family. On the contrary, his explanation of justification by faith is designed to show why Gentiles *should* be included, thus discrediting the Judaizers' position. His allegory of Hagar and Sarah (Gal 4:21–5:1), however, is more problematic.

The Allegory of Hagar and Sarah

In Genesis, the women are presented as feuding competitors for the seed of Abraham (Gen 16:1-16; 21:1-21), but in the allegory Paul uses them to represent the two sides of the covenantal divide: Hagar represents descendants of Abraham who follow the Torah (the covenant of Sinai), whereas Sarah represents heirs to God's promises through faith in Jesus Christ (the covenant of the new Jerusalem). Hagar is in slavery with her children, whereas Sarah is free and is the mother of the children of faith. Citing the Genesis account, Paul draws an unfortunate parallel between the crisis in the Galatian churches and the fates of the two women and their offspring.

> Now you, my friends, are children of the promise, like Isaac. But just as at that time the child who was born according to the flesh persecuted the child who was born according to the Spirit, so it is now also. But what does the scripture say? "Drive out the slave and her child; for the child of the slave will not share the inheritance with the child of the free woman." So then, friends, we are children, not of the slave but of the free woman. For freedom Christ has set us free. Stand firm, therefore, and do not submit again to a yoke of slavery. (Gal 4:28–5:1)

The persecution of the child refers to Ishmael's teasing of Isaac (Gen 21:9). On its face, Paul's allegory appears to exclude Jews from God's plan because they are "slaves" to the Mosaic Law, and many supersessionist Christians— both then and now—have interpreted his words that way. The third-century theologian Origen offers one classic example.

> Agar [Hagar] therefore, "was wandering in the wilderness" with her child and the child was crying and Agar cast him forth saying, "Lest I see the death of my son." After this, when already he had been abandoned as dead and had wept, the angel of the Lord is present with him "and opened Agar's eyes and she saw a well of living water."
>
> How can these words be related to history? For when do we find that Agar has closed eyes and they are later opened? Is not the spiritual and mystical meaning in these words clearer than light, that that people which is "according to the flesh" is abandoned and lies in hunger and thirst, suffering "not a famine of bread nor a thirst for water, but a thirst for the word of God," until the eyes of the synagogue are opened? This is what the Apostle says is a "mystery": that "blindness in part has happened in Israel until the fullness of the Gentiles should come in, and then all Israel should be saved." That, therefore, is the blindness in Agar who gave birth "according to the flesh," who remains blind until "the veil of the letter be removed" by the angel of God and she see the "living water." For now the Jews lie around the well itself,

but their eyes are closed and they cannot drink from the well of the Law and the prophets.[11]

For Origen, the meaning of the allegory is clear: God has abandoned the Jews (Hagar's children), who are blind to the truth of Christ, the "living water." This blindness is the result of their literal interpretation of the Old Testament and the Mosaic Law. The children of Hagar will remain in a state of spiritual starvation and carnal excess until the eschaton when an "angel of God" permits them to convert to Christianity, which will remove "the veil of the letter." Origen's reference to Romans 11:25-26 reflects the common belief that Christians have taken the place of Jews as the true Israel of God. Writing centuries later, Martin Luther uses the allegory to make similar claims.

> The Apostle sheweth by this allegory of the prophet Isaiah, the difference which is between Agar and Sarah, that is to say, between the Synagogue and the Church, or between the law and the Gospel.... [The Jews] although they be fruitful, have many disciples, and shine in the righteousness and glorious works of the law, yet notwithstanding are not free, but bondservants; for they are the children of Agar, which gendereth to bondage. Now if they be servants, they cannot be partakers of the inheritance, but shall be cast out of the house; for servants remain not in the house for ever (Jn 8:35). Yea they are already cast out of the kingdom of grace and liberty: "For he that believeth not, is condemned already" (Jn 3:18). They remain therefore under the malediction of the law, under sin and death, under the power of the devil, and under the wrath and judgment of God.[12]

As with Origen, Luther excludes Jews from "the inheritance," but he offers no hope of redemption. Their rejection of Jesus Christ condemns them to the futile bondage of the Law.

The problem with these kinds of interpretations—and many others in the Christian tradition—is that they assume that legalism is the norm for Jewish piety rather than the exception. In other words, both Origen and Luther assume that *all* Jews consider the works of the Law to be the true and complete expression of their faith and thus they strive to become "Pharisees" as caricatured in the gospels. In collapsing the distinction between Judaism and legalism, they place all Jews under the "malediction of the law." But is that Paul's position? If it is, then Paul is clearly contradicting his previous statements about the inclusive nature of the Abrahamic family, as well as his understanding of God as the unbiased rectifier of the ungodly. How could God abandon and disinherit the Jews, who were the original recipients of the promise? Is that the action of a righteous God who is trying to save all human beings? The apparent contradiction disappears, however, if we understand that the allegory is not referring to Christianity and Judaism but to the conflict between Paul and the Judaizers.[13] Many scholars now believe that Paul is using the allegory to contrast the fates of

Gentile Christians who have faith in Jesus Christ and the Judaizers who insist that Gentiles adhere to the Mosaic Law. The next section of the letter details how faith in the Christ-event frees the Galatians from the Mosaic Law. What emerges from his teachings is a program for Christian faith and ethics that parallels Jesus' teachings in the Sermon on the Mount.

The intertextual connections between the two are indeed striking, particularly since Paul rarely mentions the teachings of Jesus in his letters. Nevertheless, like Jesus before him, Paul is rejecting a strict rule-centered ethic for an Abrahamic form of faith that fears the Lord. Yet Paul's teachings exceed Jesus' program in one vital respect. In light of the Christ-event, Paul claims that the kind of faith practiced by Abraham is the key to salvation for both Jews and Gentiles.

The Meaning of Christian Freedom

Returning to the issue of circumcision, Paul restates his argument against the Judaizers in forceful, straightforward terms:

> Listen! I, Paul, am telling you that if you let yourselves be circumcised, Christ will be of no benefit to you. Once again I testify to every man who lets himself be circumcised that he is obliged to obey the entire law. You who want to be justified by the law have cut yourselves off from Christ; you have fallen away from grace. For through the Spirit, by faith, we eagerly wait for the hope of righteousness. For in Christ Jesus neither circumcision nor uncircumcision counts for anything; the only thing that counts is faith working through love. (Gal 5:2-6)

The crucial point here is that Paul is not addressing Jewish justification per se; rather, he is arguing that Gentile Christians must not follow the way of the Judaizers because faith in the Christ-event changes their relationship to the Mosaic Law. The Christ-event is the divine gift that assures the faithful of God's love and acceptance. Through faith they become part of God's covenant community. Moreover, baptized into the faith and empowered by the gift of the Spirit, the faithful are called to emulate God's generosity, giving to others as God has given to them. The radical shifts in perception and motivation that characterize "faith working through love" are the basis for Paul's instructions to the Galatians on the meaning of Christian freedom. What is important to understand about Paul's teaching is that while he rejects the Mosaic Law for Christian salvation, he clearly believes that the Law is the proper means through which Christians respond to God's grace and maintain peace and unity in the churches until Jesus returns. The pedagogical challenge for Paul is to clarify for the Galatians how they should approach the Law for ethics.

> For you were called to freedom, brothers and sisters; only do not use your freedom as an opportunity for self-indulgence, but through love be-

come slaves to one another. For the whole law is summed up in a single commandment, "You shall love your neighbor as yourself." If, however, you bite and devour one another, take care that you are not consumed by one another. Live by the Spirit, I say, and do not gratify the desires of the flesh. For what the flesh desires is opposed to the Spirit, and what the Spirit desires is opposed to the flesh; for these are opposed to each other, to prevent you from doing what you want. But if you are led by the Spirit, you are not subject to the law. (Gal 5:13-18)

Paul's reference to "self-indulgence" hints at the same issue that troubled Jesus, namely, self-serving interpretations of the Law that ultimately compromise true obedience. As Paul makes clear, the call to freedom requires a fundamental shift from the self to the other, from self-indulgence to a deep and abiding concern for the common good. The slavery of desire (in which the Law plays a part) is thus replaced with a different kind of slavery, one that freely binds the Galatians in love and service. Yet Paul warns them that the call to freedom is not without its challenges, for the ongoing battle between the Spirit and the flesh can lead to confusion, doubt, and backsliding, invariably resulting in abusive behaviors that prevent them from fulfilling their call. To reinforce this point, Paul offers a lengthy and oft-quoted list of vices and virtues that further highlight the difference between the Spirit and the flesh.

Now the works of the flesh are obvious: fornication, impurity, licentiousness, idolatry, sorcery, enmities, strife, jealousy, anger, quarrels, dissensions, factions, envy, drunkenness, carousing, and things like these. I am warning you, as I warned you before; those who do such things will not inherit the kingdom of God. By contrast, the fruit of the Spirit is love, joy, peace, patience, kindness, generosity, faithfulness, gentleness, and self-control. There is no law against such things. And those who belong to Christ Jesus have crucified the flesh with its passions and desires. If we live by the Spirit, let us also be guided by the Spirit. Let us not become conceited, competing against one another, envying one another. (Gal 5:19-26)

This passage contains many interesting and subtle insights into human motivation that echo those of the antitheses and "hard sayings" of Jesus. The first verses list the works of the flesh and cover quite a range of sinful activities. Paul's inclusion of the passions of jealousy, anger, and envy is significant because it suggests that these "works" of the flesh are conscious choices on our part. We *choose* to be jealous, angry, and envious and then, having "worked up" these emotions, we use them as motivational springs for fornication, quarrels, carousing, and other activities that corrupt and splinter the community. Feelings of envy and jealousy spring from a sense of emptiness that drives the quest for objects of the flesh and that justifies actions that are needed to acquire them—usually at the expense of others. Paul's warning about conceit and competition is intended to break this destructive cycle.

In contrast to the grasping and aggressive behaviors of the flesh, the fruit of the Spirit is the emotional response to God's initiative in Jesus Christ. Receiving the unexpected and unmerited gift of salvation motivates the faithful in a very different way. Instead of experiencing a gnawing sense of emptiness, they experience a sense of fulfillment and completion, expressed in feelings of love, joy, peace, patience, generosity, and so on. Instead of grasping after objects of desire, recipients of the gift are filled with the desire to serve others, to give to others as God has given to them. For Paul, the fruit of the Spirit is the source of the "miracles" experienced by the Galatian churches. In believing Paul's gospel, the Galatians experienced a *metanoia* (Gk. "a change of mind") that transformed their communities for the better, but now their earthly progress and their ultimate salvation are threatened by the false teachings of the Judaizers.

When Paul states that "there is no law against such things," he is making another important point. The Law is powerless in matters of virtue or character development because it cannot reach into the human heart. The old adage, "You can't legislate morality," acknowledges this serious limitation. The purpose of all law—whether political or religious—is to protect public and communal values and safeguard public order. Law cannot generate the motivational fruit of the Spirit; only faith in God's promises as witnessed in the Christ-event can transform the heart and redirect the will.

The final section of Paul's ethical teachings confirms this reading, offering the Galatians additional guidelines for judging their behavior and for building up the faith community.

> My friends, if anyone is detected in a transgression, you who have received the Spirit should restore such a one in a spirit of gentleness. Take care that you yourselves are not tempted. Bear one another's burdens, and in this way you will fulfill the law of Christ. For if those who are nothing think they are something, they deceive themselves. All must test their own work; then that work, rather than their neighbor's work, will become a cause for pride. For all must carry their own loads. Those who are taught the word must share in all good things with their teacher. (Gal 6:1-6)

Here Paul emphasizes the humility that attends a life of the Spirit—the self is subsumed for the sake of others. Paul's instruction on fulfilling the "law of Christ" may be connected specifically to love of neighbor, which he cites earlier in the letter (Gal 5:14), or it may refer to the general intention of Jesus' teachings. Whatever the case, Paul's choice of words is used to make yet another contrast between faith and the Law.

In contrast to the Mosaic Law, the law of Christ is not an external prescription; rather, it signifies the fruit of the Spirit, namely, the virtuous dispositions that inform Christian freedom. Over time, these virtues become operational habits that act *like* a law. For example, in this passage Paul is urging the Galatians to treat each other with kindness so that they can forgive transgressions and bear each others' burdens. Over time, this generosity of spirit will become a stable disposition within each of them, arising spontaneously and naturally. The Galatians will be able to police themselves, without fear of the Law's catalogue of transgressions. In this respect, the law of Christ is very similar to Jesus' command in the sermon to be perfect "as your heavenly Father is perfect" (Mt 5:48). Both instruct the faithful to emulate God's generosity. Until that happens, however, Paul counsels vigilance and constant self-evaluation so that the Galatians won't backslide.

Paul concludes on a cautious but hopeful note in his final instructions:

Do not be deceived; God is not mocked, for you reap whatever you sow. If you sow to your own flesh, you will reap corruption from the flesh; but if you sow to the Spirit, you will reap eternal life from the Spirit. So let us not grow weary in doing what is right, for we will reap at harvest time, if we do not give up. So then, whenever we have an opportunity, let us work for the good of all, and especially for those of the family of faith. (Gal 6:7-10)

Taking a final slap at the Judaizers, Paul warns the Galatians of the consequences of their weakness, but then softens his tone, offering a much-needed morale booster to his chastened flock. Paul's reference to the traditional proverb: "You reap what you sow" and to "harvest time" conjure images of the final judgment, when the fates of all human beings are decided. While Paul's final instruction on good works emphasizes the welfare of the "family of faith," he makes it clear that Christian charity must be extended to all persons—whether Jew or Gentile.

Paul and the Jews

Our analysis of Paul's gospel and his teachings on the Law and Christian freedom help clarify the intention and meaning of the allegory of Hagar and Sarah. Rather than promoting the exclusion of the Jews from God's plan, the allegory functions as a theological prelude to Paul's ethical teachings, contrasting in a dramatic way the fates of those who practice Abrahamic faith (Sarah) and those who follow the way of the Judaizers (Hagar). For Paul, the command to "drive out the slave and her child" is not directed at Jews, but against the Judaizers—or any agitators for that matter—who give in to the temptations of the flesh, namely, to the transitory requirements of the Mosaic Law. When viewed together, Paul's gospel of justification by faith, his theological interpretation of Hagar and Sarah, and his ethical teachings present the Galatians with a mutually reinforcing program for Christian belief and practice that will help them avoid this disastrous pitfall.

The inclusive character of Paul's gospel is further reinforced in the concluding blessing of the letter in which he bestows peace and mercy upon "the Israel of God" (Gal 6:16). The phrase harkens back to the righteous remnant—the "priestly kingdom and a holy nation" (Ex 19:6) idealized at Mount Sinai and preached by the prophets. For Paul, the bond that unites Jew and Christian is the Spirit of God, which is received through an Abrahamic form of faith that saves. Our reading of Galatians is confirmed in Paul's letter to the Romans, which is the last and most detailed statement of his theology. A brief consideration of Romans 2:21-29 is particularly helpful to our study because it articulates the Jewish side of the bond.

The Letter to the Romans

In the letter to the Romans, Paul presents a diatribe against an imaginary Jewish opponent—probably a Pharisee—who prides himself on obeying the letter of the Law and boasts of his special relation to God. Accusing his opponent of hypocrisy, Paul asks the "corrector of the foolish" and the "teacher of children" a series of pointed questions:

> While you preach against stealing, do you steal? You that forbid adultery, do you commit adultery? You that abhor idols, do you rob temples? You that boast in the law, do you dishonor God by breaking the law? For, as it is written, "The name of God is blasphemed among the Gentiles because of you." Circumcision indeed is of value if you obey the law; but if you break the law, your circumcision has become uncircumcision. So, if those who are uncircumcised keep the requirements of the law, will not their uncircumcision be regarded as circumcision? Then those who are physically uncircumcised but keep the law will condemn you that have the written code and circumcision but break the law. For a person is not a Jew who is one outwardly, nor is true circumcision something external and physical. Rather, a person is a Jew who is one inwardly, and real circumcision is a matter of the heart—it is spiritual and not literal. Such a person receives praise not from others but from God. (Rom 2:21-29)

Paul's questions make the point that no one is exempt from accountability to God—the Pharisee must practice what he preaches if he is to be truly righteous. Moreover, the "requirements of the law" involve more than external observance. Like Jesus before him, Paul argues that obedience to the Law is valuable if and only if the motive and the act (i.e., the Spirit and the letter) are in harmony, but if the heart is corrupt, then the act—no matter how perfectly executed—is a transgression against the will of God and worthy of condemnation. This condition holds for both the circumcised (the Jews) and the uncircumcised (the Gentiles). This is why Paul claims that "a person is a

Jew who is one inwardly," and that real circumcision (which is the mark of God's chosen people) is "a matter of the heart—it is spiritual and not literal." Inclusion in the new "Israel of God" is thus a matter of character rather than self-serving obedience, which is why Paul declares that God will "justify the circumcised on the ground of faith and the uncircumcised through that same faith. Do we then overthrow the law by this faith? By no means! On the contrary, we uphold the law" (Rom 3:30-31).

Paul's exchange with the Pharisee thus confirms the centrality of Abrahamic faith for both Jews and Christians; the difference lies in how each group receives the transforming power of the Spirit. Jews receive it by trusting in God's covenantal promises; Christians receive it by trusting in the reality of the Christ-event. In response to these gifts, Jews and Christians strive to emulate God's generosity and to fulfill the Law in both Spirit and letter in accordance with God's good intentions.

Further confirmation of Paul's inclusive scheme is found in Romans 11:25-36. The passage forms the climax to a larger block of material (Rom 9–11) that explains to the Gentile Christians of Rome God's complex relationship with the Jews and how they fit in with his overall plan of redemption. John Gager tells us why Paul included this rather lengthy section in his letter:

> Romans 9–11 belongs to Paul's attempt to correct what he takes to be a profound misreading of his views about Israel and the Torah, or law of Moses. Apparently some Gentiles in the Jesus movement had taken him to be an advocate of what we have called the rejection-replacement view, namely, that the Jews and their law have been rejected by God and that the Jews had been replaced as the chosen people by Gentile followers of Christ. In Romans 9–11 Paul repudiates this view in the clearest possible terms.... [14]

Misinterpretations of Paul's views were quite common among the early Christian communities; hence his many letters—but what is so distressing about this particular case is that Christians (not only in his own day but also later, e.g., Origen and Luther) continued to misread Paul's attempt to correct earlier misinterpretations of his teachings! We can only imagine Paul's response to such a turn of events. Fortunately, his words are still with us, providing the light to help us get back on the right path.

Weaving all the threads of his theology, eschatology, and ethics together, Paul begins with a plea for Christian humility.

> So that you may not claim to be wiser than you are, brothers and sisters, I want you to understand this mystery: a hardening has come upon part of Israel, until the full number of the Gentiles has come in. And so all Israel will be saved; as it is written, "Out of Zion will come the Deliverer; he will banish ungodliness from Jacob. And this is my covenant with them, when I take away their sins." As regards the

gospel they are enemies of God for your sake; but as regards election they are beloved, for the sake of their ancestors; for the gifts and the calling of God are irrevocable. Just as you were once disobedient to God but have now received mercy because of their disobedience, so they have now been disobedient in order that, by the mercy shown to you, they too may now receive mercy. For God has imprisoned all in disobedience so that he may be merciful to all. (Rom 11:25-32)

Citing Isaiah 59:20-21, Paul affirms God's intention to save both Jews and Gentiles, but the process necessitates "hardening" a part of Israel until the full number of Gentiles can be brought into the fold. The "part" of Israel that is causing all the trouble is the segment of the Jewish population that has fallen into the trap of legalism, whether they are individual Pharisees, Sadducees, Essenes, farmers, shopkeepers, or itinerant preachers. Their "hardening" is the result of the externalizing of righteousness, which obscures the kind of faith and obedience practiced by Abraham. For Paul, the delay of the final judgment is a blessing in disguise (hence his reference to "mystery"), because God in his mercy has used the disobedience of these wayward Jews to send "the Deliverer" so that the faith of Abraham can be retrieved and proclaimed to Gentiles through Paul's gospel. But the need for and significance of the delay does not stop with the success of Paul's mission to the Gentiles, for he argues that just as Jewish disobedience enabled Gentiles to be adopted into Abraham's family, it now offers Gentiles a chance to help their Jewish brethren return to the faith of their ancestors. The phrase "by the mercy shown to you" tells them how. As faithful Christians, they know that God's mercy and the attendant gifts of the Spirit were bestowed upon them through their faith in the Christ-event. Paul is telling them that by setting a good example, by living a life of the Spirit, Christians will show all Jewish legalists the benefits of a life of faith—a life they cannot obtain through the works of the Law. But their example doesn't mean that Jews will or should convert to Christianity. On the contrary, they only have to look to the irrevocable "gifts and the calling of God" to find their way back to Abraham and to the kind of faith that will "banish ungodliness from Jacob."

Before leaving the passage, however, we should acknowledge the eight-hundred-pound gorilla in the room and ask the obvious question: Did Paul himself view Jesus as God's prophet-Messiah? His reference to Jesus in the passage strongly suggests that he did. Paul describes Jesus as the "Deliverer" sent by God to save all of Israel, which includes both Jews and Gentiles. Jesus' mission as the Deliverer can be accomplished only if his prophetic ministry and his death and resurrection embody multiple initiatives to the peoples of the world. Paul's deep and abiding concern for the Jewish people was not about whether they would convert to Christianity—time was simply too short for that. His concern was whether they would heed the teachings of Jesus (and Israel's other prophets) and return to the roots of their faith so that God's efforts to rectify the ungodly could be fully realized.

Conclusion

Paul's letter to the Galatians is a bold and brilliant attempt to justify his apostleship and theological vision and to save his churches from the false teachings of the Judaizers. As a historical and theological document, the letter has been invaluable to this study because it illuminates the religious and cultural conflicts within the early church that have fueled anti-Jewish sentiments. While it is true that Paul's teachings have been and continue to be used by some Christians to support exclusionary theologies, it is equally true that Paul himself did not embrace or promote such views. He did not insist that Jews convert to Christianity, or preach that the Christ-event nullified the Jewish covenant, or advocate hatred of his people. On the contrary, in illuminating the intertextual connections between Abrahamic faith and the Christ-event, Paul revealed God's intention to redeem all God-fearing Jews and Gentiles and to include them in his kingdom.

In this respect, the letters of Paul support the possibility that God's salvific initiative in Jesus has indeed taken multiple forms. As the Galilean prophet, Jesus revitalized God's gift of the Law, focusing on the spirit of the Law and the interior dispositions that are required to fulfill the Law, thus making the kingdom of God a genuine possibility on earth as it is in heaven. As the Christ of faith, Jesus was the suffering Messiah, who sacrificed himself for the sake of others. Paul articulated the implications of this great gift for human salvation and Christian ethics. Our analysis has shown that the gift of Christ does not alter Jesus' emphasis in the sermon; it merely shifts the object of faithful concern from God's covenant promises to the Christ-event. Both are intended to promote an Abrahamic form of faith and the kind of interior dispositions that trigger the shift from the self to the other—a shift that God, the prophets, and Jesus all advocated long before Paul developed a different theological rationale for it. The prophet-Messiah thus succeeds in holding God's multiple initiatives together—it is our theological biases and on limited, either-or thinking that disrupt this delicate balance.

Ultimately, this means that both Jews and Christians will have to revise their answer to Jesus' question: "Who do people say that I am?" For Jews, Jesus is a legitimate Jewish prophet whose teachings reaffirm the meaning of faithful obedience to the will of God; for Christians, Jesus is the Messiah, whose death and resurrection serve as a new vehicle for Abrahamic faith. In his teachings as God's prophet and in his death and resurrection as God's suffering Messiah, Jesus shows both traditions how faith saves without privileging one tradition over the other. The common ground between the traditions is the Bible's model of Abrahamic faith and the Jewish-Christian ethics that spring from it.

Having completed our reading of Matthew and the letters of Paul, we shall next consider the results of our study and what our project of biblical liberation means for the interpretation and use of the Bible as a spiritual and moral source and for furthering interfaith dialogue.

Questions for Reflection and Discussion

1. Write a brief paragraph that answers the following question: What do you think it means to say, "I have faith in Jesus Christ?" What claims are being made with this statement? How has this chapter affirmed, challenged, or altered your understanding of faith in Jesus Christ?

2. Paul and the other leaders of the early church engaged in many debates about the nature of the new faith. What were these conflicts about? Were they satisfactorily resolved? What do early church experiences reveal about role of tradition, innovation, and dissent in faith communities? How might you apply this process in your own community?

Recommended Reading

Chilton, Bruce. *Rabbi Paul: An Intellectual Biography*. New York: Doubleday, 2004. A lively and readable biography of Paul.

Gager, John G. *The Origins of Anti-Semitism: Attitudes toward Judaism in Pagan and Christian Antiquity*. Oxford: Oxford University Press, 1985. A coherent and well-documented study of Jewish-Christian relations that also considers Paul's argument regarding the Jews.

Keck, Leander E. *Paul and His Letters*. 2nd ed. Philadelphia: Fortress Press, 1988. An influential scholar offers a comprehensive interpretation of Paul's life, letters, and theology.

Meeks, Wayne A. *The First Urban Christians: The Social World of the Apostle Paul*. New Haven: Yale University Press, 1983. An authoritative study of the daily life, practices, and conflicts of the early Christian communities founded by Paul.

Roetzel, Calvin. *Paul: The Man and the Myth*. Minneapolis: Fortress Press, 1999. A scholarly reconstruction of Paul's life and theology that attempts to fill in some of the gaps in Pauline research.

9

THE BIBLE LIBERATED

Now that we've completed our exegetical journey through the biblical world, it's time to take stock and figure out what it all means. We began our biblical rescue mission with three central goals in mind: First, to make the Bible less intimidating and more accessible to all the Bible-curious, regardless of their spirituality or religious affiliation; second, to liberate the Bible from Christian interpretive traditions that limit and distort its revelatory message, and, third, to liberate the Bible from its reputation and use as a divinely sanctioned rulebook. Using a variety of exegetical tools, we embarked on a series of close readings from a global, theocentric perspective, focusing on God's redemptive activity through major portions of the Christian canonical narrative. The central question guiding our readings was a methodological one: How does God develop and use the gifts of creation, covenant, the Law, the prophets, and Jesus as the prophet-Messiah to help human beings fulfill the divine intentions, grow and mature in their faith, and construct their own moralities within the biblical world?

A review of the biblical narrative and God's evolving pedagogy and governance structure will provide the answer, revealing a promising method and model for contemporary Christian ethics that not only discredits the rulebook model, but reveals the Bible's significance for all human beings, regardless of their spirituality or religious affiliation. As we "connect the dots" in the biblical narrative, we'll also make the rather startling discovery that Jesus is not only God's prophet-Messiah, he is also the new Abraham—the quintessential God-fearer—whose example of humble obedience and doubt affirms and epitomizes the program God first introduced with the patriarch.

Connecting the Dots

When we entered the biblical world, we immediately encountered the God of Israel, the central character of the story. Yahweh is depicted as a powerful, mysterious, but very accessible deity who creates and continually hones a progressive program for human development (part of God's economy of the gift) that coincides with the divine plan for salvation. The program combines universal values and norms with concrete practical strategies to address the needs and failings of the biblical characters within their particular literary contexts. As the narrative unfolds, Yahweh finds it necessary to revise the program, offering new gifts as the need arises to help human beings move toward spiritual and moral maturity. In each case, God presents them (either directly or through his agents) with an ideal to strive for and then provides a practical program to help them realize it.

In Genesis, Yahweh offers the fundamental gift of a good creation. In bringing the world into being, God's providential economy establishes a moral order that is grounded in the core values of justice, respect, mutuality, and solidarity and that is initially governed by a strict rule-centered ethics of obedience. As creatures born with innate goodness and dignity, human beings are meant to live together as equal partners, to create and nurture families, and to fulfill their calling as stewards of creation. Unquestioned obedience to God ensures that human beings will realize the ideal of the garden, but Adam and Eve's willful disobedience of the divine command shows the weakness in this model, for with the gift of freedom comes the possibility of rebellion against God and the corruption of the core values that sustain the moral order. Rather than abandon or destroy creation (an option that God later tries but finds unsatisfactory), Yahweh offers humanity the gift of the covenant to address this fundamental weakness.

In establishing a covenant relationship with Abraham, God takes a more "hands-on" approach, promising the patriarch that he will make him a model of righteousness through whom "all the families of the earth shall be blessed" (Gen 12:3). To realize this ideal, God introduces a more flexible, mentoring model that focuses on character development and that encourages critical thinking, debate, and even religious doubt. Surprisingly, rather than undermine the divine-human relationship, these activities serve as a catalyst for Abraham's moral and spiritual growth. Through his ongoing and often contentious relationship with Yahweh, Abraham acquires "fear of the Lord," a religious disposition that is characterized by humility, gratitude, obedience, worship, and unselfish service to others. As a God-fearer, Abraham trusts in God's providential care and obeys the will of God freely and authentically—even when God commands the sacrifice of his beloved son, Isaac. Abraham's obedience and desire to serve others are not prompted by an unreflective assent to authority (as was expected of Adam and Eve) or by calculated self-interest (as was initially practiced by the patriarch). Instead, Abraham's actions are prompted by genuine respect for the will of God and a sense of gratitude for everything God has provided over the years. Thus, with Abraham, righteousness before God is no longer limited to obedience to divine commands but is redefined and expanded to include the interior dispositions that motivate moral action.

While God's mentoring program is successful—Abraham is indeed transformed into a model of righteousness—changing circumstances require that God further refine his program to address the unique challenges presented by the plight of the Hebrew slaves.

After years of enslavement by the Egyptians, the Hebrews are ill-equipped to become the "priestly kingdom" and "holy nation" God envisions. To achieve this ideal, God combines the gift of the Sinai covenant (the rule-centered model) with a three-stage training program (the mentoring model). This flexible hybrid transforms the Hebrews from a group of fearful and overly dependent slaves to a responsible and unified people eager to obey God's will and to secure their future in the Promised Land. With the leadership and guidance of Moses, the people enter into the Sinai covenant with God and agree "in one voice" to uphold all the covenant laws, thus accepting complete responsibility for the use of their freedom. As God's chosen people, they understand that they must remain loyal to Yahweh, practice just relations with each other, and show compassion and charity for the vulnerable (as represented by the widow, the orphan, and the stranger). In accepting these terms, the people agree to a theocratic form of government, living together as one nation under God.

Although the people pledge their loyalty and obedience to the Lawgiver, their longing for the old ways (signified by the murmurings and the golden calf incident) reveals a fundamental truth about moral agency that is often overlooked; namely, that the righteousness of the Abrahamic model—or any model for that matter—cannot be automatically duplicated and solidified. Genuine moral and spiritual growth is a lifelong process that requires ongoing training, constant reinforcement, vigilance, and time. This ethical truism plays itself out in the turbulent and tragic history of Israel, prompting God to introduce new refinements into his program in the prophetic books.

With God's ongoing care and assistance, the people conquer the land, establish the Davidic monarchy, and achieve considerable prosperity and power in Canaan. But in their quest for wealth and prestige they forget those pesky covenant requirements, incurring God's righteous wrath once again. Rather than destroy them outright (as he did with the golden calf idolaters), God sends the gift of the prophets to remind the people of their covenant obligations and to warn them of the consequences of their idolatrous and abusive behavior. Unfortunately, the people stubbornly refuse to listen to the prophets. The book of Isaiah recounts God's righteous punishment of the people (via the Assyrians and Babylonians) and the efforts of the three Isaiahs to rehabilitate them. Whether by accident or design, the combined Isaian writings construct a progressive program of spiritual and moral reform that mirrors the Sinai covenant in its form and intention. This time the goal is to transform the people of Israel from demoralized victims of war and exile to chastened and much wiser God-fearers who strive to realize the ideal of the new Jerusalem.

Collectively, the prophets' efforts at reform introduce two significant additions to God's economy. First, the God of Isaiah is presented as a cosmic deity who extends the scope of his salvific activity to include pagan nations. In the new Jerusalem all persons are potential vehicles for and recipients of God's grace. Second, the mysterious and innovative nature of God's activity introduces a critical or objective moment into the pedagogical structure. The rise, fall, and restoration of Israel attest to the fact that human beings can never assume they know God or the ways of God, for Yahweh is a mysterious deity who is often willing to use unorthodox means to achieve his aims and to punish anyone—even his "chosen people"—if they fail to uphold God's justice. A chastened and humble people—a people who truly fear the Lord—will always question their own assumptions and motives before embarking on any plan of action, knowing full well how easily they can become complacent, overly confident, and corrupt.

Despite the adjustments in God's program, the new Jerusalem described by the prophets fails to materialize. Instead, infighting among Israel's ruling families leaves the country vulnerable to the expansionist plans and military might of the Greeks and later the Romans, who burden the people with heavy taxation and oppressive laws and social policies. To make matters worse, over time Israel's religious identity is threatened by internal squabbles among religious groups (primarily Sadducees, Pharisees, and Zealots) that vie for power and influence. Rather than intervene directly, Yahweh once again sends the gift of prophecy. This time his chosen messenger is Jesus of Nazareth. Embedded in Matthew's gospel is a new program for religious reform and renewal that addresses Israel's increasing fragmentation and alienation from the Torah.

In his role as religious reformer, the Matthean Jesus proclaims the coming of the kingdom of God, a kingdom where suffering is alleviated and where the poor, the meek, and the peacemakers are comforted and honored. His teachings in the Sermon on the Mount are designed to realize the ideal of God's kingdom on earth—despite the power of world empires—and to challenge the legalistic interpretations of the Torah by some of his fellow Jews (represented by the Pharisees and scribes). To retrieve God's true intention in crafting the Law, Jesus introduces a number of antitheses and "hard sayings" in the sermon, antitheses that shift the focus away from the act itself (the legalistic emphasis) to the motive behind the act (the Abrahamic emphasis). While Jesus never uses the phrase "fear of the Lord," his attention to interior dispositions and the fundamental connection between motive and act reflect the kind of faith and obedience to God's will that Abraham practiced but that was lost with the rule-centered approach of Jewish legalists.

In retrieving fundamental elements of God's progressive program, Jesus makes another important contribution. His teachings show that the relationship between love and justice—between compassion and the essential egalitarianism that grounds legal justice—must be placed at the very center of ethical reflection because both are needed for God's justice to be fully realized in the kingdom. The virtue of equity, which balances the often conflicting claims of love and justice, thus becomes a central feature of God's program.

Jesus' teachings on the kingdom of God, as well as his healings, exorcisms, and other worthy deeds, attract quite a following, but his success brings only further division to Israel. In fact, his ministry causes such a stir (particularly after the Temple incident) that Jewish leaders eventually bring him to trial before the Sanhedrin, and he is later executed by the Romans for sedition. But the death of the prophet does not deter God's efforts to save human beings. On the contrary, it provides him with the opportunity to introduce his most innovative and daring gift to date: Jesus as prophet-Messiah. In Jesus of Nazareth, God places the roles of prophet and Messiah in creative tension, extending their salvific power to Jews and Christians through their respective covenants. But bitter conflicts about the identity of Jesus blind both groups to the complex nature of the gift. God's response is brilliant and a little cheeky, to say the least. He chooses one of the most zealous persecutors of the early church to reveal the significance of Jesus Christ for Gentile salvation and for Jewish-Christian relations. In making his case, Paul's writings reinforce key components of God's pedagogical program while illuminating others.

In his letter to the Galatians, Paul argues that the death and resurrection of Jesus (the Jewish Messiah) is the event that enables Gentiles to be included in God's kingdom, thus reasserting God's intention to save all human beings. The human response that opens the door to the kingdom is an Abrahamic form of faith first established with the patriarch. For Paul, faith in God's providential power is the key for both Jews and Christians because it makes the Mosaic Law and the Christ-event effective vehicles of God's grace and Spirit. That is to say, faith in God's salvific intentions—as modeled by Abraham and witnessed in the Sinai covenant and the Christ-event—is the necessary condition that enables both Jews and Christians to obey God's commandments in both letter and Spirit, thus making them righteous before God. The centrality of Abrahamic faith for salvation finds further confirmation in Paul's ethical teachings.

Like Moses, the prophets, and Jesus before him, Paul envisions an ideal society where the faithful freely and joyfully obey God's will. For Paul, the ideal is the Spirit-filled church; the practical program to realize this ideal is a Christian ethics grounded in Abrahamic faith, informed by the Mosaic Law, and motivated by the Spirit of God (as opposed to the desires of the flesh). Similarly, Paul's teachings on Christian freedom emphasize character development and harmony between motivation (the Spirit) and action (the letter of the Law), thus reaffirming the program established with Abraham, retrieved in the teachings of the prophets (including Jesus) and completed (at least in the Christian biblical narrative) in the church.

In reaffirming God's universal intention, Paul also illuminates another, more controversial feature that challenges the anti-Jewish theologies that were taking root in the early church. His interpretation of God's redemptive plan in Romans 9–11 establishes that God's salvific initiative can indeed take multiple forms: for Jews it is the Sinai covenant (properly understood and practiced, of course) and for Gentile and Jewish Christians it is the Christ-event. This means that Jews who follow the Sinai covenant do not have to convert to Christianity to be saved—they have the Law. But no matter the number or nature of the forms, they are all made effective through an Abrahamic form of faith that fears the Lord.

While the intertextual connections Paul makes between Abraham and the Christ-event confirm the centrality of faith and the inclusive character of God's kingdom, they also shed light on two other features of God's program that are not explicitly developed in Paul's writings but are revealed when we consider his work within the intertextual dynamics of the biblical economy as a whole.

The Necessity of Conflict and Struggle

As noted in the previous chapter, in his letter to the Galatians Paul argues that Abraham was deemed righteous before God because of his faith—a faith that existed *prior* to the Sinai covenant and the Mosaic Law. For Paul, the priority of faith made circumcision and other covenant requirements unnecessary for Gentile converts to enter the church. If we accept Paul's reasoning regarding the priority of faith, then we must also consider the *process* by which Abraham acquired it—a process that we know was anything but smooth. While Paul never refers to this process in his letters, his insistence on the centrality of faith raises a crucial question for Christian ethics: Is Abraham's ongoing struggle with God the model that the faithful should expect and even hope to emulate? A brief comparison of the lives of Abraham and Jesus strongly suggests that it is.

Abraham's story depicts the transformation of the patriarch from a self-interested and often manipulative opportunist to a humble and obedient servant of God. He achieves this status toward the end of his life, only after many misjudgments and mistakes. As depicted in the gospels, Jesus of Nazareth is the new Abraham because he shows what it means to fear God from the very beginning of his life. In living out the Abrahamic ideal, Jesus is showing his followers what it means to live a life of humility, gratitude, obedience, worship, and unselfish service to others.

While Jesus is definitely the new and improved Abrahamic model, he also experiences dramatic changes in his relationship with God that test his faith. Recall that in Matthew's baptism scene, the Father-Son relationship appears strong and secure. Jesus is anxious to please the Father, telling John that his baptism is necessary, "to fulfill all righteousness" (Mt 3:15). God is duly impressed, bestowing upon Jesus the gift of the Spirit, which empowers him throughout his earthly ministry. In the garden of Gethsemane, however, we encounter a very different divine-human exchange.

> He took with him Peter and James and John, and began to be distressed and agitated. And he said to them, "I am deeply grieved, even to death; remain here, and keep awake." And going a little farther, he threw himself on the ground and prayed that, if it were possible, the hour might

pass from him. "Abba, Father, for you all things are possible; remove this cup from me; yet, not what I want, but what you want." He came and found them sleeping; and he said to Peter, "Simon, are you asleep? Could you not keep awake one hour? Keep awake and pray that you may not come into the time of trial; the spirit indeed is willing, but the flesh is weak." (Mk 14:33-38)

Here is a Jesus who doubts, who cries out to his Father in heaven in fear and trembling, but the Father is silent. In this garden (a familiar setting for catastrophe), there are no words of praise from heaven, no dove signaling divine approval. Jesus' admonition to his disciples is heavy with irony, for he is suddenly aware of the weakness of his own flesh. Faced with his own mortality, he knows and fears the pain and prolonged torture of crucifixion—a punishment he no doubt witnessed under Roman rule. Yet, despite God's silence, Jesus doesn't run away from the test. Like Abraham at Mount Moriah, Jesus trusts God and obeys the Father's will without a word of protest (Mk 14:61; Mt 26:63; Lk 23:9). The dutiful and obedient Son fulfills the scriptures (Mk 14:49) just as he did at his baptism, but at a far greater cost.

The depth of Jesus' faith commitment is clearly witnessed at the moment before his death. He cries out, "My God, my God, why have you forsaken me?" (Mk 15:34; Mt 27:46). Initially, these words seem to indicate a resurgence of doubt, but nothing could be further from the truth, for Jesus' words are taken from Psalm 22. While the opening verses of the psalm describe the pain and suffering of one who feels utterly abandoned by God, the psalmist's hope for rescue is soon realized, transforming the lament into a song of gratitude and praise to a merciful God.

> From the horns of the wild oxen you have rescued me.
> I will tell of your name to my brothers and sisters;
> > in the midst of the congregation I will praise you:
> You who fear the LORD, praise him!
> > All you offspring of Jacob, glorify him;
> > stand in awe of him, all you offspring of Israel!
> For he did not despise or abhor
> > the affliction of the afflicted;
> > he did not hide his face from me,
> but heard when I cried to him.
> From you comes my praise in the great congregation;
> > my vows I will pay before those who fear him.
> The poor shall eat and be satisfied;
> > those who seek him shall praise the LORD.
> > May your hearts live forever!
> All the ends of the earth shall remember
> > and turn to the Lord;

and all the families of the nations
    shall worship before him.
For dominion belongs to the Lord,
    and he rules over the nations.
To him, indeed, shall all who sleep in the earth bow down;
    before him shall bow all who go down to the dust,
    and I shall live for him.
Posterity will serve him;
    future generations will be told about the Lord,
and proclaim his deliverance to a people yet unborn,
    saying that he has done it. (Ps 22:21-31)

As it was with Abraham, Jesus' moment of doubt at Gethsemane is the catalyst for a deeper faith and trust in God, a trust so great that in the hour of his death he is confident that God will deliver him from evil. The resurrection confirms that Jesus' faith is not misplaced, for like Abraham before him, Jesus knows that Yahweh is a trustworthy God who always provides.

The Necessity of a Global, Theocentric Perspective

In the first chapter of this book, we likened the global dimension of biblical revelation to an orchestra performing a symphonic work. The canon is the musical score and the individual texts are the instruments that work together—in harmony and conflict—to tell a story. The emergence of Jesus as the new Abraham confirms the power and truth of this metaphor. Comparing their lives reveals not only the necessity of conflict and struggle for the development of authentic faith but also the necessity of interpreting the Bible from a global, theocentric perspective instead of the traditional christocentric one. Only by tracing God's activity throughout the economy of the gift do we discover the full extent of God's intentions in Abraham and Jesus. In connecting their narratives, we discover that Jesus is not only the prophet-Messiah, but he is also the new Abraham, whose life, death, and resurrection confirm and fully realize the Abrahamic model of righteousness.

A global, theocentric perspective also exposes the folly of limiting biblical analysis to the key teachings of Jesus or to particular moments in his life, such as the crucifixion or resurrection, for just as the sacrifice of Isaac is a culminating point for Abraham, so the Christ-event is the culminating point for Jesus. By exploring and comparing their narratives we see a likely trajectory for our own. By grasping the totality of their lives we understand that we, too, shall change and grow and have doubts, but as God-fearing human beings we can expect nothing less, for faith is not about absolute certainty or having all the answers. Faith is about trust in God's intentions for the world and in God's promises as revealed in the many gifts offered throughout the biblical story and throughout our own lives. Thus we must have a grasp of the whole if we are to make any sense of the individual parts.

THE BIBLE'S PROGRAM FOR CHRISTIAN FAITH AND ETHICS

Throughout the narratives of the Bible, God offers a variety of gifts to help readers realize this goal. The result is a program for spiritual and moral development that contains the following components:

- a goal or ideal to strive for
- practical strategies to realize the goal or ideal
- traditional or foundational values and norms
- flexibility, innovation, and balance
- love, justice, and equity
- doubt, struggle, and prophetic insights
- inclusivity, innovation, and openness
- a moral litmus test

For contemporary Christians, following this program means using a variety of sources (scripture, tradition, reason, and experience) for ethical reflection and accepting the challenge and responsibility of biblical interpretation. It also means that, while they are fully committed to their own faith tradition, they recognize that all world religions have revelatory truth and value for the moral life.

The Bible as a Revelatory Text and Moral Source

From an ethics perspective, the significance of these intertextual connections and global revelations cannot be overstated, for they strongly suggest that the governance structure and pedagogical program Yahweh develops in Genesis and Exodus, refines in Isaiah, and extends in the New Testament are *canonical*, that is, they function together as an authoritative paradigm or model for faith communities to construct their own ethics and morality. In crafting the program—which holds the polarities of faith and doubt, virtue and duty, love and justice, mystery and certainty, and tradition and innovation in creative tension and balance—God's intention is not to produce unreflective rule-followers who parrot the dictates of a divine-command morality. On the contrary, God's strategy is designed to transform readers of the Bible into God-fearing servants of the creation who think critically about their faith, who are open to innovation, change, and doubt, and who have the ability to construct moralities that uphold justice and foster peace for their own time and place.

Thus, contrary to the rulebook model espoused by many Christians, the Bible is best understood as a revelatory text that illuminates rather than legislates. Its authority is derived not from its status as a religious text per se or from the divine command morality it initially presents, but from its power to reveal new modes of being and new approaches to living that have existential significance and truth value for all human beings, regardless of their religious affiliation.

Although we can never hope to perfect the Abrahamic model as Jesus did, we can look to Abraham, Jesus, and other biblical figures for help and guidance. The structures, values, ideals and innovative strategies of God's economy are there, ready to be explored, debated, appropriated, and practiced. But appropriating the biblical texts requires careful and responsible exegesis. This means that we cannot adopt literal readings that limit biblical meaning, or ignore the theological biases of interpretive traditions, or restrict ourselves to certain key texts, or pull biblical teachings out of their original contexts and apply them directly to our present situation—such practices contradict the purposes of God's biblical economy. Instead, as critical discerners we must be open-minded and free enough to explore the Bible in multiple ways, using a variety of literary, historical, cultural, and theological approaches to unlock its revelatory content. The global, theocentric reading used in this book is just one example of a more eclectic approach to biblical interpretation that offers new insights for developing Christian ethics for our own time and place.

Liberating the Bible from its interpretive prisons and limitations is not without restrictions and safeguards, however. Guarding against eisegesis and the misapplication of biblical teachings requires not only the use of the accepted tools of biblical criticism but also the adoption of the simple but powerful maxim: "the tree is known by its fruit" (Mt 12:33). Whenever we use the Bible as a moral source, we must be sure that we are upholding God's intentions. This means that we must ask ourselves—both as individuals and as members of faith communities—some very tough questions. For example, does the morality we construct teach fear of the Lord as practiced by Abraham and Jesus? Does it uphold justice and foster compassion and peace among persons, whether Jew or Gentile, Christian or non-Christian? Does it promote and protect the inherent dignity of all God's creatures, as well of creation itself? If the answer to any of these questions is no, then we must acknowledge and confess that we have corrupted God's intentions on some fundamental level and thus must return to the biblical drawing board.

Responsible use of the Bible also requires that the appropriation of specific ethical content be integrated with and tempered by other moral sources. The Bible does provide some universal values and norms that can and should be used in ethical reflection. The teachings of the Decalogue, the social justice command, and the love command, for example, constitute the foundational structures of biblical ethics and are vital to distinguishing

Christian ethics from moral philosophy. That being said, it must be acknowledged that much of the moral content of the Bible is too historically and culturally conditioned to be useful in many contemporary settings. The validity of biblical teachings on homosexuality, gender relations, abortion, war, and marriage, for example, have been and continue to be challenged and debated by theologians, scientists, and ethicists, as well as "regular folks" who are simply trying to live decent and faithful lives in today's world. In these matters, the power of human reason and experience may carry far greater weight in moral decision-making than the Bible. Yet, instead of rejecting these biblical teachings entirely, we could use them as imaginative illustrations to help us understand the principles, values, and norms that constitute biblical morality, with an eye toward assessing and appropriating similar (but not identical) building blocks for contemporary Christian ethics.

Responsible appropriation also requires that we consider the dynamics of biblical revelation. The divine-human relation depicted in the Bible shows that both God and human beings are deeply affected by the exchange—the unpredictability of human freedom means that God learns from human beings just as human beings learn from their God. God's revelation is thus an ongoing, open-ended, dynamic process that incorporates both tradition and innovation. As disciples of the text, we must acknowledge the dynamics of God and God's revelation and be vigilant for new gifts of the Spirit that may appear to help us in our own situation. The new revelations and gifts arising from the text and from our own experience of God may challenge us to revise traditional understandings, and we must be open to that possibility. This book itself may offer such a challenge, for in observing how biblical moralities are constructed within the biblical world, we are given the gift of a moral methodology that guards against ethical relativism and that provides the means to respond appropriately to particular historical and cultural situations. It is our contention that such an understanding of the Bible will yield more consistency in and credibility to the Christian witness and to the discipline of Christian ethics because the focus will shift from the "what" of the Bible to the "how" of the Bible, offering a method of appropriation that is more in line with God's spiritual and pedagogical intentions.

Implications of This Study for Interfaith Dialogue

In liberating the Bible as a spiritual and moral source, our study of the biblical economy also opens up possibilities for interfaith dialogue because it affirms the existence of a cosmic Being or Sacred Power who infuses creation with structure and purpose. The name of this deity—whether it is Yahweh, Allah, the Tao, Brahman, or any other name we care to use—is not as important as the divine intention, which is revealed in the sacred literature of all the great world religions. The divine communication, as articu-

lated in the Bible, the Qur'an, the Bhagavad Gita, the Tao Te Ching, and
other authoritative texts, teaches the primacy of the divine-human relation,
the centrality of faith, the necessity of humility, obedience, justice, and compassion, the importance of intention, and the possibility of salvation from
the human predicament. The shared content of these revelations can and
should help us live together in peace, justice, and general prosperity, yet one
of the tragic ironies of human history is that religion is more often than not
a source of fragmentation, intolerance, injustice, and hatred. Today, anti-
Semitism still seethes below politically correct speech, and conflicts between
Jews and Muslims in Palestine, Hindus and Buddhists in Sri Lanka, and the
most recent battle between the Judeo-Christian "West" and radical Islam
present a serious threat to all the peoples and nations of the earth.

Engagement with the Bible's economy of the gift offers hope for genuine dialogue and rapprochement among people of faith because it not only
illuminates common ground but it also exposes the limitations of all organized religions. The history of Jewish-Christian relations is a classic example
of how human thought and conceptual biases—as well as the competitive
struggle for religious survival—can trap human beings in untenable positions that generate sectarian hatred, violence, and war. The God of the Old
and New Testaments rejects such divisive, either-or thinking, offering Jews
and Christians multiple initiatives in Jesus that effectively overcome the
schism without privileging one faith over the other. The stubborn refusal of
both groups to leave the armed camps of their own exclusionary theologies
and consider God's revelation in the prophet-Messiah only perpetuates their
collective fall from grace and its tragic consequences.

The Bible's intertextual complexity also challenges simplistic understandings of divine revelation, which contribute to and often exacerbate tensions among religions. Regardless of culture, religious tradition, or language,
all revelatory texts are the product of divine-human interaction and the creative power and limitations of religious language and human concepts. As a
historical phenomenon and cultural artifact, each sacred text has made the
transition from oral to written form and has undergone an extensive period
of reflection, revision, and development prior to and even after canonization.
With respect to the Bible, the historical and dynamic nature of divine revelation as charted in the economy of the gift challenges all supersessionists
who believe that successive stages of revelation somehow negate or usurp
previous ones, and religious fundamentalists who believe that sacred texts
are ahistorical and that a particular tradition or interpretation (usually
theirs) is the correct or definitive one. Regardless of the canonical content
and structure of a particular religious tradition, divine revelation cannot be
pigeonholed or limited by human concepts, space-time configurations, textual interpretations, or redactions. On the contrary, the Sacred is constantly
revealing itself to us in new and innovative ways while affirming enduring
truths about the divine-human relation. The constant interplay between tradition and innovation found in all sacred texts means that no person, group,

or institution can define or control the Wholly Other—it is far too mysterious, elusive, and transcendent for such heavy-handed hubris.

The complex nature of divine revelation also means that all world religions can be legitimate and effective paths to God and salvation because they all spring from the same sacred source. Contrary to the triumphalist rhetoric of religious zealots (which surfaces in all world religions), there is no hierarchy in God's self-communication, only unity in diversity. Thus, the teachings of the Jewish and Christian canons, as well as the Qur'an, the Bhagavad Gita, the Tao Te Ching, and other sacred texts are all worthy of careful study and consideration, for they all offer human beings insights into the divine-human relation and the meaning and value of human (and non-human) existence.

As we come to the interfaith table with our sacred texts and good intentions, we must all remember that we are human beings first, members of faith communities second. We must also remember that the litmus test of our collective will remains the same. Do our religious traditions uphold the divine intentions? Do they further peace, justice, compassion, charity, and solidarity in the human family? If not, then we must have the humility and the good sense to recognize the error of our ways, to understand that our grasp of the Sacred is always partial and limited, and to take heart in the knowledge that the Sacred is always with us, revealing itself to us in infinite ways. But we must be prepared to accept the challenge, the uncertainty, and the struggle of faith. Joining our brothers and sisters at the table, we would do well to consider the wisdom of the great Hindu sage, Ramakrishna. His prayer to the Sacred Mother is as timely today as it was when first uttered over a century ago.

> Mother, Mother, Mother! Everyone foolishly assumes that his clock alone tells correct time. Christians claim to possess exclusive truth.... Countless varieties of Hindus insist that their sect, no matter how small and insignificant, expresses the ultimate position. Devout Muslims maintain that Koranic revelation supersedes all others. The entire world is being driven insane by this single phrase: "My religion alone is true." O Mother, you have shown me that no clock is entirely accurate. Only the transcendent sun of knowledge remains on time. Who can make a system from Divine Mystery? But if any sincere practitioner, within whatever culture or religion, prays and meditates with great devotion and commitment to Truth alone, Your Grace will flood his mind and heart, O Mother. His particular sacred tradition will be opened and illuminated. He will reach the one goal of spiritual evolution. Mother, Mother, Mother! How I long to pray with sincere Christians in their churches and to bow and prostrate with devoted Muslims in their mosques! All religions are glorious![1]

Amen to that!

Recommended Reading

Childress, James F., and John MacQuarrie. *The Westminster Dictionary of Christian Ethics*. Philadelphia: The Westminster Press, 1986. An essential reference for theological and applied Christian ethics.

Gill, Robin, ed. *The Cambridge Companion to Christian Ethics*. Cambridge: Cambridge University Press, 2001. This helpful collection of essays from noted ethicists and theologians examines conceptual foundations, approaches, and issues in Christian ethics.

Johnson, Luke Timothy. *Scripture and Discernment: Decision Making in the Church*. Nashville: Abingdon Press, 1983. Johnson's innovative study employs biblical patterns to guide discernment and moral decision making in Christian ethics.

Schweiker, William. *Power, Value, and Conviction: Theological Ethics in the Postmodern Age*. Cleveland: The Pilgrim Press, 1998. A theocentric approach to practical moral reasoning that considers the dynamics of tradition and innovation.

APPENDIX

Cultural History and the Development of Biblical Texts

*2500–2000 BCE   **The Early Migration of Israel's Ancestors:** The ancient ancestors of Israel were a mixed people of Northwest-Semitic (possibly Amorite) stock who migrated to Canaan from Mesopotamia (the land between the Tigris and Euphrates Rivers) during the first half of the second millennium BCE.

2000–1700 BCE   **The Period of the Patriarchs (Genesis 12–50):** Upon entering Canaan, the ancestral tribes followed traditional practice and adopted the local Canaanite gods. While most of the tribes remained in Canaan, others continued on, settling in northern Egypt as refugees or guest workers. Some of them would eventually become state slaves to the pharaohs, setting the stage for the exodus. During this time the first oral traditions about God's revelation to Israel's ancestors (Abraham, Isaac, and Jacob) emerged.

1300–1250 BCE   **The Exodus from Egypt and the March to Canaan (Exodus; Numbers; Deuteronomy):** The exodus likely occurred during the reign of pharaoh Rameses II (1290–1224). Moses' revelation centered on Yahweh, a tribal god from the land of Midian, who promised the Hebrew slaves liberation from Egyptian bondage. The exodus from Egypt, the events at Mt. Sinai, and the sojourn in the desert were central to Israel's development as Yahweh's chosen people and as a covenant community.

1200–1050 BCE   **The Period of the Conquest and the Judges (Joshua; Judges; 1 Samuel):** As the people reentered Canaan, they introduced Yahwism to the local tribes, who found the new religion appealing. Eventually, they formed loose tribal federations that were united in their worship of Yahweh and their mutual struggle for survival. Tribal leaders would periodically meet at central sanctuaries (such as Shechem and Shiloh) to renew their religious and tribal loyalties and settle disputes. Charismatic judges would assume leadership in times of crisis. During this period oral traditions about the patriarchs, Moses, the exodus, and the tribal judges took shape.

---

*All dates are approximate.

1050–930
BCE

The United Monarchy of Israel (1, 2 Samuel; 1, 2 Kings):
Under Saul, David, and Solomon, the tribal federations
eventually evolved into a united monarchy with Jerusalem as
the capital city and site of Yahweh's Temple. Under royal
sponsorship, writers collected and edited the various oral
traditions, forming a narrative about Israel's origins that
promoted the kingdom's political and religious worldview (the
Yahwist, or J Source). Priestly and prophetic schools generated
additional materials, reflecting the changing fortunes and
theological development of the people of Israel.

922–722 BCE   The Kingdom Splits in Two (1 Kings 12, 17–21): In 922 BCE,
internal squabbles between Solomon's successor (the inept
Rehoboam) and the northern tribes split the empire into the
Northern Kingdom of Israel and the Southern Kingdom of
Judah. The Israelites established their own capital city of
Samaria and developed traditions that reflected their religious
outlook. Reworking the Yahwist's materials, the Elohist (the E
source) constructed a theological narrative that was critical of
kingship and that stressed the centrality of the covenant for
proper worship and righteous governance. Northern and
southern prophets (such as Amos, Hosea, Micah, Isaiah) were
also active during this period.

722–721 BCE   The Destruction of Israel (2 Kings 17, 18–20; Isaiah 1–39): The
Assyrian Empire began a systematic campaign of conquest in
the region, eventually crushing the Northern Kingdom. The
Assyrians deported the bulk of the Israelite population to other
parts of their empire while moving foreign peoples into Israel.
Survivors who escaped deportation fled to Judah, taking their
Elohist traditions with them. To explain the calamity, First
Isaiah argued that Yahweh was a cosmic God who sent the
Assyrians to punish Israel for its many sins.

Judah survived as a vassal state of Assyria. To avoid
Israel's fate, priests, prophets, and other leaders organized a
religious reform movement (the Deuteronomic School) that
emphasized loyalty to Yahweh and the covenant. The reformers
combined materials reflecting the Yahwist and Elohist traditions
with legal traditions and sermons to form the book of
Deuteronomy (the D source). When reform failed, the book
was hidden away in the Temple. Years later, King Josiah
(640–609) discovered the book and attempted to enact the
reforms, but he was killed before they could be fully instituted.
During these years the basic materials of the Pentateuch and
the Deuteronomistic History were collected.

605–586 BCE   The Destruction of Judah (2 Kings 23–25; 2 Chronicles 36):
After destroying the Assyrian Empire in a series of battles, King

Nebuchadnezzar of Babylon secured Judah as a vassal state. When Judah's kings resisted Babylonian rule, Nebuchadnezzar destroyed the kingdom in two invasions (598 and 587), deporting the Judean upper classes to Babylon and sacking Jerusalem. Survivors who escaped exile migrated to Egypt, the Arabian Peninsula, and other lands. Thus began the dispersion of the Jewish people (the Diaspora) throughout the ancient world.

586–539 BCE   **The Babylonian Exile (Isaiah 40–55):** The writings of Second Isaiah offered a message of hope to the exiles, who remained in captivity for over fifty years. Rather than adopt the gods and culture of Babylon, Jewish leaders fought to maintain Israel's identity and history. One school of priests and Levites (the Priestly, or P source) gathered all the Pentateuchal materials, as well as laws, cultic requirements, genealogies, and other materials not found in the earlier works to form the Pentateuch (Genesis, Exodus, Leviticus, Numbers, Deuteronomy). Around the same time, the writer-redactors of the Deuteronomic School edited the historical books (Joshua, Judges, 1, 2 Samuel, 1, 2 Kings) to form the Deuteronomistic History (DH), which recounts Israel's history (in cycles of sin, punishment, and repentance) from the conquest to the exile. The editorial work on these projects continued into the postexilic period.

539–390 BCE   **The Postexilic Period (Isaiah 56–66; Ezra 1–6; Haggai; Nehemiah 8):** The exile ended with the victories of the Persian king, Cyrus, who permitted the Jews (a name derived from "Judeans") to return home. They found a desolated Judah. The writings of Third Isaiah addressed the social and religious challenges faced by the Restoration community.

To regain Yahweh's favor, the prophets Haggai and Zechariah pressed the returning exiles to rebuild the Temple, which was completed in 515. Later, under the leadership of Ezra (458–390) and Nehemiah (445–433), the community instituted programs of religious and political reform that restored the foundations of Yahwism and reestablished Israel as a community committed to the Mosaic Law. The text Ezra read to the people at a great assembly was likely an early version of the Pentateuch, which had been completed during this period.

336–200 BCE   **The Greeks in Palestine:** The Persian Empire (539–330) crumbled under the military might and genius of Alexander the Great, who instituted a program of Hellenization to bring Greek culture to the world. After his sudden death, part of his empire was divided between his loyal generals Ptolemy (Egypt and Judea) and Seleucus (Syria and the eastern territories). Under the Ptolemies, Jewish scholars translated their sacred texts into Greek (the Septuagint). In 200 BCE, the Seleucid king Antiochus the Great (223–187) wrested control of Judea from the Ptolemies.

200–164 BCE **The Maccabean Revolt (1 Maccabees 1–6; 2 Maccabees 5–10; Daniel 7–12):** The Syrian king's successor, Antiochus IV Epiphanes (175–164), embraced Hellenization. His intolerance of Jewish customs and religious practices and desecration of the Temple sparked the Maccabean Revolt (167). In 164, the Hasmonean leaders of the revolt regained control of the Temple and rededicated it to Yahweh (the feast of Hanukkah). Antiochus died at the time of the Temple rededication. The apocalyptic book of Daniel was composed during Antiochus's persecution of the Jews.

142–63 BCE **The Hasmonean Dynasty and "The Big Mistake" (1 Maccabees 13–16):** In 142 BCE, the Jews achieved independence from the Seleucids. The Hasmonean Dynasty was plagued by political intrigue and infighting among members of the Jewish aristocracy and emerging Jewish factions (Pharisees, Sadducees, and Essenes). Their collective fate was sealed when the Hasmoneans made "the big mistake" of asking the Roman general Pompey to mediate a dispute over the Hasmonean throne. When attempts at peaceful negotiation failed, Pompey attacked Jerusalem in 63 BCE, ending Jewish independence.

63–6 BCE **The Roman Occupation:** The power of the Hasmoneans rapidly declined and in 40 BCE the Romans appointed the Herodians of Idumea to rule Judea, installing Herod the Great as the first Herodian king. The brutal policies of the Romans and the Herodian rulers gave rise to Jewish insurrectionist groups (Zealots and Sicarii) and fueled the eschatological hopes of many Jews who prayed for the Messiah to come and destroy the Romans and their puppet regimes and redeem Israel.

6 BCE–32 CE **Jesus and the Jesus Movement:** Jesus of Nazareth was born between 6 and 4 BCE to a poor Jewish family in Galilee during the reign of Augustus and before the death of Herod the Great. His brief and controversial ministry attracted a following among people from diverse backgrounds and the swift condemnation of the Jewish authorities. Days after his execution by the Romans for sedition (30–33), his disciples reported his tomb empty and their leader resurrected by God. Soon afterward they began preaching the good news that Jesus was Israel's suffering Messiah whose death and resurrection had redeemed his chosen people, offering them a place in God's kingdom. Oral traditions about the life and work of Jesus and the rationale for Christian supersessionism began to take shape.

32–62 CE   **Jewish-Christian Tensions and the Early Church (Acts; Galatians):** Initially, the Jesus movement was a Jewish sect based in Jerusalem under the leadership of Peter, John, and James, the brother of Jesus, but Christian missionaries soon spread the faith throughout Palestine. They met active resistance from other Jews (most notably, Paul) who rejected their claims about Jesus, hauling many before Jewish authorities for punishment. The religious rift between Jews and Christians turned abusive and occasionally violent (e.g., Stephen's martyrdom).

Peter's conversion of the Gentile, Cornelius, and Paul's own conversion and mission to the Gentiles transformed the Jesus movement into a Jewish-Gentile faith that accepted converts from different religions and backgrounds. Paul established and guided house churches in Asia Minor and the Mediterranean region, chiefly through extended visits and letters (45–58). Paul's interpretation of the Christ-event, which rejected the salvific efficacy of the Law for Christians, increased tensions between Jews and Christians, and between Paul and the Judaizers, who challenged his authority as an apostle. Despite Jewish-Christian animosity, Paul's letter to the Romans specifically argued against Christian hardliners who excluded Jews from God's kingdom. During this time, Paul's letters, as well as oral and written traditions about Jesus, were being preserved, interpreted, and circulated. Roman authorities launched periodic persecutions of Jews and Christians, ultimately leading to the deaths of Peter and Paul in Rome (62–64).

66–73 CE   **The Jewish Revolt (Mark 11:27–13:37):** Nero's ordered confiscation of silver from the Jerusalem Temple sparked a riot, forcing the Roman authorities to flee Jerusalem. Zealots and Sicarii launched an armed revolt against Romans, Greeks, and the Jewish aristocracy that quickly spread throughout Judea. Christians refused to participate, which many Jews interpreted as an act of national betrayal, leading to further violence. The Romans put down the revolt, destroying Jerusalem and the Temple and slaughtering thousands of Jews (70). The mass suicide of Jews at Masada (73) marked the end of Jewish resistance. Mark's gospel (66–70), which incorporated oral and written traditions about Jesus, was completed during this period. The gospel's condemnation of Jewish leaders reflects the anti-Jewish sentiments within the Markan community.

80–160 CE   **The Council of Yavneh and Early Christian Writings (Matthew 15:1-9, 23:13-39; Mark 14:55-65; Acts 2:36, 3:14-15; John 8:43-49, 9:22, 16:2):** After the revolt, the Pharisees became the dominant Jewish party. Vespasian granted them permission to establish a rabbinic school at the coastal city of Yavneh. Between

75 and 100 CE, rabbis engaged in debates about the Jewish canon and other matters of communal worship and practice. The *Birkath ha-Minim* (a prayer against the heretics), the alleged letters of the rabbis slandering Jesus, and the spread of anti-Christian gossip further exacerbated tensions between Jews and Christians, leading to the expulsion and voluntary exclusion of Jewish Christians from some of the synagogues.

During this time, the writers of Matthew (85–90) and Luke-Acts (85–90) used the gospel of Mark, the Q Source, and their own materials (Special M and L) to develop gospels that reflected their understanding of Jesus for their respective communities. The anti-Jewish rhetoric, Christ-killer accusations, and supersessionist thinking contained in the gospels and other early writings (such as the book of Barnabas, the Gospel of Peter, and the Gospel of John) and the hatred spawned by the Bar Kochba Revolt (132–135 CE) would eventually lead to a parting of the ways between Jews and Christians and the establishment of Christianity as a distinct religion.

The remainder of New Testament texts (the general epistles and the Book of Revelation) were largely pseudonymous writings produced during the Roman persecutions of the late first and early second centuries CE, but by the fourth century Christianity had become the state religion of the empire. The anti-Judaism of the New Testament texts and other early Christian writings would form the basis for anti-Jewish legislation (both in the church and Roman state) and Christian anti-Semitism.

NOTES

1. What Is the Bible Anyway?

1. In recent years scholars have been questioning the historicity of such biblical events as the exodus and the conquest, but at this time the consensus is that these events did occur in history. For historical background on the Bible, see Michael D. Coogan, ed., *The Oxford History of the Biblical World* (New York: Oxford University Press, 1998).

2. Roger Haight, *Dynamics of Theology* (New York/Mahwah, NJ: Paulist Press, 1990), 29.

3. Rudolf Otto, *The Idea of the Holy* (London: Oxford University Press, 1958), 12–13.

4. Haight, *Dynamics of Theology*, 24–25.

5. Ibid., 25.

6. Paul Ricoeur, "Structure, Word, Event," in *The Conflict of Interpretations*, ed. Don Ihde, trans. Robert Sweeney (Evanston: Northwestern University Press, 1974), 85.

7. Sandra M. Schneiders, *The Revelatory Text: Interpreting the New Testament as Sacred Scripture* (New York: HarperCollins Publishers, 1991), 35.

8. Roger Haight, *Jesus Symbol of God* (Maryknoll, NY: Orbis Books, 1999), 202.

9. For a helpful discussion of the different canons and their formation, see Mark Z. Brettler and Pheme Perkins, "The Canons of the Bible," in *The New Oxford Annotated Bible with the Apocryphal/Deuterocanonical Books*, 3rd ed., New Revised Standard Version, ed. Michael D. Coogan (Oxford: Oxford University Press, 2001), 453–60.

10. In Judaism, *Torah* refers to the first five books of the Bible (the Pentateuch) and to the divine law or instruction given at Mt. Sinai.

11. Paul Ricoeur, "Biblical Time," in *Figuring the Sacred: Religion, Narrative, and Imagination*, ed. Mark I. Wallace, trans. David Pellauer (Minneapolis: Fortress Press, 1995), 171.

12. See Paul Ricoeur, "Ethical and Theological Considerations on the Golden Rule," in *Figuring the Sacred*, 293–302.

13. All biblical citations are taken from *The New Oxford Annotated Bible with the Apocryphal/Deuterocanonical Books*, 3rd ed., New Revised Standard Version, ed. Michael D. Coogan (Oxford: Oxford University Press, 2001).

14. Clarence Walhout, "Narrative Hermeneutics," in *The Promise of Hermeneutics* by Roger Lundin, Clarence Walhout, and Anthony C. Thiselton (Grand Rapids: Wm. B. Eerdmans Publishing Company, 1999), 122.

15. Michael J. Gorman, *Elements of Biblical Exegesis: A Basic Guide for Students and Ministers* (Peabody: Hendrickson Publishers, Inc., 2001), 9–10.

2. The Economy of the Gift

1. See John Bright, *A History of Israel*, 3rd ed. (Philadelphia: Westminster Press, 1981) and Wayne T. Pitard, "Before Israel: Syria-Palestine in the Bronze Age," in *The Oxford History of the Biblical World*, ed. Michael D. Coogan (New York: Oxford University Press, 1998), 25–57 for background on the origins of Israel.

2. Lawrence Boadt, *Reading the Old Testament* (New York/Mahwah, NJ: Paulist Press, 1984), 216.

3. See Daniel L. Smith-Christopher, "Returning to the Sources: The Hebrew Bible," in *The College Student's Introduction to Theology*, ed. Thomas P. Rausch (Collegeville: Liturgical Press, 1993), 24–44, for a survey of Israel's historical and religious development.

4. Stephen L. Harris and Robert L. Platzner, *The Old Testament: An Introduction to the Hebrew Bible* (Boston: The McGraw-Hill Companies, Inc., 2003), 64.

5. Lawrence E. Stager, "Forging an Identity: The Emergence of Ancient Israel," in *The Oxford History of the Biblical World*, 105.

6. See Harris and Platzner, *The Old Testament*, 79–91, for an excellent summary of the Documentary Hypothesis and the sources for the Pentateuch.

7. Mordechai Cogan, "Into Exile: From the Assyrian Conquest of Israel to the Fall of Babylon," in *The Oxford History of the Biblical World*, 270.

8. Boadt, *Reading the Old Testament*, 130.

9. See Boadt, *Reading the Old Testament*, 109–32, for an interesting and detailed discussion of the influence of Babylonian writings on the primeval history in Genesis.

10. Stephanie Dalley, ed., *Myths from Mesopotamia: Creation, the Flood, Gilgamesh, and Others* (Oxford: Oxford University Press, 1989), 254–56.

11. Ibid., 261.

12. See Harris and Platzner, *The Old Testament*, 41–42.

13. Bruce C. Birch et al., *A Theological Introduction to the Old Testament* (Nashville: Abingdon Press, 1999), 61.

14. See the commentaries of Robert Alter, *Genesis* (New York: W. W. Norton & Company, 1996) and Richard Elliott Friedman, *Commentary on the Torah* (San Francisco: HarperSanFrancisco, 2001) for insight into the Babylonian connection.

15. Boadt, *Reading the Old Testament*, 131–32.

3. The Gift of the Covenant

1. Wayne T. Pitard, "Before Israel: Syria-Palestine in the Bronze Age," in *The Oxford History of the Biblical World*, ed. Michael D. Coogan (New York: Oxford University Press, 1998), 27.

2. Robert Alter, *Genesis* (New York: W. W. Norton & Company, 1996), 48.

3. Marc A. Jolley, "Fear," in *Eerdmans Dictionary of the Bible*, ed. David Noel Freedman (Grand Rapids: Wm. B. Eerdmans Publishing Company, 2000), 457.

4. The Gift of the Law at Sinai

1. Carol A. Redmount, "Bitter Lives: Israel in and out of Egypt," in *The Oxford History of the Biblical World*, ed. Michael D. Coogan (New York: Oxford University Press, 1998), 63–64.

2. In the Hebrew, the location of the rescue is called *yam suf* (traditionally translated as "Red Sea"). The most common meaning of *suf* is "reed," which has led many biblical scholars to translate the phrase as "Reed Sea" or "Sea of Reeds."

3. Michael Walzer, *Exodus and Revolution* (New York: Basic Books, 1985), 44–45.

4. Ibid., 47.

5. Timothy P. Jenney, "Holiness, Holy," in *Eerdmans Dictionary of the Bible*, ed. David Noel Freedman (Grand Rapids: Wm. B. Eerdmans Publishing Company, 2000), 598.

6. John Courtney Murray, *The Problem of God* (New Haven: Yale University Press, 1964), 6–7.

7. Walzer, *Exodus and Revolution*, 51.

8. Ibid., 53.

9. Richard Elliott Friedman, *Commentary on the Torah* (San Francisco: HarperSanFrancisco, 2001), 280.

10. Ibid., 281.

11. Walzer, *Exodus and Revolution*, 61.

12. Bruce C. Birch et al., *A Theological Introduction to the Old Testament* (Nashville: Abingdon Press, 1999), 134–35.

5. The Gift of the Prophets

1. Lawrence Boadt, *Reading the Old Testament* (New York/Mahwah, NJ: Paulist Press, 1984), 307.

2. See Gerald T. Sheppard, "Isaiah," in *The HarperCollins Bible Commentary*, ed. James L. Mays (San Francisco: HarperSanFrancisco, 2000), 489–97, for a helpful summary of scholarly attempts to determine the authorship and structure of Isaiah. See also A. Joseph Everson, "Isaiah," in *Eerdmans Dictionary of the Bible*, ed. David Noel Freedman (Grand Rapids: Wm. B. Eerdmans Publishing Company, 2000), 648–52.

3. John Bright, *A History of Israel*, 3rd ed. (Philadelphia: Westminster Press, 1981), 271.

4. Ibid., 275.

5. Ibid., 286.

6. There is much scholarly debate about whether Sennacherib conducted one campaign or two. John Bright offers a convincing argument for the two-campaign theory. See Bright's "Excursus I," in *A History of Israel*, 298–309.

7. Stephen L. Harris and Robert L. Platzner, *The Old Testament: An Introduction to the Hebrew Bible* (Boston: McGraw-Hill, 2003), 209–10.

8. See "The Martyrdom of Isaiah," in *The Apocrypha and Pseudepigrapha of the Old Testament*, vol. 2, ed. R. H. Charles (Oxford: Oxford University Press, 1964), 155–62. The book is a Jewish pseudepigraphal work that details the ghastly death of Isaiah by order of Manasseh. See also 2 Kings 21 for a description of the excesses of Manasseh's reign.

9. See annotation for Isaiah 7:14 in *The New Oxford Annotated Bible, with the Apocryphal/Deuterocanonical Books*, 3rd ed., New Revised Standard Version, ed. Michael D. Coogan (Oxford: Oxford University Press, 2001), 988.

10. Aaron W. Park, "Zion," in *Eerdmans Dictionary of the Bible*, 1421–22.

11. Harris and Platzner, *The Old Testament*, 234.

12. Adele Berlin and Marc Zvi Brettler, eds., *The Jewish Study Bible* (Oxford: Oxford University Press, 2004), 860.

13. Boadt, *Reading the Old Testament*, 364–65.

14. *The Jewish Study Bible*, 782.

15. Boadt, *Reading the Old Testament*, 418.

16. *The Jewish Study Bible*, 877.

17. Bright, *A History of Israel*, 365–66. The hostility between the Samaritans and the returning exiles would persist for centuries and would be immortalized in the parable of the Good Samaritan.

18. Leonard J. Greenspoon, "Between Alexandria and Antioch: Jews and Judaism in the Hellenistic Period," in *The Oxford History of the Biblical World*, ed. Michael D. Coogan (Oxford: Oxford University Press, 1998), 344.

19. See Paul Hanson's classic study, *The Dawn of Apocalyptic: The Historical and Sociological Roots of Jewish Apocalyptic Eschatology* (Philadelphia: Fortress Press, 1979) and Mary Joan Winn Leith, "Israel among the Nations: The Persian Period," in *The Oxford History of the Biblical World*, 300–2.

6. Between the Testaments

1. See Edward H. Flannery, *The Anguish of the Jews: Twenty-three Centuries of Antisemitism* (New York/Mahwah, NJ: Paulist Press, 1985), for an excellent and unflinching examination of the roots of Christian anti-Jewish bias and anti-Semitism, the anti-Jewish writings of the church fathers, and the systematic abuse of the Jews over the centuries.

2. Paula Fredriksen and Adele Reinhartz, "Introduction," in *Jesus, Judaism, and Christian Anti-Judaism: Reading the New Testament after the Holocaust*, ed. Paula Fredriksen and Adele Reinhartz (Louisville: Westminster John Knox Press, 2002), 2.

3. John Bright, *A History of Israel*, 3rd ed. (Philadelphia: Westminster Press, 1981), 378–79.

4. Ibid., 390.

5. See Paul Cartledge, *Alexander the Great: The Hunt for a New Past* (Woodstock: Overlook Press, 2004), 201–18, for a review of Alexander's policies.

6. Bright, *A History of Israel*, 420.

7. Leonard J. Greenspoon, "Between Alexandria and Antioch: Jews and Judaism in the Hellenistic Period," in *The Oxford History of the Biblical World*, ed. Michael D. Coogan (New York: Oxford University Press, 1998), 335.

8. Dennis C. Duling and Norman Perrin, *The New Testament: Proclamation and Parenesis, Myth and History*, 3rd ed. (Fort Worth: Harcourt Brace & Company, 1994), 48.

9. Amy-Jill Levine, "Visions of Kingdoms: From Pompey to the First Jewish Revolt," in *The Oxford History of the Biblical World*, 365.

10. Ibid., 366.

11. Cited in David C. Rapoport, "Fear and Trembling: Terrorism in Three Religious Traditions," *The American Political Science Review* 78, no. 3 (September 1984): 670.

12. John Bright suggests the origins can be found in Iranian or Persian theological concepts, whereas Paul D. Hanson believes it developed within the prophetic tradition of Israel. See John Bright, *A History of Israel*, 454–57, and Paul D. Hanson, *The Dawn of Apocalyptic: The Historical and Sociological Roots of Jewish Apocalyptic Eschatology* (Philadelphia: Fortress Press, 1979), 1–31. The debates continue.

13. See Lawrence Boadt, *Reading the Old Testament* (New York/Mahwah, NJ: Paulist Press, 1984), 506–15, for a helpful discussion of Jewish apocalyptic.

14. R. H. Charles, ed., *The Apocrypha and Pseudepigrapha of the Old Testament*, vol. 2 (Oxford: Oxford University Press, 1964), 214–15. The use of parentheses indicates that the word or words enclosed are supplied by the editor for purposes of clarity; bracketed phrases indicate an intrusion into the original text.

15. See Levine, "Visions of Kingdoms," 367–69, for a helpful discussion on the Essenes and the Dead Sea Scrolls.

16. Michael Wise, Martin Abegg, Jr., and Edward Cook, *The Dead Sea Scrolls: A New Translation* (San Francisco: HarperSanFrancisco, 1996), 139.

17. Bright, *A History of Israel*, 463.

18. Paula Fredriksen, "The Birth of Christianity and the Origins of Christian Anti-Judaism," in *Jesus, Judaism, and Christian Anti-Judaism*, 14.

19. Scholars still debate the extent of Jewish proselytism and how it contributed to Jewish-Christian tensions in the Greco-Roman period. For background, see Albert I. Baumgarten, "Marcel Simon's *Verus Israel* as a Contribution to Jewish History," *The Harvard Theological Review* 92, no. 4 (October 1999): 465–78; Shaye J. D. Cohen, "Crossing the Boundary and Becoming a Jew," *The Harvard Theological Review* 82, no. 1 (January 1989): 13–33; Jerry L. Daniel, "Anti-Semitism in the Hellenistic-Roman Period," *Journal of Biblical Literature* 98, no. 1 (March 1979): 45–65; Louis H. Feldman, "Reflections on Rutgers's 'Attitudes to Judaism in the Greco-Roman Period,'" *The Jewish Quarterly Review*, New Ser., 86, no. 12 (July–October1995): 153–69 and "The Contribution of Professor Salo W. Baron to the Study of Ancient Jewish History: His Appraisal of Anti-Judaism and Proselytism," *AJS Review* 18, no. 1 (1993): 1–27; John G. Gager, "Jews, Gentiles, and Synagogues in the Book of Acts," *The Harvard Theological Review* 79, no. 1/3, Christians among Jews and Gentiles: Essays to Honor of Krister Stendahl on His Sixty-Fifth Birthday (January–July 1986): 91–99; Leonard Victor Rutgers, "Attitudes to Judaism in the Greco-Roman Period: Reflections on Feldman's 'Jew and Gentile in the Ancient World,'" *The Jewish Quarterly Review*, New Ser., 85, no. 3/4 (January–April 1995): 361–95.

20. Stephen L. Harris, *The New Testament: A Student's Introduction*, 4th ed. (Boston: McGraw Hill, 2002), 91–92.

21. Daniel N. Schowalter, "Churches in Context: The Jesus Movement in the Roman World," in *The Oxford History of the Biblical World*, 397.

22. Levine, "Visions of Kingdoms," 380.

23. P. Cornelius Tacitus, *The Annals of Imperial Rome*, Book XV, 44, in *The Annals and The Histories by P. Cornelius Tacitus*, ed. Robert Maynard Hutchins, Great Books of the Western World Series, vol. 15 (Chicago: Encyclopaedia Britannica, Inc., 1952), 168.

24. Levine, "Visions of Kingdoms," 381.

25. Harris, *The New Testament*, 140.

26. Duling and Perrin, *The New Testament*, 60.

27. See Solomon Zeitlin, "The Tefillah, the Shemoneh Esreh: An Historical Study of the First Canonization of the Hebrew Liturgy," *The Jewish Quarterly Review* 54, no. 3 (January 1964): 208–49.

28. Cited in Duling and Perrin, *The New Testament*, 91.

29. See Steven T. Katz, "Issues in the Separation of Judaism and Christianity after 70 C.E.: A Reconsideration," *Journal of Biblical Literature* 103, no.1 (March 1984): 43–76; see also Daniel Boyarin, "Justin Martyr Invents Judaism," *Church History* 70,

no. 3 (September 2001): 427–61. The Bar Kochba Revolt (132-135 CE) was sparked by the plans and policies of Emperor Hadrian (117–138 CE), who wanted to build a temple to Jupiter on the former site of the Jerusalem Temple. He also decreed a complete ban on the practice of circumcision. The Jews were outraged. Led by the charismatic young Jew, Shimon bar Kochba ("son of a star"), rebel bands swept across Palestine, capturing many towns and villages, including Jerusalem. Some leaders of the revolt believed that Shimon bar Kochba was the long-awaited Messiah and tried to persuade Christians to join them, but they refused on religious grounds. Their unwillingness to deny Jesus led to further bloodshed that hampered the rebel cause. Meanwhile Hadrian dispatched his best general and a sizeable army to suppress the revolt. The results were devastating for Jews and Jewish Christians alike. Those who survived were exiled or sold into slavery and the city of Jerusalem once again lay in ruins.

30. Katz, "Issues in the Separation of Judaism," 74.

31. Flannery, *The Anguish of the Jews*, 32.

32. Shaye J. D. Cohen, *From the Maccabees to the Mishnah* (Philadelphia: The Westminster Press, 1987), 227.

33. Bart D. Ehrman, ed., *The New Testament and Other Early Christian Writings: A Reader*, 2nd ed. (New York: Oxford University Press, 2004), 125.

34. Thomas A. Idinopulos and Roy Bowen Ward, "Is Christology Inherently Anti-Semitic? A Critical Review of Rosemary Ruether's *Faith and Fratricide*," *Journal of the American Academy of Religion* 45, no. 2 (June 1977): 202–3. See also, Rosemary Ruether, *Faith and Fratricide: The Theological Roots of Anti-Semitism* (Eugene: Wipf & Stock Publishers, 1996); John G. Gager, *The Origins of Anti-Semitism: Attitudes toward Judaism in Pagan and Christian Antiquity* (Oxford: Oxford University Press, 1985).

35. Gager, *The Origins of Anti-Semitism*, 203.

7. The Gift of the Gospel

1. For a range of positions on the nature and distinctiveness of Christian ethics, see David Fergusson, *Community, Liberalism and Christian Ethics* (Cambridge: Cambridge University Press, 1999); Paul J. Achtemeier, *Inspiration and Authority: Nature and Function of Christian Scripture* (New York: Hendrickson Publishers, Inc., 1999); Charles E. Curran and Richard A. McCormick, eds., *The Distinctiveness of Christian Ethics*, Readings in Moral Theology No. 2 (New York/Mahwah, NJ: Paulist Press, 1980); Gareth Jones, "The Authority of Scripture and Christian Ethics," in *The Cambridge Companion to Christian Ethics*, ed. Robin Gill (Cambridge: Cambridge University Press, 2001).

2. Michael J. McClymond, "Jesus," in *The Rivers of Paradise: Moses, Buddha, Confucius, Jesus, and Muhammad as Religious Founders*, ed. David Noel Freedman and Michael J. McClymond (Grand Rapids: Wm. B. Eerdmans Publishing Company, 2001), 341–42.

3. Stephen L. Harris, *The New Testament: A Student's Introduction*, 4th ed. (Boston: McGraw-Hill, 2002), 10.

4. See Jonathan L. Reed, "Q," in *Eerdmans Dictionary of the Bible*, ed. David Noel Freedman (Grand Rapids: Wm. B. Eerdmans Publishing Company, 2000), 1102.

5. The most recent and controversial attempt to settle the debate about the historical Jesus is the "Jesus Seminar." Convened in 1985, the seminar brought together a self-selected group of several dozen scholars to analyze and evaluate evidence about

Jesus. In 1993, the seminar published *The Five Gospels: The Search for the Authentic Words of Jesus*, which assessed the authenticity of fifteen hundred sayings attributed to Jesus. During the meetings, participants would cast public votes on the authenticity of each statement using beads that followed a color-coded rating system. When all was said and done, only about 18 percent of the words attributed to Jesus made the cut. Many noted scholars have criticized the seminar for its questionable methodology, its interpretive bias, and its narrow focus. For an excellent summary of the history of Jesus scholarship and the Jesus Seminar, see McClymond, "Jesus," 309–51.

6. Harris, *The New Testament*, 273.

7. E. P. Sanders, "Jesus Christ," in *Eerdmans Dictionary of the Bible*, 704.

8. See Mark Allen Powell, "Matthew," in *HarperCollins Bible Commentary*, ed. James L. Mays (San Francisco: HarperSanFrancisco, 2000), 868–71.

9. Warren Carter argues that Matthew's hand washing-scene was not intended to condemn the Jewish people as much as to expose how the Roman authorities and the Jewish leaders manipulated the people so that they willingly accepted responsibility for Jesus' death. Unfortunately, this subtlety was lost on generations of Christian readers, many of whom interpreted the scene as a condemnation of the Jews. See Warren Carter, *Pontius Pilate: Portraits of a Roman Governor* (Collegeville: Liturgical Press, 2003), 96–99.

10. Warren Carter, *Matthew and the Margins: A Sociopolitical and Religious Reading* (Maryknoll, NY: Orbis Books, 2001), 36.

11. Harris, *The New Testament*, 152.

12. Jack Dean Kingsbury, "The Structure of Matthew's Gospel and His Concept of Salvation-History," *Catholic Biblical Quarterly* 35, no. 4 (October 1973): 451–74.

13. Dennis C. Duling and Norman Perrin, *The New Testament: Proclamation and Parenesis, Myth and History*, 3rd ed. (Fort Worth: Harcourt Brace & Company, 1994), 341.

14. John Bright, *A History of Israel*, 3rd ed. (Philadelphia: Westminster Press, 1981), 434–35.

15. McClymond, "Jesus," 376.

16. See Duling and Perrin, *The New Testament*, 339–43, and Dale C. Allison, Jr., "Sermon on the Mount/Plain," in *Eerdmans Dictionary of the Bible*, 1186–87.

17. Bright, *A History of Israel*, 441–42.

18. Ibid., 439. Legalism generally has a pejorative sense and has been used to characterize (and caricature) Jewish piety for centuries. While the stereotypical depiction of all Jews as hypocritical Pharisees is rightly rejected, there is no question that the legal grounding of the Mosaic Law made and continues to make Judaism and Christianity particularly vulnerable to this ethical trap. This book argues that Israel's prophets (including Jesus), the author of Matthew, and Paul all addressed this problem to some extent in their teachings

19. Paul Ricoeur's essay "Ethical and Theological Considerations on the Golden Rule," in *Figuring the Sacred: Religion, Narrative, and Imagination*, ed. Mark I. Wallace, trans. David Pellauer (Minneapolis: Fortress Press, 1995), provided invaluable guidance in understanding the dynamics of the golden rule and the love command in the Sermon on the Mount.

20. Aristotle, *Nicomachean Ethics*, trans. Martin Ostwald (New York: Macmillan Publishing Company, 1962), 141–42.

21. Paul Ricoeur, "Love and Justice," in *Figuring the Sacred: Religion, Narrative, and Imagination*, ed. Mark I. Wallace, trans. David Pellauer (Minneapolis: Fortress Press, 1995), 325.

22. Ibid., 326.

23. Ibid., 301.

24. Ibid.

25. Amy-Jill Levine, "Matthew, Mark, and Luke: Good News or Bad?" in *Jesus, Judaism, and Christian Anti-Judaism: Reading the New Testament after the Holocaust*, ed. Paula Fredriksen and Adele Reinhartz (Louisville: Westminster John Knox Press, 2002), 97.

8. The Gift of Jesus

1. See Tertullian, *Adversus Marcionem*, Book 5:4, 8 in Tertullian: *Adversus Marcionem*, Books 4 and 5, vol. 2, ed. and trans. Ernest Evans (Oxford: Oxford University Press, 1972); Origen, "Homily VII," in Origen, *Homilies on Genesis and Exodus*, trans. Ronald E. Heine, The Fathers of the Church Series, vol. 71 (Washington, DC: The Catholic University of America Press, 1982); Augustine, "Tractate 11" (John 2:23–3:5) in *St. Augustine: Tractates on the Gospel of John, 11–27*, trans. John W. Rettig, The Fathers of the Church Series, vol. 79, vol. 2 (Washington, DC: The Catholic University of America Press, 1988); Martin Luther, *A Commentary on St. Paul's Epistle to the Galatians*, ed. Philip S. Watson (Westwood: Fleming H. Revell Company, 1961).

2. For background on Paul, see Calvin Roetzel, *Paul: The Man and the Myth* (Minneapolis: Fortress Press, 1999), 11–12, and F. F. Bruce, *Paul: Apostle of the Heart Set Free* (Grand Rapids: Wm. B. Eerdmans Publishing Company, 1977), 41–44.

3. Bruce, *Paul*, 71–72.

4. Stephen L. Harris, *The New Testament: A Student's Introduction*, 4th ed. (Boston: McGraw-Hill, 2002), 289.

5. See Roetzel, *Paul*, 19–22, for a summary of the debates.

6. Ibid., 92.

7. Leander E. Keck, *Paul and His Letters*, 2nd ed. (Philadelphia: Fortress Press, 1988), 114–15.

8. Bruce, *Paul*, 70.

9. Harris, *Paul*, 333.

10. See Keck, *Paul and His Letters*, 95–109, for an illuminating discussion of Paul's understanding of the Spirit-flesh relation.

11. Origen, "Homily VII," in *Homilies on Genesis and Exodus*, 134.

12. Martin Luther, *A Commentary on St. Paul's Epistle to the Galatians*, 423.

13. See Frank J. Matera, *Galatians*, Sacra Pagina Series, vol. 9 (Collegeville: The Liturgical Press, 1992), 172–79.

14. John Gager, "Paul, the Apostle of Judaism," in *Jesus, Judaism, and Christian Anti-Judaism: Reading the New Testament after the Holocaust*, ed. Paula Fredriksen and Adele Reinhartz (Louisville: Westminster John Knox Press, 2002), 73.

9. The Bible Liberated

1. Philip Novak, *The World's Wisdom: Sacred Texts of the World's Religions* (San Francisco: HarperSanFrancisco, 1994), 42.

INDEX

Of Related Interest

Liberating Jonah
Forming an Ethics of Reconciliation
Miguel De La Torre
ISBN 978-1-57075-743-3

Reconciliation among peoples—why we need it, why it's possible, and how to bring it about.

When a reluctant Jonah finally entered Nineveh to announce God's grace to the powerful Assyrian empire, God brought about reconciliation between the oppressors and the oppressed. Our world today, inhabited by both oppressors and oppressed, is also in need of reconciliation—between different ethnic backgrounds, socio-economic levels, and gender and sexual orientations.

A Sacred Voice Is Calling
Personal Vocation and Social Conscience
John Neafsey
ISBN 978-1-57075-748-8

How do we distinguish between an authentic calling and the competing, counterfeit voices in our culture? How can we balance the inward listening *to* our hearts and listening *with* our hearts to the needs of our world? Drawing widely on the wisdom of saints and sages, John Neafsey describes a path to living in the place, as Frederick Buechner has put it, "where our deep gladness and the world's deep hunger meet."

"A perceptive combination of spiritual wisdom, psychological insight, and biblical passion."
—*Marcus Borg, author,* The Heart of Christianity

Please support your local bookstore or call 1-800-258-5838.
For a free catalog, please write us at
Orbis Books, Box 308
Maryknoll, NY 10545-0302
or visit our website at www.orbisbooks.com.

Thank you for reading *Liberating the Bible.*
We hope you profited from it.